Contemporary Italian Philosophy

SUNY series in Contemporary Italian Philosophy
Silvia Benso and Brian Schroeder, editors

Contemporary
Italian Philosophy

Crossing the Borders of Ethics, Politics, and Religion

Edited by
Silvia Benso and Brian Schroeder

Translated from the Italian by
Silvia Benso

STATE UNIVERSITY OF NEW YORK PRESS

Published by
State University of New York Press, Albany

© 2007 State University of New York

For information, contact State University of New York Press, Albany, NY
www.sunypress.edu

Production by Marilyn P. Semerad
Marketing by Fran Keneston

Library of Congress Cataloging-in-Publication Data

Contemporary Italian philosophy : crossing the borders of ethics, politics, and
    religion / edited and translated by Silvia Benso ; edited by Brian Schroeder.
        p. cm. — (SUNY series in contemporary Italian philosophy)
    Includes bibliographical references and index.
    ISBN-13: 978-0-7914-7135-7 (hardcover : alk. paper)
    ISBN-13: 978-0-7914-7136-4 (pbk. : alk. paper)
    1. Philosophy, Italian—20th century. I. Benso, Silvia. II. Schroeder, Brian.

B3601.C65 2007
195—dc22   2006024605

10 9 8 7 6 5 4 3 2 1

For Erik Aren Schroeder

Contents

Preface

The predominance of French and German thought in contemporary continental philosophy has resulted in an unfortunate overshadowing, if not a veritable exclusion, of much thinking from Mediterranean Europe. Several countries in this region have sizeable and vibrant philosophical communities, and Italy arguably stands in the forefront both historically and contemporarily. It is true that much recent Italian philosophy is and has been engaged with its northern neighbors' great traditions, for example, to name some meaningful representatives of the twentieth century, with idealism (Benedetto Croce, Giovanni Gentile, Piero Martinetti), phenomenology (Antonio Banfi, Sofia Vanni Rovighi, Enzo Paci, Pier Aldo Rovatti), French and German existentialism (Augusto Guzzo, Armando Carlini, Federico Sciacca, Nicola Abbagnano, Luigi Pareyson, Pietro Chiodi), Marxism (Galvano Della Volpe, Lucio Colletti, Antonio Gramsci, Enzo Paci, Giulio Preti), hermeneutics (Luigi Pareyson, Carlo Sini, Gianni Vattimo), and neopositivism (Ludovico Geymonat, Giulio Preti). It is also true that at least part of Italian philosophy is rooted in the tradition of historiography, historicism, and the history of philosophy (Nicola Abbagnano, Mario Dal Pra, Eugenio Garin, Cesare Vasoli, Giovanni Reale, Paolo Rossi, Pietro Rossi, Sergio Moravia). Nevertheless a considerable body of original work is now occurring in Italy, extending well beyond mere commentary on or conversation with the principal figures of ancient through contemporary thought. And although this is quite naturally not so pronounced within Europe itself, relatively little attention is paid currently to Italian and other Mediterranean thinking in the United States.

Contemporary Italian philosophy is a long overdue and much needed supplement to continental thinking, and while certain Italian thinkers have been and are continuing to make noticeable contributions, at least in the United States remains a general lacuna with regard to the broader recognition of the Italian philosophical community. Italian philosophers are quite active in presenting and participating in conferences and colloquia in continental Europe. Yet partly because of linguistic difficulties due to a system of general education that has privileged Greek, Latin, French, and German as *the* philosophical languages (whereas English is the language of sciences), and partly because of the prevalent perception of American philosophy as essentially analytic and pragmatic in orientation, Italian philosophers have generally been absent from professional activity in the United States. The problem of language stands as a barrier also for most Americans. Unlike French and German, Italian is not regularly offered at many American colleges and universities, to say nothing of the high schools, and this has produced a limited number of qualified translators and an ensuing lack of interest by many publishers to pursue such translations. What makes this all the more astonishing is that the single greatest exodus in modern history has been that of Italy, and primarily to the United States, which, as a result, boasts the largest number of Italian expatriates and those of Italian descent, outside of Italy.

Geographically, culturally, and politically, Italy is uniquely located in the world, poised between Europe, Africa, and the Middle East, and, consequently, impacted by all three areas. This positioning was not lost on the ancient Romans, who built their empire largely because of this, and so is it also recognized by Italians today, and thus by their philosophical community. Particularly at this juncture of world history, which is witness to the emerging European Union, the continuing development of democracies, and the changing face of such important and decisive alliances such as the North Atlantic Treaty Organization, introducing Italian philosophy to the English-speaking world is critical. Indeed, a unique attribute of contemporary Italian philosophy has been its predisposition toward availing itself of the current debates in non-Italian philosophy while never losing its sense of cultural and intellectual independence. This has resulted in a strength often not found in the dominant German and French traditions, which have tended to be more insular in their focus, therein situating Italian philosophy as a genuine global model of thinking, one both open to world philosophy and yet firmly grounded in its own historical and cultural identity.

The question of whether a specific national identity exists for Italian philosophy has been nevertheless much debated, and not only because the discourse on national identities may sound inappropriate, dangerous, or even obsolete in the contemporary world context. On the one hand, the issue is whether contemporary Italian philosophy can be said to have a unitary character that affords it a strong national identity. Certainly during the years of fascism, as for instance the historian of philosophy Carlo Augusto Viano argued, the hegemony of Croce's and Gentile's neoidealism seemed to give Italian philosophy a uniform character. From such a perspective, the tradition of Italian philosophy was traced back to the experience of the Italian Renaissance, which, through Bruno and Vico, was seen as a fundamental influence on the development of modern European thought. This hegemony was followed, after World War II, by a process of "deprovincialization" that, through the engagement with foreign philosophical movements such as existentialism, Marxism, and neopositivism, de facto erased the unitary character of Italian philosophy. If neoidealism was the prevalent philosophical culture during the Fascist era, it is also true that, as another historian of philosophy, Eugenio Garin, has remarked with ample documentation and in fundamental agreement with among others the political philosopher Norberto Bobbio, it was precisely during those years of alleged hegemony that a constant debate with foreign thinkers developed to the point of corroding such a presumed hegemony. For example, beside his and Gentile's readings of Hegel, Croce's own philosophy unfolded in constant conversation with the thought of Marx, Simmel, and Weber; existentialism and neopositivism had already become topics for conversation among Italian philosophers before the outbreak of the war; and Gramsci's writings, written before the 1940s although published only later, were in opposition to but also in dialogue with the philosophy of neoidealism. Thus, a unitary character does not seem to have been fully actual, even during the only historical period when it seemed to be more likely present. Certainly it is not present in current Italian philosophy, if by "unitary" one means the predominance of a specific philosophical tradition capable of making itself hegemonic. Despite its fundamental importance in the years following the war up until the 1970s, not even the traditional distinction between Catholic (or more religiously oriented) and Marxist (or more secular) thought holds any current validity, and the apparent Marxist cultural hegemony during the 1960s was in any event always somewhat precarious and frail. In current Italian philosophical debate one therefore finds phenomenological, historicist, Marxist, analytical, hermeneutic, and various metaphysical and epistemological positions. In short, Italian philosophy is permeated by a continuous conversation with all the great philosophical (religious and nonreligious) traditions that one can find anywhere else in the philosophical world.

A second aspect, on the other hand, regarding the issue of Italian philosophical identity has to do with the question of whether Italian philosophy retains its own originality and creativity. Some, such as Lucio Colletti, have spoken of Italy as a "philosophical province of the Third Reich," that is, of a scarcely creative and original community dominated by German thought from Hegel to Marx, Fichte to Nietzsche, Schopenhauer to Dilthey, Jaspers to Heidegger. Viano has supported such a position and has written not so much of a tributary "provincialism" of contemporary Italian philosophy, which ultimately suggests closure and lack of dialogue with non-Italian thinkers, but a "dependency of Italian philosophy on foreign philosophy" (a dependency that, for Viano, was not there in the case of Croce and Gentile). Whereas, with the possible exception of Gramsci, recent Italian philosophy has not produced figures the stature of Husserl, Heidegger, or Sartre, that is, thinkers capable of having a worldwide impact, several Italian philosophers have produced highly original and creative compositions (by some, for example by Antimo Negri, called "theoretical centaurs") of quite disparate philosophical tendencies, approaches, and interests. Thus, for example,

Marxism and phenomenology unite in the thought of Giulio Preti and Enzo
Paci, Christian existentialism and hermeneutics in that of Luigi Pareyson,
hermeneutics and nihilism in Alberto Caracciolo and Gianni Vattimo, existentialism and Marxism in Cesare Luporini, Marxism and nihilism in
Massimo Cacciari, neopositivism and Marxism in Ludovico Geymonat,
neoscholasticism and phenomenology in Sofia Vanni Rovighi, and Christianity and Marxism in Italo Mancini. Such a "synthetic attitude" (Viano),
syncretism, eclecticism, "cosmopolitanism" (Vattimo), or "renewed Alexan-
drinism" (Vincenzo Vitiello), as it has been variously called, constitutes perhaps the highest point of strength of Italian philosophy, what gives it both its
unitary and national identity—an identity, however, that although nationally
grounded, does not close itself off to the larger, worldwide philosophical context, but rather is nourished by the conversation with such a context.

    *Contemporary Italian Philosophy: Crossing the Borders of Ethics, Politics,
and Religion* marks a significant advance toward deepening American-Italian
relations on both the intellectual and cultural levels. Indeed, the works of a
few contemporary Italian philosophers, most notably Giorgio Agamben,
Norberto Bobbio, Massimo Cacciari, Adriana Cavarero, Mario Perniola, Carlo
Sini, and Gianni Vattimo have been translated into English. Despite the
importance of such translations and the undoubted philosophical relevance
of these authors, these translations represent isolated, discrete, and somewhat
random occurences, due more to individual philosophical personalities and
personal situations than to a desire to approach, appreciate, and diffuse Italian philosophy in its overall context and richness. The only volume in English
that engages Italian philosophy in its own right is Giovanna Borradori's
edited collection *Recoding Metaphysics: The New Italian Philosophy*, published
in 1988. This volume focuses explicitly on the issue of metaphysics via
Heidegger's criticism of it and organizes the Italian debate (and hence the
philosophers included in the volume) around two positions that both pivot
around Heidegger: the position of those who interpret the Heideggerian
conceptual framework by means of philosophical hermeneutics, and the
opposing position of those who, moving from Heidegger's critique, attempt to
construct a form of positive thinking capable of subtracting Being from the
nihilistic, technological destiny that has characterized Western metaphysics.
Because of its narrow theme and grid of interpretation, Borradori's volume is
rather specific, however, and in that sense represents a limited exposure to the
depths of Italian philosophy. Far from replacing such a volume, this collection
complements, supplements, and opens Borradori's scope and themes by meditating on topics situated at the crossing of ethics, politics, and religion through
the authoritative voices of a vast array of contemporary Italian philosophers,
the majority of whom are not part of Borradori's collection.

    Rather than attempting a historical overview, or even a survey of
contemporary Italian philosophy, which to be comprehensive would both
necessarily have to span several decades and include thinkers working in

areas as varied as aesthetics (Luciano Anceschi, Gianni Carchia, Umberto Eco, Dino Formaggio, Mario Perniola), philosophy of language and analytic philosophy (Andrea Bonomi, Aldo Gargani, Diego Marconi), philosophy of science (Evandro Agazzi, Dario Antiseri, Francesco Barone, Giulio Giorello), and history of philosophy (Mario Dal Pra, Paolo Rossi, Pietro Rossi, Carlo Augusto Viano), to name a few, this volume intends to be a work *in* contemporary Italian philosophy. As such it offers some living and lively examples of the original thinking now occurring within the Italian philosophical scene— as said before, not exhaustively nor even in general but at the crossing of themes of ethics, politics, and religion. Without claiming to be a conclusive representation even with respect to these more specific areas of intersection, this anthology brings together seventeen leading philosophers whose theoretical work and activity are situated at the crossing of such disciplines. Of course, choices had to be made and with them arguable exclusions for which apologies are not always sufficient; but an effort was made to provide a wide selection of original thinkers belonging to different philosophical lineages and affiliations so that the collection could be, within temporal, thematic, and editorial limitations and constraints, as representative as possible of what in the United States is generally termed the "continental" tradition. Regrettably, a clear preponderance of male contributors will be noticed. This reflects an unfortunate situation within the Italian philosophical scene, which has only recently started to be rectified. Although Italy today has a growing number of very talented women philosophers (for example, Maria Cristina Bartolomei, Laura Boella, Silvana Borutti, Adriana Cavarero, Franca D'Agostini, Roberta De Monticelli, Donatella Di Cesare, Luisa Muraro, Chiara Zamboni), few have yet amassed the scholarly record that the contributors herein have. On this basis alone were certain thinkers included over others. Some of the chapters have been written specifically for this volume, and where this is not the case, they were written very recently and never before published in English translation. All the contributions are therefore not only current, but also often address directly issues that are confronting both academics and the larger *socius* today.

Italian and other European philosophers in fact often assume a more visible and hence prominent role in social and political life than in the United States, where nonscientific academia is frequently marginalized and excluded from the public eye by an increasingly politicized corporate media machine. Encompassing as wide a range of interests as any tradition in the world, but similar to practically all other European traditions, and perhaps even more so given its Renaissance ancestry, Italian philosophy has never compartmentalized itself professionally in the way that recent American philosophy has, that is, by identifying itself in terms of specific areas of specialization. Philosophers in Italy tend to be broadly published, and finding them writing on topics ranging from the history of philosophy, to metaphysics, epistemology, politics, art and aesthetics, language theory, the philosophy of

religion, theology, anthropology, and cultural analysis is not unusual. Moreover, beginning in the latter part of the twentieth century, in a move par-
alleled by more prestigious American universities, Italian philosophy has
increasingly resisted identifying itself according to traditions represented by
individuals or individual universities, so-called schools of thought (the historicist and idealist traditions at the universities of Rome and Naples, the
historiographical approach coupled with an attention to cultural history at
Florence, philosophy as a discipline capable of orienting political activity at
Università Statale di Milano, the neoscholastic tradition and its concern for
metaphysical issues at the Università Cattolica del Sacro Cuore in Milan,
the Aristotelian approach to metaphysics and the attention to the political
discourse of Marxism at Padua, the dialogue with non-Italian philosophies
and the interest for scientific and political cultures at Turin). Although
allegiances clearly remain, this doctrinal and academic independence has
resulted in an extraordinary freedom of thought that is continuing to gain
new ground and forge pathways for thinking that have traditionally often
been tangled by old allegiances and loyalties, fostering what might be characterized as a "new" Renaissance-like approach to philosophy. These varieties of approaches, their crossings, and intersections are, among others things,
what *Contemporary Italian Philosophy: Crossing the Borders of Ethics, Politics,
and Religion* intends to portray in the variety of figures herein.

After a general primarily historical introduction describing thematic
aspects of the development of Italian philosophy in the twentieth century up
to the contemporary panorama, the work is arranged in three parts, corresponding roughly to a historical unfolding of past, present, and future thinking. The chapters comprising the first part situate the discussion of ethics,
politics, and religion within the context of the legacy bequeathed by the
tradition. Rather than offering a strictly historical overview, however, for the
most part these contributions are highly theoretical in nature; they provide
indications of themes and topics that have guided the tradition but that now
need to be rethought and suggest philosophical figures that may inspire a
reconfiguration of possible ways of addressing ethics, politics, religion, and
their intersection. The task of rethematizing past concepts and relations is
addressed decisively in the speculative chapters in part two. Here religious
themes are declined in the direction of an ethical thinking wherein such
concepts as finitude, responsibility, and human existence assume a clearly
innovative valence. The chapters in part three address the challenge the
contemporary political and philosophical scenario pose and attempt to delineate more fully concepts such as ethics, justice, and subjectivity, concepts
capable of withstanding the demands of the globalized world in which philosophy, and not only in its Italian variation, today finds itself at work.

Although each contribution in this collection stands on its ground,
this volume serves largely as a selective introduction to contemporary Italian
philosophy—not to provide an overview, but rather to present an example

of Italian philosophy at work on some specific themes and their intersections. Struggling with its organization, we editors made a conscious effort to avoid a false characterization of the contributors as being essentially ethical, political, or religious in their orientation. The overall philosophical work of the authors here gathered stretches across borders, and so do their contributions as presented in this volume. Therefore, any subdivision, including the one here suggested, is somewhat fictional and arbitrary, and other intersections may be designed, and other borders imagined. This work, moreover, neither intends to limit the importance of Italian philosophy to the abovementioned themes or thinkers, nor purports that the philosophers included have the final say on any of these topics. Why these and not other philosophers were included is due solely to the choice of the editors based on familiarity with their work and research in the area of contemporary Italian philosophy. All of the philosophers presented here are well established and highly published; several of their names are already known in the United States, and the others deserve to be. All of them, however, are proximate insofar as they can rightly be considered as "continental" philosophers, and excellent ones at that.

Silvia Benso
Brian Schroeder
Editors

Acknowledgments

We have received great encouragement and support from many along the way, and for that we are very grateful; several institutions and individuals in particular deserve specific acknowledgment. This volume would not have been possible without the assistance of a Fulbright Senior Research Fellowship and a Miller Research Fellowship, which permitted extended research time in Italy. Brian Schroeder would like to thank the J. William Fulbright Scholarship Commission for its crucial funding of this project in its initial stages, and Paul and Francena Miller, for their generous support of the College of Liberal Arts at the Rochester Institute of Technology. Silvia Benso would like to thank Siena College for granting her both financial assistance and leave time to work on this project. Gianni Vattimo and Maurizio Pagano, who have been behind this work from the start and have also contributed richly to this volume, deserve special mention, as do Hugh Silverman and Jason Wirth. We are especially indebted to Jane Bunker, Marilyn Semerad, and the staff at SUNY Press not only for their enthusiastic support of this volume, but also for establishing the new SUNY Series in Contemporary Italian Philosophy. And last but not least, we extend our sincere and deepest appreciation to the contributors of this volume for their constant support, encouragement, and patience.

Introduction

Contemporary Italian Philosophy

The Confrontation between Religious and Secular Thought

MAURIZIO PAGANO

In the first thirty years after World War II (1945–1975), the Catholic and secular [laica] cultures in Italy lived in a regimen of separation. This does not mean that no relations occurred between the two sides. What was missing, however, was mutual acknowledgment, the conviction that the other side's issues and theoretical proposals were meaningful and relevant. Secular culture tended to consider religion as a topic of confessional interest, and thus it excluded it from the issues worthy of discussion, whereas Catholic culture lived somewhat as if it were in a separate enclosure. This was mirrored also in the modes of circulation of culture because the important publishers and most well-known bookstores offer mainly secular products, whereas religious, philosophical, and theological themes are confined in a separate and marginal space.

This situation is a legacy of Italian history. The country had been unified in 1870 with the capture of Rome, a move against the temporal power of the Church. The new Kingdom of Italy had developed as a secular, liberal state. The teaching of theology was banned from state universities and that of religion from all schools. On its side, the Church situated itself almost always against the state and modernity. Moreover, unlike in the United States, the Protestant presence was very small, so Catholics did not find themselves conversant with Christians from other confessions, but only with representatives of a culture indifferent or hostile to their religious perspective.

To evaluate how the debate around religion develops on philosophical grounds, one must first consider the figures of Benedetto Croce and Giovanni Gentile, the greatest representatives of Italian philosophy at the beginning of the twentieth century. Croce and Gentile played a lively part in that vast movement of European thought that arose at the end of the nineteenth

1

century, looking for new avenues of philosophy after the crisis of positivism. For both, the starting point was a critical confrontation with positivism and Marxism, which at the end of the nineteenth century had itself come very close to positivism. Both Croce and Gentile put forth their proposals as critical renewals of Hegel, even as a "reformation" of his dialectic. Croce, with his solid grounding in history and literature, had a passion for concrete analyses, and in his philosophy looked for an articulate picture to support and frame his particular inquiries. Gentile, on the other hand, was a speculative mind who wanted to further the modern philosophy of the subject and make it coherent by constructing a rigorous, unitary system.

The issue on which both philosophers completely agree is the idea that one should eliminate any element of transcendence from philosophy. Both aim at delineating a totally immanent conception of Spirit [Spirito]. The whole of reality is resolved in the experience of Spirit, in the history through which Spirit creates and realizes itself. Both Croce and Gentile mean to elaborate a secular thought that, one should note, does not despise religion, but rather wants to retrieve within itself the best and truest meaning of religiosity. Their outlet will thus be a secular religion, or rather a religious secularity.

According to Croce, Hegel's system is too unitary, too monolithic. It is not true that Spirit unfolds along a single path culminating into philosophy. On the contrary, it consists of spheres that are linked to and at the same time distinct from one another. These spheres, or degrees, are four in number: two of a cognitive character (art and logic) and two of a practical nature (economics and ethics). As one can see, religion does not have a specific place. It is reduced to aesthetics as far as liturgical elements are concerned and to ethics and conceptual thought as far as other aspects. Croce does not actually give any special consideration to the autonomous features of religious experience. In this respect, his position remains greatly inferior to Hegel's philosophy of religion. As critics have amply acknowledged, the best and most fecund aspect of Croce's work does not lie in his systematic framework, but rather in his concrete work of analysis of the human world in its various forms. Of his work, one should say that it has always been sustained by a deep ethico-religious drive, which brought Croce, especially in his last years, to question intensely the presence of evil and the negative in history. The same inspiration guided him in his political opposition to fascism and defense of liberalism, which in him became a "religion of freedom."

Unlike Croce, Gentile finds that Hegel's system is not coherent enough. The great enemies of idealism are realism and naturalism; in short any theory that admits as its presupposition something else that is located outside and before thought. Idealism can maintain itself and win its fight only if it is coherent to the end and denies that any reality (whether idea or nature) exists outside thought thinking of it. The only reality is thus Spirit, and this reduces itself to the act of thought. Certainly thought, as subject, always comes across an objective reality opposed to itself; yet it realizes itself precisely by bringing it back to itself time after time in an infinite process of spiritualization of the world. Such a radical position finds its confirmation in the history of philosophy. From Descartes to Berkeley, from Kant to Hegel, modern thought has asserted the centrality of the subject in an increasingly clearer manner and has progressively reduced the meaning of reality to it. Gentile's absolute idealism advances itself as the most coherent form in which this line of development finds its climax. Because the whole of history is the history of Spirit, the history of philosophy is the core of history. On this ground the entire experience of modernity is read as an irresistible movement toward radical immanence and thus toward the elimination of any transcendence.

Unlike Croce again, at the climax of his system Gentile retrieves Hegel's triad of art, religion, and philosophy. Yet, his conception of religion is much more schematic and hasty than the German philosopher's. For Hegel, religious experience has at its center the relation, full of tension, between the freedom of the finite subject and the infinite divine object. It stretches itself therefore from the moment of rupture, in which the subject asserts its autonomy, to the moment of reconciliation, in which the two extremes reunite. For Gentile, religion is simply the sphere within which the Absolute is asserted as object entirely independent from and opposed to the subject. Religion is characterized by a dogmatism that denies freedom; yet religion is also a spiritual experience, so here too does Spirit gradually assert its rights. This occurs in part already in religion itself, especially with Christianity and the dogma of the unity of God and humanity in Christ. The process, however, fulfills itself only in philosophy, in absolute idealism, which in the experience of Spirit, finds again the unity of divine and human. Gentile thus proposes his thought as the true theology, a totally immanent theology that denies any revelation and alterity; only thereby one that can fully assert the freedom of Spirit. Gentile advances a radical demythologization of Christianity in which religion is considered as an inferior philosophy. His entire thought and work, however, are supported by a strong ethico-religious drive, which brings him to understand his own historical task as that of a religious reformer who aims at realizing the liveliest legacy of Italian *Risorgimento* (Mazzini's secular religion) against the degenerations of the liberal state and against socialism, forgetful of the young Marx's humanism. Given this perspective, Gentile adhered to fascism and was the minister of education in the first Mussolini government. In that role, he introduced the teaching of religion in elementary schools, understanding religion as an inferior philosophy apt for children, whereas in the high schools the entire learning process would find its climax in philosophy. According to Gentile, education must be secular and nonconfessional. Yet secularity must be understood not as an agnostic and purely neutral attitude, but rather as a faith realized in the free quest of Spirit.

Croce and Gentile's neoidealism exerted a dominating, although not exclusive, influence on Italian philosophy and culture in the first part of the twentieth century. Among the alternative voices, the most important is certainly Antonio Gramsci, the prestigious communist leader whose main work only became known after World War II. Born in Sardinia, Gramsci was educated in the extraordinary climate of 1915–1920 Turin, where he led the workers' fights at Fiat and planned the democracy of workers' councils. Here he worked with Togliatti and came to be on the same wavelength as the leftist liberal Piero Gobetti. After Mussolini's rise to power, Fascists murdered Gobetti. Together with other communist leaders, the regime condemned Gramsci to prison in a mock trial in 1927. He remained in prison until close to his death in 1937 due to a disease his imprisonment had worsened. His main thoughts are contained in the *Prison Notebooks* [*Quaderni dal carcere*], written between 1929 and 1934, and published in Italy in 1948 by Togliatti's initiative. In these notes, Gramsci deeply rethinks "the philosophy of praxis" (how he refers to historical materialism). On the one hand, he strictly connects it to his politically revolutionary project; on the other, he inserts it in the tradition of modern, especially Italian, thought. For Gramsci, Marxism is an integral historicism, which represents the climax of modern history. The decisive turn on this path is brought about by Hegel, who eliminates any dualistic and naturalistic residue, thereby giving birth to a philosophy of the subject. Marx makes such a subject concrete, and Croce retranslates into speculative terms the philosophy of praxis, definitively eliminating any transcendence and thus reaching the highest climax of bourgeois thinking. Gramsci in turn eliminates the idealistic elements within Croce's thought, thereby realizing a completely immanent vision, focused on human being as a concrete and social subject who indissolubly links his or her theoretical understanding to his or her praxis of transformation of the world.

Another name worth mentioning for his exemplary value is Piero Martinetti. Inspired by Plato, Schopenhauer, and especially Kant, he delineates a dualistic and pessimistic vision, in which reason gradually elevates itself to a principle of absolute and transcendent unity, which reason itself however can never fully possess. Furthermore, Martinetti was one of the first Italian philosophers seriously to study Indian thought. He severely criticized neoidealism, but also the Catholicism of his times. Martinetti was one of the eleven professors who refused to pledge allegiance to the fascist regime. Thus in 1931 he had to relinquish the position he held in Milan, where he had founded an important school, which through his student Antonio Banfi and his disciples exists to this day. After returning to his country house near Turin, Martinetti lived in solitude, cultivating the land; yet, he remained a point of reference for many young anti-Fascists. He was also arrested in 1935 for a few days. To the police officer who had arrested him and asked for his identification, he replied disdainfully: "I am a European citizen, who by chance was born in Italy." With his rigorous coherence, Martinetti is a spiritual master, and a source of inspiration both for secular philosophers such as Norberto Bobbio and Ludovico Geymonat, and for Catholic thinkers such as Augusto Del Noce and Luigi Pareyson. He is perhaps the only figure with whom both secular and Catholic thinkers can identify with equal devotion and admiration to the point that one often hears of a Turinese "Martinettism."

The only organized and efficacious opposition to Gentile's predominance in philosophy was in the Catholic area, and precisely in the neoscholastic trend that went back to Thomas Aquinas and had its center in the Università Cattolica del Sacro Cuore in Milan. This orientation dominated Catholic thought in the first thirty years of the twentieth century, but it did not bring new results at the theoretical level.

The entire panorama of Italian thought started to change in the 1930s, both because new foreign trends, such as phenomenology and especially existentialism, became known and discussed, and because Gentile's school started to split internally. For both theoretical and political reasons, some of his students moved closer to Croce and then later to Marxism. Other thinkers close to him developed an interest for the religious dimension that was inspired by Augustine and Antonio Rosmini and privileged the interior experience of the subject. From this tendency, whose representatives were especially Armando Carlini, Augusto Guzzo, and Federico Sciacca, a second area of Christian thought developed, which was an alternative to neoscholasticism and which, although it was not a real school, was qualified with the collective name of "spiritualism." Some years later, an important thinker who was developing his own formation at that time at Guzzo's school, Luigi Pareyson, will reevoke that experience by saying that the diaspora of Gentile's school repeated in Italy, 100 years later, the division in the Hegelian school between the left and the right. The Hegelian attempt to reconcile Christianity and modernity had failed, according to Pareyson, and opened the way for the alternative between Feuerbach's atheistic humanism and Kierkegaard's rediscovered Christianity. The same choice presented itself again more urgently after the exhaustion of Gentile's thought. This alternative was the theme with which Italian thought found itself confronted, according to Pareyson, at the end of the war.

The panorama one encountered immediately after the end of the war presented a sharp division between Catholic and secular thought. Because the latter was in turn split between the supporters of Marxism and those of a liberal-democratic orientation, one can properly say that Italian philosophy in the first decades after the end of the war unfolded within three sharply distinct areas: the Catholic, the Marxist, and the one that defines itself as "secular" in the strict sense. The common element in all is the conviction that in the previous period, because of the fascist dictatorship and the predominance of idealism, Italian culture had closed itself off to the external world and lost its contacts with the most vital movements of the European culture. The urgent task presenting itself after the war was that of intensively resuming such relations, and building a new and more open culture. This shared inspiration was lively and efficacious in the first two years after the Liberation, and even caused some collaboration among the various areas.

The climate changed abruptly in 1947 when De Gasperi under pressure from the United States expelled communists and socialists from the government, and worsened with the excommunication of the communists, which Pius XII decreed in 1949. For the entire period of the cold war, the three areas conversed almost exclusively within themselves. Contacts resumed around the 1960s, when conditions were favored by the de-Stalinization of the communist world and by the renewal brought about by John XXIII and the Second Vatican Council among Catholics. During this period an intense dialogue between Catholics and Marxists developed in the search for points of convergence that might enable a shared involvement in society.

The main theme on which postwar Italian Marxism focused was the confrontation with Gramsci's thought. By prominently publishing Gramsci's *Prison Notebooks* beginning in 1948, Togliatti imposed his own theoretical and political views, which saw Marxism as a historicism capable of both continuing the Italian cultural tradition and of renewing it in a democratic direction. An alternative line of thought, which failed to gain influence, was promoted by intellectuals such as Elio Vittorini and by philosophers such as Galvano Della Volpe and Giulio Preti, who were especially active in northern Italy and who proposed a sharp break with the past and a radical opening of Italian culture to new trends coming from the United States and from the most advanced European countries.

In the secular area a program of retrieval and reassertion of a critical and antimetaphysical conception of reason prevailed. This was the area most involved in the effort of importing into Italy the best results of European and American thought, from historicism to existentialism, from pragmatism to neopositivism and analytic philosophy. The most vibrant center was Turin, where Nicola Abbagnano and Norberto Bobbio led the movement of "neoilluminism," which was greatly open to the contributions from human sciences and especially from sociology. Abbagnano was well known to the public because by the end of the 1930s he had started to develop his own original formulation of the philosophy of existence. In a polemic with Heidegger, Jaspers, and later with Sartre's positions, who emphasized the negative character of possibility, and with Marcel's religious existentialism, who anchored the ultimate guarantee for the realization of human projects in transcendence, Abbagnano advanced a "positive existentialism," which focused on the finitude of human projects and on the open and undecided character of possibility. In the new, postwar climate, Abbagnano was mainly concerned with discerning how, and with which instruments and which techniques, thought can cooperate to the enactment of the best possible choices, to the realization of possibility. For this reason, his philosophy opened up to cooperate with natural and human sciences, to deepen methodological studies, and to listen to the most current foreign voices. Among these, he privileged John Dewey's thought. On this path, his existentialism ended up with neoilluminism.

Another representative of positive existentialism, next to Abbagnano, was Enzo Paci, a student of Banfi's in Milan. In these years, Paci moved to a form of relationism that Whitehead inspired, and finally ended up with a thought attempting to combine Husserl's phenomenology and Marxism. In 1951, he founded *aut aut*, one of the most well-known and successful Italian philosophical journals, which Paci's student, Pier Aldo Rovatti, now directs. Several other thinkers who retain an important place within the Italian contemporary panorama have been educated at Paci's school: Carlo Sini, who, among other things, has deeply studied the philosophy of Charles Peirce, and Salvatore Veca, who has devoted himself especially to political philosophy, introducing in Italy the theories of John Rawls and other overseas thinkers. With respect to neoilluminism, the most genuine and coherent interpreter of this line of thought was Norberto Bobbio, who recently died. A philosopher of rights and politics linked to the legacy of Piero Gobetti's "liberal socialism" and attentive to Hans Kelsen's and analytic philosophy's contributions, Bobbio defended and reasserted the great themes of modern liberal and democratic thought. He engaged repeatedly in a constructive dialogue with the Marxists, spurring them to review their most dogmatic and extremist positions. With regard to religious themes, both neoilluminism and Marxism proved to be substantially insensitive to this dimension of existence.

Within the area of Catholic thought, the discussion between neoscholastics and spiritualists, who tended to prevail, continued. Both tendencies aim to show how a path leading to God, to a transcendent dimension, unfolds from experiences common to everyone. Neoscholastics, which Gustavo Bontadini led, start from the most general experience, that of becoming, and try to provide a rigorous and incontrovertible proof for the existence of God. Spiritualists, on the other hand, want to start with human experience with the dimension of the subject. With its peremptory need, which also generates some degree of anxiety, to provide a final and cogent proof, neoscholastic thought is certainly more rigorous, but also more distant from the issues and questions rising in a human world and in an increasingly lively and autonomous society. The spiritualist discourse is less solid on the level of argumentation, but as a whole is more attentive to catch the various and novel questions arising within human experience. Thus, its line fell apart sooner, but as a whole its experience prepared the establishment of a new, more mature, and open climate within the Christian thought of the following years.

This new generation of philosophers, educated between the end of Fascism and the beginning of the postwar period, soon distanced itself not only from idealism, but also from spiritualism. Through this path, it came into contact with the great European philosophies and also with the most important theologies, and it became a significant and in some cases original interlocutor within the international debate. Starting in 1961, Enrico Castelli organized in Rome a long series of meetings which world-class philosophers, from Bultmann to Gadamer, Ricoeur to Levinas, attended. In this way, he introduced in Italy the interest for demythologization and biblical hermeneutics. Alberto Caracciolo, a thinker not connected to any Christian denomination, but strongly interested in the religious experience and in the themes of evil and nihilism, first developed a philosophy of religion aimed at showing, following Schleiermacher's example, the autonomy of this sphere in relation to other fields of experience. Moving from neoscholastic thought Italo Mancini and Virgilio Melchiorre opened an engagement with phenomenology and hermeneutics. The former also confronted himself with the entire German theology from Barth on, and he introduced the thought of Bonhoeffer to Italy.

One of the most original and incisive voices is that of Augusto Del Noce, who radically confronted the problem of atheism and its connection with modern thought. Faced with the enigma of existence and the problem of evil, one is called to a radical option: either one chooses a naturalistic vision, according to which evil is reduced to finitude, or one embraces the religious view, which takes evil back to human choices and sin. Already at the beginning of the history of the West, the myth of Anaximander and that of Genesis present these two alternatives. The issue presents itself again at the origin of modernity when Descartes asserts, on the one hand, the subject's centrality and autonomy, and on the other, God's absolute freedom. From here two alternative lines unfold: the one largely prevailing being the philosophy of the subject, the climax of which is Hegel, and which finds its actualization in Marx's atheism. This is the perspective that most decisively denies all transcendence and finds its most consequent formulation in Gentile's absolute idealism. For Del Noce, the failure of Gentile's thought affects this whole line and opens the way for a retrieval of the religious trend, which is minoritarian but truer moving from Pascal and Malebranche and through Vico coming to Rosmini and Gioberti. Rather than innovating, this second way represents and develops on modern grounds the insurmountable legacy of traditional Christian thought.

For Luigi Pareyson, too, Hegel is the climax of the main line of modern thought, which tends toward immanence and secularization. Unlike Del Noce, who in the end wants to retrieve traditional philosophy, Pareyson situates himself decisively on the ground of modernity, which is that of a philosophy of freedom. To the line of immanence he opposes a richer (although still minoritarian) series of thinkers, which goes from Pascal and Vico to Fichte and Schelling, Kierkegaard and Dostoevsky. According to Pareyson, the conciliation that Hegel offers to Christianity is a kiss of death; in the end, it is an equivocation that comes to light immediately after the death of the philosopher. On the one hand, there are those who continue Hegel's philosophy and realize it as ending in radical atheism, such as Feuerbach and Marx. On the other hand, there are those who, against Hegel, find again genuine Christianity, as is the case with Kierkegaard. In this light, after the dissolution of Hegel's synthesis or, 100 years after, of Gentile's, the decisive issue for philosophy itself is that of a choice in favor of or against Christianity. In this picture, Pareyson, a Christian thinker, situates himself on the side of existentialism, which he develops in the direction of an ontological personalism. The human being is not to be thought as a subject of knowledge, but rather, and more radically, as a person: as such, it is constitutively in relation with being and open to the truth. Nevertheless, it is itself an interpretation of the truth.

On these grounds and rethinking Heidegger's, Jaspers's, and Marcel's teachings, Pareyson develops a hermeneutic philosophy that unfolds in an autonomous and parallel manner with respect to Gadamer's and Ricoeur's. At its center is the idea that the truth is not to be conceived of as object, which thought may reproduce from the outside, but as inexhaustible origin, which thought interprets at its own risk. In this picture, different interpretations are entirely legitimate, and a dialogue is thus guaranteed that recognizes in the other a different, but equally genuine, perspective on truth. With these developments, Pareyson provides a decisive contribution to the introduction of hermeneutics in Italy and to the raising of the Italian philosophical debate to a more mature level. The last years of his life were devoted to a further deepening. Because the relation of human beings to being and truth always has the feature of interpretation and because this is a free act always exposed to the risk of failure, the issue is that of focusing on this knot of freedom, on its double-edged and risky character, which involves both the human and the divine being, and which, in the end, is revealed as the very face of being. This is the stage of the "ontology of freedom," in which, following the example of the later Schelling, philosophy realizes itself as hermeneutic of the religious experience. Here, the discourse focuses on the theme of evil, on sin and suffering, and it finds in the religious myth the only language capable of approaching these themes without reducing their thickness. The task of philosophy then is that of resaying the truth of myth by transferring it on the universal ground of thought that is common to everybody, both believers and nonbelievers.

The novelty that imposed itself after the second half of the 1970s was the end of the division in the three areas and the fading of the separation between Christian thought and secular culture. First was the crisis of Marxism, which quickly lost its position of prominence after 1945. Immediately after this, the debate focused on the "crisis of reason," understood as modern reason, rigid and projectual. The retrieval of reason was the banner of neoilluminism, the movement that had dominated postwar secular philosophers. This very orientation was thus called into question. In general, a crisis of the great visions of synthesis, of totalizing discourses claiming to unveil the global sense of history and experience, arose so that what was asserted were perspectives that accepted as a starting point a situation of radical pluralism, devoid of synthesis. Hermeneutics came to replace dialectics and metaphysics. In this horizon, the rigid separation between secular and Christian thinking fell apart, and philosophers met and separated on the basis of the themes they addressed.

The new situation is introduced by Cacciari's "negative thought" [pensiero negativo] and finds a guide in the hermeneutics of Gianni Vattimo, a student of Pareyson, who together with Pier Aldo Rovatti develops a "weak thought" [pensiero debole] in which the themes of nihilism and the postmodern condition are central. The crisis of modern reason in its claim to dominate the world and the fading of the metaphysical view that thought of being as presence have started a process of weakening which, according to Vattimo, is to be read as a positive *chance*. In fact, it can free us from the authoritarian and substantially violent perspective that was implied in the entire Western thought. Along this path hermeneutics meets again the biblical legacy: the Christian God, who in the incarnation consigns his absoluteness to the weakness of the flesh, to the risk of history and interpretation, is located at the origin of the process of weakening. On these grounds, one can read the whole history of the West as a process of secularization, that is, of interpretation and application of the Christian message. Thus, hermeneutics acknowledges its own origin in the core of Christian religion. In this way, however, Vattimo seems to advance again a global vision of history, seen as a linear process that, from a strong and authoritarian beginning, moves toward a development increasingly entrusted to the free interpretation of the human being. In this sense his proposal comes close to the move toward immanence that Gentile exalted and that Del Noce and Pareyson criticized, although Del Noce and Pareyson understood this unfolding as the main direction of modern thought and experience.

The need for a confrontation with the Christian tradition and in general with the religious dimension is largely common among the most significant contemporary philosophers. This tendency is particularly evident in Massimo Cacciari, who had started out with Marxism, and also in Vincenzo Vitiello. Something similar is true for Mario Ruggenini and for Salvatore Natoli, whereas their teacher, Emanuele Severino, remains strongly polemical against the Christian faith. After his formation at the Università Cattolica del Sacro Cuore in Milan at Bontadini's school, Severino clamorously broke from it, asserting the need of a "return to Parmenides," that is, to a thought capable of asserting being and radically denying nothingness, and emphasizing a reading of the history of the West as a progressive path toward nihilism, which ensues from Plato's choice of asserting the reality of becoming. The religious inspiration, however, is explicit in Sergio Givone, who develops the legacy of Luigi Pareyson's "tragic thought" especially on aesthetic grounds. The philosophy of religion is at the center of the interests of the late Marco Maria Olivetti, a student of Enrico Castelli, who among other things kept the tradition his teacher started alive, and regularly organized in Rome important series of international conferences. The proceedings of these are published in *Archivio di Filosofia*, a philosophy journal under Olivetti's direction. More distant from the religious themes is Remo Bodei, who is, however, very sensitive to ethical and political issues. He is among the most attentive intellectuals trying to grasp the transformations of the current society and reflect on the destinies of the individual within the new horizon of the contemporary world. These authors frequently enter in conversation with Italian theologians, who have left neoscholasticism behind and in their turn widely engage international theological thought. Particularly distinguished among them are Bruno Forte, Piero Coda, and the Milan group of Giuseppe Colombo and Pier Angelo Sequeri.

In this new horizon, not only a dialogue but also a cooperation and in some cases a real convergence between philosophy and theology occurs. This ground has been deepened especially by Giovanni Ferretti, a philosopher whose formation occurred at the Università Cattolica del Sacro Cuore in Milan but who later worked at length with Pareyson's students, Claudio Ciancio and Ugo Perone. In this way, he approached hermeneutics. According to him, "critical hermeneutics" can be the shared ground for a kind of reason that has given up the claims to totality and for a theology that subtracts itself to confessional dependency to develop its reasons on a ground accessible to all. After the engagement in the 1960s and 1970s with the themes of history and eschatology, politics and secularization, now the common issues are those of evil and freedom, finitude, subjectivity, spirit, and the question of ethics on a planetary scale. Theology advances the themes of Christology and of the Trinity, philosophy those of intersubjectivity and alterity. Since 1987, *Filosofia e Teologia*, a journal regularly devoted to the confrontation between theology and philosophy has been published with editorial sites across Italy.

In the 1990s, the Italian cultural situation described herein, characterized by the nearing of secular and Catholic thought and by the convergence of philosophy and theology within a hermeneutic horizon, faces a new, greater challenge: the confrontation between religions and cultures, and the theme of globalization. Italian philosophy has been slower to detect the new horizon, partly because it lingered in the discussion between the supporters of modernity and of postmodernity, which today appears to us as a rearguard debate. This time theology has moved more quickly, spurred by the international debate on pluralism and inclusivism that began in the United States and in Great Britain. I think that one can indicate at least three needs that the new situation imposes as urgent for philosophical thought: first, in-depth work on the issue of intercultural relations is required; second, a renewed reflection on the theme of universality is needed; and, finally, a style of thought that is attentive and sensitive to the dimension of conflict in all its various forms is in order.

As for the first point, the prevailing hermeneutic climate with its opening to dialogue among different positions seems to offer a favorable starting point. An important premise to tackle the new tasks consists in the acknowledgment that Western reason is at its core a dialogical reason. In its modern path, it is marked by the long and at times harsh confrontation between philosophy and theology, as well as by the debate between secular and religious thought, the path of which has been here delineated for the last century in Italy. To evaluate this aspect deeply, Hegel's lesson remains essential, especially in the pages in the *Phenomenology* devoted to the fight of Enlightenment against faith, where he has shown the decisive relevance of this confrontation between religious dimension and autonomous reason.

This recognition of the pluralistic and dialogical character of Western thought is the premise to approach the confrontation with other cultures. The most recent discussions on this theme have convincingly shown that the dialogue with other cultures cannot be carried out by an objectifying thought that claims to have a panoramic view of its own and other traditions. We are situated in a determined situation, and we relate to others moving from there. In this sense the situated and perspectival aspect of thought and therewith its hermeneutic nature have been recognized. Theology has particularly emphasized the relational character qualifying the Christian revelation and the Absolute it proposes. More generally, several authors have claimed that this relational character affects our entire experience, and thus must orient our thinking. On these issues, the contributions of John Hick, John Cobb, and David Tracy meet those of French theologians such as Claude Geffré and Jacques Dupuis as well as the philosophical perspective of Paul Ricoeur.

The dimension of universality must be also thought in relational terms. The concept of universality, which becomes timely again in the epoch of globalization, has been traditionally conceived of as an a priori construed notion, as a category that reduces any particular to its homogeneous measure, according to a preconstituted and nonmodifiable norm. For this reason, nineteenth-century philosophy has rightly criticized and abandoned it already. Today it is making a comeback, especially in the discussions on world ethics, where it is understood as a regulative principle, as a set of criteria and norms that may obtain an intercultural acknowledgement and orient action. Time and again in the history of the West, starting as far back as with Xenophanes, the observation that other cultures and other religions exist has spurred one to look for a universal dimension of thought where one could understand one another. The universal is something that is elaborated in relation to the concrete experience, that allows it to enter a more adequate and richer relation with it to make it stand out in its specific features. At the roots of the genesis of the universal is always a break with respect to concreteness; by taking distance from it, one enters a more formal dimension in which the concrete is not obliterated but rather transposed and put in the condition to communicate with another concrete. In this sense the universal should be thought as a formal dimension that does not require rotation around a single center. Thus, a "universal without one" is one that enables exchange among particulars without forcing them to become homogeneous.

Following the line here advanced, we can distinguish between the properly universal dimension, which has a formal character, and its concrete realizations, which develop on historical grounds. Think, for example, of the unity of the divine Xenophanes claimed, of the minimal element common to religions the deists sought after, of universal human rights the Enlightenment formulated. What is universal in these formulations is the formal element that lives in the distancing from the concrete. It supports, time after time, a historical concretization that is universal only in this formal ground, and which nevertheless is historically necessary to give life to that formal element. One can thus understand why various historical claims, even when they energetically claim universal validity, may be failing and come into conflict with one another. To examine them and to evaluate critically the reasons for their conflict, one must then refer to the formal dimension, which is properly universal. Here, however, we are not talking about a monocentric universal in which in the end there is room only for one contestant who as winner dominates the others. In the "universal without one" is room for a true "struggle for recognition" in which my particular claim fights not to annihilate the other, but so that the other acknowledges my needs. The other should not abandon his or her needs, but he or she must widen his or her horizon to be able to coexist with me. In this perspective, the universal is conceived of as a wider sphere that can embrace within itself the opposed reasons for the conflict without its own self-destruction and can offer the conditions for the conciliation of such reasons.

Part 1

Marking the Borders

Historical Legacies

The five chapters comprising Part 1 engage ethical, political, and religious themes within the more general context bequeathed to twentieth-century philosophy by the tradition. The borders marked here are those of the legacy that the history of philosophy has consigned to contemporary thinking, but also the borders within or across which contemporary philosophy needs to think to retain its timeliness. All five authors shared similar consideration and concern despite their difference in formation and approach: the acknowledgment that old models of thinking have become obsolete and that new paradigms are needed to face the current crisis in which contemporary philosophy finds itself. Rather than providing a historical overview, these chapters adopt a highly theoretical approach, indicating themes that contemporary thinking is obliged to reconfigure to remain current with its epoch, while suggesting categories, movements, or figures of thought that might be inspirational for such a rethinking.

The roots of the Western configuration of ethics, politics, and religion, whether understood as separate areas of inquiry and action, or as fields intersecting to various extents to the point of overlapping, lie in the philosophy of that seminal thinker of the antiquity named Plato, and to him the opening chapter by Carlo Sini (Università di Milano), "The Desire for Eternal Life: The Platonic Roots of Western Political Science and Its Ethical and Theological Consequences," is devoted. Sini was educated in the tradition of the Università Statale di Milano, where he studied under Enzo Paci, a phenomenologist, existentialist, and Marxist thinker with a strong interest in Sartre and Whitehead. The themes of semiotics and pragmatism, especially Peirce's semiotics, are at the core of Sini's own meditation, which develops also through a reflection on Heidegger's hermeneutics in the direction of an "infinite semiosis" wherein semiotics and hermeneutics meet. An imaginative interpretation of Plato's *Republic* leads Sini to retrace in it the site of the staging of political science—a site that is opposed both to archaic conceptions of power (as exemplified through the story of Gyges's ring) and to the

political rhetoric of the Sophists (as in Thrasymachus's speech). Plato's gesture, Sini argues, is characterized by a deep identification of politics, philosophy, and pedagogy, united in the shared goal of removing the instance of
sexual desire and establishing in its place the supersensible site of the theoretical truth of the soul. The aspiration toward eternal life, which has always
ruled human speech and legitimizes its political power, acquires in Plato a
new meaning that, for Sini, will remain fundamental to all subsequent elabo-
rations of political theory. The dissolution of such a Platonic thread and the
surfacing of the backgrounds of its staging and characters are indicated by
Sini as the marks of the current political crisis, which is by no chance
centered around the crucial issues of generation, the social role of women,
and the political function of the communicative sign ruled by semiotic sciences and cybernetic technologies. Ultimately, Sini understands such a political crisis as the last consequence of Platonic metaphysics and science,
identifies its overall feature in the "theological" character of the entire Western
science, and finally indicates the opening of a new political scene in the
mutual recognition based on the currently unequal desire characterizing the
constitutive relationship between men and women.

The consideration which Sini already advanced, that philosophy finds
itself in front of a crisis, a change of paradigms, even a rotation of its traditional ways of proceeding is presented also in "Philosophy, Poetry, and Dreaming," by Sergio Givone (Università di Firenze). Educated in the Turin tradition
and formed under the guidance of hermeneutician and existential philosopher Luigi Pareyson, Givone has extensively explored the dimension of the
tragic, in its romantic and not simply Nietzschean variation, as the hermeneutic model adequate to a historical epoch hanging over the abyss of nihilism understood in both its philosophical and religious meaning. According
to Givone, we are observing an increasingly widespread aesthetization of
knowledge and the identification of philosophy with a literary genre among
others. Such an outcome was foreshadowed in the idea that science is a form
of knowledge to be contextualized in a wider historical and linguistic horizon
and in the thesis that philosophy is not at all a form of knowledge but rather
a self-understanding of ethico-religious choices if not simply a form of literary invention. For Givone, this is not so much a tendency as it is a given—
not only ontology but also the very scientific enterprise has been ascribed by
several sides to a mythopoietic horizon. Although variously contested, such
an ascription has been developed in somewhat opposite directions: on the
one hand, the alleged crisis of foundational reason has seemly brought about
the banning of the notion of truth (which if anything was reintroduced
within a merely apophatic if not mystical or merely tautological conception);
on the other hand, such a crisis has been declined positively in the direction
of an opening to the truth that is no longer truth but rather source of
dialogue, communicative exchange, infinite conversation, and so forth. Yet,
Givone asks, is it true that by renouncing demonstration, philosophical rea-

son finds itself confronted with the alternative of either silence or an irremediably equivocal arguing? The answer Givone provides is that everything depends on the genealogical deconstruction of the question, whether one starts with Nietzsche or with the romantic project. If one starts with Nietzsche, Givone argues, then truth is eliminated with the consequence that interpretative (and nondemonstrative) thought ends up being dissolved in fabulation. But if one starts with the romantic project, then fable, tale, and narration become the very site of philosophy. Givone's suggestion is that a way escaping the abovementioned alternative would thus present itself, a way in which philosophy and narration are neither in an irreducible conflict nor superimposed one on the other; rather, they rest in a deeper relation, as Novalis indicates when he is read backward in the direction of Vico and forward in that of Horkheimer and Adorno.

The legacy of Nietzsche's thought, most notably in its nihilistic variation, is implicitly in the background of "Christianity and Nihilism," by Vincenzo Vitiello (Università di Salerno), who was educated in the historicist tradition of Naples. A scholar of German classical idealism, Nietzsche, Heidegger, and the Christian and Neoplatonist traditions (especially Plotinus and Augustine), Vitiello has focused his research on some crucial theoretical questions such as the interpretation of time, the concept of difference, and the relation between dialectic and hermeneutics, arriving thus at his own hermeneutic theory—which he names "topology"—founded on a reinterpretation of the notion of space. Through a topological and not historical analysis of several historical figures (Matthew, Paul, Augustine, Kant, Dostoevsky, Mann), Vitiello shows how the conflict between paganism and Christianity is irresolvable because in each exists a seed of the other and vice versa. According to Vitiello, if, as Schelling claims, there is an eternal Christianity, a Christianity occurring "before" historical Christianity, then there is an eternal paganism, one taking place "after" historical paganism. Hegel, Nietzsche, and Dostoevsky testify to this. Today, in the age of seemingly complete nihilism marked by the overwhelming presence of technology and the apparent victory of the economical over the ethical, in the age of globalization, what is required is, for Vitiello, a different mode of political thinking, one that accepts the abandonment of the plan of ethically ruling the world not simply as a lack or fall, but rather as a challenge. Through a radicalization of the nihilistic experience, Vitiello attempts a different interpretation of Christianity, one that separates Jesus's word from that of Paul, and finds in the zero-point of existence a possibility of salvation—not of redemption Vitiello emphasizes. It is not a matter of redeeming the world from evil, but rather of preserving the finitude of the finite, and thus of suffering evil (of suffering, not welcoming it, which would be to justify evil as an instrument for the good). What Vitiello advances is a "morality of imperfection" to save the world from the absoluteness of the good—from the ever new Grand Inquisitors of whom Dostoevsky narrates. The chapter concludes with the evocation of Hans Kelsen's juridical philosophy as pointing to a feeling of universal *philia* emerging from the experience of suffering as an irrefutable witness to finitude. Not a neopaganism, but a new Christianity aware of the fragility of everything is Vitiello's suggestion for our contemporary epoch.

The great themes of paganism or nihilism and Christianity (reinterpreted under the categories of philosophy and Christian theology) and their legacy to our philosophical times are at the core also of "Philosophy and Christian Theology Today: Hermeneutic Circularity as Fact and Task," written by philosopher of religion Giovanni Ferretti (Università di Macerata). An astute scholar of Max Scheler and Emmanuel Levinas, Ferretti, who also holds a degree in sacred theology, was educated in the Neo-Thomist, neoscholastic, and phenomenological tradition of the Università Cattolica del Sacro Cuore in Milan (University of the Sacred Heart), where he studied under the guidance of Sofia Vanni Rovighi, one of Italian major phenomenologists; Ferretti has also become very close to the tradition of hermeneutics through his collaboration with some of Pareyson's students, most notably Claudio Ciancio, Ugo Perone, and Maurizio Pagano. Through an abundance of details and references both to philosophers and to theologians, Ferretti describes the move from a disjunction between philosophy and theology to a nearing of the two disciplines that compels both to a reinterpretation of crucial theoretical knots constitutive of each. This situation, which Ferretti names "hermeneutic circularity," forces both philosophy and theology to welcome the mutual aid they can offer in the addressing of fundamental issues posed to both by contemporary culture, such as the relation between the one and the many (or totality and fragments), the emergence of a new subjectivity of an emotive-vital kind, the positivity of finitude, weakness, mortality of being, and the new dimension of ethics in relation to the globalized world.

The urgency for philosophy to confront contemporary philosophical themes consigned to it by the tradition of metaphysics is addressed in "Ontology of Actuality," by Gianni Vattimo (Università di Torino). Vattimo, who was educated at the hermeneutic school of Luigi Pareyson, develops much of his initial philosophy through a reflection on Schleiermacher, Heidegger, and Nietzsche, focusing on an interpretation of hermeneutics in an antimethodological, antifoundational register. The nexus "hermeneutics-nihilism" in its destinal, epochal character later leads Vattimo (and Pier Aldo Rovatti) to formulate a "weak thought" (*pensiero debole*) from which arises an ethics of *pietas*, and the refusal to engage in the features of reactive nihilism as Nietzsche described. In his chapter, Vattimo appeals to Foucault's notion of an "ontology for the current times," or an ontology of actuality, as the only adequate possibility for philosophy in the epoch of the end of metaphysics. He meditates on Heidegger's notion of an *Überwindung* (overcoming) of metaphysics in relation to its meaning as *Verwindung* (twisting or distortion) to claim a postmetaphysical thinking that has no other sources than its own legacy, that is, the legacy of modernity that, following Nietzsche, takes up the features of secularization or of the dissolution of ground. In Weber's theory of modernization, claims Vattimo, a concept of secularization escaping the metaphysical horizon can be found. What comes to light is a negativity or weakness characterizing being itself so that the ontology of actuality Vattimo ultimately invokes is in the end configured as a negative ontology that also marks the passage to an overcoming of metaphysics into ethics.

Chapter 1

The Desire for Eternal Life

The Platonic Roots of Western Political Science and Its Ethical and Theological Consequences

Carlo Sini

In Book II of *Republic*, Plato has Glaucon narrate the strange tale of Gyges, a shepherd serving the king of Lydia. After a tempest and an earthquake, a chasm opens where Gyges was grazing his herd. Descending into the chasm, the shepherd discovers wonderful things: a bronze horse through whose small windows one can see a huge corpse covered only with a gold ring. Gyges takes the ring and runs away, putting it on his finger. At a meeting with other shepherds to decide who would go to the king and give account of the herds, by casually rotating the ring on his finger, Gyges realizes that the ring has the magical power of rendering him, at his pleasure, invisible to the others. Managing to become part of the mission, Gyges goes to the palace, seduces the queen, and then with her help kills the king and seizes power.

An ancient tale, Gyges's story has other versions. Among them is Herodotus's version, of which Plato was certainly aware. According to Herodotus, Gyges is the squire of the king of Lydia, Candaulis. Proud of his wife's beauty, the king wants Gyges to admire the queen's naked body. He instructs him to hide by the door of the nuptial room, covered by the darkness of the night, when the queen undresses. Suddenly turning, however, the queen sees Gyges, and addresses him thus: "Since you have seen what you were not supposed to see, and to prevent you from seeing other wonderful and prohibited things, you have only two possibilities: either you die, or you kill the king, take his place, and marry me." Surmising Gyges's choice is not difficult. He coupled with the queen on the nuptial bed, and then they waited together to kill the king. In this way, Gyges the squire became in turn the king.

Glaucon resorts to the story of Gyges to expose his thesis relating to our political essence. By nature, all human beings desire to predominate over other human beings. As Thrasymachus claimed before Glaucon, human society is born out of the predominance of strength: the strong subdue the weak, thereby finding reason to impose those laws that sanction their own superiority and interest. The issue of justice, the central theme in *Republic*, is for Thrasymachus all right there. Those who, like Socrates, would defend justice in abstract "moralistic" arguments, to the point of even claiming, against common experience, that the unjust person is unhappy, either have understood nothing or take pleasure in vain rhetorical exercises. The one who is stronger determines what is just and unjust, what is legal and illegal, that is, the law, and does so to one's own advantage, that is, to consolidate one's power on the ground of one's own pleasure and happiness.

Fascinated by the intellectual lucidity and courage of Thrasymachus's thesis, Glaucon would like, at the same time, to see Socrates refute it. First, however, he defends it by making it more flexible and subtle. Indeed, human beings desire supremacy by nature; they desire exclusive and unconditional possession. Yet they experience also the dangerousness of such a natural desire: even the strongest may happen to succumb, for example, to suffer violence by another without the possibility of avenging themselves of it (which, for a Greek, is the most intolerable thing). It then happens that, at least in appearance, social and political society is not founded on a declared violence, but rather on a shared agreement obliging everyone not to exercise violence with the reciprocal guarantee that one will not suffer it as established precisely by the laws. This is the public pact on which the political community is grounded. However, it cannot and actually does not cancel our natural desire for supremacy. Hence, we see that in public everyone praises and shows obedience to the laws established by the social contract; yet in private where nobody sees, everyone gives free rein to their natural desire. Thus political aggregations and factions are formed; in word they respect the laws, but secretly they are ready to use any means, from lies to money to homicide, to make their own interests actually prevail within the state. To ratify this thesis, Glaucon recounts the story about Gyges: Let us suppose we give Gyges's ring to an unjust man, that is, to one who follows natural violence, and to the just man Socrates invoked (that is, to one who does not want to commit injustice, and who at the limit would prefer to suffer rather than to exercise it because only thereby, he thinks, he will not be unhappy). Certain of not being seen, both the hypothetical just and the unjust man would commit exactly the same actions, according to Glaucon; they would steal goods from the market, free their friends from chains, go into homes and sexually mate with whomever they like. If one were to possess such a power, which makes one similar to the blissful gods who do all what they want, and were not to use it, then one would simply be a mad person. Instead of being happy, one would be an unhappy person who has lost his or her mind.

Plato devotes the entire monumental *Republic* to the confutation of this thesis, which in the West will see famous retrievals, from Thrasymachean Hobbes to Locke to Rousseau, and so on. To overcome it (at least in theory), however,

Plato will have to imagine, on the one hand, a total revolution in political and social human life thanks to the institution of an ideal state philosophers rule. Without it, he says, the evils of the city and human unhappiness will never end. On the other hand, he has to grant with reasonable arguments and suggestive stories a life in the beyond in which the unjust are punished and the just rewarded. As everyone knows, this is the famous Platonic "utopia." That this hasty judgment does not give justice to what is instead realistic and still timely in it, is the point we will try to suggest synthetically.

One should first recall that the ideal city Plato described is founded on three essential steps. The first concerns the hierarchical structure of society, which is grounded on the spontaneous inclination of the soul and not on blood heritage. Political and military power is entrusted only to those who display a love of wisdom and the good more than anything else, being then aptly educated in them (the philosophers). All other citizens are subjected to these individuals. However (second step), the class of the rulers cannot possess anything, unlike the other citizens. In fact, they receive frugal sustenance from the ruled. Furthermore (third step), such a class is formed of men and women who are chosen on the basis of their natural "philosophical" inclination; however, they cannot exercise their sexuality according to their own desires, but only according to criteria of eugenics that are established with respect to times and persons by the older rulers. The children who will be born will be raised in public orphanages, so that among the rulers will be found no more fathers, or mothers, or natural children. Among themselves all rulers will be, according to their age, fathers and mothers, sons and daughters, brothers and sisters. As is well known, Plato does not fail to underline the enormity and the presumable scandal of such ordinances according to the common judgment of the time. And it is a fact that even we as readers are disturbed, to say the least. What induced Plato to propose a solution as drastic as presumably unrealizable (as he himself acknowledges)?

Developing the argument in an analytic and detailed manner is not possible here. I limit myself therefore to suggesting some essential points.[1] We must not overlook the pregnancy of the first dialogue of the work (the beginning of Plato's dialogues often has symbolic meaning and hiddenly prefigures the sense of what follows). Such an introductory dialogue takes place between Socrates and old Cephalus, in whose home the entire conversation of *Republic* occurs. Socrates asks Cephalus what characterizes old age, to which Cephalus replies: the fading away of desire. The old would like to go on desiring the pleasures of life, especially food, drinks, and sex, but they are no longer able truly to enjoy them. Hence their unhappiness: desire itself weakens and for them life no longer has meaning. Afterwards Socrates asks whether wealth provides consolation to the condition of old age. Yes, Cephalus replies, but not so much because money allows one to buy those practical comforts that are necessary to old age; rather, because being rich allows one not to commit violence and do injustice to anyone. But what is justice, then?

Here the general theme of *Republic* is set out, whereas Cephalus leaves the discussion to his friends and exits the scene. Taken as he is by religious mania, he spends his days sacrificing to the gods, fearing he will suffer in the afterworld those punishments one variously hears of. Evidently the rich Cephalus is not sure that during his lifetime he has not committed some injustice, and in any case he is looking for some heavenly protector.

What does all this mean? Synthetically, that the question of political justice has its foundation in desire. Consistently Cephalus does not take part in the dialogue because having freed himself from the desire for mundane things, and especially from sexual pleasure (so he says), he is no longer a political subject. He already lives in the beyond, caught up in his religious obsessions.

Yet, in the exchange with Cephalus, Plato admirably classifies the objects of desire, which with a modern terminology can be listed thus: objects of oral eros, genital eros, and anal eros (that money that allows buying anything: a real "transferal object" of any desire). The political question is thus one and the same with desire, which is a wild master, a ferocious and insatiable wolf of which Thrasymacus will be the explicit incarnation. But what does desire really mean? Why does the human being find himself or herself originarily inscribed in the incoercible passion of supremacy and possession? Plato shows this amply in *Republic* and in all his writings. But we will let Aristotle also say it synthetically, he who, while not sharing his teacher's political solution, inherited his philosophical ground of reasoning.

In the first book of *Politics*, Aristotle says that in nature females and males cannot exist separately, therefore they mate. They are in fact subject to the irrepressible impulse to generate, that is, to leave behind themselves another similar to them. In *De Anima*, Aristotle specifies that such an impulse derives from the desire, on the side of corruptible and mortal beings, to imitate the eternal life of the eternal gods. Precisely with the economy of life and death in sight, in nature sexual pleasure is the most intense, powerful, and desirable (Freud will say the same). Hence the entire familial and social organization. Because man is by nature the most intelligent, that is, the most capable of foreseeing the results of actions aiming at survival, he subdues both animals and women. As Hesiod used to say, in its essence the home is the woman and the plowing ox. The same occurs with master and slave, and then with Greeks and barbarians, hence the birth of the highest and most civilized state: the one of rational men, educated in arts, sciences, and philosophy. As a side note: despite much debate, this is still in fact the predominant opinion in the West.

The real political issue, then, is that of desire and eternal life, which is represented or "simulated" by blood descent, hence the old obsession of giving one's name to one's children, who will perpetuate the father's life, that is, will literally live in the name of the father, making his lineage eternal. From this one can notice how, very recently, our epoch is going through an anthropological and thus political revolution of the greatest and most immeasurable importance, testified by two events unthinkable up until a short while ago: the weakening of desire for descendents in favor of other more immediate desires, such as social self-affirmation, personal wealth, and the like; and the juridical recognition of the transmission of the name from the mother to the children. In particular, humankind, which has for centuries relied on amulets and magical practices of all kinds to secure for itself fecundity in mating, today does everything it can to obstruct it or at least plan it with many limitations.

What is important to stress here, however, is the role of woman in the traditional conception that grounds social and political life. If political union, as we have said, is a guarantee for eternal life, then the "chief" must be the one who with his own generating ability embodies and distributes it for everyone. The chief, the sovereign, the king (precisely an immortal figure: "The king is dead, long live the king!") is the one who makes cattle, fields, and our sexual unions fecund by his very presence alone. The only witness of this fecundity, however, is the woman: she makes manifest the "magical" potency of the man, his ability to produce in woman "wonderful things," that is, the birth of a new being. For this reason, however, to be certain, such "wonderful things" must remain prohibited and secret, that is, exclusive. In other words, woman cannot have a public life like man. Rather, she must live segregated in his exclusive possession, excluded from any participation in the political dimension of the community. Meanwhile, testifying to man's fecundity, woman is in substance the one who confers on him the right to royalty and possession. For this reason the sovereign, the embodiment of eternal life of which his woman is the guarantee, is the owner of everything: fields, cattle, life and death of the subjects. He is thus the owner of any primogeniture and the receiver of any offering. In fact, he is the symbolic link between earth and heaven. That is, he is the one to whom the gods give fecundity and life for everybody. At a minor level, this function is repeated in any family group by the father.[2]

Innumerable ethnological testimonies for this political-social-religious structure exist, which is obviously neither the only one nor the oldest known to human beings, yet it is typical of patriarchal societies. The tale of Gyges is evidently connected to it. By possessing the king's woman not only does the shepherd, or squire as he may be, acquire royalty from her and thus the right to exercise life and death, but also all images previous to the final scene reassert it. The shepherd descends into the womb of mother Earth and steals her precious hidden treasure: a symbolically incestuous act that realizes the dream of the living to rejoin one's origin and thus become immortal (analogously, in Plato's ideal city, all citizens consider themselves to be born directly from the Earth without any male sexual intermediation). The subtracted treasure (the ring) gives the power to let the invisible appear and at the same time disappear. This possession of the invisible is reasserted also in Herodotus's version, where the squire sees what he was not supposed to, that is, the secret

of the generation that founds royalty; the sovereign embodies this preroga-
tive, that is, the mystery and secret of life. It is a gift of the invisible gods;
it is the gift that makes everything visible appear on earth. Blood generation
testifies to this primordial incarnation, from which derives blood right, which
is certainly among the oldest rights we know. The ring, symbol of royalty
(and of marriage) is the transferal object thereof. That the ancient sources
refer the beginning of "tyrannical" royalty in Lydia and the invention of
money to Gyges is significant: that gold that his descendant Croesus, in his
avidity, will discover to be rather indigestible, that is, not exactly equivalent
to life.[3]

When one takes all this into account (and there would be much more
to say), the Platonic operation takes up a clear meaning. By evoking the tale
about Gyges, which is not by chance recalled also at the end of *Republic*[4] at
the completion of the path, Plato proposes a new and unheard of political
organization, which is no longer founded on blood right, and, moreover, on
the sexual desire that lies at its origin. To this goal, philosophy is instituted;
it is an educational and formative program that must yield a class of human
beings free from desire for sex, paternity, gold, and any other visible possession. Men and women of the invisible, the philosophers are educated to the
vision of the suprasensible, that is, of that invisible that Plato represents in
the light of the Good: the good end to which the generation of all visible
things is ordered—from human to cosmic things, as explained in *Timaeus*,
the explicit continuation of *Republic*.[5]

Essential to the Platonic operation is obviously the transfiguration of
desire into desire for knowledge (philosophy), that is, into the ability to see
the invisible law of everything (what Plato calls "idea," which will then
come to mean precisely "vision") and ultimately in the ability to produce it.
In the end, philosophical politics is nothing else than the *science* of the
production of souls and bodies, and of the rational administration of life and
death (addressed to those who must not be born and to those whom, having
been born, is in the "common interest" to suppress. This is all *literally* explained in *Republic*).

When considered in this way, Plato's proposal in *Republic* is something
completely different than a simple utopia because much of it, not to say the
essential, has in fact been realized in the political theory and practice of the
Western world. Let us briefly discuss this with reference not so much to the
history of this filiation (this topic is too long and complex to address it here)
as mainly to our actual times.

First is the alliance of rationality and mysticism characterizing the
political tradition in the West, making all science in general and then all
political science an explicit or masked theology. The Platonic foundation of
the concept, that is, of rational knowledge, has its essential groundings in
Republic (emblematic in this respect is the myth of the cave). The concept
is the suprasensible, that is, that universal viewpoint expressing the truth of

all things. Because the reference is not to any particular individual, the place is also sexless, despite the fact that its foundation is due to a group of men reflecting at Piraeus on how to solve the evils of politics and human life. This is a theological place in all senses because it aims at a panoramic and supramundane vision. That is, it aims at the truth in itself of everything that is, human beings included. This is still the ideological claim of modern science (a claim rather different from what it actually does, which is much more important and fecund, although it does not know how to think of it yet): to see things *sub specie aeternitatis*, that is, as God would see them. It is a theological and teleological notion of the scientific method. For this to make sense, however, the "suprasensible place," as Plato calls it, must exist: the mystical side of the concept, which is complementary and consubstantial to its truth.

At the political level, rational mysticism expresses itself in the charismatic investiture of power, whether assigned to the ecclesiastic power, the mystique of "enlightened sovereignty," "general will," representation of the sovereign people, or, finally, to the citizen's universal right to vote. All these components concur to form public sovereignty, the sensible representation of which is visible (the soldiers still stand even when the republic replaced the king), the "arcanum" of which, however, remains invisible, that is, the secret of power which, as Glaucon claimed, is rather consigned to the backstage intrigues of politics and its substantial "economic" choices of life and death.

The process aiming at the manifestation of the arcanum, however, has been on its way for a while now (this is substantially what is called "modernity"). Power desubstantializes itself, manifests itself to the public "democratically," opens the doors of palaces, and lets public information come in. Power makes itself known and transparent in its "signs," aptly dematerialized; even money is more and more suprasensible and "computerized." Believing that all this obeys solely moral reasons or that it is out of love for justice, however, would be naïve or at least insufficient. The case is that of the path of the concept, which imprints every feature of communitarian and social life: the suprasensible in the idea (that is, in the "*video*," as the word says in its etymology) descends on earth and takes root there. Everything thus becomes public and suprasensible, including the private lives of the powerful and the humble, sounded and mimed by the unlimited eye of television.

The end of the transferal objects of traditional desire and power, their assimilation to pure signs of information available to everybody is by no means, however, the end of the political theology of the West; in some respects, it is rather its most efficacious realization. Power, in fact, now transfers itself on the sign itself. In other words, information becomes the real place of power and its reaffirmed arcanum. Today information is a universal category applicable to natural and economic sciences, to human sciences and to the media's semiotics and cybernetics, to genetics and to artificial intelligence. At its ground are still, and always, those things Glaucon mentioned:

lies, money, violence, and death. More than preventing these things, as it thought it would do, the Platonic project has made them scientific, that is, more efficient and even more or less shared by all in the common conviction that, after all, this is the best possible political organization. In many, although not all, respects, this is the myth of universal democracy, which is actually supported by the supersensible of financial capital, "smart" bombs, and atomic weapons, possessed primarily by the West.

At least two aspects, however, are important to mention. The first, already noticed, is that the dialogue of *Republic* is a gathering of men, of free and wealthy citizens (in truth, it is an impressive meeting of dead characters, some dead of violent death, whom Plato with unparalleled art resurrects to reflect on the disasters of Athens and Greece following the devastating Peloponnesian War). It is a gathering of patriarchal men who nevertheless dare to equate themselves with women. This is certainly an extraordinary yet not so peacefully shared fact. On this issue, however, it is also easy to equivocate. It is by no means a matter of "woman's liberation"; rather, it is a matter of her complete elimination. It is the elimination of her problem and, first of all, of the problem of that recognition that, in the ancient political conception, ambiguously assigned to woman the origin itself of sovereignty. I say ambiguously because such a recognition did not go back to a woman's act of choice or free election. To obtain it, constriction or rape were very well sufficient. The mere fact was enough to testify for itself, regardless how a woman welcomed it. Plato's scandalous and titillating proposal of "women in common" (this is how Socrates and his friends express themselves, despite the fact that it is also a matter of "men in common," but this expression does not come to their lips, which is comprehensible as much as eloquent) is in fact a gelid and, in its own way, naïve proposal. By instituting a public vagina and an impersonal phallus, scientifically planned, as a matter of fact Plato pretends to erase desire at its roots. He does this by completely "virilizing" woman and by assimilating her soul ("logic") to the male logic of philosophical rationality. Any modern woman's vindication that walks on this path, aware or not, does not know what it says or does. That is, it ignores that it is repeating within itself, and is thus caught by it, the rational metaphysics of the West, which was actually inaugurated for political purposes by the male sex, that is, by undoubtedly exceptional and extraordinary Greek men.

Plato wants to uproot desire, at least from politics and science, for our personal and social happiness. Only in this way will we have a just society and a just political order. The fact is, however, that once the matter is set out in this way, which appears to be very difficult to Plato himself, it is also insufficient. In fact, more than educating oneself to suppress desire through its transvaluation in rational exercises and mystical visions, it was a matter of understanding it. What does desire desire? And why does it desire it? These questions are largely unaddressed.

To Thrasymachus, who argues out of the unquestionable and evident desire for overwhelming, that is, out of the desire for power and force that enables one to attain it, Socrates opposes several insufficient objections until he comes to imagine, as Nietzsche put it, a world behind the world in which tyrants suffer the pains of hell and the just attain their desired happiness (which is doubtful, as Socrates acknowledges, that they achieve in this life and remain just). That is, in the end Socrates resembles a little bit old Cephalus, only he is much smarter and more imaginative (what game is here Plato really playing?). Yet, the only proper question that one should have asked Thrasymachus and all those who think like him is not raised and perhaps not imagined by Socrates: Why is power so desirable?

If one looks at the depth of this abyss, then power (of subduing the plowing ox, woman, and any other person) shows to be what it actually is: a mere transferal sign of something it itself is *not* (for example, money, logic, the suprasensible vision, information). What it is not is indeed the very movement and nature of desire, which consists only in desiring to be desirable. This originary exchange, by its own nature unequal and incomparable (among equals there is in fact nothing that can be exchanged or, more exactly, donated), is the real motor of desire: what links the infant to the parents and the parents to the infant, man to woman and woman to man, the lover to the beloved and the beloved to the lover (Plato has indeed said something about it in various dialogues). I desire your desire, that is, your recognition. I am something for and by virtue of your desire, and likewise you are something for mine in the unequal exchange of the two poles each desiring his or her other, inassimilable and incontrollable, from whom they derive their own very identity. This reveals the mystification of "force" and its transferal objects, starting with the bewitching and rhetorical use of speech (of which logic too is part, when it does not realize its prejudices) and ending with money.

Everyone's identity, therefore, is nothing "in itself." Rather, it is always in the relation with the desire for the other, whom one cannot truly desire to subdue because this would imply the failure of one's own desire and one's subsequent unhappiness. The fear of unhappiness and of the failure of one's recognition, however, is such that the superstitious appeal to the possession of transferal objects, from which one can draw an albeit imaginary and precarious illusion of happiness and perhaps even justice, becomes very common. Philosophy should liberate us from this superstition, as it has partly contributed to do. It is for this involuntary or voluntary injustice that what today we call democracy should make itself responsible (as it partly does).

The provisional conclusion could then be this: the relation of desire linking, despite everything, man to woman, and, in general, human beings among themselves, is the implicit meaning of Western politics. Plato has at least hinted as much, and this Aristotle has already stiffened in his "phenomenological" observations (man lies on top, woman below; the master orders, the slave obeys; the Greek rules, the barbarian is subject). As its implicit meaning, this is at the same time the presumable future of politics in its epoch of planetary expansion. The unequal exchange of sexuality and desire, however understood, is when correctly understood the current political issue. The problems of capitalism, finance, globalization, desertification, cultural homogenization, and the spreading (never known to human beings to this degree) of injustice and poverty are nothing except its congruent aspects.

Notes

1. For an exhaustive treatment of the issues I here raise, see Carlo Sini, *La virtù politica* (Milan: Cuem, 2000). Some of the themes there addressed are also discussed in different thematic contexts in Carlo Sini, *La libertà, la finanza, la comunicazione* (Milan: Spirali, 2001).

2. Francesca Calabi writes, "the passage of royalty through a woman is a strong element in many myths about sovereignty; it is not only a reference to matrilinear succession, but also a memory of legends and myths in which a woman assigns power to a man chosen by her"; Francesca Calabi, "Gige," in *Platone: La Repubblica*, ed. M. Vegetti (Pavia: Pubblicazioni del Dipartimento di Filosofia dell'Università di Pavia, 1995). The acquisition of power through a woman who is subtracted from another man also presents several examples. It is enough here to mention the rape of the Sabine women, from which comes the Roman ceremony of the faked matrimonial rape; Oedipus and Jocasta, Aegistus and Clytemnestra, the Suitors and Penelope, and so on. One should also recall, in James George Frazer, *The Golden Bough: A Study in Magic and Religion* (London: Macmillan, 1980), the fight with the old king of the young man aspiring to power.

With regard to the tale of Gyges, one should also keep in mind the theme of the chasm, abyss, or cave (*chasma*), which too has a clearly sexual connotation. The descent into the *chasma* is an archaic image linked to ritual transformation and to the rites of initiation: the descent into the abyss has cognitive and prophetic goals. Normally, at the end of the abyss is the encounter with a female goddess: Mother Goddess, Prophetess, Nocturnal Goddess, Mnemosyne, and so on. According to Walter Burkert, at the end of the *chasma* a confrontation between life and death takes place: *Mysterium der Wiedergeburt*. Eternal rebirth or eternity of the rebirth. Many examples can be provided for this meaning of the descent into the *chasma*: Epimenides, Orpheus, and Pythagoras (whom Apuleius considers to be "magicians"). The shamanistic and orphic features of such descents have also been stressed. One can think of the emblematic instances of Empedocles, who disappears into Etna, and of Parmenides and his goddess, who is situated beyond the abyss of the gateway of day and night, that is, beyond mortal time.

3. See *Oxford Classical Dictionary* (New York: Oxford University Press, 1996).

4. Mario Vegetti, in *Platone: La Repubblica*, has brilliantly shown the circular structure of *Republic*, which is marked by a path downward and a final going back up, or upward path. In particular, he has shown how the entire path of *Republic* is articulated by four descents into the *chasma*. The first, very famous, is Socrates's descent to Piraeus, Athens's harbor ("I went down to Piraeus yesterday . . . "), to attend the festival in honor of the Thracian goddess Bendis, a barbarian and noctur-

nal goddess, comparable to Hecates, the Greek goddess of infernal abysses. Here, Piraeus takes up the symbolic value of a disquieting and dreadful place. In it, people of all provenance and social origin go by. According to Plato, from the sea there comes a "disorderly variety of bad customs." Moral and social confusion, associated with the tumultuous events of trading and commerce. In *Timaeus*, Plato symbolically assigns Piraeus to the inferior parts of the human body (the womb and sex), the hysthmus to the neck, and Athens's acropolis to the head. This psychosomatic topography hints to the return to the mainland that is the homeland, which is accomplished precisely with *Timaeus*, under the sign of the festival in honor of Athena, clearly opposed to Bendis.

With reference to Vegetti, he has shown that in *Republic* the descent (*katabasis*) to Piraeus is followed by three other descents: that of Gyges, that of the myth of the cave, and that of the myth of Er. Four symbolic descents into the *chasma* that ultimately lead to the going back up (*anabasis*). At the end of book ten, Socrates speaks in fact in lieu of Er, replacing him in the role of *angelos*, of messenger, and he invites to "always hold to the upward path (*tes ano odou*)."

5. On the meaning of the continuation of *Republic* in *Timaeus*, I refer to Carlo Sini, *Raccontare il mondo* (Milan: Cuem, 2001).

Chapter 2

Philosophy, Poetry, and Dreaming

Sergio Givone

"That which cannot be proven must be narrated." This could be the slogan expressive of a change in paradigm if not even a kind of rotation in the speculative axis: from the increasingly widespread aestheticization of knowledge to the identification of philosophy with one literary genre among others. This outcome is already present in the idea that science too is a form of knowledge to be contextualized within a wider historical and linguistic horizon. Yet, it can also be recognized in the thesis that philosophy (and especially the philosophy of history) is not at all a form of knowledge, but rather a self-understanding of ethical-religious choices if not simply a form of fantastic invention.

More than a trend, this is a fact. It is a fact that from several sides one has witnessed the attempt to reconsign not only ontology (that is, philosophy when it has the meaning of being as its object, as its unobjectifiable object), but also the very scientific enterprise to an originarily mythopoietic dimension. Analogously, despite various contestations, this attempt has developed in opposite or almost opposite directions. The alleged failure of foundational and demonstrative reason has seemed to imply, on the one hand, the banning of the notion of truth, which was instead newly put forth within an apophantic, if not mystical or merely tautological conception; and, on the other hand, the declination in a positive sense of this very failure, through its understanding as an opening to a truth that is no longer the truth, but rather communicative exchange, infinite conversation, source of dialogue, and so on.

Yet, are we sure that, by giving up proofs, philosophical reason necessarily comes to be confronted with the alternative according to which either it is forced to silence or it appeals to an irremediably equivocal arguing (equivocal in the sense that it demands consensus on behalf of truth, but

A version of this work appears as "Filosofia, poesia e sogno," in *Annuario Filosofico* 17 (2001): 191–205.

after truth has been denied; that it claims to keep knowledge and narration separate, but after it has collapsed one into the other; that it wants to have demythologizing value, but without being aware of its own mythical charac- ter, that is, not only argumentative, but also hermeneutic, symbolic, meta- phorical)? Everything rests on the genealogical deconstruction of the question—whether one starts with Nietzsche or with the Romantic project. In the first instance, truth is removed with the result that interpretative, nondemonstrative knowledge ends up being resolved into fabulation. In the second instance, truth is situated at the core of the fable, and thus fable, tale, or narration becomes the very site of philosophy. This does not mean at all a reduction of philosophy to mythology. Rather, it means to consider "myth" (fable, tale, narration) as philosophy's most proper content and ground with which it originarily stands in relation. What comes to delineate itself is a path that escapes the abovementioned alternative. And, rather than bring- ing to a site where philosophy and narration stand in an irreducible contrast or are superimposed one to the other, it signals a deeper connection between the two.

Nietzsche claims to explain how the "true world" has at last become a fable by tracing the "history of an error," thereby showing the dissolution of truth while holding onto its concept.[1] Holding onto it only provisionally, however, that is, until the opposition between appearance and reality fades away. Hence, also truth (and error) fades away. What kind of story is this, then?

The true world is nothing other than illusion, belief, object of faith. For this to surface, a long process is needed. At first, the true world seems to belong to the wise, pious, virtuous human being, but then it becomes increasingly elusive and turns into a promise of future happiness, a reward for virtue, or a product of atonement. Later, its location in the afterworld no longer seems worthy of faith. Yet, to this the idea is counterposed that it nevertheless holds true as a consolation, as a regulative ideal. Just an idea: that is, something unreal, pale, vague, having the nature of dreams. Not only this, it is also unreachable and unknowable. And if unknowable, how could it still hold the value of an obligation? Idea that is nothing more than an idea: useless, empty, something to be disposed of.

In the end, therefore, it is the true world, the truth that reveals itself as an illusion. Yet, who reveals what to whom? Truth reveals itself to itself (to whom, otherwise?) as illusion, as nontruth. Hence, a contradiction. Nietzsche, however, avoids this in two ways. On the one hand, he distin- guishes between the true world and truth: the former is the object of the will (it is we who want it to be, even if it actually is not); the latter is instead the result of an attitude of a different order because it is the product of a "rigorous method" in front of which, as one reads in *Human, All Too Human*, the dogmas of religion and metaphysics are no longer believable.[2] In fact, truth and the will that something be true belong to different and opposed

worlds,[3] without mentioning that "there are also facts, and not only interpretations."[4] On the other hand, he pushes the truth beyond itself to where
there is no more truth because everything is an interpretation. Thus, in *The
Will to Power*, Nietzsche recognizes the will to truth as one of the forms of
the will to power,[5] and finally in *Twilight of the Idols* he simultaneously
abolishes the true world and the false world.[6]

It is an odd story, the story of truth. According to Nietzsche, throughout the centuries truth fights a huge battle against itself. In the end, it
emerges victorious, except that its victory consists in its own self-destruction.
Truth triumphs by annihilating that which has no longer reason to be: truth.
For the entire period of the battle, truth remains in relation with itself; it
even remains indissolubly tied to itself. In the name of truth is truth first
challenged, and then vanquished by humans. From this standpoint, God and
truth perfectly coincide, are equivalent in everything and all; in the end they
are synonyms. What holds true for truth holds true for God and vice versa.
As humanity kills God in the name of God, in the same way it is in the
name of truth that humanity declares it outdated, untimely. If of God one
can only say that he "is dead" (*The Gay Science*), of truth one will say that
it "is no longer" (*Twilight of the Idols*).

The analogy, however, does not end here. The God who is dead and the
truth that is no longer are not simply facts to be acknowledged within a history
whose narrative plot is finally revealed. They are paradoxes, and precisely this
paradoxical element shows the meaning of what has happened. When the
madman comes to announce that God is dead and receives sneering smiles in
front of what looks like an obvious matter (who does not know that God is
dead?), in truth he knows that his thought is very far from being understood
because it is not the case of acknowledging what everyone witnesses in the
secularized world, but rather of measuring oneself with a disquieting and highly
dramatic event: God has been killed by us in the name of God; thus God dies
in God, God whom God himself lets die, as taught by Christian dogmatics.
Commenting on this passage from *The Gay Science*, Heidegger writes that this
does not mean that the Godhead has nothing more to do with human existence. Rather, it means that it goes on towering above it, yet in a different form:
not in the form of fullness, but rather in the form of the going under and of
the eclipsing, and then he remarks that "giving up the ancient gods and
enduring this renunciation is the safeguard of their divinity."[7]

It is what happens to truth. Truth that is no longer is not merely and
simply truth that has disappeared, faded away. Rather, the truth disappears,
fades away, annihilates itself out of what remains of the truth, out of its
becoming trace, emptiness, nothingness. A paradox pushed to its extreme
limit? Certainly. But also the only one that can account for the parabola
connecting "Truth and Lie in an Extramoral Sense" and the *Nachlaß*, and
that is entirely comprised under the sign of the slogan "dreaming knowing
that one is dreaming."[8]

Here what is in question is not only the overcoming of the (typically metaphysical, as Nietzsche would say) opposition between true and false, reality and appearance, being and nonbeing, but also the access to an onto-logical dimension that is actually "beyond," in which one can move freely *en artiste*, albeit as an artist who no longer needs art because art and life are one and the same and are such by virtue of an infinite mythopoiesis (the grand style) that has finally found its principle (the will to power). Dreaming is this dimension. It is such within the horizon of a nihilism that wants to be programmatic and positive and not merely reactive to the going under and dissolution of truth. Life, Nietzsche says, does not stop losing attraction, intensity, problematicity when truth encounters nothingness. On the con-trary—as long as one learns to dream knowing that one is dreaming. That the dream is grounded in nothingness does not make it less beautiful, less worth of being dreamt. That the dream falls back into nothingness: this is nihilism. This is so because truth can no longer be declined in the past: God is dead, the world has become a fable.

"The world must be romanticized. Thus one can retrieve the originary mean-ing (*den ursprünglichen Sinn*)."[9] According to Novalis, truth must be declined in the future, we could say. Only by falling into the mirror of the fable will the world give off that truth that is otherwise destined to remain hidden.

For Novalis, fable and dream are in the end one and the same. "All fables are nothing else than the dream of that natal world which is every-where and nowhere. The higher powers in us which one day will realize our will like genies are now muses who nourish us with sweet memories along this fatiguing path."[10] Fables are thus an anticipation and a prefiguration of dreams. What will be realized in dreams is announced in fables thanks to the fact that fables, like dreams, draw from the source, "which is everywhere and nowhere." The source of meaning, the source of truth. This source can in-deed be identified with nothingness to the extent that it refers neither to reality, reality as objectively given in some place, nor to unreality, unreality of which one can only say that it is not. It can be identified, however, with nothingness insofar as nothingness is groundlessness, abyss, and inexhaust-ible source—that is, simultaneously place and nonplace of the "powers" that in fables reveal themselves as muses and in dreams as genies. Both fables and dreams imply an actual transcendence of meaning. That is, the world is not fable, it is not dream; if anything, it will be, or better, it will have to be. It will be such when the immemorial that has been awakened to memory and retrieved from latency (thanks to fables) rejoins the world to the origin (in dreams that are realized, in dreams that have become real).

"Dreaming and nondreaming" will be one and the same. "Dreaming and *nondreaming at the same time*—the activity of the genius is synthesized—through which both strengthen each other mutually."[11] Is this a dreaming knowing that one is dreaming? Yes and no. Yes, because the one who dreams, and simultaneously does not dream at all, evidently knows that he or she is dreaming. No, because this "knowledge" is not at all part of the dream, thus undermining it at its roots, that is, revealing its character of illusion, even if an illusion that helps to live. On the contrary, such "knowledge" turns the dream into a place (a place that is a nonplace) of an experience of truth. Unlike what will be the case in Nietzsche, for whom dreaming knowing of one's dreaming will in the end mean to dream with open eyes, and thus dreaming in a certainly inventive and fantastic, but substantially meaningless, way (hence, the Nietzschean nihilism), Novalis seeks after a higher fullness of meaning. Moreover, if in Nietzsche we find no difference between dream and fable, dream and poetry, and if actually, by becoming aware of its being dream and nothing else than dream, life turns itself into grand style, in Novalis, on the contrary, the fable is prophetic anticipation of what will be brought to fulfillment only in the future in dream (and in dream after dream); thus poetry as cipher or divinatory narrative of the world-to-be remains necessary. "The *true fable* must be at once *prophetic representation*— ideal representation—absolutely necessary representation. The authentic fable poet is a seer of the future."[12]

The dream as we experience it here and now (and not in the world of the powers in act, the world of genies) also reveals all its deep affinity with poetry. "The dream is often meaningful and prophetic, since it is an effect of the natural soul—and *thus* it rests on the order of association—It is meaningful like poetry—but for that reason also it is meaningful in an irregular way—*throughout free*."[13] On the contrary, poetry seems to be like the dream: "Tales, without connection, but built through association, like *dreams*. Poems—*well resounding* and full of beautiful words. At the most, true poetry can have an overall *allegorical* meaning and can produce an indirect effect, like music."[14] In summary, dream and poetry, dream and fable spring out as if from nothingness. Musically. That is, freely. Yet, this freedom is truth because the essence of truth is freedom. At the moment when Novalis seems to come most showily close to nihilism, or to anticipate one of its possible outcomes, he more radically takes his distances from it.

Nietzsche, however, prevails on Novalis. Besides, why *should* the world become fable, as Novalis proposes, if, as Nietzsche says, it has already become such in actuality? That it has become such seems to be proven by the events, even the processes that are still occurring, which have radically transformed the idea of art and the idea of reality. Aestheticization, derealization, and depersonalization are the main features of a truly epochal movement.

Not only the Cartesian subject, the I to whom being becomes transparent, the transcendental and impersonal principle of knowledge, but the very person, the person as an irreducible singularity able to make itself style, way of living and shaping is put into question, according to a contemporary scholar, Mario Costa. It is revoked, moreover, through the application of new art technologies. According to Costa, synthetic products, that is, the products of digital techno-science, whether they are specifically computer art, no longer make reference to an empirical subjectivity; they do not claim to express the individual personality. They exist rather on their own; they refer only to themselves; they are true "selflessnesses." Thus, "new technologies have caused an irreversible crisis for the old way of understanding artistic activity and the whole set of aesthetic categories related to it: artistic personality, expression, personal style, inspiration, intuition . . . have definitely exhausted their historical path."[15]

If things are this way, the depersonalization of art is an accomplished fact. What kind of object is an object, like the aesthetic one, that has neither author nor world? What is the referent of an object that is constituted through the suppression of any link with its producer, and of which one cannot even say that it comes from some place because it has no rootedness whatsoever, no history, no place, but rather it presents itself as fundamentally unrelated in addition to its not meaning anything else? Evidently (as has been said with much consistency), it refers to nothing other than itself. Yet this means that depersonalization is accompanied by an even more relevant event at the ontological level, that is, by derealization. To define it, Mario Perniola has resorted to the concept of the simulacrum—the image that does not reflect something other than itself, but rather rests perfectly on itself: nonimage image, image that is neither real nor unreal, but, if anything, hyper-real, virtual. In fact, its reality consists in its being that which it is; thus, it is more than reality, it is virtuality always in act. Proper to the simulacrum is transit, that is, the movement "from the same to the same." This is differing, differing of oneself from oneself. According to Perniola, at the moment when the work ceases to have the value of a spiritual or metaphysical revelation, at least when it no longer claims to be rooted in a subject and its historical world, but rather simply stands there, a thing among things, silent, sphinx-like, then it becomes anonymous, cold, and indifferent, but simultaneously it accesses a dimension of pure enigma: "Today more than ever, art leaves behind itself a shadow, a less shining shape into which what belongs to it that is disquieting and enigmatic retreats. The more violent the light with which one claims to invest works and the artistic operations, the sharper is the shadow that they project; the more diurnal and trivializing is the approach to artistic experience, the more does what is essential in it retreat and protects itself in the shade."[16]

Aesthetization becomes the key word. In itself, it is a poor and ambiguous word. Yet, it lends itself to saying the double movement that, on the one hand, sees the aesthetic model come out of its field and spread, imposing itself on the most diverse forms of experience in an exclusive and contradictory manner; on the other, it sees the artistic subtract itself to the beautiful and aim at the safeguard of a space in which something like dismay and wonder are still possible. This occurs to the extent that this event is linked with the spreading of a technological rationality of which it is not simply the reflex, but on the contrary is the cause, the engine. According to Wolfgang Welsch, technics and its dizzying development show in an evermore clear manner what tradition has been unable to recognize adequately; that is, the fact that it is rationality that has to do with derived structures (*Folgestrukturen*), whereas the aesthetic is encountered at a deeper level and represents something fundamental (*Grundschicht*). Hence, according to Welsch, "an epistemological aestheticization—a fundamental aestheticization of knowledge, of truth, and reality—from which no issue escapes."[17] The showy aestheticization of the world that has followed—according to which only what is beautiful or at least is part of an artistic dimension seems to be worth existing, has value, is approved (confirmation of the prevarication of the aesthetic over the ethical)—is the natural consequence of this situation. This does not mean that art limits itself to supporting the process of aestheticization of the world, which in turn would be a secondary effect of the aestheticization of the scientific and technological undertaking. On the contrary, art works in countertendency. If in times when beauty was something rare art has been capable of producing sublime beauty, and if when the Industrial Revolution was in danger of obscuring a whole spiritual world, dulling sensitivity, stupefying perception, and vulgarizing taste, art has been able to take on itself the safeguarding of such a world and has consigned it to us intact—and even enriched it—today it is art, and perhaps art alone (to say it with Adorno) that poses a strenuous resistance to the invasion of media images and opposes their otherwise uncontested domination. No longer made to please and even less to gratify, today art strikes, upsets, hits. Welsch's conclusion is that "there is no longer a way to describe adequately what happens in the artistic realm, without taking into account an aesthetics which is beyond aesthetics."[18] One must here take into account the fact that nothing will ever be the same as before.

In sum, aestheticization, derealization, and depersonalization define an event at the end of which the opposition between reality and appearance collapses because the opposition of art and technics disappears. In the world in which technics discovers its irreducibly artistic, aesthetic foundation, and, vice versa, art operates exactly like technics, that is, in an anonymous, impersonal way under the sign of a virtuality for which everything is possible, reality and appearance pass one into the other; there is no longer reality, no longer appearance, but rather a still unnamed (unless we call it cyber) third that results from the suture of an ancient incision. "The dream of a thing," Marx said. Could this be, in the world now become a fable, Nietzsche's daydream, the dream of one who knows that he or she is dreaming (and thus one is no longer oneself but neither is one outside oneself because one is simply no longer an I, a subject, a personal identity)? Whatever the answer to this question may be, in the background is the dissociation of art and technics, and its typically modern manifestation within a history that starts

when art and technics are one and the same and ends when art and technics
go back to appear originarily united. From this perspective, a mandatory
passage is the thought of Vico.

On the one hand, we find the "theological poets," according to Vico; on the
other, are the "*famuli.*" Rather, first the one, then the other. First are those
who, in the ancient wood where everyone is a prisoner of the brutality of the
state of nature, look for the signs of a superior destination or provenance that
frees the human being from the violence and misery in which it dwells. The
signs are sought and found on the ground of a purely fictitious knowledge,
which is yet rooted in truth. They would not even search for them if their
condition of blindness and total ignorance were natural and not instead
rejected, decayed. The fact that the decoding of the signs implies the reinvention of a fantastic world, where, on the one hand, the cause of natural
phenomena is attributed to "simulated and faked" *idola*,[19] and where, on the
other hand, the design of the divine providence remains hidden in the symbols and allegories that hint to it: nothing takes away from the fact that the
reconquest of the human and thus of the lost paradise proceeds through this
stage. Myths and rites, laws, institutions, social practices have their ungrounded
ground in poetry. Yet, the life worthy of human beings, and thus truly corresponding to their humanity, is not the wild life but rather the civil life; the
theological poets thus invent, simulate, feign, and meanwhile tell the truth
with respect to both the provenance and the destination of the human being.
Per mendacia poetae veritatem [truth comes through the poet's lies].
        Then come the *famuli*, the servants, those whose task is that of grant-
ing the satisfaction of material needs: they must act on reality, bend it to
their goals, which is possible only by effectively understanding how things
work. What is here necessary is not a theological and mythological knowledge, but rather a manufacturing, operative, let us in the end say technical
knowledge, even if this implies the adoption of a linguistic order that removes from itself all reference to the hidden meaning and transcendence. It
is a sacrifice that pays off. If the world is emptied of its enchantment and
irreducible enigmaticity, existence nevertheless becomes less arduous, less
painful, and, moreover, less frightening. This is a truth divested of magic and
mystery, yet it is a truth without which the human being cannot do.
        From myth to *logos*, then? At the threshold of the next enlightenment?
Nothing of this. For Vico it is not so much the case of a passage from the
time of superstition to the time of reason as is the case of the antithesis of
two modalities of language that confront and contradict each other. His is
not a progressive but rather a tragic conception of history because the history
of human beings is an oscillation between conflicting forms of knowledge
that cannot be mediated. Yet it is also a sacrificial conception of truth. The
truth that the human being experiences is demediated [*dimidiata*], and it is
such by function of this experience: only by renouncing knowledge of how

things truly are can the theological poets let emerge the hidden thread governing the world; only by renouncing ungrounded hypotheses can the *famuli* discover how things are and intervene on them. Always only a part of truth, never truth in its whole, is given to human beings, and the part that is given to them is given at the cost of the rest. Either mythopoietic truth, which is so close to a lie, and yet is the only one capable of saying something about the unfathomable mystery wrapping us before divine revelation; or the truth of science and technics, undoubtedly true, yet indifferent to the meaning of life and the destiny of the human being. It does not cast light on Vico's notion of fable that he, a Christian thinker, envisions for the end of times a conciliation of the two perspectives, when we will speak the language that God used to create the world and thus the truth will be entirely unveiled to us. His notion of fable is "true fabulation," narration that remains tragically related to truth, and it is not thus the place of its complete dissolution but rather, on the contrary, the place of its agonic manifestation, at the limit of contradiction and even within contradiction.

Vico's position could be understood as an answer to Nietzsche before Nietzsche. But we can also find a post-Nietzschean answer to the Nietzschean "dreaming knowing that one is dreaming." It comes from Freud: "Dreaming not knowing that one is dreaming," or even, "Dreaming dreams that have never been dreamt."

Freud writes, "I shall demonstrate that there is a psychological technique which makes it possible to interpret dreams, and that on the application of this technique, every dream will reveal itself as a psychological structure, full of significance, and one which may be assigned to a specific place in the psychic activities of the waking state."[20] He then clarifies his thesis in the following manner: the dream "is a perfectly valid psychic phenomenon, actually a wish-fulfillment; it may be enrolled in the continuity of the intelligible psychic activities of the waking state; it is built up by a highly complicated intellectual activity."[21] Thus Freud does not hesitate to distance himself from those, such as for example the physiologist Burdach, who think that dreams take us to a world that has little or nothing to do with this one; or from those, such as I. H. Fichte, who think that precisely for that reason they have a cathartic, liberating function—a function that liberates precisely from daily pains and anxieties. On the contrary, Freud claims that dreams have a revelatory significance, insofar as they are the satisfaction of the desire that is revealed, brought to light. Freud points to dreams' unmistakable content of truth, that is, their ontological rooting, their deep connection with reality. He does not hesitate to appropriate the naïve and popular opinion according to which dreams always reveal something about our life: if not in the sense of attributing to them a prophetic and divinatory value, then certainly in the sense of acknowledging an anamnesic meaning in the staging that they make us observe as viewers and at the same time as

protagonists. The idea of the divine origin of dreams (which has been retrieved in modern times by Schelling) gives more to thought than the assertion of their irrelevance to the goal of an understanding of the world in
which we live. And if Aristotle is right when he says that, if anything,
dreams have a "demonic," that is, physiological, natural character, one should
not forget that for Aristotle such is nature and, moreover, the *psyche*, insofar
as they are both oriented toward the divine. In sum, the soul (the soul and
its dreams) is the place of an experience of the truth. That such an experience has more to do with the inferior world than with the world of the gods
is of little importance. *Flectere si nequeo Superos, Acheronta movebo* [if I cannot bend the Higher Powers, I will move the infernal regions].[22]

The dream has a revelatory character; therefore, it lets the deep (which
is truth and reality) surface to the extent that it denies itself to reality and
truth not only by escaping in a world of ghosts and of at least apparently
arbitrary connections, but also by refusing to become aware of being what it
is: a dream. When we dream we do *not* know we are dreaming. This holds
true for real dreams, "nocturnal" dreams. But this holds true also for "diurnal"
dreams, for the *Tagträume* or daydreams. In them is obviously a certain
awareness, but it is almost suspended, rather negated, and in any case con-
cealed by the "indulgence" that the I reserves for itself, Freud says. In any
case, it is always a matter of satisfaction of desire.

This not-knowing holds true also for those daydreams that are not
private but public, and that are the substance of poetry. This is the thesis
that Freud advances in his 1907 essay, written eight years after the *Traumdeut-
ung*, which he devotes to W. Jensen's *Gradiva*. In this work, "dreams that have
never been dreamt . . . dreams created by imaginative writers and ascribed to
invented characters in the course of a story"[23] belong simultaneously to three
classes: to that of the dreams of poetry (and Jensen's is in fact a poetic invention); to that of daydreams (the main character of the story projects his own
removed desire on reality); to that of dreams with closed eyes (although the
main character is not in a state of unawareness, it is almost as if he were in
one, so hallucinatory and fantasmatic the "vision" is).

It is well known which vision it is—the apparition of a maiden who
seems to come out of an ancient bas-relief and walk through the streets of
Pompeii with the same pace and gestures that the artist has fixed on marble
in a unique instant. What is this? The hallucination of someone who is
raving and is prey of a nightmare from which he cannot wake up because he
is already awake? The irruption of a ghost into the real world? No, it is
nothing of this. The maiden is a living person. That she is such is proven by
the fact that the main character, who is recognized by her, recognizes her,
and this recognition does not disturb at all the reality to which they both
belong; rather, it perfectly explains the enigma. At the origin lies a childish
love, a removed love. As a consequence, it inhabits his unconsciousness
under the form of an unsatisfied desire. It is not the maiden in flesh and

bones who animates and enlivens the bas-relief; it is rather the bas-relief, which evidently the main character has invested with his own desire, that reveals to the main character what the maiden is for him. That is to say, it is not the maiden who embodies and enlivens the bas-relief; rather, the bas-relief tells what the maiden "truly" is. The bas-relief reveals the hidden truth. The recognition is not so much of the bas-relief in the maiden, but rather of the maiden in the bas-relief. In fact through the bas-relief, the main character comes to clarify his feelings for her.

What looked like an escape from reality toward the realms of unreality (toward dreams or the fable) thus appears instead as a return to reality, and even more as a conquest of its true meaning by virtue of the dream, by virtue of the fable. Paradoxically, what is true for Novalis (and for Vico!) is also true for Freud. But not for Nietzsche. Whereas for Nietzsche reality dissolves into fabulation, for Freud fabulation, the plays of imagination, as well as all forms of dreams, are expressive, and even more revelatory of reality. They reveal what constitutes the secret of reality. By becoming fable, reality unveils it. And it reappropriates itself to itself. We are at the antipodes of Nietzsche's "dreaming knowing that one is dreaming."

And yet, some persist in doing so, like the eternal Odysseus whom, according to Horkheimer and Adorno, we encounter at the beginning and at the end of the history of the West.

In the end, Odysseus is nobody else than the one who expresses and realizes the intention of dreaming knowing that one is dreaming. He knows very well that this is *almost* impossible. Yet, he finds a way (in fact he is more ingenious and shrewd than anyone else), and we know what the way is: he plugs the ears of his sailors with wax and has himself tied to the mast, so that he can listen to the song of the Sirens in its quality of purely aesthetic simulation without interference from either moral consciousness or desire. The presupposition for this is the separation of the real and the oneiric, or pure daydream world. On the one hand is reality (which concerns the sailors, who can be concerned insofar as they are cut off, excluded from that superior spiritual region that is dreaming); on the other are dreams (which the hero enjoys with open eyes, but only on condition that he self-excludes himself from reality, from the life in which one lives and dies truly and irrevocably). And so, on the one hand is technics, servile work, the possibility of intervening on things; on the other hand is the vacation of spirit, the evasion into the unreal as luxury and sterile enjoyment.

> Whoever would survive must not hear the temptation of that which is unrepeatable. . . . The laborers must be fresh and concentrate as they look ahead, and must ignore whatever lies to one side . . . they become practical. The other possibility Odysseus . . . reserves to himself. He listens, but while bound impotently. . . . The bonds with

which he has irremediably tied himself to practice, also keep the
Sirens away from practice: their temptation is neutralized and becomes a mere object of contemplation—becomes art. . . . Thus the
enjoyment of art and manual labor break apart as the world of
prehistory is left behind.[24]

This means that the extreme and fulfilled attempt at a conciliation of
reality and dream, reality and fable, as well as art and technics, that is, the
Nietzschean attempt (in the world where reality is dream, is fable, art and
technics collapse one on the other and are in fact the same thing, both being
linguistic constructions that are grounded on no natural or objective order
of things), brings scission, unaware, with itself. Dreaming while knowing
that one is dreaming: this undoubtedly rational awareness that the world is
a fable because it has become such in an irrevocable way, belongs to the one
(Nietzsche starting from *Truth and Lie in an Extra-Moral Sense*) who removes
the latent opposition between reality and dream, art and technics, and reconciles them. Yet, if technics reveals itself to be nothing else than art,
nothing else than a fabulous reinvention of the world, nothing else than one
of the possible stories thanks to which we discover, or believe that we discover, a meaning that is not there, then art seems to be destined to disappear
in front of the exclusive domination of technics, to be absorbed by technics,
at most to hide itself in it. And yet art represents, at the same time, a manner
of resistance to universal meaninglessness, a witness in favor of reality on
behalf of unreality, a warden of the truth that is *not*. This is exactly what
Horkheimer and Adorno propose (Adorno especially insisted on this in his
writings after *Dialectic of Enlightenment*).

Horkheimer's and Adorno's thesis, according to which "the enjoyment
of art" and "manual labor," art and technics, "break apart as the world of
prehistory is left behind," literally recalls Vico's thesis about the relation
between the "theological poets" and the *famuli*. What is here important to
stress, however, is that Vico as well as Adorno and Horkheimer hold onto
the aporetic character of separation. The difference is, at most, that for Vico
the aporia is destined to remain such until the end of times, when truth and
language (myth, poetry) will return to be the same for both God and human
beings, whereas for Adorno and Horkheimer the aporia is hidden and denied
by the false aesthetic consciousness.

Today, one considers Nietzsche more than both Vico on one side and
Adorno and Horkheimer on the other. And the whole discourse revolves
around the Nietzschean thesis and the two aspects that characterize it. Once
they realize that the world has become fable, some emphasize that at the
origin technics and, even beforehand, science are also forms of mythopoiesis;
others deduce from this the proof for the irrelevance of art with respect to
meaning and reality (which on the contrary concern science and technics).
Postmodernism and scientism share the field almost exclusively between

themselves: they are two opposite and noncommunicating yet intertwined and mutually supportive perspectives.

For postmodernism not only technics but also the scientific enterprise in its entirety (and thus science and philosophy) are brought back to their inventive—in a word, to their aesthetic—components, and thus to a substantially fabulatory form of experience. Analogously, art, particularly the art of narration, ends up being identified with a light and ungrounded play, a play devoid of truth, like narrative is, even when narrative looks like the last expedient able to snatch the chaotic movement of existence from the absurd. What truth is there if, in the world that has become fable, everything is in the end art, and if even life is, in the best cases, dream, and remains such, even if it is not the dream of a madman, but that of a good storyteller? For neoscientism (which appropriates the thesis of the death of philosophy from postmodernism and maintains that philosophy has no longer a reason to be when confronted with science, whereas postmodernism claims that philosophy no longer has a reason to be when confronted with the aestheticization of knowledges), only science remains capable of saying something meaningful and even true about the world that, having become fable, has become such insofar as virtual reality, product of technics, and scientific construction. The objectivity of science is not doubted; at most it becomes one with effectuality.

A more or less hidden nexus, however, keeps together postmodernism and neoscientism in their aporetic separation. Postmodernism needs neoscientism. In fact, it nourishes itself with the denial that something such as objective knowledge, nonmediated by history, language, and so forth exists. In its turn, neoscientism needs postmodernism, so much so that it constitutes itself starting from the unmasking of the aestheticizing nihilism that is implied in it. Yet, the two perspectives remain opposite and, moreover, unaware of their common derivation, even when this is evident. It is not by accident that today we find those who go back to Nietzsche as the philosopher who has reduced truth to fabulation, as well as those who see in Nietzsche the theoretician of positivism and thus of truth as the destruction of idols and mythologies.

This is apparently a no exit. And this holds true in the case of postmodernism as well as in that of neoscientism because they are so entangled in a suffocating embrace. Why not try, then, as suggested here, a different way? That is, not the way of a return to Nietzsche and his affirmation that the world has become a fable (to which corresponds dreaming knowing that one is dreaming), but rather the way of a return to Novalis and his idea of the world that *must* become a fable (it must because only this way will dreaming and not dreaming, that is, dreaming and experiencing reality, become the same thing). From here follows a widening of the gaze toward directions abyssally far and yet in many respects very close: backward toward Vico, and forward toward Horkheimer and Adorno (it has been unavoidable and certainly not accidental that the attempt at a renewed reflection on myths, starting with the so-called *Mythos-Debatte*, moved on the one hand from Adorno but, on the other, headed toward Vico). One would at least gain a different reconstruction of the issue and maybe some new light on the relation linking philosophy, poetry, and dream to the notion of truth.

Notes

1. Friedrich Nietzsche, *Twilight of the Idols/The Antichrist*, trans. R. J. Hollingdale (Baltimore: Penguin, 1968), pp. 40–41.

2. Friedrich Nietzsche, *Human, All Too Human*, trans. R. J. Hollingdale (Cambridge: Cambridge University Press, 1986), pp. 60–61.

3. Nietzsche, *The Antichrist*, p. 123.

4. Friedrich Nietzsche, *The Will to Power*, trans. W. Kaufmann and R. J. Hollingdale (New York: Random House, 1968), p. 267. (Trans. note: In Nietzsche's text, however, the quotation does not appear in the form the author reproduces.)

5. Ibid., p. 314.

6. Nietzsche, *Twilight of the Idols*, p. 41.

7. Martin Heidegger, *Hölderlins Hymnen "Germanien" und "Der Rhein,"* *Gesamtausgabe* (Frankfurt, Germany: Klostermann), vol. 38, p. 95.

8. On this, see especially Friedrich Nietzsche, *The Gay Science*, trans. W. Kaufmann (New York: Vintage, 1974). (Trans. note: Nietzsche further develops the idea of dreaming knowing of one's dream, which appears first in section 54, in sections 57–59 of the same book.)

9. Novalis, *Das philosophische Werk*, in *Schriften*, ed. P. Kluckhon and R. Samuel (Stuttgart: Kohlhammer Verlag, 1960), vol. II, p. 545.

10. Ibid., vol. II, p. 564.

11. Ibid., vol. III, p. 63.

12. Ibid., vol. III, p. 281.

13. Ibid., vol. III, p. 452.

14. Ibid., vol. III, p. 572.

15. Mario Costa, *Dall'estetica dell'ornamento alla computer art* (Sarno: TempoLungo, 2000), p. 141.

16. Mario Perniola, *L'arte e la sua ombra* (Turin: Einaudi, 2000), p. Xff.

17. Wolfgang Welsch, *Grenzgänge der Ästhetik* (Stuttgart: 1996), p. 96.

18. Ibid., p. 160.

19. Giovan Battista Vico, *The New Science*, trans. T. G. Bergin and M. H. Fisch (Ithaca, NY: Cornell University Press, 1970).

20. Sigmund Freud, *The Interpretation of Dreams*, in *The Basic Writings of Sigmund Freud*, trans. and ed. A. A. Brill (New York: Random House, 1938), p. 183.

21. Ibid., p. 208.

22. Trans. note: The epigraph is at the beginning of Freud's *Interpretation of Dreams*.

23. Sigmund Freud, "Jensen's 'Gradiva,'" in *The Complete Psychological Works of Sigmund Freud*, trans. J. Stratchey (London: Hogarth Press, 1959), vol. IX, p. 7.

24. Max Horkheimer and Theodor W. Adorno, *Dialectic of Enlightenment*, trans. J. Cumming (New York: Herder and Herder, 1972), p. 34.

Chapter 3

Christianity and Nihilism

Vincenzo Vitiello

Nolite conformari huic saeculo, continete vos ab eo.

—Augustine, *Confessiones*, XIII, 21

Within recent history, 1989 marks an important date, the symbolic meaning of which is destined to increase in time. It has been said— and the assertion has become almost commonplace—that it closes the "short century," which started with the October Revolution of 1917 or with the beginning of World War I in 1914.[1] In truth, the year of the fall of the Berlin wall closes a longer historical period. Certainly, it closes the age that began with the Declaration of the Rights of Man, during which the great and noble ideal of the human self-foundation of community and history arose and matured. This ideal—which had its highest philosophical formulation in Hegel's theory of the ethical state—has shipwrecked in both of its 1900 "realizations": the Nazi-Fascist one in 1945 when the Red Army occupied Berlin, thereby ending the Third Reich; and the communist one in 1989 with the dissolution of the Soviet empire. Berlin is somehow the town sym- bol of this double failure, in a confirmation of Thomas Mann's thesis that Germany has been the battleground of all spiritual conflicts in Europe.[2]

With the failure of the human self-foundation of the *polis* and history, the function of religion within the human community has again become prominent. One should only think of the role played in this part of the century by the Church of Rome, and particularly by the papacy of John Paul II, and of the reawakening of Islam. The close dialogue that philosophy today entertains with religion has thus very real motivations—if the task of

This chapter first appeared as Vincenzo Vitiello, "La spada, l'amore, e la nuda esistenza, ovvero: Cristianesimo e nichilismo," in *Nichilismo e politica*, ed. R. Esposito, R. Galli, V. Vitiello (Bari: Laterza, 2000) pp. 221–246.

philosophy is to apprehend *"its own* time . . . in thoughts."[3] Yet—one should
ask—what is the time of philosophy? Is it sufficient to widen the historical
horizon to the past two centuries? Or should one go farther backward? And
backward only?

When, at the beginning of the sixteenth century, Christian Europe
split, all the great reformers, from Luther to Münzer, to Calvin and many
others with them, starting with Melanchthon, began again to ponder on the
meaning of Nebuchadnezzar's dream, to meditate on the prophecy of the
collapse of the great statue with the pure gold head, silver chest and arms,
bronze belly and thighs, and partly iron, partly clay feet.[4] In epochs of crisis,
thought goes back to its origins. To be on top of the events in our recent
history, to understand what really happened and happens, we Europeans
have to go back to our Christian origins. We also have to ask whether in
them nests that "necessary evil" that by subtracting itself to our sight confuses us and leads us astray.

It has been often said[5] that the ideal of the human self-foundation of the *polis*
and history is historically connected to the Christian idea of the *Civitas Dei.*
Yet, as the author who is the most involved in this connection has remarked,
"das bekannte überhaupt ist darum, weil es bekannt ist, nicht erkannt" [Quite
generally, the familiar, just because it is familiar, is not cognitively under-
stood].[6] One cannot in fact stop at the assertion that Hegel's philosophy of
history is the secularization of the Augustinian theology of history. One
should still explain why, in Christian thought, such a theology affirmed
itself. And returning to the Jewish roots of Christianity is not sufficient. The
relation between Christianity and Judaism is extremely complex and even
contradictory. In the synoptic Gospels we find statements by Jesus that are
difficult to bring back to the historical conception of the chosen people. First
is the fundamental claim that the Kingdom [of God] is not of this world, not
to mention the conflictual relation between the first Christians and the Jewish
community. In truth, the one who introduced Jesus's words into the Jewish
tradition, and not only into this, was Paul, the historical founder of Christianity. The issue is then that of understanding the reason that grounds Paul's
operation of recovery of the Jewish tradition of the Law within Christ's Word.

Matthew 10:34, *"non veni pacem mittere sed gladium"* [I did not come to bring
peace but a sword]. Jesus's sword separates humans from the world, from all
relations constituting human kinships: from the living as well as from the
dead. To the young man who asked him to bury his father before following
him, Jesus replied, "Leave the dead to bury their own dead" (Matt. 8:22).
The very relation with God must be kept hidden from the eyes of others.
Jesus exhorts us to pray secretly (Matt. 6:5–6). Even the Word, however
worldly and human, knows the destiny of separateness. It does not expose
the Truth, it hints to it, *"aperiam in parabolis os meum"* [I will open my mouth

in parables] (Ps. 78; Matt. 13:35). Silence remains beyond—different. Thus, the total remission of the Son to the Father—*non sicut ego volo, sed sicut tu* [not as I will but as You will] (Matt. 26:39)—is followed by the cry of forsakenness (Matt. 27:46). The Father reveals himself as such, as Father, in difference. Forsakenness marks the infinite difference that is present in the trinitarian relation between Truth and Word.[7]

Jesus's opposition to the entire tradition of Judaism as well as that of the Gentiles could not be sharper. The sword separates *religio* and *saeculum* in the most radical way: "Render . . . to Caesar the things that are Caesar's, and to God the things that are God's" (Matt. 22:21). Needless to say, Jesus is not against the law. He demands rather that those who follow him respect it even more scrupulously than the Scribes and the Pharisees (Matt. 5:17–20). Yet, even the most rigorous observance of the law by all human beings would not make this world the house of God. Human beings do *not* dwell in God's proximity. Christ's disciples will never be able to welcome a guest in their house with the words with which Heraclitus, warming up by the domestic hearth, received the strangers who came to visit him, "*einai gar kai entautha theous*" [here too are the gods].[8] This is indeed so not because God shuns humble places, but rather, because God, the God of Christ, is and remains far from the world. Other. Transcendent.

According to Heidegger—the Heidegger who looked at the pagan world with nostalgia—Christianity is at the origin of the modern *Entgötterung der Welt* (dedivinization of the world).[9] In truth, such is not Christianity, but rather Christ. The distinction is essential to understand the meaning of Paul's work. The old doctor of the Law gave himself an enormous task: to regulate the Christian community after Christ's death to prevent the Word from becoming dispersed in the multiple interpretations of the various groups or sects that referred themselves to it. Paul retrieved the old Law. In this manner, he gave certainty of the divine presence and help back to the world, now emptied of the gods. To the *world*: not only to the "present," to the world that had heard Jesus's word, but also to the "past," to the world before the announcement. The old Law, he said, was the pedagogue of humankind until the Son's advent. Yet, after the announcement, the Law has not ceased to hold true; rather, it has acquired a new value on the ground of faith. Not only of human faith, but also of the faith from which everything comes, of the faith that makes one just, insofar as it justifies; of the faith that is God's faithfulness to the covenant with Abraham, which has been renewed with the death of the Son (Gal. 3).

To understand the enormous relevance of Paul's operation, one must leap over centuries. The relation Law-Faith-Law is still Hegel's model, who in the *Rechtsphilosophie* translates it into the dialectical scheme: external right, abstract morality, ethics. It is not by chance that ethics, which comes last, is the ground of right itself. That is, it works secretly ever since the first moment,[10] not unlike the faith in the true God, in the God announced by

Christ, who still supports the old Law: "If the root is holy, so are the branches" (Rom. 11:16). Paul's doctrine, however, lies at the origin also of Hegel's project of reconciling Athens and Jerusalem, Greekness and Christianity. For the apostle Paul, in fact, Jesus's message is addressed to everyone, to the Gentiles—to the pagans—not less than to the Jews because the Law given by God to Moses is present also in nature (Rom. 2:14–15).

With this, we do not simply mean that Paul reunited what Jesus's sword had separated. Paul's relation to Jesus is far from simple. The difference[11] must not deny the continuity. Otherwise, one could not explain the reason why Paul presents himself as a faithful interpreter and apostle of Christ's Word. In Jesus's preaching, division, sword, and conciliation of love are together. And it is such a love that it does not exclude anyone. In explicit opposition to the old Law that prescribed loving the neighbor and hating the enemy, Jesus exhorts us to behave like the Father who is in Heaven, who lets the rain fall on those who are just and those who are unjust, and the sun shine on both the good and the evil ones (Matt. 5:43–45).

Christianity is this internal tension between separation and reconciliation, this alternation of sword and love. Paul does not deny separation; indeed, on the contrary! However, he subordinates it to reconciliation. This subordination is not in Jesus's teaching. The words on the dividing sword follow, not precede, those on the love for everyone and everything.

That Paul's interpretation of the Word of Christ has prevailed is testified by the history of Christianity; yet, never as in modern and contemporary philosophy and theology has the principle of reconciliation had such a decisive upper hand on the opposite principle of separation or the sword. This must make one think, because bitter divisions and even ferocious contrasts mark the modern and contemporary ages. Inferring that precisely the hardness, if not the ferocity of the conflicts of our times, has contributed to the prevailing of the principle of reconciliation is not illegitimate. Faith in a love that welcomes and redeems all, in a God who having historical destiny in his hands turns evil into an instrument of good enables one to withstand any human evil. A very high testimony of this is Bonhoeffer's *Ethics*, which finds in *Kantian* morality, in the claim of an *autonomous human* morality, the first separation from God, the first "evil." The conclusion it reaches is the total remission of human action and its entire history into God's hands: "Ultimate ignorance of one's own good and evil, and with it a complete reliance upon grace, is an essential property of responsible historical action. The man who acts ideologically sees himself justified in his idea; the responsible man commits his action into the hands of God and lives by God's grace and favor."[12]

Augustine, to whom one owes the first great project of a theology of history, which was developed under an urgency of times certainly no less cruel than ours, was more cautious. Although he claimed that not only Biblical history but also the history of the Gentiles is led by the hand of the true God; although he saw also in the expansion of the empire of evil the plan of the divine providence, which had thus ensured the widest diffusion to the Good Book, Augustine remained perplexed when reading this passage from the Second Letter of Paul to the Thessalonians (2:3–10):

> Let no one deceive you in any way; for that day will not come unless the rebellion comes first, and the man of lawlessness [*ho anthropos tes anomias*; *homo iniquitatis*] is revealed, the son of perdition, who opposes and exalts himself against every so-called god or object of worship, so that he takes his seat in the temple of God, proclaiming himself to be God. Do you not remember that when I was still with you I told you this? And you know what is restraining him now [*to katechon*; *quid detineat*] so that he may be revealed in his time. For the mystery of lawlessness is already at work; only he who now restrains it [*ho katechon*; *qui tenet*] will do so until he is out of the way. And then the lawless [*ille iniquus*; *ho anomos*] will be revealed, and the Lord Jesus will slay him with the breath of his mouth and destroy him by his coming appearance. The coming of the lawless one by the activity of Satan will be with all power and with pretended signs and wonders, and with all wicked deception for those who are to perish, because they refused to love the truth and so be saved.

It is not the lawless, the *iniquus*—the Antichrist whom some Christians identified with Nero, or more generally with the Roman Empire, with its persecutions—who is a source of perplexity for Augustine. Rather, it is what or who restrains—*qui tenet*—his revelation.[13]

Bonhoeffer instead does not show any perplexity. He turns into something positive what for Paul is negative and evil. For Bonhoeffer, *to katechon* is "the force of order, equipped with great physical strength, which effectively blocks the way of those who are about to plunge into the abyss." What is in question here is not the philological accuracy of the interpretation, but rather what derives from this interpretation:

> The "restrainer" is the force which takes effects within history through God's governance of the world, and which sets due limits to evil. The "restrainer" itself is not God; it is not without guilt; but God makes use of it in order to preserve the world from destruction. The place where the miracle of God is proclaimed is the Church. The "restrainer" is the power of the state to establish and maintain order. The two are entirely different in nature, yet in the face of imminent chaos they are in close alliance, and they are both alike objects of the hatred of the forces of destruction, which see in them their deadliest enemy.[14]

Bonhoeffer makes God the only true responsible being for what happens in history. And thus also for the action of the state. We know of Bonhoeffer's opposition to Nazism and of his sacrifice.[15] Precisely this, however, allows us to see more clearly the dangers of his theory. Nothing better than Bonhoeffer's life teaches that the State, rather than being a power opposed to chaos, to the forces of destruction, is often exactly the incarnation of these. When we read, therefore, in the quoted passage from *The City of God* that Paul's words "only he who now restrains, let him restrain until he be taken out of the way" can be interpreted in this way: "only he who now reigns, let him reign until he be taken out of the way," let us not identify "he who now reigns" with the Roman Empire, or even more restrictively with Nero.[16] If the Antichrist is the exemplary figure of the tyrant, the *katechon* is the people of "evil and hypocrisy" who nest within the Church itself—as Augustine warns, interpreting Paul's words through those of John the Evangelist. *Ho katechon, to katechon* is the lawless one, *ho anomos* at one's highest degree; indeed, what and who hides lawlessness thereby makes fighting more difficult. And what better hides lawlessness than the doctrine that claims that the power of the State, of the Law, rests on a divine foundation?

The "ideal" image of our time's tyrant is that which Dostoevsky prophetically sketched in Ivan Karamazov's poem "The Grand Inquisitor."[17] To understand it completely, in all its terribleness, we must distance ourselves from our empirical, factual knowledge, from our historical experiences. The Grand Inquisitor is not Hitler, Stalin,[18] or Mao. They are too wretched, too humanly wretched. The relation between them and the Grand Inquisitor is the same as between the fact and the idea. The Grand Inquisitor is the metaphysical idea of their historical being. Only on the strength of this "idea" could they, in their infinite human-all-too-human wretchedness, realize their demonic enterprises. *Diabolus simia Dei* [the devil apes God]: if it did not hide under the guise of the good, then evil could not realize itself. The Grand Inquisitor unveils the identity of *ho anomos* and *ho katechon*.

The Grand Inquisitor is a "perfect" Christian, if perfect, "fulfilled" is his love. He loves creatures to such a complete degree that he cannot stand that they may suffer from a burden as heavy as the one assigned to them by the Creator, that is, freedom. Only the Elect, not the many could stand it. And he, the old leader of the Church of Seville, who was among the few predestined, chosen to celebrate the glory of the Lord, able to accept that measure, to be measured by it, rejected it. He rejected it out of love: oh, not love of himself—the old man does not know what *philautia* is—and not of one individual or individuals, but out of love for everyone: for the rejected, especially, whose destiny of condemnation he has decided to share. For them he has chosen the hell of the present lie against the Truth of the future heaven. The Grand Inquisitor is the Antichrist who hides in any "perfect Christian," in any Christian who claims to realize the Kingdom on earth.

To katechon is, in its essence, love; perfect, complete, total love: the love of what is as it is. *To katechon* is, in the deepest sense, the renunciation of the future; the subordination of the future to the present, to the present of "always the same things." In this light, "representative democracy" constitutes a more astute *katechon* because it realizes a more subtle hiding of the *anomos*. It deceives, in fact, about a future that is not there, that not only it does not guarantee, but also cannot even promise. It is like the history of historicism in which facts change but the form remains unchanged.

One understands, then, why *ho katechon* hides in the Church itself. The iniquity of realizing the Kingdom on this earth—this iniquity is hidden by the one who wants to realize the Kingdom. The one who denies the invisible in favor of the visible Church. Yet the same way as the Antichrist hides himself in the Church, likewise in the Antichrist are the seeds of his own defeat. The invisible Church lives in the visible churches. It both sustains and denies them.

This dialectic of the Antichrist, who contains in himself the seeds of his own negation, is present also in Dostoevsky's work. It has the face of one of his demons: Kirillov.[19] He does not pray to ask; he does not pray so that something that is not, that is not yet, may happen. He prays to give thanks for the fact that what is, is, is already. Better, he does not pray *to* give thanks. No "goal," no "to" is conceivable where everybody is happy because everyone is good. He would still be giving thanks if, rather than praying, he were cursing! Nevertheless he prays. He gives thanks by praying because he now knows, but unfortunately only he knows that everything is good and everybody is happy. If humans are unhappy it is because they do not know that they are happy! And because they do not know it, they commit evil deeds! Knowledge divides humankind into good and evil, happy and unhappy ones. To eliminate this scission, everyone must know that they are happy. And good. To be good, one must know that one is good; that one is already what one is not. The being-already projects itself as future. The eternal present, the *anulus aeternitatis* [ring of eternity] is the task, the project—the future. "*Werde, was du bist!*" [Become what you are!] Nietzsche will say, retrieving an expression from medieval mysticism.

These are the paradoxes of poets, moreover poets with a sick imagination who think of one more than the devil—this is what some pious democratic spirit will think, hurting because suspected of hiding "iniquity"! The paradoxes of metaphysicians—this is what some cold rationalist will say, mindful of that philosopher of science who in metaphysicians only saw *Musiker ohne musikalische Fähigkeit* [a musician without musical any ability]. Unfortunately, one cannot easily get rid of these paradoxes if one can find some similar ones even in that philosopher who is a model of rationality and philosophical *Nüchternheit* [sobriety]: Immanuel Kant.

Giovanni Gentile once said that Kant was "the first sincere interpreter of the philosophy" of Christian *ethics*.[20] The statement seems paradoxical. But it only

seems such. Kant's moral philosophy, founded on the irreconcilable opposition
of morality and nature, cannot be understood without the *Entgötterung der Welt*
[dedivinization of the world], which Christ brought about.

To understand the radical opposition of Christian morality to pagan
ethics, one need only open the *Groundings for the Metaphysics of Morals* and
compare them with the *Nichomachean Ethics*. What in Aristotle decides for
the goodness of acting is the "result" of the action. *Phronesis*, prudence, is
distinguished from *deinotes*, mere ability, because of the "goal," the good,
which, however, like sight, is "by nature." A good man, *euphues* (literally, of
good nature), is the one who has "good nature": *euphuia*. This "nature" which
one has is not possessed, nor is it learned; at best, one can improve it through
practice.[21] Of course, the "nature of the soul"—*phusis tes psuches*—is different, the *phusis* of the stone is different, but this distinction does not take
away from the "naturalness" of ethics, of the ethical "disposition" (*hexis*). It
is a distinction internal to *phusis*. Very different is Kant's separation between
morality and nature—clearly nature that is impulse, desire, appetite, not
mechanical nature. This radical separation is radical opposition, to the point
that the preservation of life itself is a moral duty if and when it is accompanied by no pleasure.[22] Only out of this opposition can one understand why
in Kant that which decides is not the result of the action, but rather the pure
"intention" of the acting.

Kant breaks the bond of subject-predicate. Against Leibniz, the
Intellektualphilosoph, he denies the "tautology" of "*praedicatum inest subjecto*"
[the predicate inheres to the subject].[23] What follows from this break is the
deeper rift between phenomenon and noumenon. Not by chance does Hegel
criticize together Kant's theory of judgment—while searching for the way, in
"syllogism," to recompose the predicative nexus more steadily[24]—and the
concept of noumenon, marked as the "*caput mortuum*" of thought.[25] However, what gives Kant a central role in Western metaphysics—that is, in
philosophy as well as in theology—is represented by the internal tension
within his thought. Precisely the assertion of the absolute difference between
the human being as a moral being, that is, as a free subject, and nature brings
Kant extremely close to Spinoza's pantheism, and thus close to a renewed
form of the pagan acceptance of destiny. If freedom is unconditionedness,
then there is no freedom when the past conditions the action. Yet, where
there is no past, there is also no time. And where there is no time, "*nichts
geschieht*"—nothing happens.[26] The natural world, the world that unfolds in
time, is only the "schema" of the noumenal world. This is the phenomenon:
the schema.[27] Behind Spinoza one can see Plato: time as ever-being (*aionios*)
moving icon of the eternal (*a-idios*, literally: unimaginable) that remains in
unity.[28] Again, the supreme tautology, "always the same things": *tauta aei*.[29]

Kant soon realizes the risk his conception of freedom runs. He takes to
the extreme, therefore, the opposition between "what ought to be" and "what
is," between moral freedom and physical world. As free subjects, human

beings perceive their extraneousness to nature most when what they perceive as duty is not realized or even cannot be realized.[30] More than the failure of the intention, the very impossibility of its realization testifies in favor of freedom!

The *Critique of Practical Reason* is dominated entirely by this tension-opposition between destiny and freedom. The task Kant proposes himself is paradoxical: to show the freedom of a finite rational being; that is to say, to show the unconditionedness of a conditioned being. This pure rational being is, moreover, unconditioned when it frees itself of its conditionedness. Here is the paradox, however: the conditioned can free itself of its conditionedness only when already free from it. The categorical imperative can in fact only be abided by one who can listen to it. But one who can listen to it is only one who has already done what it orders: liberation from conditioning sensible (natural) inclinations. The imperative orders one to do what one has already done! This does not mean that the imperative is useless, but rather that its function must be rethought. The imperative works as a "memento" for the moral will. It helps to remember that the fight against inclinations, the conflict between moral freedom and nature, is always in action, and is always open; that the moral will is not the saintly will; that is, it has not turned its freedom into nature, into a new nature. Or better still, it has not turned its freedom into its only nature, as it happens to the saintly will. This is so because even the moral will is—in its own way—"nature." It is nature—if by this term we mean what is not the object of a choice but rather a "given." *Given*: like sight for the eyes, to use Aristotle's example; *given*: like the *euphuia*, the good *nature*, which one does not possess because one is possessed by it.

In Kant the terms of the tension-opposition are such that each is born from the other, and meanwhile it flows back into the other while denying itself. The freedom-principle affirms itself within nature, as the need for a condition sufficient to explain the totality of the phenomena, that is, nature itself. This principle, however, cannot impose itself, turn itself into the explicative principle of nature because in the end it itself is revealed as "given," going back into the opposite from which it arose and from which it cannot but resurrect for the need has not been satisfied. One thus observes the continuous oscillation between "to be" and "ought to be," between destiny and freedom, between nature and morality—and vice versa. The antinomy does not rest. This oscillation is not, like Hegel's relation, a third moment that resolves within itself the two previous moments. It is not a synthesis that overcomes and reconciles thesis and antithesis. To be an internal opposition to each term, the oscillation is an oscillating oscillation in itself. If we still wanted to use Hegelian language, we would have to resort to the expression characterizing the "*setzende Reflexion*": "*absolute recoil* upon itself" (*absoluter Gegenstoß in sich selbst*).[31] This oscillation, in itself oscillating, cannot be escaped. No "external reflection" comes to break the intrinsic link of the opposites, their uniduality, so that they can be reconciled in a third moment.[32] Because each term is a relation inclusive of the other, the relation of relations knows no other destiny than the one pertaining to the individual terms.

Because it does not exit from itself but rather repeats itself, the oscillation certainly produces ever new historical figures. Yet these are structurally, *topologically*, not equal but rather identical. This means that "to be" and "ought to be," destiny and freedom, nature and morality are not historical determinations, but instead history-producing forces, *transcendental topoi* of historical being.[33] They certainly always give themselves in different "historical figures"—and this difference of "figure," "image," is what characterizes and defines their historicity—but their structure, to repeat, is what remains identical in the change.

When we wanted to stress the historicity of these *topoi*, we indicated them with other, more historically related names: those of "paganism" and "Christianity." Now, when we want to call attention to the topological character of these historical figures, we intend to emphasize the following: First, that to go back to the origins, as we said at the beginning, does not at all mean to return to what is ancient as to the place of the originary good, a mythical golden age from which humanity would have departed because of the evilness of one, a few, or all—according to a pattern that goes from Hesiod to Rousseau to Heidegger (a certain Heidegger, at least). Against this reading of history as "decadence," I am fond of recalling that *degnità* [axiom] of Vico's according to which "the origins of all things must by nature have been crude,"[34] and I hope that the memory of this passage does not make one fall into the opposite vision of progressive history. Thus, if in epochs of crisis one feels the need to return and meditate on Nebuchadnezzar's dream, or on the *katechon*, it is not to return to a remote past, to what is ancient. Rather, it is to go back to the "archaic," to the place of the *archai*, which is not a mythical site, born out of the poets' fervid imagination. It is rather the deep structure of historicity, that which explains what happens on the surface. For the philosopher, then, to understand one's epoch in thought does not mean to widen the horizon of history beyond the immediate present—this is the certainly indispensable task of any thinking historian. The philosopher has the further task of inquiring into the "underground" of history—Vico's "ideal eternal history traversed in time by the history of every nation in its rise, development, maturity, decline, and fall"[35]—to understand what really happens.

Second, the topological analysis of Christianity allows for freeing religion from too tight a relation, almost a link, with history. Schelling remarked that a Christianity existed before historical Christianity, before the coming of Christ, a Christianity as old as the world.[36] This is an eternal Christianity, which, to belong to theocosmogony, cannot not be present even in paganism. Without this eternal Christianity, without this Christianity before Christ, we could not understand the median, "Christ-like" character of the Theban Dionysus, which is an intermediary figure between Dionysus

Zagreus and Dionysus Iaccus.[37] Consistent with this claim, one must speak of a paganism after historical paganism and its end, a paganism that is nestled within Christianity, that is the product of Christianity itself: total love that becomes welcoming of everything, of everything that is as it is. Fulfilled love that denies difference, the Other—that denies the future, the essential future, the future that breaks with historical time. The relation between Matthew 5:43–45 and 10:34–35 defines not the historical but the eternal condition of human beings, the oscillating oscillation between love and sword, the complete welcoming of everything, of everything as it is, and the separation of the world, and the judgment on the world. This oscillation, oscillating in itself, defines simultaneously the universal human character of the Christian message. It says both our connection to the earth and our insatiable *Sehnsucht*, desire and nostalgia together for the "other," for transcendence. This defines our creatural finitude. This, too, Augustine grasped in the deepest and most elevated manner: *Hic esse valeo nec volo, illic volo nec valeo, miser utrubique* [Here I have the power but not the wish to stay; there I wish to be but I cannot; both ways, miserable].[38]

Now we can say we know what *to katechon* is and who *ho katechon* is. *To katechon*, what hides the iniquity of denying finitude; *ho katechon*, the one who makes oneself the author of such hiding within the human community, within history. That this possibility of hiding resides in the very Christian *Sehnsucht* shows, as we have said repeatedly, that overcoming history through a topological inquiry into the deep structures of historicity helps also to show the "religious" roots of the shipwrecks, of the failures of human society along its entire history.

To avoid the possibility that the topological going back to the "religious" roots of historicity may reduce itself to the identification and definition of purely formal, general, and devoid-of-history features, we must now identify what determined historical figure in our time assumes the oscillating tension between destiny and freedom, nature and morality, "paganism" and Christianity. Or, to say it well, what historical figure of oscillation-tension determines and characterizes our time, the present age, the one in which we now live.

Before dealing directly with this topic, recalling the conclusion of Ivan Karamazov's poem, which recalls—and overturns—Jesus's episode in front of the Sanhedrin, seems appropriate. After having sharply contested Jesus's entire work, the Grand Inquisitor tells the Prisoner he will not allow him to render futile his and his predecessors' work, which has cost so much effort and blood. Thus, he condemns him to be burned at the stake. We have said earlier that the Antichrist hides in Christian love itself, and the old leader of the Church of Seville is a magnificent example of this. We have also added that in the Antichrist are also the seeds of his own destruction—as Kirillov's tragic logic shows. The same dialectic sustains the story of the Inquisitor; however, the movement is exactly the opposite. The great old

man has not entirely lost the sense of truth: at the climax of his tirade, after
having recalled that he too had been in the desert and had eaten roots and
locusts, towering in all his faith in front of the Prisoner, he screams to his
face: "Condemn us,[39] if you can and dare!" The *hubris* of the challenge does
not erase the recognition of the one who only has the right to judge. And
the Prisoner, who has been silent the whole time, understands the suffering
of the old man. After the verdict of condemnation, he goes near him and
kisses him on his pale lips. The Inquisitor too understands. He understands
that his suffering has affected the Prisoner. He opens the prison, and, sending
him away, warns him never to come back, never again. The Prisoner—and
this is the conclusion—"disappears in the obscure meanders of town."

Renunciation of judgment, acceptance of the world as it is? Definitive
victory of Matthew 5:43–45 over 10:34–35? Of the divine love that welcomes everybody—just and unjust, good and evil—over the sword? Of the
present over the future?

This is too simple an answer. Too simple even for Alyosha, let alone
for Ivan. Let alone for Dostoevsky, who is at once all the Karamazovs, including Dmitri, and the old father Fyodor Pavlovich, and Smerdyakov!

No, Dostoevsky hints at something that he only glimpses and soon
confuses: the relation between Christianity and nihilism characterizing our
epoch. To introduce us to this problematic relation, we choose as a guide and
mentor another novelist.[40]

Der Zauberberg. The magic mountain: this is the mountain where all enchant-
ments and disenchantments of Western—and not only Western—culture
are "ironically" unveiled. It starts with the ancient enchantment of ascent
and *askesis*. The truth is not on high on the mountains any more than it is
below in the plane. It is not in science any more than it is in common life,
in love, or in mystical intuition. In science is maybe only a radiological slide,
which is accurately preserved in a wallet pocket: life reduced to the shadow
of a skeleton. The rest, whether time or space, biology or chemistry, matter
or spirit, is only a hypothesis that, while asserting itself, denies itself, and
once denied it comes back to repropose itself. *Der absolute Gegenstoß in sich
selbst*. But this is not new at all—we know it. What is new is the character
who is called on the stage as the first actor: an antihero, a well-to-do young
bourgeois who is brought by chance to live an experience of estrangement
from his world—an experience that ends in "nothing." The form of the story
is that of the *Bildungsroman*. Yet this form is not the ultimate object of
the author's ferocious irony, an irony the more ferocious the more detached
its author is.

Thomas Mann publishes the story of Hans Castorp, the antihero of the
novel, in 1924. The story ends with the beginning of World War I. Yet the
author speaks of it as of a distant story "already . . . covered with historic
mold," and therefore a story that must be told "in the tense best suited to a

narrative out of the depth of the past" (*in der Zeitform der tiefsten Vergangenheit*)! Years do not matter; what matters is the events. In 1930 Ernst Jünger will say that the Great War has a greater influence on world history than the Revolution of 1789 itself.[41] In some measure, Thomas Mann anticipates such a claim: what is before 1914 belongs to a remote past, to another history. Observing it from the outside, then, from a place estranged from the world, from a sanatorium in the high mountains, makes sense. It is like observing history, at least a history—one should say that at the end of *a* history one never knows whether it is *only* one story that comes to an end—in the last stage of its decadence. To be faithful to the time of which he narrates, the author could only observe history through the eyes of his hero, or antihero, thus, he sketches his moral character at the beginning of the narration. The "good Castorp," consciously, unconsciously, was part of the feeling of his epoch. And this was an epoch of crisis, "if his own time seem[ed], however outwardly stimulating, to be at bottom empty of . . . food for . . . aspirations."

> In an age that affords no satisfying answer to the eternal question of "Why?" "To what end?" a man who is capable of achievement over and above the average and expected modicum must be equipped either with a moral remoteness and single-mindedness which is rare indeed and of heroic mold, or else with an exceptionally robust vitality. Hans Castorp had neither the one nor the other of these; and thus he must be considered mediocre (*mittelmäßig*), though in an entirely honorable sense.[42]

Mittelmäßig. Mann's term is the very same one that, in one of Zarathustra's "speeches," Nietzsche uses when with sharp irony he criticizes Aristotle's "just mean," the virtue that renders "modest and meek." "That, however, he says, is mediocrity [*Mittelmäßigkeit*], although it is called moderation [*Mäßigkeit*]."[43] Thomas Mann was too educated, and in turn too "ironical" toward Nietzsche—and especially so in the *Zauberberg*[44]—for us not to be induced to think that, when he defines Castorp as *mittelmäßig*, he may not have Nietzsche in mind. The addition "though in an entirely honourable sense" rids of any doubt in merit. In reference to Castorp, however, *mittelmäßig* does not mean "moderation," although Castorp is "moderate." It means something other. The novel continuously hints to this "other," even if it never says so explicitly. Let us begin by saying that it certainly indicates a median position. Castorp, the "good Castorp," is the one who *stands in the middle*. He stands in the middle because he does not decide, does not take a stand between the pedagogue Settembrini, *der Drehorgelmann*, and the mystigogue Naphta, *der häßliche*. Divided about everything, the one a Copernican, the other a Ptolemaian, not only in matters of cosmology, but also of religion, art, history, politics, in sum, in life in general, Settembrini and Naphta both have the same *hubris*, that of dreaming—they cannot do more, there, on the "magic mountain"—the reordering of the world and the history of the world according to their own ideas. To this goal, even war is for both a just mean. They agree on only one thing: defense by weapons. Meanwhile, below in the plain the "great furnace" was being prepared.

Castorp remains in the middle: the mediocre, good Hans Castorp. He remains in the middle also in his solitary meditation on the great themes of science, time, and life. And his is a middleness [*medietà*] that does not mediate; it does not reconcile. Rather, it rejects the extremes, between which it yet oscillates. Uncatchable, ungraspable middleness, which however always presents itself "in a figure." It will be the figure of the *healthy* bourgeois that goes from Hamburg to Davos to visit his sick cousin, and the first thing he learns is that thinking of oneself as healthy is already a sign of sickness. It will be the improvised and disorganized reader of science books who nevertheless reveals himself as capable of deep reflections on time and space, matter, life. It will be Madame Chauchat's uncertain timid lover or the soul over which Settembrini and Naphta fight. It will be one of the very many young men who in the mud of the trenches will know certainly the end of a world, but it is unknown whether one will survive that end or whether one will die with that ruining world—certainly something other remains in all these "figures." None defines him; he withdraws from all, although he crosses them all.

The theme of "middleness" has always been at the center of Thomas Mann's poetic and literary reflection; however, it is linked with the themes of "decadence" and "sickness." In this connection lies his distance from Hegel and from everything Hegel has meant and means. The *Zauberberg* represents the climax of this reflection. Mann had come close to it in *Kröger* as far as issues of art are concerned, and in *Königliche Hoheit* as far as political matters go.[45] Only the experience of World War I, however, could bring him to touch on the real core of the matter. In a fundamental passage in *Betrachtungen eines Unpolitischen*, after having asserted as we said initially that Germany has been the center of Europe's spiritual fights, Mann adds, "*Der Begriff 'deutsch' ist ein Abgrund, bodenlos*" [the concept "German" is an immense abyss][46] The abyss, then, is in the center. Not the origin, not the end—the center is the abyss. Now we understand why Hans Castorp's *Mittelmäßigkeit* is called *ehrenwert* [honorable]. Because in his self-presentation "in figures," while subtracting himself from them all, because in his "mediocrity," all figures are for him no more determinant than smoking a "Maria Mancini" after lunch or dinner. Because in his pure existence there is "nothingness." Pure "standing in the middle" is "nothingness." It is the abyss of nothingness. Yet, it is an abyss that is confused with the surface itself because this nothingness is not "*quiddam majus quam cogitari potest*" [something greater that what can be thought] but rather the exact opposite: "*quiddam minus quam cogitari possit*" [something smaller than what might be thought]. The choice of Hans Castorp, of the mediocre man, neither a moral hero nor endowed with robust vitality, responds to this need of thought: to show the naked existence, the *Null-Punkt* of the historical being.[47] To show it in its very nonshowing, in its withdrawing from all "figures" in which only it is; or, better, from all figures that it is. Thus Mann has staged not an artist, or a prince, or an exceptional man, a man who fulfills himself, who lets himself be absorbed in the historical and ideal image he aims at realizing and realizes. Rather, he has staged an average man, very average, "median," whose "head-piece sustained without undue strain the demands made upon it by the course at the Real-gymnasium—strain, indeed, was something to which he was quite definitely disinclined, whatever the circumstances or the object of his effort; less out of fear of hurting himself than because he positively saw no reason, or, more precisely, saw no positive reason, for exertion."[48]

At the end of the narration, the author himself enters the scene to give a last salute to his antihero. He confesses that he narrated the story not out of love for him—"for you were simple," he says with marked detachment—but for the story itself, which he defines *"eine hermetische Geschichte"* [a hermetic tale].[49] One cannot access naked existence directly, but only through hints, references, allusions. The final salute belongs to these:

> Farewell—and if thou livest or diest! Thy prospects are poor. The desperate dance, in which thy fortunes are caught up, will last yet many a sinful year; we should not care to set a high stake on thy life by the time it ends. We even confess that it is without great concern we leave the question open. Adventures of the flesh and in the spirit, while enhancing thy simplicity, granted thee to know in the spirit what in the flesh thou scarcely couldst have done. Moments there were, when out of death, and the rebellion of the flesh, there came to thee, as thou tookest stock of thyself, a dream of love. Out of this universal feast of death, out of this extremity of fever, kindling the rain-washed evening sky to a fiery glow, may it be that Love one day shall mount?[50]

The final question attests that nihilism is not pessimism, negativity, renunciation of life—if still in the fires of war one perceives the need for love. Nihilism is, rather, the sense and feeling of being's finitude—of the existent that is never in self-control, never *subject of* . . . , but rather, always, in its own depths, in its naked existence, *subject to.* . . . To what? To whom? The question remains a question. To answer it would mean to cross the threshold of the finite. This may well happen. Moreover, when one rejects this possibility, the possibility of crossing the threshold of the finite, finitude would already be betrayed because it would be turned into an absolute position that contradicts and denies it. Finitude denies its own absolutization; it denies the absolutization of the negation of the absolute. The absolute *is not*; the absolute *is-possible*: it is insofar as it is a possibility that is always possible. It is clear, then, why "where danger is, grows the saving power also"[51]: what "saves" is "danger" itself. That possibility itself—the ultimate, extreme, properly eschatological possibility, the possibility of the absolute—which, when actualized, "redeems" the finite from finitude, from imperfection, from unfulfillment in no other way than by canceling the finite into the perfection of the One, the Indistinct, or the Indeterminate; that very same possibility, insofar as [it is] pure possibility, "saves" the finite from an absolutization of itself.

A "positive" task for nihilism is here sketched: "salvation"—which is care, not redemption—of the finite in its *insecuritas*, in its *infirmitas*, that is, in its always being only possible, a possible possibility.

What is the "political" form appropriate to such care?

It is the political form that does not obliterate "naked existence," but rather starts out of it. It is the political form that does not seek *Nomos* in *Phusis*, that in this search even sees the *katechon*, that which and the one who hides *anomia, iniquitas*.

The possibility that is possible not only in relation to other, but also in relation to itself is that which does not have a structure, a *phusis* that determines it. It is that to which attributions do not belong; rather, they come to it from other, *ab extra*. Insofar as this "possibility" is always "less than any less," naked existence is not, cannot be free—if and when freedom is attributed to it. It is not responsible, although it may be, if and when it is recognized as such. It is not social, political, or historical—although it may be, if and when. . . . Kant's break with the subject-predicate link, his opposition to the Aristotelian tradition, aims precisely at this: grasping the "purity" of existence, its being "other" in reference to everything that is predicated of it.[52] This is what Hegel has not at all understood, but what, in truth, Kant himself has not deepened and developed, and precisely where it should have been mostly deepened and developed: in the field of morality.

This task has been accomplished by our century's juridical philosophy, when with Hans Kelsen it has posed the issue of the autonomy of the juridical. The problem is not only epistemological, but also, it has a fundamentally ethical relevance.

Kelsen moves from the traditional distinction between the logic of being, which is descriptive, and the logic of the "ought-to-be," which is prescriptive. He understands this distinction as an ultimate given of consciousness, that is, a given that cannot be further explained, and yet is irrefutable: "nobody can assert that from the statement that something is, follows a statement that something ought to be, or vice versa."[53] The distinction, however, does not exclude that relations exist between the two "logics." The difference itself between the principle of causality—proper to natural sciences—and the principle of imputation—proper to normative sciences—is not absolute. The real difference between the two logics is in the inversion of the temporal order. In the logic of being, the past dominates; in the logic of the ought-to-be, the future dominates. Against "the view that determinism and moral-legal responsibility can be considered to be compatible only by referring to the fact that our knowledge of the causal determination of human behavior is inadequate," Kelsen notices, "it is not freedom, i.e., nondetermination of will, but its very opposite, causal determinability of will, that makes imputation possible." That is, "one does impute a sanction to an individual's behavior because he is free, but the individual is free because one imputed a sanction to his behavior."[54] Kant had established a circle between freedom and moral law by making the former the *ratio essendi* of the latter, and the latter the *ratio cognoscendi* of the former.[55] Kelsen breaks the circle: only the imputation (the law) determines juridical and moral freedom. He breaks the circle because he moves, and means to move, only within the "phenomenal," that is, within the historico-empirical world. The two logics, of nature and of the law, are even. Neither transcends the epistemological horizon of the "phenomenon," the *Erscheinung*. Because he does not distinguish and does not want to distinguish juridical law from moral law, because his problem is *only* epistemological—the definition of pure knowledge of right, or more generally, of normativity—Kelsen, in turn, integrates Kant's project. His epistemological "methodologism" enables that political-juridical order that better respects the "naked existence" that is the deepest need of moral Kantianism.

This methodologism, however, has nothing to do with conventionalism. Kelsen is a fine logician. If he breaks the Kantian circle of freedom-law (which, in any event, gives an ontological foundation, the *ratio essendi*, to the ought-to-be; having granted this, one is unable to distinguish normative sciences from natural ones), this is certainly not to fall into the metaphysics of the subject, which in any case postulates a "power" that is before the norm and as "existentiell" [*esistentivo*] foundation of the norm. Before the norm, however, there is nothing except the norm. The notion of *Grundnorm*, of fundamental norm, indicates nothing other than this: that the foundation of the norm is normativity.[56]

Kelsen's methodologism reveals a sharp awareness of its own limit. The acceptance of the mere factual-being of normativity entails the recognition that the occurrence of the norm, normativity, remains unexplainable because to explain it would mean to reduce normativity to a norm. The consequence is that of an opening up of an infinite process because this norm, to which normativity has been reduced, should then refer to another, additional normativity.

The pure—nonmetaphysical, that is, nonontological—doctrine of right is therefore as open as possible because on the one hand, by referring any determination of imputability to the norm, it recognizes that all imputations are valid exclusively within the normative horizon within which they arose. Thus, because they do not define the being of it, these imputations respect the naked existence to which nevertheless they attribute freedom, responsibility, rights, duties, authorizations, and permissions. On the other hand, such a doctrine says nothing about the being there itself (the occurrence) of normativity to avoid the paralogism of reducing normativity to a norm.

This conception of right, and of the political organization that it entails, will certainly not prevent human beings from harming one another. Yet, perhaps, if human beings convince themselves that what really matters is "other," that "other" that the norm does not name, and that nevertheless is always at stake, one will be able to hope for a reduction of the evil that human beings because of their *ungesellige Geselligkeit* [unsocial sociality] love to exchange among themselves. This is the evil of wanting to impose one's own norm, considered as the only one endowed with true normativity because *kata phusin* [according to nature], if not, even, because willed by God.

Conciliation (*irenismo*) or indifference? Or both, together?

Neither this nor that, one hopes. One wishes, rather, a feeling of universal *philia* arising from the experience of suffering: irrefutable witness to finitude—and to contradiction.[57]

Notes

1. See Eric Hobsbawm, *Age of Extremes: The Short Twentieth Century* (New York: Penguin, 1994).

2. See Thomas Mann, *Betrachtungen eines Unpolitischen* (Frankfurt: Fischer, 1956), p. 46. See also Vincenzo Vitiello, "La conciencia europea frente a la primera guerra mundial: Thomas Mann y Benedetto Croce," *Revista de Occidente* 160 (1994): 37–56.

3. G. W. F. Hegel, *Hegel's Philosophy of Right*, trans. T. M. Knox (London: Oxford University Press, 1967), p. 11.

4. See *Daniel* 2, 32–35. On this theme, see the interesting work by Mario Miegge, *Il sogno del re di Babilonia: Profezia e storia da Thomas Müntzer a Isaac Newton* (Milan: Feltrinelli, 1955).

5. See Wilhelm Dilthey, especially *Introduction to the Human Sciences*, trans. R. Betanzos (Detroit: Wayne State University Press, 1988), pp.130, 135–137, and Karl Löwith, especially *Meaning in History* (Chicago: University of Chicago Press, 1949), pp. 52–59.

6. G. W. F. Hegel, *Phenomenology of Spirit*, trans. A. V. Miller (Oxford: Oxford University Press, 1977), p. 18.

7. On this theme, see Vincenzo Vitiello, *Cristianesimo senza redenzione* (Bari: Laterza, 1995), pt. I, chap. III, "Trinità come nihilismo."

8. For an interpretation of this fragment by Heraclitus in relation to the other, *ethos anthropo daimon*, see Martin Heidegger, "Letter on Humanism," in *Basic Writings* (New York: Harper and Row, 1977), pp. 233ff.

9. Martin Heidegger, "The Age of the World Picture," in *The Question Concerning Technology* (New York: Harper and Row, 1977), p. 116.

10. This is a constant theme in Hegel, who has not failed to theorize it; see especially G. W. F. Hegel, *Science of Logic*, trans. A. V. Miller (Atlantic Highlands, NJ: Humanities Press, 1969), pp. 577–578.

11. The difference is highlighted especially by Jacob Taubes in *The Political Theology of Paul*, trans. D. Hollander (Stanford: Stanford University Press, 2004), p. 51.

12. Dietrich Bonhoeffer, *Ethics*, trans. N. Smith (New York: Macmillan, 1965), p. 234. On this issue, see Vincenzo Vitiello "*Religio et saeculum*: L'etica di Dietrich Bonhoeffer," in *Dietrich Bonhoeffer e la comunità del cuore*, ed. R. Panattoni (Padua: Il Poligrafo, 1999), pp. 35–52.

13. Augustine, *The City of God*, trans. M. Dods (New York: Random House, 1950), bk. XX, 19, p. 738ff.

14. Bonhoeffer, *Ethics*, p. 108.

15. An excellent testimony of this are Bonhoeffer's "letters from prison," edited by his friend Eberhard Bethge under the title *Letters from Prison*, trans. R. Fuller (New York: Macmillan, 1967).

16. Heidegger too interprets it this way in his commentary on Paul's Second Letter to the Thessalonians; see Martin Heidegger, *The Phenomenology of Religious Life*, trans. M. Fritsch and J. A. Gosetti-Ferencei (Bloomington: Indiana University Press, 2004), pp. 75ff.

17. See Fyodor Dostoevsky, *The Brothers Karamazov*, trans. R. Pevear and L. Volokhosky (New York: Farrar, Straus and Giroux, 2002). The bibliography on the topic is vast; I will therefore limit myself to indicate the texts that are mostly present in the previous reflections: V. Rozanov, *La leggenda del Grande Inquisitore*, trans. N. Caprioglio (Genoa: Marietti, 1989); Nicolas Berdaev, "La rivelazione dell'uomo nell'opera di Dostoevskij," in *Un artista del pensiero*, *Saggi su Dostoievskij*, ed. G. Gigante (Naples: Cronopio, 1992), pp. 37–73; René Girard, *Dostoievski, du double à l'unité* (Paris: Plon, 1963).

18. On the relation between Dostoevsky's thought and the Bolshevik revolution, see F. Stepun, who, however, had *The Demons* as his reference, in the abovementioned volume *Un artista del pensiero*, pp. 75–102.

19. See Dostoevsky, *The Demons*. On the topic, see Vincenzo Vitiello, *Topologia del moderno* (Genoa: Marietti, 1992).

20. See Giovanni Gentile, *I fondamenti della filosofia del diritto* (Florence: Sansoni, 1955), p. 15. The term "ethics" used in this context is significant.

21. Aristotle, *Nichomachean Ethics*, 1114b6–10.

22. See Immanuel Kant, *Foundations of the Metaphysics of Morals*, trans. L. W. Beck (Indianapolis: Bobbs-Merrill, 1959), p. 14.

23. See Immanuel Kant, *Critique of Pure Reason*, trans. N. Smith (New York: St. Martin's Press, 1965), pp. 280–281. As far as Leibniz is concerned, see especially *Discours de Métaphysique*, § 8, in *Werke* (Darmstadt: Wissenschaftliche Buchgesellschaft, 1985), I, pp. 72–76.

24. See G. W. F. Hegel, *Faith and Knowledge*, trans. W. Cerf (Albany: SUNY Press, 1977), p. 73, and *Science of Logic*, pp. 664–704.

25. See G. W. F. Hegel, *Logic*, trans. W. Wallace (Oxford: Clarendon Press, 1975), § 44, p.72.

26. Kant, *Critique of Pure Reason*, p. 469.

27. Ibid., p. 476.

28. Plato, *Timaeus*, 37d–38b.

29. Aristotle, *Metaphysics* XII, 1072a7–9.

30. See Kant, *Critique of Pure Reason*, p. 473.

31. Hegel, *Science of Logic*, p. 402.

32. In Hegel too, however, the "passage" from the posing reflection to the external reflection remains completely unexplained. See Vincenzo Vitiello, *La voce riflessa. Logica ed etica della contraddizione* (Milan: Lanfranchi, 1994), pt. I, chap. 1.

33. Here I cannot explain the terminology I use (*topoi; transcendental topology*); I refer to what I have written on the "Svolta topologico-trascendentale dell'ermeneutica" in part II of Vincenzo Vitiello, *La favola di Cadmo. La storia tra scienza e mito da Blumenberg a Vico* (Bari: Laterza, 1998), where, in chap. 3, "Oltre la topologia: l'ou-topia," there is also an indication of the limit that *rechtfertigt* transcendental topology as a hermeneutic of the finite (in both the subjective and objective sense of the genitive).

34. Giovan Battista Vico, *The New Science*, trans. T. G. Bergin and M. H. Fisch (Ithaca: Cornell University Press, 1970), "Degnità" 367, but also "Degnità" 123.

35. Ibid., "Degnità" 349.

36. "*Das Christenthum ist vor Christus in der Welt, ja so alt als die Welt*" [Christianity is in the world before Christ, it is certainly as old as the world], F. W. J. Schelling, *Philosophie der Offenbarung* (Frankfurt: Suhrkamp, 1993), lecture IX.

37. Ibid., lecture XXI.

38. Augustine, *Confessions*, trans. R. Warner (New York: Penguin, 1963), bk. X, 40, p. 253.

39. Trans. note: The English translation has "Judge us."

40. This is so because we have the grounded opinion that the "truth" of our time has revealed itself more in the varied and multiple language of art than in that of philosophy. Another *anti-Hegelian* motif, as one can see.

41. See Ernst Jünger, *Die totale Mobilmachung*, in *Sämtliche Werke* (Stuttgart: Klett-Cotta, 1980), vol. VII, pp. 119–142.

42. Thomas Mann, *The Magic Mountain*, trans. H. T. Lowe-Porter (New York: Random House), p. 32.

43. Friedrich Nietzsche, *Thus Spoke Zarathustra*, in *The Portable Nietzsche*, trans. and ed. W. Kaufmann (New York: Viking, 1976), p. 282.

44. The "magic mountain" is 5,000 feet above sea level, 1,000 feet lower than the place where Nietzsche had the first revelation of his deepest thought, the thought of the "eternal return." On the complex notion of "irony," also in relation to Mann's interpretation of Nietzsche, see Mann, *Betrachtungen eines Unpolitischen*, Preface. Mann will readdress Nietzsche in a 1947 critical essay, "La filosofia di Nietzsche alla luce della nostra esperienza," in *Nobiltà dello spirito e altri saggi*, ed. A. Landolfi (Milan: Mondadori, 1997), pp. 1298–338.

45. On this issue, I refer again to the already mentioned Vitiello, *Cristianesimo senza redenzione*, pt. II, chap. II: "La malattia dello spirito."

46. Mann, *Betrachtungen eines Unpolitischen*, p. 47.

47. The naked existence, like Plato's *exaiphnes*, is not in time (*en oudeni chrono oûsa: Parmenides* 156e). Yet, this "zero-point of the historical being" cannot be interpreted as the "instant" in which "time is constantly intersecting eternity and eternity constantly permeating time"; Søren Kierkegaard, *The Concept of Dread*, trans. W. Lowrie (Princeton, NJ: Princeton University Press, 1967), p. 80. The "naked exist-

ence," like the *exaiphnes*, is indeed *metaxu*; however, it is *atopon metaxu* (*Parmenides* 156d), and its *atopia* consists in the fact that, if it links, it also separates the one and the many, stasis and movement, eternal and time. In truth, naked existence "suspends" both time and eternity.

48. Mann, *The Magic Mountain*, pp. 31–32.

49. Ibid., p. 715.

50. Ibid., p. 716.

51. "*Wo aber Gefahr ist, wächst/das rettende auch*": Friedrich Hölderlin, *Sämtliche Werke und Briefe* (Darmstadt: Wissenschaftliche Buchgesellschaft, 1989), vol. I, *Patmos*, verses 3–4, p. 379.

52. See especially Kant's passage on the *Sachheit*, or *transzendentale Materie* in the doctrine of schematism (Kant, *Critique of Pure Reason*, pp. 183–184), and also those passages devoted to the *Antizipationen der Wahrnehmung* (Kant, *Critique of Pure Reason*, pp. 201–208).

53. Hans Kelsen, *Pure Theory of Law*, trans. M. Knight (Berkeley: University of California Press, 1967), p. 6.

54. Ibid., p. 98.

55. See Immanuel Kant, *Critique of Practical Reason*, trans. M. Gregor (Cambridge: Cambridge University Press, 1997), p. 4 note. Heidegger's interpretation of Kant's moral philosophy is entirely centered on the theme of the circle: as long as one conceives of human acting and will in the same way as natural processes (*als physische Vorkommnisse*), he says, one will not be able to understand "the fact of the ought-to-be" (*das Faktum des Sollens*). "*The actuality of willing only exists in the willing of this actuality*"; see Martin Heidegger, *The Essence of Human Freedom*, trans. T. Sadler (London: Continuum, 2002), p. 197 (emphasis added by Heidegger). This interpretation is the logical consequence of the reduction of *Möglichsein* to *Ermöglichung*, of "being-possible" to "being-possibilitating" [making-possible] (see the immediately preceding lecture course of winter semester 1929/30, *The Fundamental Concepts of Metaphysics*, trans. W. McNeill and N. Walker [Bloomington: Indiana University Press, 1995], esp. p. 363), which characterizes the real "*Kehre*" after *Sein und Zeit*, the turn that will bring Heidegger closer and closer to the Hegelian horizon. Of this *Kehre*, Heidegger has given several nonmatching interpretations. This is a sign of an oscillation that it is not inappropriate to frame within the context of the topological contrast between destiny and freedom, *ethos* and *lex*, "paganism" and "Christianity" of which we have spoken. This seems true especially if one keeps in mind the most tense and labored pages of Martin Heidegger, *Contributions to Philosophy (From Enowning)*, trans. P. Emad and K. Maly (Bloomington: Indiana University Press, 1999).

56. Hans Jonas, in *The Imperative of Responsibility* (Chicago: University of Chicago Press, 1984), claims that facing the immense power that today human beings hold in their hands is possible only through an ethics that, overcoming the modern prejudice according to which there is no passage from being to ought-to-be, finds the ground of *Sollen* in *Sein*. Thus, Kant's "*Du kannst, denn du sollst*" (you can because you ought to), must be turned around into "*Du sollst, denn du tust, denn du kannst*" (you ought to because you act—which you do because you can) (p. 128). The enormity of contemporary human "power," which is capable of changing the ecosystem, imposes that one finds in power itself the principle that rules it, limiting it responsibly. Jonas believes he has identified it in the preferability of being to nonbeing. This is not an abstract but a concrete possibility; that is, it is immanent to being. In short,

it is a matter of Goethe's "long live the one who creates life!" But because life destroys as well as it creates, because power has in itself the force that can deny it, then finding in the "object" of the will (of power) the ontological ground the force that binds power to being is necessary. Jonas cites as an example "the newborn, whose mere breathing uncontradictably addresses an ought to the world around, namely, to take care of him." I will not dwell on the example, the persuasive force of which is only equal to the moral naïveté that dictated it, but rather on what Jonas immediately adds: "I say 'uncontradictably,' and not 'irresistibly': for of course the force of this, as of any, 'ought' can be resisted" (p. 131). Thus, not even the ontological foundation of the "object" of the will power guarantees protection from the danger of "nonbeing" any more than pure normativism.

57. "*Wenn man sagt, daß der Widerspruch nicht denkbar sei, so ist er vielmehr im Schmerz des Lebendigen sogar eine wirkliche Existenz*" (it is said that contradiction is unthinkable; but the fact is that in the pain of a living being it is even an actual existence); Hegel, *Science of Logic*, p. 770.

Chapter 4

Philosophy and Christian Theology Today

A Hermeneutic Circularity as Fact and Task

GIOVANNI FERRETTI

A Historico-Cultural Novelty

Here we will analyze today's situation with respect to the relation between philosophy and Christian theology. The goal will be that of understanding better what should or could be the right attitude of philosophy when confronted with Christian faith, and, on the other hand, what might be the legacy that Christianity can still offer to contemporary philosophy as a richness that enlivens its own quest for truth. We will not fail to bring to light also the decisive enrichment that comes, or rather may come, to theology as a consequence of its confrontation with contemporary philosophy according to that "fusion of horizons" characterizing the hermeneutic circle also with respect to the relation between philosophy and theology.

The reflections we would like to propose start by recalling an interesting historico-cultural novelty, which is by now widely present in the concrete proceeding of philosophical and theological work, even if it is rarely perceived or thematized at the level of reflection. This is that particular process of reciprocal "epistemological" nearing between philosophy and theology, which implies an increasingly marked coming together and/or intertwining of the method or methods employed by philosophers and theologians in their concrete work. Consequently, this induces a progressive move from the status of sharp distinction, sometimes pushed to "separation" in fact and in principle, to a meaningful convergence or methodological affinity that undoubtedly renders more urgent, although not always easier, a mutual dialogue and confrontation.[1]

In the past, the sharp distinction between philosophy and theology has been explained in various ways. For example:

1. Starting from the *different source* of truth at which each attains: philosophy at a source springing from below, that is, human reason alone; theology at a source springing from above, that is, divine revelation. Thus, one spoke of a *duplex ordo cognitionis* [a double order of knowledge] characterizing them in reference to the faculties activated in them: reason or faith. This is a position that has joined the medieval Catholic Thomas Aquinas and the twentieth-century Protestant Barth.

2. On the ground of the *different object* each studies: insofar as it is metaphysico-speculative science, philosophy should in fact be interested in the necessary transcendental structures of being or of consciousness; whereas because it has as its object a particular historico-revelatory event, theology should configure itself as a historico-positive science. This is a position that in the twentieth century is shared, for example, by the philosopher Heidegger and by the theologian Rahner.

3. For the *different results*: because with respect to the great themes of the meaning of existence, philosophy could only formulate human questions, whereas theology alone would be capable of offering God's answers. One should think of the method of correlation between philosophy and theology the philosopher and Protestant theologian Tillich proposed, but widely present in the structure of the constitution *Gaudium et Spes* by the Second Vatican Council.

4. For the *specific methods* that as a consequence would characterize the respective procedures: the speculative-critical method for philosophy, which would be mainly committed to producing universally valid rational argumentations, and the hermeneutic-positive method for theology, which would be committed to interpreting the particular historical datum of divine revelation in a faithful way.

One cannot doubt the strong influence that these distinctions have had on the concrete, historical self-configurations of philosophy and theology in the Western Christian tradition. We think that today, however, if one looks carefully, a series of progressive acquisitions, both on the side of theology and on the side of philosophy, have challenged such forms of distinction in various ways, bringing to that meaningful form of epistemological convergence we have mentioned and that we would like now to illustrate.

Most recently theology has, for example, increasingly emphasized its specific character of "*critical radical reflection* on the experience of faith," to the point of appropriating as its own the requests for absolute *radicalness* and never ceasing *problematicity* that have always characterized Western philosophy. Not only in philosophy, but also in theology, one now claims that nothing should be taken as a presupposition or for granted once and for all. One should be committed to test, rather, always and anew the ultimate, grounding foundations of the truth of faith one professes.[2] Faith, to whose source of truth theology resorts first of all, is not in fact a matter of blind assertion, nor does it exclude the intention to understand (*intelligere*, the medievals said) its object. In fact, it claims to have its own good "reasons," which it can and should exhibit to everyone, in the conviction that everyone can understand them. And theology feels always and newly committed to clarify such reasons, taking into consideration all forms of opposite argumentation that historically can be opposed to faith. Certainly, for theology, faith is also indissolubly a gift from God, which culminates in the offer of grace in the historical person of Jesus of Nazareth as God's highest revelation; it is also and always a free act of acceptance of such a gift, which no argumentation could ever impose on our freedom. Yet, the moment of the gratuitous gift and that of freedom are not to be considered as opposite for the intelligent understanding of the truth of faith. They are rather at its very origin. The same occurs in several other situations, for example, in the access to the truth of the intimate mystery of the other person, which is accessible only if the other offers to me the gift of his or her self-revelation and if I am freely disposed to welcoming it by trusting him or her.[3]

On its side, over the course of the last two centuries, philosophy has progressively discovered a series of elements that, while they characterize better its way of searching for the truth, actually make it closer to theology. We are going to recall some among the principal:[4]

1. The discovery, especially with Vico and Hegel, that the truth for which philosophy searches, and especially the meaning of the totality in which the meaning itself of human existence is inscribed, can come to philosophy also from history and not only from a consideration of the immutable structures of being. Philosophy thus cannot disinterest itself in the truth-relevance of the great historical events, among which is, undoubtedly, the Christian event.

2. The emergence of the hermeneutic-critical character of its procedure with regard to any human experience of the truth, be this in the artistic, literary, scientific, or religious field. That is, not necessarily must or can philosophy make the truth that concerns it arise directly from itself. Truth can also be received from the various fields of human experience in which it expresses itself, without exclusion of the religious experience. For this reason, as the later Schelling has acknowledged and as contemporary authors such as Ricoeur, Pareyson, and Levinas have advanced, it cannot always proceed in an autonomous, logico-deductive manner. Especially when the matter is that of the great issues of human existence, such

as freedom, evil, and the ultimate destiny of the human being and the cosmos, philosophy must also know how to proceed in a hermeneutic fashion, that is, trying to question with a critically aware spirit the sites of the emergence and self-objectivation of the human consciousness of truth, committing itself to clarify and universalize the meaning of it. This is in fact the specific function of philosophy with respect to human experience. This is recognized, for example, also by John Paul II's encyclical letter, *Fides et ratio*: "Moreover, theology needs philosophy as a partner in dialogue in order to confirm the intelligibility and universal truth of its claims."[5]

3. The becoming aware—which also belongs to the achieved "hermeneutic age of reason"[6]—of the ineliminability of certain presuppositions or, perhaps better, "moments" of faith in the very path of reason. Despite the dutiful commitment of philosophy to proceed "without presuppositions," it must, in fact, recognize that at the basis of its path always exists an element of choice of faith, that is, a free act of trust in the reality that presents itself to us as a gift; an originary giving that reason can in no way redeem through its argumentations. This holds true especially for existential truths or for those truths that commit ethically where the truth is not of an "objective" (in the Kantian sense of "phenomenal object"), but rather of a "subjective" order (in the Kantian sense of the noumenal consciousness of the ethical imperative, to which corresponds the subjective experience of freedom). Kant wrote of "rational faith" as the ethical way of philosophical access to the existence of God; and Jaspers wrote of the indispensability of "philosophical faith" as way of access to all truths of an existential order.[7]

These progressive acquisitions on the side both of philosophy and of theology have, as a matter of fact, largely reduced the difference *in principle* between the two disciplines. The distinction, which is in fact nevertheless found especially in the academic environment, seems to be due not so much to a real question of principle, but rather to their historical reference to two textual traditions (on the one hand, the Holy Scriptures and the literature involved in their interpretation; on the other, the texts of the classical "philosophers" and those of their interpreters and/or continuators), including the respective "history of their effects";[8] and it is also due to the prevalence within theology of the pastoral-confessional instance, regulated by the Magisterium of the Church, and within philosophy of the critical instance. In the twentieth century we see an increasing interest in philosophizing out of the Jewish faith (for example, Rosenzweig, Buber, and Levinas) or out of the Christian faith (Blondel, Pareyson, Ricoeur, and Henry) with results that have undoubtedly deeply characterized philosophy in our century. Hence, the progressive becoming aware of the deep mutual influence between philosophy and theology in the course of the history of Western thought to which we would like to refer in the following section.

The Becoming Aware of the Deep Mutual Historical Influence between Philosophy and Theology

The reciprocal epistemological nearing of philosophy and theology has made possible *the* and, indeed, has been made possible *by* the progressive becoming aware of the deep mutual historical influence that has occurred between philosophy and theology in Western thought. Beside the proclaimed reciprocal autonomy, the erection of separating boundaries of a political-academic nature, and the multiple tensions and/or conflicts that have occurred, theology and philosophy have mutually conditioned and influenced each other not only in the patristic and medieval ages, but also in the modern and contemporary epochs.[9] As the abovementioned *Fides et ratio* recognizes, between philosophy and theology exists something like a "relationship" [*interazione*],[10] a "circle,"[11] a fecund "reciprocity,"[12] a "mutual support,"[13] an "exchange of their respective insights,"[14] "as they offer to each other a purifying critique and a stimulus to pursue the search for deeper understanding."[15]

For the patristic and medieval periods, this mutual influence is absolutely evident, and generally has been always recognized, although with diverging evaluations regarding its result (we are referring in particular to the debate on the so-called Hellenization of Christianity). Theology has undoubtedly assumed and at the same time transformed the main categories of Greek philosophical thought, and it has used them "to think" the very contents of the Christian faith. One can think, first of all, of the concept of "being," which has been taken up to think absolute divine perfection, or of the notions of "nature" and "hypostasis," which have been taken up to think the unity and distinction of the three divine Persons or the unity and distinction of Christ's two dimensions, human and divine. Without a doubt, however, the Christian faith has offered new themes first of all to medieval philosophy, such as those of creation, original fall, personal freedom, absolute dignity of the human being, noncircular but rather *eschaton*-oriented history, and so on. It has even created the conditions of possibility in the modern period for the birth of a philosophy and a science somewhat autonomous from the religious sphere. A first and decisive desacralization of the cosmos, which as such is assigned to human rational inquiry, has been correctly identified in the narrative of the creation. And, as a fundamental principle of his entire thought, Aquinas could assert that grace "does not suppress nature, but rather brings it to fulfillment."[16] Consequently, God must be considered as being at the origin both of reason, as the capability of searching for and finding the truth, and of faith, as the possibility of accessing the mystery of the divine plan of salvation.

In the modern and contemporary epochs, despite the progressive process of autonomy from the religious sphere carried out not only by science and politics, but also by philosophy up to the reclaiming of forms of sharp "separation,"[17] the mutual influence or, as it were, the reciprocal "fusion of horizons" between philosophy and theology has not stopped. As a matter of fact, it has taken up the form of a genuine "hermeneutic circle," which we want to document here in some of its most relevant aspects, starting with the influence on theology and then moving on to philosophy.

With respect to theology, we would like to highlight the following issues, which converge in attesting the fruitful contribution made by modern philosophy for the development of modern and contemporary theology.

1. *Through its confrontation with the critical reason of the Enlightenment, Christian theology has been able to avoid uncritical fundamentalism and/ or authoritarian fideism.* In fact, it has understood not only that it needed philosophy to think about faith, and thus that it was steeped in philosophy in its very practice, but also that, as "faith's critical conscience," it is intimately pervaded by the same critical instances belonging to philosophy up to the need of radically questioning the foundations of its own knowledge. Consequently, it has succeeded in avoiding being content with a faithlike self-foundation of a mystical-irrationalistic kind, which would have certainly rendered it immune from any sort of philosophical criticism, but which, at the same time, would have placed it outside the common human horizon of truth.

2. *Through its confrontation with the modern totalizing horizons of meaning (existence, history, utopia, politics, liberation praxis), Christian theology has turned itself into existential theology, theology of history, theology of hope, political theology, theology of liberation, and so on.* Thus, it has accepted to measure the truth of faith against all dimensions of human truth, to show concretely that Christian faith does not annihilate or lessen but rather valorizes and strengthens all aspects of what is human. According to what has been called the "anthropological turn" of theology, which the Catholic theologian and philosopher Karl Rahner championed, but which has ended up asserting itself in the main occurrences of nineteenth-century theology (one can think of Protestant theologians such as Bultmann, Pannenberg, and Moltmann, or of Catholic theologians such as Guardini, Metz, and Schillebeeckx),[18] any understanding of the truths of faith theology proposed must be proven with reference to the human being by asking, for example: Does it free or suppress human beings? Does it

help them grow, or does it alienate them? The truths of the Christian faith in fact understand themselves as life truths for the human beings; only in relation to life can they thus manifest their authentic meaning. The objection of anthropocentrism, which has been moved against this theological vision,[19] is successfully overcome were one to recall that human beings are essentially "beings in relation," in relation with the truth of being and, ultimately, in relation with God. Thus, the more they realize themselves the more they tend, rather than folding on themselves, toward the truth and toward God. In accordance with such an anthropological turn, *Fides et ratio* asserts that human beings can be defined as "the one[s] who seek the truth."[20] And it appropriately remarks from the outset that their journey of search for the truth "has unfolded—as it must—within the horizon of personal self-consciousness."[21]

3. *Through a confrontation with the crisis of ontotheology, Christian theology, especially in the twentieth century, has rediscovered the sense of "divine mystery" of its own mystical-apophantic tradition.* The criticism that Heidegger, undoubtedly among the most representative and influential thinkers of the twentieth century, has moved against "ontotheology" is well known. By forgetting the ontological difference between being and beings, ontotheology would have thought of God as of any other being, be it as of the being above all other beings, the most perfect being, which must be thought as the uncaused cause (*causa sui*) of being and of the order of the universe.[22] Interacting with such a criticism, in addition to the Marxist criticism of onto-theocratic transcendence that would be at the origin of the alienating domination of a human being on another, twentieth-century theology has tried to think of God as the *cipher* of that "inexhaustible mystery" that is at the origin of any of our cognitive and volitional acts and that precisely thus goes beyond any of our powers of understanding and saying.[23] Far from having to be thought of as an impending metaphysical height that crushes us with his omnipotence, God must rather be thought as that "radical alterity" in no way available or manipulable that comes toward us from the future and that thus opens up an unlimited space of free planning and utopian hope for human beings.[24] It is an absolute alterity that at the same time hides and reveals itself in the mystery of the alterity of the other, of the alterity of the other human being (in whom both our birth and our death are rooted). Thus, it confers to human beings that dimension of absolute dignity and ultimateness of meaning that simple empirical observation could not validate, and that nevertheless imposes itself to the existential experience of all human beings in a way that cannot be disregarded.

4. *Through a confrontation with the hermeneutic turn in contemporary philosophy, Christian theology has found again the pluralistic possibilities of its originary truth status.* The truth that the Christian faith announces, and the theological-magisterial tradition of the Church has fixed in binding and yet historically variable formulations, is not exhausted in any such formulations. Rather, it lives in them all as itself inexhaustible and, at the same time, as capable of provoking innumerable others. Since the beginning, the sole Gospel has been formulated in four Gospels. In each of them is the whole truth of the Gospel without its being exhausted in any of the four, thus leaving room for the formulations of the others. Thus *dogmatism* is avoided, which by identifying the truth with one of its particular formulations excludes all other formulations of the truth as false. But *relativism* is also avoided, which by identifying truth and its subsequent historical formulations proclaims the historical relativity of truth itself, thus losing its originary or root unity.[25]

In the wake of this hermeneutic framework, theology has not only become aware of the possibility that the Gospel may be incorporated in contexts other than that of Western culture in its Greek guise,[26] but it is also becoming increasingly aware that the truth is not exhausted even in the context of Christian theological truth. Theology thus becomes attentive to the testimonies of truth that one can have in other religions and more generally in the various expressions of wisdom belonging to different human cultures.

What is retrieved in this way is that attitude toward the truth that is connatural to the originary Christian inspiration: on the one hand, the commitment to the testimony of the truth that has revealed itself in Christ and that in faith is welcomed and lived; on the other hand, the attentive listening to the testimonies of the truth that can come from any side in the conviction that truth cannot contradict truth and that any authentic formulation of it can only contribute to its deepening. Aquinas expressed this attitude with this formulation, which follows the Ambrosiaster: "*omne verum a quocumque dicatur a Spiritu Sancto est*" [all truth comes from the Holy Spirit regardless of who states it].[27]

In light of this originary inspiration, appropriately brought back to light by contemporary theology, truthfully discerning the lights and shadows of Christian history is also possible. On the one hand, recognizing that Christian truth has not asserted itself primarily through the force of political power, but rather and above all through the testimony of its martyrs and more in general through the testimony of "good life" of Christians themselves is possible. In fact, this accompanied and certified the value of the "arguments" and "proofs" that the apologist Fathers formulated based on the sacred scriptures and the communicative-rational reflection. On the other hand, recognizing that when, starting with the Constantinian period, the so-called Christian governments thought they had to use force to impose the Christian truth because they thought of religion—in this case Christianity—as a factor of social cohesion and stability, Christianity came on a contradiction within itself is possible. If Christianity has not completely broken down and disappeared, this is because at its core has always remained alive the originary instance, according to which faith can be only the product of a free adhesion, and in no way can it be imposed through force. From here comes the continuously renewed prophetic "protest," on behalf of Christianity itself, against impositions of faith out of political reasons, be it "ecclesiastical politics" (one could think for example of the sad defense of the Native Americans by the missionaries on the occasion of their forced Christianization and/or enslavement by the Spanish political power) and their definitive condemnation by the Church.

The process has occurred not only in the direction of an influence of modern philosophy on theology, however, but also in the opposite direction, of an influence of Christian faith, theologically rethought, on modern and contemporary philosophy. To dispel the common place of this latter's becoming in a completely "separate" way from the instance of Christian faith, that is, from its "horizon of truth," we will indicate some aspects where such an influence is more evident with no pretension to completion or to coherence of exposition.

1. *Faced with the irreducibility of Christian faith to anything other than itself, both in philosophical-rational and psychological, historical, economic, and generally scientific terms, philosophy has been pushed to challenge the claim of modern rationality to self-constitution as absolute autonomy.* One can think even only of the position of the later Schelling, and then of Kierkegaard, in their reaction to Hegelian panlogism, which aimed at reencompassing positive Christian religion itself within the dialectical process of reason. But even earlier, one can think of Pascal and of Kant himself, in relation to the impossibility of understanding the presence of radical evil in human beings in purely rational terms. The later Schelling in particular maintains, for example, that the historical Christian event imposes a self-modification to philosophy, which commits itself to think through it: from "negative"—or logical dialectical—philosophy, it must turn into "positive"—or historico-hermeneutic—philosophy, no longer constructive of its objects but rather, first of all, "receptive" and interpreter of what history effectively offers it to think.[28]

2. *Faced with the always newly claimed "absolute theological difference-ulteriority," philosophy has been confirmed in its resistance against total scientific objectification of meaning, accomplished technical manipulation*

of human beings, and any absolutization-deification of worldy realities.
In the early twentieth century, the Protestant theologian Barth,
following on a Kierkegaardian theme, forcefully advanced once again
the fundamental theological theme of the "qualitatively infinite
difference" between God and humanity, emphasizing the qualification of God as the "wholly other."[29] Undoubtedly this theological
theme has influenced Heidegger's thesis of the "ontological difference" between being and beings, which is at the basis of the criticism of the scientific-technical reduction of being to a ready-at-hand
or manipulable being—a reduction that belongs to the scientific
attitude toward the world. This is a criticism that both existentialism
and personalism developed independently in various ways. We could
also recall, however, on a different side, the theological inspiration
that is at the basis of the "negative dialectic" of thinkers such as
Adorno and Horkheimer. Here mentioning Horkheimer's renowned
work, *Die Sehnsucht nach dem ganz Anderen,*[30] where the absolute
theological difference-ulteriority becomes the unavoidable point of
reference for the criticism of any absolutization of a particular social
status quo, which inevitably blocks the dialectical process of human
emancipation is sufficient. As Rahner writes, "the Christian conception [of God] will always express God's passionate protest against
every kind of polytheistic or pantheistic deification of the world."[31]

3. *Being provoked by Christian eschatology (not only of fulfilled justice, but
also of full human realization up to a beatifying community with God),
philosophy has found itself committed to avoid a banalization of the
humanum and its subordination to the historical totality; thus, it has
safeguarded the character of never instrumentalizable "end" of the human person, which is as such endowed with inalienable rights and duties,
as well as with that unfillable opening to the future signified by its desire
for the infinite.*

Among the philosophers who have received this provocation
the most, one should undoubtedly mention the Marxist philosopher Ernst Bloch, the author of the grandiose three-volume work,
The Principle of Hope.[32] In it among other things we find the expression "religion in heritage,"[33] which Moltmann already addresses in
1959 to propose an anthology of essays by Bloch on religion.[34]

Bloch borrows from Christianity especially the Christological-
messianic and eschatological motif to avoid the reduction of Marxism into the simple economic outcome of a classless society, as if
in it the great problems of human desire were automatically solved
and the great antiutopia of death were definitely overcome. To
avoid withering, Marxist hope must appropriate the Christian perspective of the final insertion of human beings in God himself, that

is, in the mysterious transcendence that is always beyond any human historical actualization. It is a perspective that impregnates with itself those "great mysteries of desire" such as the Christian mysteries of Christ's resurrection, ascension to heaven, and glorious return. But it is also the unexpected and unhoped-for mystery of the Incarnation, which presents God both as present in the smallest child of human beings and, at the same time, as the one who, out of love, takes on himself mortal life to give his very own life for human beings. The God of the Old Testament could not in fact have given his life for his people!

In truth, the matter is that of an appropriation that means to be "more than religious," that is, capable of realizing what Christianity could only promise. On the one hand, it eliminates any theocratic motif from the notion of transcendence, transforming it in a "transcending without transcendence"; on the other hand, it interprets the messianic eschatological motif in a militant sense, that is, as a historical commitment for its realization. While it brought about a deep transformation of Marxism, such an appropriation helped Christian theology free itself of any solidarity with static-contemplative ontotheological metaphysics, which is strictly linked with an ideology of conservation. This is a clear example, then, of a hermeneutic circle between theology and philosophy.[35]

Beside Bloch, a retrieval of the Jewish-Christian eschatological motif is present in other various twentieth-century philosophers, for example, in Emmanuel Levinas and Luigi Pareyson. This is so, however, not in view of an overcoming or fulfillment of Christianity, but rather in a hermeneutic universalizing function. Levinas, for example, intends "to translate" into Greek, that is, into the universal language of philosophy, the eschatological message of the Jewish prophets, who have been able to give voice to all the oppressed of the earth. This is a proposal the outcome of which is a real overturning of Greek thought, essentially contemplative, toward a rediscovery of the primacy of the ethical instance coming to us from the face of the other human being as the ultimate origin of the very meaning of the contemplation of the truth of being. Therefore, from "love of wisdom" philosophy must rediscover itself as "wisdom of love."[36]

4. *Enlightened by the Christian notion of freedom (in God and in human beings), philosophy has opened up for itself the way to elaborate an ontology that identifies freedom as the very core of being.* In this respect, we think of that trend of modern philosophy that Pareyson knowledgeably addresses, which starting with Descartes and moving through Pascal, Kant, Fichte, Schelling, Kierkegaard, Dostoevsky,

and finally contemporary existentialism, has tried to develop a *philosophy of freedom* as a global alternative to the *philosophy of necessity* of Greek kind. From here come both the rise of the fundamental philosophical question—unknown to the Greeks—"Why is there something rather than nothing?," and the direction in which the answer is sought: not only in the theorem of God's free creation of beings, but also in the vertiginous perspective of the gratuity of the originary being itself, which is thought as self-generating out of free choice insofar as it is free "lord" of its very being.[37]

5. *Being provoked by the Christian conception of the original fall and redemption through christological kenosis, modern and contemporary philosophy has finally seriously faced the issue of evil, up to the elaboration of a "tragic thought" that does not let itself be soothed by any consolatory nihilism.*

Unfortunately, the history of the philosophical meditation on the Christian doctrine of the fall and the original sin is still entirely to be written. This is so both on the side of its *reception* because it is considered as enlightening the effective human condition in which evil always already precedes and questions us, and even seems always to intertwine ambiguously with the good; and on the side of its *rejection*, insofar as it is considered to be incompatible with the individual's free personal responsibility. With regard to acceptance or rejection, one finds the alternative positions of Pascal and Voltaire, Kant and Goethe, Schelling and Hegel, Kierkegaard and Marx, to name several of the most famous. As Augusto Del Noce has highlighted, such a history cannot be expunged as secondary or uninfluential from the course of modern and contemporary philosophy.[38]

Today's philosophical renewals of such a theme, as for example in Nabert, Ricoeur,[39] and Pareyson, are very significant. Mentioning here some cadences of Pareyson's "tragic thought" is sufficient. For him, philosophy has for the most part tried either to rationalize evil, making of it a necessary moment in history, or to eliminate it through the nihilistic negation of God. If there is no Good, that is, no absolute, originary Good, source and measure of all good, then there is not even evil, what should not be. Yet evil imposes itself with undeniable evidence to our experience, and Christianity has the merit of having been able to hold it in its mysterious and tragic reality, finding its root in the freedom of the originary fall and denouncing its ruinous effects throughout the history of humankind. This is so to the point that it introduces evil in God himself, who in Christ has been involved in our very passion and death. The event of the cross thus represents something much more tragic than the "death of God" itself in our culture as Nietzsche proclaimed! At the same time, as we know, Christianity has been able to open up the hope of overcoming evil because it sees the fall as a universal event of human history always and only in light of the universal relevance of the salvation offered by God and anticipated in the figure of the resurrected Christ.[40] This is so not to offer a banal consolation in front of our tragic negative experiences, but rather to give solid support to the "hope against all hopes" (Romans 4: 18) that in the end there will be justice for all the oppressed of the earth. This is in accordance with the fundamental ethical imperative that forcefully emerges in front of the oppression of a human being by another human being, which gives meaning to all of our life: "It cannot, it must not be this way!"

This list of Christian motifs positively "inherited" by modern and contemporary philosophy could be helpfully prolonged because many are the fruitful contributions that the Christian faith has been able to give to Western philosophical thinking. We still mention, for example, the development of a real "philosophical Christology," which has been emphasized with special care in these latest years by Xavier Tilliette,[41] or the most recent proposals of a "trinitarian ontology," committed to a philosophical-theological rereading of being in an essentially triadic-relational manner.[42] It is time, however, to move to the third part of our discourse, that is, to the indication of some themes emerging within the context of our contemporary culture. Such themes represent real challenges both to philosophy and to theology because they implicate both in the attempt to answer by focusing their respective attention more on "the thing in itself" under scrutiny than on the defense of their respective methodological differences or fields of competence; by remaining fully available to welcome, no matter where they come from, contributions capable of helping the individuation of the solution. Here the matter is that of a "hermeneutic circularity" that joins both in front of contemporary culture, or better, in front of the most pressing and deepest expectations of today's human beings. It is a hermeneutic circularity that not only provokes both directly, but also pushes them to welcome gladly the mutual aid they can give each other to fulfill their task with full responsibility.

Common Themes of Reflection in Front of Some Challenges from Contemporary Culture

1. *First of all, the theme of the relation "one-many," "totality-fragment."* This theme, among the most characteristic of the postmodern period,[43] has come to the fore as the necessity to find some "third way" between the equally unsatisfying alternatives of the unity/ totality of meaning, which is already experiencing a crisis in many ways, and the simply unrelated fragmentation of meanings, which

seems to abandon any intention of universal communicability, and thus of truth as such.[44] In this regard, one could wonder whether the Christian vision of God as uni-trinity, which invites to think plurality within the divine unity itself, could not be in some way "inherited" also in philosophical terms. For example, through a commitment to think being at the same time as the One and the Many because the One must be thought of not as a self-centered and exclusive totality, but rather as communion in the love relation. And the Many must be thought of not as unrelated monadic separateness, but as difference that constitutes itself in its identity only through a recognition coming to it from the other's alterity and through a self-donation to the other as practice of its own very identity. It would seem that a philosopher such as Levinas has been able to give fecund indications in this direction when he criticizes the Greek conception of being as uni-totality and meanwhile proposes to identify the ultimate meaning of being in the interhuman relation, where the I finds its identity only if it carries within itself the other who constantly questions out of his or her radical alterity. In any event, we are in front of a theme that involves both philosophy and theology and that may perhaps be better addressed if both the one and the other are mutually able to welcome and put to work mutual suggestions.

2. *The problem caused by the emergence of the so-called new subjectivity, which is not of an essentially cognitive-rational, but rather an emotive-vital kind.* Nietzsche and Freud are the main references in this respect. Will one truly have to surrender to the uncontested primacy of the blind rights of the vital impulse as the only alternative to the various repressive-sacrificial conceptions of the vital, of a rationalistic/bourgeois and/or religious/sacral kind? Or will walking the path of the retrieval of the veritative intentionality of the vital sentiments themselves be possible? Today, philosophers and theologians are fruitfully moving on this path, which Scheler has already shown with his rediscovery of the axiological intentionality of the emotional life. Far from being considered as a totally blind impulse with respect to values, corporeal vitality, for example, the site of the so-called passions, is studied as symbolic-expressive field of the other's ethical appeal as well as of the availability to self-donation. Yet, after centuries of philosophical as well as theological intellectualistic rationalism, which has done nothing except to dismiss any positive value of the emotive-passional realm, the path in this direction is still for the most part to be trod on.[45]

3. *The problem posed by claiming the positivity of finitude, weakness, mortality of being, in opposition to the traditional ontology of transcendence*

as immutability and powerfulness. Will the only outcome of this claim, which has one of its main sources in Heidegger, be necessarily ontological and theological nihilism, which claims that the finite should be thought without any relation with the infinite? Or will welcoming the instance of the truth by walking the path of overturning the traditional meaning of being itself, to the point of thinking being and/or God no longer as theocratic, imposing transcendence, but rather as gratuitous and unconditioned donation to the other than oneself be possible? In other words, on the side both of philosophy and of theology, will keeping open the tension between finite and infinite, immanence and transcendence, which seem to be constitutive of the very humanness of human beings, without giving up either their constitutive finitude or their essential relation with the infinite be possible? The christological symbol of the Word made flesh, and flesh that, in the death on the cross, is donated out of love to the point of complete self-emptying (*kenosis*), has been already conceptualized in the Chalcedonian formulation of the inseparable unity of the humanness and divinity of Christ, albeit in the unmistakable difference of the two natures. Even today this symbol may perhaps help us to interpret correctly the mysterious relation of human beings' finite being to God's infinite being. Will the "true human being" not perhaps be the one who entrusts oneself completely to God as did Jesus? And will the "true God" not perhaps be the one who gives himself completely to human beings as he has done in Jesus? In both cases, in the mutual self-donation neither (God nor humanity) loses identity; if anything, they find it in its deepest truth.[46]

4. *The problem posed by the new dimensions of ethics, which is no longer individual (or individualistic), but rather social and planetary.* The criticisms, which have spread in contemporary culture, of an ethics founded on a metaphysical-Platonic transcendence (God, or values, or both) have not been able to silence the ethical provocation constantly coming to our freedom/responsibility from our consciousness of the presence of evil always preceding us: the evil of human beings deprived of their dignity by thousands of forms of exploitation, oppression, and spoliation; the evil of a society not only characterized by the spreading of usurpation or the nonrecognition of the rights of the other (not only as person, but also as race, ethnicity, people, religion, culture, social status, and so forth), but also by now capable of technically programming such usurpation and nonrecognition in a globally efficient way; the evil that presents itself as selfish pollution to the point of the inhabitability of the vital earthly environment and even as possibility of the destruction of the planet itself as life place for future generations.

In front of the urgency of the ethical provocation coming from a presence of evil such as a planetary problem, will not philosophies and theologies
be judged positively or negatively on the grounds of their ability or inability
to contribute to the elaboration of a planetary ethics that can be critically
convincing not only at the level of theory, but also of praxis?[47] Will the
salvation of the suffering human beings and of life itself on Earth not be a
criterion of truth by which to measure the plausibility if not the absolute
legitimacy of future philosophies and theologies? As a matter of fact, the
categorical imperative "to overthrow all conditions in which man is a de-
based, enslaved, neglected, contemptible being," which Marx formulated in
the introduction to the *Critique to Hegel's Philosophy of Right*[48] and which
today should be extended to the entire future of the planet, is becoming the
horizon of meaning for all philosophical and theological assertions. This
horizon of meaning is actually such only if it is freely accepted and made
one's own by everyone because meaning can be accessed only through freedom. Yet, one should not forget that such freedom, which can open or close
itself up to the ethical meaning of life, is already since the beginning an
ethically "invested" freedom. That is, it is not neutral in front of both good
and evil. Rather, it is characterized by that preoriginary "investiture" from
the Good that, as Levinas has correctly understood, questions us out of the
absolutely different (divine) Other speaking in any human being in need of
us. The words of the Gospel according to Matthew (25: 31–46), according
to which the Lord, when the final judgment comes, will say that what has
been done to the smallest, thirsty, hungry, naked has been done to him, "you
have done it to me," reveal to us, in an emblematic manner, this tight
connection between the Other and others. At the same time, they reveal the
true face of that (divine) Other who, far from being manifest as sacred
separate transcendence, has chosen to become present to our free acceptance
as the very dimension of the absolute dignity of our brothers and sisters.

    In conclusion, we can assert that today philosophy and theology can-
not think of themselves as immunized either against the challenges of the
present time, which involve both, or against mutual provocations, the neglect of which would not be critically justified. Mutual attention and dialogue—more than past conflicts—reveal themselves, in fact, as a precious
possibility on the way to the quest for the meaning of the truth, which is
dear to both, and for which each has full responsibility.

Notes

1. In this introductory paragraph, I recall what has been developed fully in
Giovanni Ferretti, "Filosofia e teologia: alla ricerca di un nuovo rapporto," in *Teologia
e filosofia: Alla ricerca di un nuovo rapporto*, ed. S. Muratore (Rome: A. V. E., 1990),
pp. 15–55, 211–307; also in Giovanni Ferretti, *Filosofia e teologia cristiana, I. Questioni*
(Naples: Esi, 2002) pp. 21–66.

2. See, for example, on the Protestant side, the work by Wolfhart Pannenberg, *Theology and the Philosophy of Science*, trans. F. McDonagh (London: Darton, Longman and Todds, 1976) and, on the Catholic side, Giuseppe Colombo, ed., *L'evidenza e la fede* (Milan: Glossa, 1988).

3. With respect to this, see Giovanni Ferretti, "Filosofia della fede cristiana," in *Le ragioni di Abramo: Razionalità e fede nel monoteismo*, ed. S. Biolo (Turin: Rosenberg and Sellier, 1999), pp. 33–58; and also, with a different introduction, Giovanni Ferretti, "Per una filosofia del 'credere cristiano,'" *Filosofia e teologia* 3, XI (1997): 435–60; now in Ferretti, *Filosofia e teologia cristiana, I. Questioni*, pp. 111–46.

4. A wider discussion is found in Claudio Ciancio, Giovanni Ferretti, Anna M. Pastore, and Ugo Perone, *In lotta con l'angelo: La filosofia negli ultimi due secoli di fronte al Cristianesimo* (Turin: SEI, 1989).

5. See John Paul II, *Fides et ratio* (Vatican City: Libreria Editrice Vaticana, 1998), n. 77.

6. The now well-known expression is due to Jean Greisch, *L'âge herméneutique de la raison* (Paris: Cerf, 1985).

7. See, for example, Karl Jaspers's essays on philosophical faith: *Der philosophische Glaube* (Munich: Piper, 1948); *Philosophical Faith and Revelation*, trans. E. B. Ashton (London: Collins, 1967); Jaspers and K. Zahrnt, *Philosophie und Offenbarungsglaube. Ein Zwiegespräch* (Hamburg: Furche, 1963).

8. The famous *Wirkungsgeschichte* of which Hans-Georg Gadamer speaks in *Truth and Method*, trans. G. Barrett and J. Cumming (New York: Crossroad, 1982).

9. A precious history of such mutual conditionings can be found in Wolfhart Pannenberg, *Theologie und Philosophie* (Göttingen: Vandenhoeck and Ruprecht, 1996).

10. *Fides et ratio*, chap. VI.

11. Ibid., n. 73.

12. Ibid., n. 99.

13. Ibid., n. 100.

14. Ibid., n. 101.

15. Ibid., n. 100.

16. See Thomas Aquinas, *Summa Theologiae*, I, 1, 8 ad 2; this passage is quoted also in *Fides et ratio*, n. 43.

17. *Fides et ratio* speaks of "fateful [It., *fatale*] separation" (n. 45), at least in principle, although it later remarks, "a good part of modern and contemporary philosophy would not exist without this stimulus of the word of God" (n. 76).

18. For an introduction to the thought of these theologians, see Franco Ardusso, Giovanni Ferretti, Anna Pastore Perone, and Ugo Perone, *Introduzione alla teologia contemporanea* (Turin, Italy: Marietti, 1980).

19. Famous is the objection levied especially against Rahner by Hans Urs von Balthasar, *Cordula oder der Ernstfall* (Einsieldeln: Johannes, 1966).

20. *Fides et ratio*, n. 28.

21. Ibid., n. 1. On the theme of the anthropological turn, see Johann Baptist Metz, *Christliche Anthropozentrik* (Munich: Kösel, 1962).

22. See, for example, Martin Heidegger, *Identity and Difference*, trans. J. Stambaugh (New York: Harper and Row, 1969).

23. *Fides et ratio*, too, follows the venerable apophantic tradition of negative theology, deeply aware of the ineffable and incomprehensible mystery of God, both by resorting to some famous formulations by Saint Anselm (see n. 42, which quotes

the text of *Monologion*, 64, where it is said that with respect to God our reason *rationabiliter comprehendit incomprehensibile esse*), and by asserting on its own that knowledge proper to faith "does not destroy the mystery; it only reveals it more, showing how necessary it is for people's life" (n. 13).

24. Among others, see E. Schillebeeckx, *God, the Future of Man* (New York: Sheed and Ward, 1967).

25. For a specific criticism of these two false alternatives, see Luigi Pareyson, *Verità e interpretazione* (Milan: Mursia, 1971), pp. 53–90.

26. With respect to this, here is how *Fides et ratio* puts it: "In preaching the Gospel, Christianity first encountered Greek philosophy; but this does not mean at all that other approaches are precluded. Today, as the Gospel gradually comes into contact with cultural worlds which once lay beyond Christian influence, there are new tasks of inculturation, which means that our generation faces problems not unlike those faced by the Church in the first centuries" (n. 72).

27. This formulation too appears in *Fides et ratio*, n. 44.

28. See Friedrich W. J. Schelling, *Philosophie der Offenbarung* (Frankfurt: Suhrkamp, 1993), vol. I, pp. 229–33.

29. The reference is obviously, first of all, to Karl Barth, *The Epistle to the Romans*, trans. E. C. Hoskyns (London: Oxford University Press, 1968).

30. See Max Horkheimer, *Die Sehnsucht nach dem ganz Anderen* (Hamburg: Furche Verlag, 1970).

31. See Karl Rahner, "Theos in the New Testament," in *Theological Investigations*, trans. C. Ernst, O. P. (Baltimore. MD: Helicon Press, 1961), vol. I, p. 85.

32. See Ernst Bloch, *The Principle of Hope* (Cambridge, MA: MIT Press, 1995).

33. Ibid., p. 1487.

34. See Ernst Bloch, *Religion im Erbe* (Frankfurt: Suhrkamp, 1959).

35. On Ernst Bloch and theology, see Giovanni Ferretti, "Utopia in eredità. Attualità e inattualità dell'interpretazione della religione in Ernst Bloch," in *Attualità e prospettive del "Principio speranza." L'opera fondamentale e il pensiero di Ernst Bloch*, ed. G. Cunico (Naples: La città del sole, 1998), pp. 45–76; also in Giovanni Ferretti, *Filosofia e teologia cristiana, II. Figure* (Naples: Esi, 2002), pp. 167–95.

36. See especially Emmanuel Levinas, *Totality and Infinity* (Pittsburgh, PA: Duquesne University Press, 1969). On Levinas, see Giovanni Ferretti, *La filosofia di Levinas. Alterità e trascendenza* (Turin: Rosenberg and Sellier, 1996). As for the taking up of Christian eschatology in Pareyson, see Luigi Pareyson, *Ontologia della libertà. Il male e la sofferenza* (Turin: Einaudi, 1995).

37. See especially Pareyson, *Ontologia della libertà*, where this theme is developed as a philosophical hermeneutic of Christian experience, not without a creative taking up of Plotinian and Schellingean themes.

38. See especially Augusto Del Noce, *Il problema dell'ateismo. Il concetto di ateismo e la storia della filosofia come problema* (Bologna: Il Mulino, 1964), and *Riforma cattolica e filosofia moderna* (Bologna: Il Mulino, 1965).

39. See especially Jean Nabert, *Essai sur le mal* (Paris: PUF, 1955); Paul Ricoeur, *The Symbolism of Evil*, trans. E. Buchanan (New York: Harper and Row, 1967), but also *Le mal: un défi à la philosophie et à la théologie* (Geneva: Labor et Fides, 1996).

40. With respect to this, see especially the essay by Luigi Pareyson, "La filosofia e il problema del male," in *Ontologia della libertà*, pp. 151–233.

41. See Xavier Tilliette, *Le Christ des philosophes* (Namur: Culture et Vérité, 1993) and *Le Christ de la philosophie* (Paris: Cerf, 1990).

42. See for example the short but important essay by Klaus Hemmerle, *Thesen zur einer trinitarischen Ontologie* (Einsiedeln: Johannes, 1976).

43. On the challenges postmodernity posed to Christian theology, see also Giovanni Ferretti, "La teologia cristiana di fronte al post-moderno," *Firmana. Quaderni di teologia e pastorale* 14 (1997): 65–91; also in Ferretti, *Filosofia e teologia cristiana, II. Figure*, pp. 231–67.

44. See for example Giovanni Ferretti, "Frammentazione storica e memoria," in *Il tempo della memoria. La questione della verità nell'epoca della frammentazione*, ed. G. Ferretti (Turin: Marietti, 1987), pp. 9–25.

45. See Giovanni Ferretti, "Soggettività contemporanea e crisi delle antropologie," in *Bollettino dell'Istituto di Filosofia della Università degli Studi di Macerata, a.a. 1977–78* (Rome: Abete, 1979), pp. 107–40.

46. On the topic of finitude, see *Ermeneutiche della finitezza*, ed. G. Ferretti (Macerata: Giardini, 1988).

47. See Roberto Mancini and others, *Etiche della mondialità: La nascita di una coscienza planetaria* (Assisi: Cittadella, 1996).

48. See Karl Marx, *Critique of Hegel's Philosophy of Right*, trans. A. Jolin and J. O'Malley (Cambridge: Cambridge University Press, 1970), p. 137.

Chapter 5

Ontology of Actuality

Gianni Vattimo

The problem of overcoming metaphysics, a way of thinking linked in various ways to the violence characterizing Western society, which is the result of the rationalization that precisely metaphysics has inaugurated and made possible, seems to imply—as one can see meditating on some exemplary itineraries, those of Adorno and Levinas no less than those of Nietzsche and Heidegger[1]—not only the assumption of a different theoretical attitude, but also a peculiar relation with that very modern society in which metaphysics seems to have concretized and, as Heidegger says, actualized itself. If the roots of metaphysical violence are ultimately in the authoritarian relation established between ground and grounded, between true being and ephemeral appearance or, which amounts to the same, in the relations of domination built around the relation subject-object, then the question of overcoming this thinking and the world that it determines cannot be conceived of as the access to another ground from which to move for a new construction. It is the very foundational "logic" (distinction between true and appearing world; grasping of the true world in the subjective experience of evidence; unfolding of the relevance of the ground both as theoretical demonstrative power and as practical projectual principle) that one should put aside. For this reason, the question *Was heißt Denken?* has always retained such a central role in the work of a philosopher such as Heidegger. The issue of postmetaphysical thinking is thus revealed as a problem that cannot be mainly theoretical. It is not a matter of accessing in theory the principles from which then to draw consequences: criteria of judgment on the existing world (critical theory), lines of behavior to apply to modify it, and so on. Even if the relation of "foundation" ever worked in the past— metaphysical epochs are "archaeological" epochs whose constitution unfolded as enactment of a principle on which basically everything depended: there

---

This chapter appeared as "Ontologia dell'attualità," in *Filosofia 87*, ed. G. Vattimo (Rome: Laterza, 1988), pp. 201–23.

are no historical unitarian "worlds" unless where there is a metaphysics at work[2]—today it can no longer be continued, exactly as metaphysics can no longer be continued. This discontinuity [*improseguibilità*][3] reveals itself precisely at the moment when the movement of reducing reality to the link grounding-grounded is realized in the fullest manner; that is, at the moment of the modern technological society, of the *Ge-Stell*, of total organization (and, more or less necessarily and logically, of extermination). From here there derive important consequences for the possibility of articulating a postmetaphysical thinking. First of all, it cannot be formulated as access to a different principle, which would still work once again as ground, reconstituting the foundational logic in all its aspects, including the relation of conflict and domination between "subject" and "object." This means that postmetaphysical thinking is, in an entirely peculiar way, "assigned" to its legacy. For it, the history of past philosophies is certainly not a progressive revealing of the truth. Neither is it, however, only a collection of examples, of experiences of other cultures and thinkers from which one can learn something to the purpose of fulfilling one's task better, that is, to the purpose of grasping—in an autonomous experience—the true, the principles, and so on. Because this access to the true, independent from the history of past thought—or with a mere instrumental or auxiliary reference to it—would still be configured as an access to the ground, the relation of postmetaphysical thinking to the history of metaphysics from which it comes is in some way determinant. Postmetaphysical thinking has no other "sources" that are not its own legacy. The unfolding of Heidegger's thought is a testimony of this peculiar relation to a rethinking (*An-denken*) of the philosophical tradition. Additionally, however, the widespread historiographic tendency that characterizes contemporary (at least "continental") philosophy and that seems more immediately connected to scientistic prejudices (by conceiving of their work as rigorous, documented historiography of past philosophies, philosophers give themselves a scientific *status*), is in truth one of the most evident symptoms of the discontinuity of metaphysics. When not lived in a radical sense, this discontinuity translates into a fetishization of "research," which under the current conditions of philosophy can only be historiographic.

Perhaps one can escape this—historiographistic, scientistic—destiny of current philosophy only by making explicit and bringing to its conclusion also a second consequence of the discontinuity of metaphysics as discontinuity of foundational thinking. Not only does it exclude that thinking may appeal to an "other" principle because this would still be a ground; because the discontinuity of metaphysics unveils itself at the moment when it "realizes" itself in a (tendentiously) total manner in modernity, the legacy to which metaphysical thinking finds itself "assigned" is not only, or mainly, the theoretical patrimony from past philosophies that one must rethink. Rather, it is modernity itself as the world in which that theoretical legacy gives itself in its most actualized manner. In the epoch of the end of metaphysics—

when metaphysics reveals itself as untenable because of its relations with violence accompanying rationalization—philosophy escapes the destiny of becoming pure and simple historiographic industriousness only if it decisively becomes—to use Foucault's expression[4]—an "ontology of actuality."[5] In which sense Foucault used here the term "ontology" is not clear. Certainly, he did not use "criticism," and we can reasonably hypothesize that he meant to avoid relocating the thought of actuality within a metaphysical dimension: the only one that, through appealing to another principle, would enable a "criticism" of the present in the traditional sense of the term.

To make some step further in the "definition" of postmetaphysical thinking, deepening the analysis of its "assignation" to its legacy, the relation linking it to the metaphysics from which it comes (and which intends to overcome) and, especially, to the world of actualized metaphysics, that is, to modernity is necessary.

This relation can very well be defined with the term "hypocrisy" in the sense Levinas used,[6] even if not with the negative connotations the word implies for him. For Levinas Western thought is hypocritical; it ambiguously lives the multiplicity of its own legacies, and it disfigures the word of the Biblical prophets by rethinking it in the language of Greek metaphysics. Hypocrisy and contamination are our Western legacy in which even the divine word darkens in mixing with metaphysics. God speaks authentically rather from another place, from an exteriority that Levinas thinks he can guarantee also insofar as he refers only to the *Old* Testament and to the people who have remained loyal to it, the Jews. However, as seems to be confirmed by the history of Jewish culture and by its presence as a lay factor within modern culture, Jewishness may not represent, as Levinas thinks, the opening of the way to an improbable listening to the radical alterity of the divine word, but rather the phenomenal element in which the nonunitarian character of Western tradition presents itself most emblematically. Jewish alterity, that is, should be perceived not as the voice of an Other, radically stranger, but as a "disturbance" to the racial, political, and cultural unity of the Western world, as a recapitulatory example of all the elements of impurity and contamination constituting the essential laity and secularism of European civilization.

Levinas's term "hypocrisy" is only one of those one can recall to describe the ambiguous and perhaps oblique position that postmetaphysical thinking finds itself occupying in relation to the legacy of metaphysics and modernity, the legacy of metaphysics that is modernity. It cannot refer to another principle unless one repeats the game of foundation (and Levinas's results, his "return" from foundational metaphysics to a relation of religious dependency on the Lord, point at least to the risk that the only way out of foundational logic may be a regression to even more violent stages of the relation of dependency on the principle). Contemporary philosophy is rich with suggestive images that try to grasp the essence of this peculiar and difficult position of thought. Levinas's description in terms of hypocrisy (which he, however, condemns as a closed path) can be compared to Nietzsche's image of a "convalescent" philosophy and perhaps also to Sartre's inevitable bad faith of thought; and then to the image—which Klossowski develops out of Nietzsche—of thinking as conspiracy,[7] and to the other image, linked to this, of perversion, which Foucault introduces to describe Deleuze's position.[8] Although in different ways, these notions and images try to grasp the condition of a thinking that perceives the need to overcome a certain configuration, the metaphysical one. This thinking, nevertheless, attains this need only as a logical development of the very configuration itself and can satisfy it only through the instruments that the situation—which it wants to exit—makes available.

With his announcement of the "death of God," Nietzsche inaugurates this conception of the situation and tasks of postmetaphysical thinking. The death Zarathustra speaks of is a real one, not the nonexistence of God enunciated in a metaphysical proposition. God has "existed," has functioned as principle of organization and rationalization of human life, making it move from the chaotic and dangerous conditions of primitive woods to organized society, which avails itself of a scientific knowledge of nature, of the technical ability for its domination, of stable social structures. Today, precisely because of this process of effective reassurance (made possible by what Heidegger would call metaphysics), God is no longer needed; humanity does not need the "extreme" reassurance of a magical kind that was provided by the idea of God or even by the idea of the dependency of the real on a unique principle, a metaphysical ground. What is significant in Nietzsche's teaching is not so much the "anthropological" criticism of religion and metaphysics, recognized as functions of reassurance in conditions of risk that social rationalization, science, and technics have not yet mitigated; all this Nietzsche could find already in the tradition, from Feuerbach to positivism and the beginning of anthropology. What is relevant, rather, is his acute awareness of the ambiguity contained in the announcement of the death of God because God dies being killed by his faithful. Precisely because of the rationalization one's faith in God made possible (or as a result of the metaphysical belief in ground and in the logic that follows) is God revealed as a superfluous hypothesis. The world in which God is dead, however, remains totally determined by that belief, as far as its possibility and provenance are concerned. In fact, Nietzsche forbids himself the thought that the belief in God has been only a step that has now been overcome on the way to discover the true structure of reality. It is not: we live today in a world which, thanks to the primitive mistake of faith in God, has *discovered* that *in reality* God *is not*. This would be an extreme way of letting the very belief in God survive as the true structure of reality. Instead, it is: we live in a world that, thanks to the belief in God, has configured itself in structures of reassurance that enable us not to need such strong beliefs any longer and to

move toward a freer, less anxious, more experimental life. This new condition of ours, however, is not "sustained" by some true structure of reality the
mistakes of the past have finally let us see. Rather, it is entirely and only
determined by its provenance. It is only, as it were, a new phase of the
primitive religiosity, definable only as a subsequent moment of that very
same process and has no other constitutive elements than this provenance.

The experience Nietzsche condenses in the announcement of the death
of God, which runs through contemporary thought in the various figures that
the ambiguity of groundless thinking therein assumes, is the *Verwindung* of
metaphysics in Heidegger. The thinking that Heidegger inaugurates in *Being
and Time* tries to rethink the meaning of being outside the horizon of presence, objectivity, and the relation subject-object. Yet, as explained in the
"Letter on Humanism," this attempt fails because of the failing of language,
a failing that has been inherited from metaphysics.

The dependency of thought on language, which Heidegger experiences
in the "impossibility" of bringing to completion *Being and Time*, ends up
coinciding in the essay on humanism with the dependency of existence on
being. It is not as Sartre thinks that we are at a level where there are only
human beings. Rather, we are at a level where, first and foremost, there is
being. This "reversal," which *Being and Time* had certainly abundantly foreshadowed, but that is enunciated in such explicit terms only in the essay on
humanism and that assigns the "priority" of being over *Dasein* precisely out
of the experience of the dependency of thinking on language, is the content
of what, with a term Heidegger employs in that very 1946 essay, is called
"*Kehre*," the turning, in his thought. *Kehre* is both the turning that Heidegger
sees occur in his philosophy, which after *Being and Time* orients itself in
increasingly less "existentialist" and more ontological terms, and the radical
change of perspective to which thinking is in general called to overcome
objectifying metaphysical thinking. The latter is also "humanistic" thinking,
insofar as by identifying being with an object it puts being in the hands of
human beings (the climax of metaphysics is the Nietzschean "will to power,"
that is, the will to plan and organize technically the world with no limit in
objective norms).

The use and meaning of the term *Verwindung* are understood on the
background defined by the experience of the turn. *Verwindung* expresses the
condition of thought which has experienced the turn in the first sense of the
term, that is, which has discovered the dependency of thought on language,
of existence on being. Precisely on the basis of this discovery, it perceives the
need, but also the impossibility, of accomplishing, out of its own decision,
the turn in the second sense, that which would lead it beyond metaphysics.
Verwindung, which literally means something like twisting, or also recovering
from a sickness, and which he accentuates in the sense of acceptance, or
deepening,[9] is in fact used by Heidegger to indicate the relation of thinking
with that metaphysics that one should "overcome" (*überwinden*), but that in

reality—exactly on the basis of the experience spoken of in the essay on humanism—reveals that it does not let itself be put aside as a mistake from which we have freed ourselves, as an opinion we no longer believe.[10]

The "turn" to which thinking is called to overcome metaphysics and its attending violence is increasingly configured in Heidegger's later essays as a "torsion," a recovery and twisting prosecution of metaphysics itself, although not as we have mentioned of metaphysics only as a patrimony of theories or as an inherited conceptual language; but rather of metaphysics in its accomplished and realized form, the Ge-Stell, that is, modernity. The step forward that Heidegger's thought takes in its proceeding toward the "identification," although never explicitly thematized,[11] of the turn with Verwindung, would not be complete if, proceeding in the direction Heidegger suggested, we were not to interpret the meaning of this latter term in light of another concept decisive for an understanding of modernity: the concept of secularization. Although he never explicitly talks of secularization (but this has to do with the more complex question of the absence of a properly theological aspect in Heidegger's reconstruction of metaphysics as onto-theo-logy), Heidegger certainly thinks of the "death of God," of which Nietzsche speaks, as a constitutive event of realized metaphysics, that is, of the Ge-Stell and of modernity. The completion and the ending of metaphysics into technics follow the same "logic": as in Nietzsche God dies being "killed" by the very religiosity of his faithful people (who recognize God's superfluity precisely out of love for the truthfulness that God has always ordered to them), likewise in Heidegger metaphysics ends precisely when it "realizes" itself fully in technics. It is not, however, only an analogy: the realization of metaphysics into technics is actually the same phenomenon that Nietzsche calls the death of God. As such for Heidegger also it is a matter of a phenomenon of secularization.

Our issue, here, is however not a question of Heideggerian philology. Showing that it is neither arbitrary nor unjustified to follow the threads that seem to connect Nietzsche's death of God, Heidegger's Verwindung, and the problematic of secularization is sufficient. Certainly, a difficulty might lie in the fact that Verwindung indicates, for Heidegger, an attitude of recovery and twisting prosecution of accomplished metaphysics, whereas secularization, as a characterizing feature of the process of formation of modernity, concerns rather the process through which metaphysics has unfolded and asserted itself in the Ge-Stell. A first solution to this problem can be found if one acknowledges that the thinking of the overcoming of metaphysics will have to conform to a "logic" that it finds in modernity itself, precisely because such thinking can only be Verwindung, that is, albeit twisting, also the recovery and prosecution of metaphysics-modernity. Of course, this is the play, dense with implications, between "torsion" and "turning," Verwindung and Kehre, which, if our hypothesis holds, has characterized the later development of Heidegger's thought. The more it tries to escape the prophetic aura in which some of Heidegger's essays put it, the more is the turn configured as a torsion that recovers and continues the dissolving, nihilistic process characterizing the becoming of metaphysics and modernity. The essential reference to modernity and the process of modernization (which, as is easy to notice when reading some essays in *Holzwege*, Heidegger describes in not only approximately Weberian terms)[12] precisely justifies a reading of the notion of *Verwindung* in terms of secularization. On the one hand, the modernity that, for Heidegger, is a matter of continuing and twisting, is the result of a process that modernity itself has described in terms of secularization (as proved by the archetypical meaning of Nietzsche's thought and of the announcement "God is dead"). On the other hand, the constitutive features of Heidegger's *Verwindung*—the prosecution and recovery of a legacy in a way that also preserves and trans/defigures it—are also constitutive of the notion of secularization as it has been used to describe the process of formation of modernity. These proximities and analogies are at least worthy enough to justify as nonarbitrary the nearing of the two terms, Heidegger's and the one theoreticians of modernity used. The outcomes of clarification as well as of true and real theoretical resoluteness that will be drawn from such a nearing will be the only ones to constitute a more complete legitimation thereof.

Between the two concepts, the effect of clarification and theoretical resoluteness is however mutual. Not only does the *Verwindung* of which Heidegger speaks exit the pure aura of prophetism in which he and many of his interpreters have too often maintained it, but also the notion of secularization in the philosophical radicalization that the reference to Heidegger produces exits the numerous equivocations in which it has often been trapped. Particularly, it is only in light of the antimetaphysical exigencies Nietzsche and Heidegger upheld that the relevance of the concept of secularization can unfold against two symmetrical equivocations threatening to obscure it. Like the notion of modernity in general, secularization oscillates in fact between the two extremes of a vision that one could call, with Nietzsche's term, "reactive" (modernization as loss of the center, of the relation with God, defiguring of the human by an objectifying techno-scientific mentality, universal standardization and manipulation) and a Faustian, triumphalistic conception that also may be colored by critical attitudes insofar as, such as Habermas's "modernism," it thinks that the secularizing program of modernity has not been accomplished (for reasons that, we must assume, are linked to the persistence of relations of domination, even if this is not so clear, especially in Habermas's most recent work), but that it is nevertheless valid and that it is a matter of bringing it to completion against any postmodern doubt and "distortion."[13] In both these positions, which can be found in many conceptions of modernity, modernity is defined, positively or negatively, in relation to *Aufklärung*, enlightenment or illumination, thought of precisely as secularization, that is, as emancipation from the authority of the religious tradition and from authority *tout court* as religious value. Either *Aufklärung* is loss of the center and drifting "toward the X" (as Nietzsche writes), or it is the substitution of a more authentic center in place of the one represented by the old subjection to God and the authority of God's representatives on Earth. At times, this latter conception of modernity even prefers to avoid the very term "secularization" because it finds it imprecise and inadequate to describe the substantial autonomy and original legitimacy of modernity.[14] This attitude too falls back perfectly into what we have called the "triumphalistic" vision of modernity. It falls so much back into it that it refuses any derivative conception of the modern, which it instead sees as a completely original phenomenon.

Both the "reactive" and the "triumphalistic" perspective on secularization interpret the phenomenon in a sense that excludes from it the elements of "provenance" and "distortion." On the contrary, these appear to be essential for the need, which leads us here, to overcome metaphysics. In the reactive vision, provenance (and the accompanying distortion) is nothing else than a dejecting phenomenon of loss, against which one must react with the retrieval of the sacral origins in their true physiognomy. In the triumphalistic vision, provenance (and distortion) is cancelled by the idea that secularization is only the position of a new beginning. In both cases, the foundational metaphysical logic is maintained: either by an appeal to return to the "lost" ground or through the thesis that the legitimacy of the modern consists in the position of a new ground.

On the contrary, it is precisely the vocation, which philosophy experiences in late modernity, to think outside of the foundational perspective that renders philosophically meaningful a discourse on modernity, or, in other words, that puts philosophy on the way of the "ontology of actuality" (which in a metaphysical perspective would make no sense). If it wants to be loyal to the need that moves it, a philosophy that meditates on its assignation to its historical legacy, that is, to modernity, will have to start with leaving aside those interpretations of the modern that read it in terms of foundation: either as a loss to be healed or as a new beginning to be asserted. If Heidegger's *Verwindung* can make us take a step forward on the way to the definition of a postmetaphysical thinking out of the acknowledgement of its own link with secularization, this will happen not on the ground of a triumphalistic or reactive notion of secularization itself. One will have to look for a conception of secularization that escapes this still metaphysical horizon. This seems to be first of all the case with Max Weber's theory of modernization.[15]

Weber's theory of modernity is not only the one that actually exercises a determinant role in the current theoretical debate on the notion and destiny of the modern. It is also the one that seems to be most able to cast light on what one can and must understand with Heidegger's term *Verwindung*. In fact, it represents the clearest formulation of the awareness that the modern world comes from its originary religious, Judeo-Christian matrix, not so much as distance and overturning, but rather as legacy, retrieval, and prosecution. This prosecution is also not linear, as shown by the evident contradictions within the process of rationalization, which entails a feature of distortion.

As is well known, Weber sought and thought to find precisely in the contents of the Judeo-Christian religious tradition the "differential" element that explains the arising of modern capitalism in the European Western world and not elsewhere. On the one hand, the disenchantment of the world monotheism (which sets aside magic and naturalistic polytheism) made possible is the condition for a conception of nature as unitary mechanism, capable of functioning according to simple laws and thus available to calculation and forecast. On the other hand, in the radical form it assumes in Calvinism (predestination, entirely intramundane meaning of works and consequently new importance of success and accomplishment in work) and in Lutheranism (centrality of professional vocation, of *Beruf*, as the axis of a divine service that no longer confers importance to the still magical rituals of sacramentality), Christian ethics has constituted the ground for the development of the modern society of rationalized economy, technics, science, and social relations regulated by no longer "organic" but rather conventional connections. In this sense, Weber's theory of modernity is first of all a theory of secularization. What in the historiography dominated by the Enlightenment notion of progress has often presented itself as an affirmation of the human, of the hither-side, and so forth, is in reality made possible, supported, and determined by that same religious tradition that the Enlightenment thought it had put aside. The arising of capitalism and more generally of the modern world does not represent, however, either the only possible outcome of Christianity or its "authentic" actualization. Weber is not interested in a definition of the essence of Christianity (even if, undoubtedly, Calvinistic ethics seems to him also more radically loyal to the Sacred Scriptures than the one still embedded with magical and superstitious elements preached by the Catholic Church), or in other probable possibilities of its historical actualization. What confronts him is the modern rationalization of Western society, and he finds the explanation for its peculiar formation in the religious tradition from which it stems. Even wondering whether the "application" of Christianity that is enacted in modernization—capitalistic economy, global rationalization of existence—is a correct or distorted application makes no sense. It is in any event a secularizing application, insofar as the meaning of Christian revelation unfolds itself not so much in terms of granting an otherworldly salvation, as in terms of modifying the worldly reality. From disenchantment up to the radicality of Calvinistic ethics, it even looks like the process is that of a progressive "reduction" of the relevance of Biblical revelation.[16] This no longer speaks of the afterlife as of a place where reward and punishment will sanction the actions done in the world; rather, it exclusively becomes increasingly an ethics of duty for the sake of duty, and thus of rationality for the sake of rationality. Insofar as the rationalization induced by Judeo-Christian religiosity in general and by Calvinistic ethics in particular has the dissolution of modernity as its outcome, one can speak in Weber's case too of secularization as distortion—in the same sense, once again, in which Nietzsche speaks of the death of God and Heidegger speaks of the end of metaphysics. Analogously, with respect to Weber's theory of rationality, one can speak of a logic of distortion. Those who speak of a "tragicity" in Weber's thought[17] refer precisely to the apparently irreconcilable contradictions that mark this notion in his work. The tragicity can perhaps be overcome if one acknowledges, as certainly Weber did not do, that the contradictions of rationality are in reality its constitutive aspects, which only continue the twisting logic that has already manifested itself in the mundanization of monotheism into rationalistic vision of the world and of Calvinistic ethics into spirit of modern capitalism. Such an outcome can be reached probably only by applying Heidegger's problematic of *Verwindung* to Weber's issue of rationalization. The effect of deepening and clarification will thus be mutual between the two terms and between the two itineraries of thought they express.

The problematic aspect of Weber's conception of rationality and rationalization focuses on the pairs of concepts "goal-oriented rationality versus value-rationality," and "formal rationality versus substantive rationality." For the purposes of our discourse here, the two pairs of concepts can be considered largely as coinciding. What in the more specific consideration of economy Weber calls formal rationality is actually goal-oriented rationality, so is substantive rationality actually value-related rationality. The two distinctions are both elaborated in a chapter of *Economy and Society*.[18] They both allude to the difference between a social acting determined by consideration and calculation of the behavior of objects and other subjects seen as possible means in view of the end to be reached, and an acting that, on the opposite, is determined on the basis of "a conscious belief in the value for its own sake of some ethical, aesthetic, religious, or other form of behavior, independently of its prospects of success."[19] Goal-oriented rationality can also be called formal rationality because it especially unfolds as a rigorous plan of action, calculation, and, in economy, is directed by a totally abstract consideration of profit, which is pursued not because and to the extent that it satisfies a certain need (which is not the tautological need for an ever larger profit), but for itself: with no consideration for any limitations, "whether they be ethical, political, utilitarian, hedonistic, feudal [*ständisch*], egalitarian, or whatever."[20] How the ideal subject of this formal-rational action is the Calvinist entrepreneur, who seeks profit not to satisfy wishes and needs, but only as a sign of his or her divine predestination is easy to see. Precisely for this reason, he or she can assume, with respect to wealth, the ascetic detachment that enables unlimited reinvestment. This constitutes the ground for the formation of the capitalistic system. When, on the contrary, action lets itself be led by the pursuit of a value considered in any event just—this is the case not only of individual actions carried out by conviction up to martyrdom, but also of economies, like the socialist one, which think of themselves as means for the realization of political goals, of equality, of satisfaction of needs—then we are confronted with substantive or value-oriented rationality.

Concretely, however, the distinction between these two types of rationality is very problematic. First of all, this is so at the conceptual level. In fact Weber construes the ideal-typical concept of substantive rationality in relation to that of formal rationality, as some sort of a notion "derived" almost by subtraction. As Pietro Rossi remarks, "goal-oriented rational acting is characterized by a greater degree of comprehensibility, by a more direct comprehensibility; it even constitutes the term of reference entailing the other forms of action."[21] What is "missing," as it were, from substantive rationality is an element that limits the acceptance of a value as absolute and of a behavior as just on the basis of the calculus of possibilities, consequences, and means. And, in the end, if one asks what constitutes substantive rationality as rationality, one must admit that it is precisely the amount of formal rationality that it implies in any case; otherwise, value-oriented rational acting could not be distinguished from actions determined only by affective or traditional motivations.[22] On its side, formal rationality does not seem to be able to subsist (not conceptually this time, but in reality) in a completely separate way from substantive rationality. First of all, its historical self-giving depends on a series of "material" conditions: at the economic level, the self-giving of formal rationality occurs only in the presence of a free market, of a conflict among competing economies, and of social subjects endowed with a certain buying power;[23] in its wider sense in which it simply coincides with capitalistic economy, formal rationality implies the existence of a series of spiritual conditions intensely marked by an orientation toward values. Such is the case for the ascetic ethics of Calvinism, which is motivated by faith. Generally, however, no system of formal rationality can do without goals that as final ends are not the object of calculation.[24] The basis for what to many interpreters has appeared as the tragic character of Weber's thought ultimately lies in this "impossibility" of completely dissolving substantive rationality into formal rationality. This impossibility means to accept a certain ineliminable degree of irrationality also in the most rationalized behaviors and political forms. An expression of this ineliminable opening up of rationality toward irrationality[25] is also the tendency of rationalism, which Weber considers with preoccupation especially in his later works, to develop in forms that do not promote rationality at all levels, but rather mortify it. Thus, the rationalization of society, as generalized diffusion and application of technology, implies a return to forms of irrational trust toward technical devices about which the majority of users knows nothing.[26] To these perverse effects of rationalization is ultimately linked also that "relapse" into the irrational, which is the return of forms of charismatic power at the climax of modern rationalization.[27]

Certainly Weber does not consider these openings of rationality toward the irrational with a neutral, purely descriptive attitude. Although he always refuses to develop his theory of modernity into a philosophy of history, the directive function that the notion of formal rationality plays in the construction of the ideal-types of social action (and first of all in the concept of value-oriented rational acting or substantive rationality) reveals itself here as something more than a simple heuristic expedient. Weber thinks that the ideal-typical concepts sociologists employ are not objective reflections of reality; rather, they are necessarily partial interpretative instruments to which among other things no real object perfectly adequate to them ever corresponds precisely because they are idealizations and in this sense a "utopia."[28] Therefore, as pure descriptive instruments, they do not have any normative relevance. Thus, at least at first sight, the notion of formal rationality only helps to order a certain field of phenomena and processes, and only in this sense in relation to it can one say that some phenomena are more or less relevant. Precisely because they are relatively arbitrary constructions of social scientists, however, the ideal-typical concepts originate within a determined situation. Both the notion of ideal type and that of formal rationality as a leading thread to reconstruct cognitively the various forms of social acting are constructions that "occur," in Weber's theory, within a rationalized society; they are linked, therefore, to the disenchanted vision of the world belonging to modernity. The tragic tone of Weber's thought is thus connected not only with the consideration of the incumbent relapse into the irrational threatening modern societies, but also with the awareness of the unavoidable tension, which arises in the social scientist between belonging to a historical world and duty to be "nonevaluative." As a scientist, Weber can only describe the processes of construction and dissolution of rationality *sine ira ac studio* [without anger or passion]. As a man of his time, however, formal rationality appears to him as a value in relation to which he cannot but commit himself: with a choice, however, that is not "rational" and that itself thus seems to contradict not so much the duty to nonevaluativeness as much as the commitment to reason.

Yet, does the qualification of tragic really fit the conclusions of Weber's thought? It is licit to doubt it, perhaps not so much for the reasons moving the rigidly functionalist interpreters of his work. It looks like a characterization that is too psychologistic, too tied to the atmosphere of a time—which, in many aspects, is no longer ours—not to be accidental with respect to the substance of his thought. Much of the tragicity of his theory can be dissolved, certainly only out of the "privileged" perspective that is granted to us from reading Weber in a different situation than his (we could say: not at the climax of modernity, but rather in an already postmodern condition), if we explicitly acknowledge that those which to him still appear as contradictions of rationality are actually constitutive aspects of formal rationality, which unfolds not through a linear development of its own premises, but rather through a logic of torsions that are the very essence of secularization. First of all, then, the nonevaluativeness that should impose an attitude of "detachment" also with respect to value and to the preferability of formal rationality ought instead to be considered as an aspect and outcome of this rationality itself. We find ourselves in a tragic condition only if we cannot overcome the conflict between duty to nonevaluativeness and the choice for formal rationality, for modernity. But these two duties are one and the same. Nonevaluativeness is not an "eternal" value. It is the same directive ideal of rationalization when it is translated into the level of knowledge and construction of science. Thus, formal rationality presents itself—certainly against Weber's intentions and explicit claims—as the leading thread of a philosophy of history. This does not, however, have the metaphysical features on the grounds of which Weber rejected its possibility.[29] It is not a necessary law imposing itself as an ontological structure outside the historical process. It results only as a *telos* that ripens in the very process itself (somewhat as the ideal of formal rationality can only originate in the already rationalized society, even if not simply as a retrospective consideration, but rather as a "destiny" opened up only by what has happened, by provenance). Insofar as it ripens only with the process to which it gives meaning, rationality is not a necessary outcome. And, second, it is not an entirely positive ideal, analogous to the final redemption that the histories of philosophy have filled with different contents, but all of them denoted by positivity, perfection, and so forth, which they inherited from the religious matrix, the kingdom of God.

Through the function of model and "internal" *telos* exercised by formal rationality no less than through the application of the notion of rationality to the study of the world visions of other cultures too (an application Weber carries out in his *Sociology of Religion*), secularization appears then as the beginning of a philosophy of history that escapes metaphysics—and that can thus be thought as possible also from Weber's perspective—insofar as it is no longer oriented toward the identification of a necessary structure supporting historicity (as ineluctable law of becoming; as a leading function for a final condition of perfection). It no longer thinks of historicity in terms of unfolded presence, whether of the law of becoming or of the prescribed *telos*. Weber sets aside the two symmetrical "metaphysical" conceptions under which, as we have seen, secularization has often presented itself. It is not loss and decadence because we do not have any history-transcending principle to judge the process that from the religious origin has led to us in this manner. The only directive principle available is that of rationalization, which is defined precisely in the process of secularization as its immanent order and possible destination of its development. This therefore excludes that the acknowledgement of the process of secularization may lead thought to the duty of recovering the origin, which is given to us in its "value" only insofar as it has produced its own secularized translation: rationality. However, and here Weber distances himself from any triumphalistic vision of modernity, this is not the autonomous self-assertion of a new and different principle; rather, it is only the development of that religious provenance. Without its "continuation"—as one can see from the fact that no formal rationality seems to hold without reference to "irrational" choices of value—the secularized order does not hold.

Not out of explicitly and primarily philosophical considerations as in Heidegger, but out of largely scientific-positive needs for comprehension and description of the social history of Western modernity, Weber develops a vision of history in which, although in a scattered and nonsystematic manner, that connection between (metaphysical) modernity and "torsion" is announced that constitutes the horizon of sense of Heidegger's *Verwindung*. It is not a matter here of "proving" anything, of showing a point-to-point correspondence between Weber's and Heidegger's notions. On the contrary, Weber is here approached as exemplary moment of a theory of modernity—in the twofold meaning, subjective and objective, of the genitive, one should recall—that exhibits the two features of *provenance* and *torsion* that more explicitly Heidegger regards as constitutive elements of the overcoming of metaphysics. Besides, the itinerary through which, from the idea of the turn announced in the essay on humanism, Heidegger reaches the idea of *Verwindung* as the only authentic possibility that such a "turn" occurs, is precisely Weber's same path: the meditation on the essence of the modern. It is not so much or not only the insuperability of the language of metaphysics that makes the completion of *Being and Time* impossible and that inaugurates the turn (from existence to being) without, moreover, being able to accomplish it. It is rather the experience of the fact, which Heidegger develops at a philosophical level precisely in the years following *Being and Time* that the dependency of thought on the language of metaphysics is only a mark of the belonging of *Dasein* (that Heidegger is and that we are) to modernity. In this move, from *Kehre* to *Verwindung*, what occurs is not only that with an act of resignation Heidegger becomes aware that the connections tying us to the metaphysical tradition are too strong, and he falls back on an oblique tactic. Conversely, the twisting prosecution imposes itself as path for thinking because it exhibits itself as the feature of the very process through which metaphysics constitutes itself and comes to its own fulfillment in the technological society. The end of metaphysics of which Nietzsche spoke with the announcement of the death of God and which Heidegger experienced in the manifest difficulty of the idea of being as presence and, consequently, as ground, is the result of the course of metaphysics itself. In the world of late modernity, the ground loses its persuasiveness, foundational thought dissolves (this too is the sense of the triumph of scientific thought—as Nietzsche had realized when he spoke of the scientist as a model of sober thought), and, in this world, *verwindend* thinking, the logic of provenance and torsion, opens itself the way as only (nonreactive) possibility. Weber is an eminent example of this process; he is not, then, the author of an objective description of modernity to which one can resort to show that, after all, Heidegger was right. The difficulties, the contradictions, the "tragicity" of Weber's thought cannot be brought back to the difficulties of development, or verification and articulation of a scientific-descriptive theory; no one probably can think of them in these terms. They are the way in which one of the emblematic thinkers of modernity lives the consumption of foundational thought and searches for an alternative way, out of provenance and no longer out of ground, the notion of which always crumbles in his hands.

Modernity is the epoch of the dissolution of ground. In this Nietzsche is right when he calls it the epoch of the death of God. This epoch cannot and does not let itself be thought according to foundational logic. Science, technology, but also ethics and collective life never, or almost never, confront us with problems of foundation. Scientific thought is the model because increasingly, and everywhere, the matter is only that of continuing a discourse the beginnings of which are lost in the night of origins, which escape us and yet determine us as destination and provenance. Also many of the aspects of collective irrationality that Weber sees looming in modern society—trust in the technical apparatus without true knowledge and control of it, and, linked to this, what we could call the overall weakening of subjects— are constitutive elements of this situation of dissolution of groundness. To take up a "tragic" attitude in front of these events—in front of the death of God—means to continue to apply metaphysical points of view in the understanding and evaluation of the process: such are those that manifest themselves in the reactive or triumphalistic visions of the modern, which Weber sets aside with his analysis. In his thought, as well as more determinately in Heidegger's, a different logic than the "tragic" one opens itself the way. It is the logic of secularization as provenance and distortion. This is the logic "required" by modernity insofar as it is modernity, that is, unfolded formal rationality that renders the ground obsolete (God dies). This request, however, presents itself because modernity itself, as process of secularization, appears as a process of provenance and distortion. This is particularly evident in Weber. He describes the becoming of the modern world (but also, indirectly and in connection with the generalization of the model of rationality to all cultures, of the other [nonmodern] worlds) in terms of formal rationality. Yet, this ideal type also is the product of rationalization. Secularization—provenance and distortion—or rationalization are at the same time the models of the new thought required by modernity (which has set ground aside) and the essential features of the process through which modernity has construed itself.

Without the meditation on the essence of modernity, Heidegger's "turn" could have remained (and has remained, at least in some interpreters of Heidegger; perhaps in some of Heidegger's own pages) only the move from the plane where there is mainly the human being (Sartre's existentialism, but also that of *Being and Time*, at least as it initially appeared) to the plane where there is mainly being: the recognition that Western thought is humanistic, metaphysical, and destined to lead to will to power. Hence, a somewhat affected Heideggerism: critique of modernity as world of nihilism, condemnation of scientism, and so forth, and, correlatively, the effort to listen to being in an authentic way. Because the occasion for the turn had been the discovery that thought depends on language, and that, ultimately, it is first of all in language that being occurs, "Heideggerian" listening to being and the new postmetaphysical thought seemed to be called to meditate on language: both in the form of a "hermeneutic ontology" like that of *Truth and Method* and in the form of the deconstruction of the words of metaphysics (Derrida's way, which however has a model in the activity of "destructive" rereading of texts from the past in which Heidegger has always engaged).

These ways of recovery and prosecution of Heidegger entail the risk of a return to metaphysical mentality; whether they unfold as negative theologies, or they end up with a redefinition of being as language, or, as in the case of Derridian deconstruction, they think of being-language as the transcendental horizon that makes historicity possible but is substantially not affected by it.[30] Through the meditation on modernity, however, the *Kehre* unfolds into *Verwindung*. Only here is the *epochality* of being announced radically as a constitutive feature of a no longer metaphysical ontology (ontology of the actuality, thus also in the subjective sense of the genitive). To speak rigorously, in fact, it looks as if there is no reason—only on the basis of the existential analytic of *Being and Time* or also of the experience of the *Kehre* (primacy of being, primacy of language)—to think being as *epochal*, that is, according to the famous page of the essay on Anaximander in *Holzwege*, as what suspends (*epoché*) and hides while giving itself, and thus makes history possible as happening of epochs. From here arises the possible "metaphysical" equivocations of Heidegger's thought: being can still be described as what determines the human being and gives itself in language, perhaps not in the consumed language of everydayness, but in the authentic language of poetry, and so forth. Yet, what thought perceived itself to be called to, already in *Being and Time*, was to repropose the question of the sense of being outside the reductivistic horizon of presence. This task is answered only by the experience Heidegger has of the *epochality* of being, of a peculiar constitutive "negativity" characterizing being itself. This negativity comes to light precisely in the meditation on modernity—on the realization of metaphysics as provenance and distortion.

The productive connection between history and theory can be found again here, outside any "Hegelian" horizon, as the coming to light of the "negativity" or weakness of being. Such a coming to light is the one that "assigns" thought to its historical legacy (because it takes meaning away from foundational thought) and is the content of this legacy itself. The acknowledgement of all this leads thought out of the equivocations of negative theologies, of a metaphysics of language, of deconstruction; and it liberates Weber, no less than Heidegger, from being enclosed within a "tragic" horizon.

The ontology of actuality here configures itself as a negative ontology, one that, we could say, takes seriously the experience to which Heidegger tries to correspond when, in *Zur Seinsfrage*, he writes *Sein* under a crossed barring.[31] This experience, which *theory* still expresses by talking of weakness and negativity, is perhaps also the start for the overcoming of philosophy into ethics. Of this, one speaks a great deal today. It can only be accomplished, however, by "consuming" the *theoretical* experience of (the end of) metaphysics up to its very end.

Notes

1. Here and later the discourse follows up on my essay to which I refer, "Metaphysics, Violence, Secularization," in *Recoding Metaphysics*, ed. G. Borradori (Evanston, IL: Northwestern University Press, 1988), pp. 45–61.

2. On this, see Martin Heidegger, "The Age of the World Picture," trans. W. Lovitt, in *The Question Concerning Technology* (New York: Harper and Row, 1977), pp. 115–54, and "What Are Poets For?" trans. A. Hofstadter, in *Poetry, Language, Thought* (New York: Harper and Row, 1975), pp. 89–142.

3. Trans. note: The Italian term indicates not so much the fact of discontinuity, but rather the inability to continue on an old path.

4. Trans. note: Like the French term *actualité*, the Italian term "*attualità*" means "current events," "current affairs," or "the state of the world," and it is commonly used to indicate the sections in newspapers, shows, and news devoted to the description or discussion of contemporary recent events or issues. Thus, an "ontology of actuality" would be an ontology of the current times or an ontology of our times. Vattimo suggested the decision to translate *attualità* with "actuality" (despite the different connotations the English term suggests) due to the connection maintained between actuality, activity, act, and action, that is, with the ethico-practical sphere.

5. See Michel Foucault, "Che cos'è l'illuminismo? Che cos'è la rivoluzione?" in *Il Centauro* 11–12 (May–December 1984), pp. 229–236. Trans. note: This text is different than the one that appeared in English, "What Is Enlightenment?" in *The Foucault Reader*, ed. P. Rabinow (New York: Pantheon Books, 1984), p. 45ff., where Foucault speaks of an "ontology of ourselves," an "*ontologie de nous-mêmes.*"

6. For a wider discussion of the theme, I refer again to Vattimo, "Metaphysics, Violence, Secularization."

7. See Pierre Klossowski, *Nietzsche and the Vicious Circle*, trans. D. Smith (Chicago: University of Chicago Press, 1997), pp. 168ff.

8. See Foucault's introductory essay to the Italian translation of Gilles Deleuze, *Differenza e ripetizione*, trans. G. Guglielmi (Bologna: Il Mulino, 1971).

9. These are senses of the term that Heidegger indicates to the French translator of *Vorträge und Aufsätze*; for a broader discussion, see my translation of Martin Heidegger, *Saggi e discorsi* (Milan: Mursia, 1954), p. 45.

10. See again Heidegger, *Saggi e discorsi*, p. 46.

11. On *Kehre*, see Jean Grondin, *Le tournant dans la pensée de Heidegger* (Paris: PUF, 1987).

12. We are referring especially to the already-quoted essays by Heidegger, "The Age of the World Picture" and "What Are Poets For?"

13. See Jürgen Habermas, *The Philosophical Discourse of Modernity*, trans. F. Lawrence (Cambridge: MIT Press, 1987), and also the controversy with Dieter Henrich, whose contribution, which first appeared in *Merkur*, is now part of the volume *Konzepte. Essays zur Philosophie in der Zeit* (Frankfurt: Suhrkamp, 1987). Habermas's contribution, "Rückkehr zur Metaphysik. Eine Tendenz in der deutschen Philosophie?" has appeared in *Merkur*, 10 (1985): 898 ff.

14. This is the case especially for Hans Blumenberg, *The Legitimacy of the Modern Age*, trans. R. Wallace (Cambridge: MIT Press, 1983). On this, see Giacomo Marramao, *Potere e secolarizzazione* (Rome: Editori Riuniti, 1983), especially the preface.

15. For a framing of Max Weber within the history of the concept of secularization, see the short but fundamental essay by Hermann Lübbe, *Säkularisierung* (Munich: Alber, 1975).

16. On this, see for example Pietro Rossi, *Max Weber. Razionalità e razionalizzazione* (Milan: Il Saggiatore, 1982), p. 53. In general, I have kept in mind Rossi's work for this entire discussion of Weber, as well as the two books by Alessandro Dal Lago, *L'ordine infranto. Max Weber e i limiti del razionalismo* (Milan: Unicopli, 1983) and *Il politeismo moderno* (Milan: Unicopli, 1985). Furthermore, see the essays by various authors collected in *Max Weber e l'analisi del mondo moderno*, ed. P. Rossi (Turin: Einaudi, 1981) and Wolfgang Schluchter, *The Rise of Western Rationalism: Max Weber's Developmental History*, trans. G. Roth (Berkeley: University of California Press, 1981).

17. This is especially emphasized by Dal Lago in the two above quoted works. See also, in a more limited sense, Rossi, *Max Weber*, pp. 43–44.

18. See Max Weber, *Economy and Society*, trans. E. Fischoff (New York: Bedminster Press, 1968), vol. I, p. 85.

19. Ibid., pp. 24–25.

20. Ibid., p. 85.

21. See Rossi, *Max Weber*, p. 21.

22. For this typology of acting, see Weber, *Economy and Society*, vol. I, pp. 24–26.

23. On this, see Rossi, *Max Weber*, pp. 34–35.

24. See Dal Lago, *L'ordine infranto*, pp. 158ff and the texts therein discussed, and Rossi, *Max Weber*, p. 37.

25. This is perhaps a feature of the spirituality of the time; one can think of Freud, Wittgenstein, and others.

26. See, for example, Max Weber, "Science as a Vocation," in *Essays in Sociology*, trans. and ed. H. H. Gerth and C. Wright Mills (London: Routledge, 1974), p. 139, and *The Methodology of the Social Sciences*, trans. E. A. Shils and H. Finch (Glencoe, IL: Free Press, 1949), pp. 299–302.

27. That it is a relapse and that Weber perceives it as such is certain. True, the figure of a charismatic leader appears necessary to modern mass democracy—the extreme form, for now, of bureaucratic rationalization, leaning toward petrification—to maintain a relation with the vital world of values (with substantive rationality without which formal rationality cannot entirely do); see, for example, L. Cavalli, "Il carisma come potenza rivoluzionaria," in the volume *Max Weber e l'analisi del mondo moderno*. However, as Rossi remarked (*Max Weber*, p. 41), in the modern world, formal rationality has already supplanted charisma (in principle, we should think) as a factor of change. It is (only?) "in traditionalist periods" that "charisma is the great

revolutionary force" (Weber, *Economy and Society*, I, p. 245). Dal Lago ("Il politeismo moderno," p. 42) notices, on the other hand, that both possibilities Weber puts forth for modern democracy (the *Führerdemokratie*, with a charismatic leader in an American style, and the one dominated by "professional politicians"; see Max Weber, *The Profession of Politics*, trans. S. Draghici [Washington, DC: Plutarch Press, 1989], p. 46) appear to be equally perverse, even if, for the German situation of the time, Weber thinks of a solution of the first kind.

28. See Weber, *The Methodology of the Social Sciences*, p. 107.

29. See Rossi, *Max Weber*, p. 42, and the texts therein discussed; and G. Calabrò, "Il rifiuto della 'storia universale' e il politeismo dei valori," in *Max Weber e l'analisi del mondo moderno*.

30. See again Vattimo, "Metaphysics, Violence, Secularization."

31. See Martin Heidegger, "On the Question of Being," in *Pathmarks*, trans. W. McNeill (Cambridge, MA: Cambridge University Press, 1998).

Part 2

Crossing the Borders

Current Thematizations

The five chapters in Part 2 welcome the challenge to contemporary philosophy the contributions in Part 1 posed, and from a variety of approaches attempt a theoretical, speculative reconfiguration of the intersection between the themes of ethics, politics, and religion. Moving from a general consideration of a metaphysics of being ultimately pointing toward the religious, the following chapters conclude through a meditation on topics such as God, the divine, the sacred, and the transcendent with the indication of the themes of the finite, existence, and ethics as the most appropriate avenues for contemporary thinking to confront the challenge of our current times.

The first chapter, "Metaphysics of Thinking, Metaphysics of Being," is by Virgilio Melchiorre, who teaches at the Università Cattolica del Sacro Cuore in Milan, the Catholic university where he was also educated in the neoscholastic tradition. Melchiorre was a student of the metaphysician Gustavo Bontadini, for whom the centrality of metaphysics thought through the question of the contradictoriness of becoming has always been a tenet even in issues of the transcendence of reality toward the "incontrovertibility" of God. For Melchiorre, the metaphysical interest inherited from his teacher has always been coupled with an existential interest so that the transcendental analysis of consciousness and the problem of ground are ultimately articulated by him in an ontological phenomenology wherein historical and poetic imagination assume a symbolic and metaphysical function. Melchiorre's chapter begins with an analysis of the life of consciousness according to the modes of transcendental phenomenology. On this ground, and going back to the conditions of possibility of knowledge, Melchiorre retrieves Kant's theorem according to which consciousness of the conditioned always implies an originary consciousness of the unconditioned, which Melchiorre however identifies as metaphysical reality. The protological reference to a metaphysical absolute constitutes the essential cipher to delineate the destiny of knowledge in all its possibilities. If human beings are essentially constituted as rational existence, then all their modes of being (perception, conception,

feeling, imagination, will, and so on) are to be understood as different modalities of a possible form of knowledge—the unconditioned condition of the
absolute determines and configures all of them. Melchiorre concludes by
raising the issue of the knowability of the metaphysical absolute. The transcendental approach arrives at the assertion of the being of ground (its *daß*)
in an argumentative manner, but remains incapable as to the determination
of its reality (its *was*), which insofar as it is metaphysical transcends the
possibility of phenomenology. On this path, Melchiorre claims, only the
analogical way opens up, the climax of which is to be sought in the symbolism belonging to poetic thinking, of which historical faiths are a testimony.

The connection between the sacred and the historical, that is, the
human dimension of existence, is a theme in "The Truth of Existence and
the Sacred (*Ethos anthropo daimon*)," by Mario Ruggenini (Università di
Venezia). A student of Emanuele Severino first at the Università Cattolica
del Sacro Cuore, Ruggenini then followed Severino to Venice after the
latter's break with his master and then colleague Bontadini. Starting with a
hermeneutic retrieval of phenomenological themes (Husserl and Heidegger),
Ruggenini's overall philosophy develops the theme of the finitude of existence in relation to the problem of alterity to replace the metaphysics of
meaning and sufficient reason with a different experience of the truth—an
experience of truth that occurs in human speech and in the conversation
with others in which the world opens up. In general three themes recur in
Ruggenini's philosophy: a rethinking of ontological issues in a hermeneutic-
phenomenological register; a new hermeneutics of the I or self made possible
out of the relation with the other and constitutes the I neither as substance
nor as self-certainty, but rather as responsibility for the other; and the appeal
of the other as opening to the dimension of the sacred. In his chapter,
Ruggenini addresses the relation between truth and the sacred of existence
from the perspective of the relation with alterity constitutive of human finite
being. Finitude, he claims, reveals something other that is not reducible to
the relation with others, but is rather the disquieting ground and also the
fundamental bond thereof. To be with others means, Ruggenini argues, that
everyone exists in something other. The irreducible experience of otherness
that makes us be, insofar as it is also experience of a truth that occurs in
human conversation, cannot be identified, according to Ruggenini, with the
god or gods of historical religions, although it does not exclude them as long
as one is ready to rethink radically the dogmatic traditions that have codified
traditional religions. This constant availability to renew one's mind and heart,
which Ruggenini names *metanoia*, is solicited by the experience of a truth
that is announced as the finite truth of existence, but that remains other,
never stated and understood once and for all. The sacredness of existence
appears as the forgotten origin of the (albeit misrecognized) questions that
have set philosophy on the way and still inspire its quest. Beyond the opposition in principles that renders philosophy sterile and religious experiences

dogmatic, the discovery of the truth of the sacred amounts for philosophy to the revelation, Ruggenini argues, of the mystery of the world. Such a dimension preserves the root of the fundamental ethicity that perhaps still calls the *homo oeconomicus* of the technological age to assume his or her responsibility in inhabiting the earth. In the end, Ruggenini concludes, *ethos anthropo daimon*—the divine is the dwelling place of the human.

The theme of responsibility in the background of the relinquishment of any illusion to be able directly to intention, conceive, constitute, or even speak of the object is taken up explicitly in "Transcendental without Illusion: Or, The Absence of the Third Person," by Marco Maria Olivetti. Olivetti attended the Università di Roma—La Sapienza where he was deeply influenced by Enrico Castelli who, during the 1940–1950s, against all intellectualistic and rationalist philosophies of solitude characterizing modern thought, proposed a Christian existentialism with specifically theological and metaphysical characters—that is, a metaphysics that speaks of the divine and is thus strictly connected to the theology of history and salvation. Castelli, who also developed an interest for hermeneutics within the context of the philosophy of religion, became famous in Italy for organizing annual colloquia (*i convegni romani*) devoted to exploring the nexus between philosophy and the philosophy of religion, and more specifically between demythologization and hermeneutics. Since his death in 1977, Olivetti, who has since greatly advanced the conversation between hermeneutics and the philosophy of religion, has carried out Castelli's legacy. In his chapter, Olivetti moves from the need to abandon the Kantian illusion of the transcendental apperception and replace it with a notion of subjectivity constituted as radically responsive and responsible. An analysis of responsibility carried out through of an analysis of the semantics of the personal (I, you) and interrogative (who?) pronouns involved in such a concept leads Olivetti to a reconceptualization of the very notion of responsibility in terms of a responsibility for responsibility, that is, in terms of a transcendental responsibility where the third, however, remains absent.

The invocation of responsibility and ethics as the most appropriate dimensions for contemporary thinking is explicitly made in Salvatore Natoli's contribution, "Finitude and Responsibility: For an Ethics of the Finite in the Time of Risk." According to Natoli, who was a student of Emanuele Severino at Università Statale di Milano where he now also teaches, the contemporary world is characterized by complexity and risk. Risk is the measure not only of the great power human beings reach, but also of the wide range of counterfinalities that such a power inserts in nature, including human nature. Within such epochal coordinates, for our preservation and survival, Natoli argues that we must consciously take on the burden of our own finitude in the conviction that, no matter how great the accomplishments, nothing and no one can relinquish us from our original limitation. From this perspective science, rather than unconditionally increasing human power, reconsigns humans to their limitations, although of a different kind. From here there follows the need, Natoli maintains, of a thought and ethics adequate to the current reality. In this sense, the proposal of an ethics of the finite, which coincides with what Natoli metaphorically terms "neopaganism" seems to be essential. This is a philosophy of a finitude no longer protected by a cosmos, but rather exposed to the a-cosmism (*acosmismo*) of possibilities.

The conviction that the ethical modality constitutes the meaning of philosophy for the current epoch is shared by Pier Aldo Rovatti (Università di Trieste), the author of the last chapter in Part 2, "Praise of Modesty." Rovatti was educated in the tradition of the University of Milan—Statale under the influence of the phenomenologist, existentialist, and Marxist philosopher Enzo Paci. He was also a student of Ludovico Geymonat, a philosopher with wide interests in empiricism, critical rationalism, and the methodology of science, which he later tried to integrate with the historicist perspective of dialectical materialism. Rovatti's area of interest is that of the condition of philosophy after the nihilistic turn Nietzsche effected. More specifically, he is interested in the condition of subjectivity in the time of the crisis of metaphysical foundations and in the transformations that subjectivity undergoes especially in fields such as psychoanalysis. The "paradox of subjectivity," that is, the need not only to take leave from subjectivity but also to hold to it in some different manner, leads Rovatti to explore, while moving within the horizon of Husserlian phenomenology, themes such as silence, modesty (*pudore*), and play (*gioco*); these are testimonies of a criticism of the purely speculative attitude in philosophy and of the need to decline the speculative gaze into an ethical direction. In his chapter, which unfolds in conversation with Vattimo, Heidegger, Husserl, Freud, and Levinas, Rovatti introduces the metaphor of modesty as a way ethically to respond to the weakening of philosophy testified by Vattimo's philosophical hypothesis—to which Rovatti himself has contributed—of a "weak thought" (*pensiero debole*). Rovatti defines "modesty" as a movement of withdrawal of thought from things and events to allow the emergence of a "shadow zone" that remains invisible and ineffable, a zone of renunciation of the claims traditional philosophy advanced to be able to grasp its objects. The contemporary weakening of philosophy thus entails an ethical aspect, which can be identified with the modesty, discretion, and lack of violence of a universe of thought deprived of its dimension of will to power. Rovatti concludes with an invitation to an "ethics of diminution," that is, an ethics of dwelling in the distance from oneself and from others.

Chapter 6

Metaphysics of Thinking, Metaphysics of Being

Virgilio Melchiorre

When considering the outcomes of contemporary thought, one who wants to wonder anew about the destiny of metaphysics might perhaps start with a decisive Kantian remark. One will remember, in fact, how Kant accompanies the project of a radical critique of metaphysics with the observation of an irreversible need for metaphysics: "[Metaphysics] is older than all other sciences, and would survive even if all the rest were swallowed up in the abyss of an all-destroying barbarism."[1] What can the meaning of such a need be when one is contesting its legitimacy, exactly as it seems to happen in Kant's first *Critique*? Is it a simply historical remark that recognizes the persistence of myths and superstitions despite the conquests of reason? The mistakes of the mind, in fact, cannot be healed all at once when they are widespread in the multiplicity of cultural traditions and customs. They resist being conquered by thought, rather, and only the long course of history will be able to defeat them. Is this precisely the case of metaphysical thinking? Kant's text certainly cannot be bent in this direction when he warns that metaphysical questions are assigned to human beings by the very nature of reason; and that, were one to talk of an absolute impossibility of metaphysics, one would then have to wonder whether a constitutive need of the mind could by itself be exposed to an irremediable contradiction. Should one then not rather think that the critique of reason questions not metaphysics as such, but rather only an incorrect way of configuring it?[2] The question not only could be addressed to Kant's text, but also to much contemporary thought. This is not the place, however, for an analysis of a historiographic character,[3] despite the fact that our question retains its particular relevance within the modern history of philosophy. What matters now is a purely theoretical evaluation of the question, yet with the *caveat* that our research must at least partly rely on the speculative framework of modernity.

First, let us specify this reference. The fact that philosophy has regenerated itself by finding in the certainty of the *cogito* its own starting point must be understood as an essentially methodological, before being an ontological, gain.[4] Ontology moves in search of the general structures of being. Yet, this search cannot be guaranteed if, first, the modes through which consciousness makes it possible are not ensured: thought is not, if not as thought of being; yet being has in thought the untranscendable condition of the possibility of its self-manifestation, of its coming to meaning. The analysis of the noetic structure is therefore preliminary. Any research on the meaning of being in general, or on the meaning of a specific region of being, must be referred to it. This analysis will perhaps enable us to answer the question of the legitimacy of metaphysical thought. It will enable us to acknowledge whether the irrepressible metaphysical tension Kant refers to is an undue overdetermination of the mind or instead whether it is immanent and coessential to the structure of the life of consciousness.

Perceptive Adumbration

If it means to be radical, our inquiry must proceed from the basic structures of consciousness, and it must do so by following the paths of transcendental phenomenology. We move thus from the analysis of perception, which constitutes the basic and thus constitutive modality of any mode of consciousness, be it awake and active or unfolded only passively. In this respect, the first, certainly fundamental given is the one that Husserl indicated as *the paradox and in some way the contradiction of the perceptive process*: the claim, by external perception, to do something that it cannot do because of its very essence.[5] Perception in fact gives us reality's flesh and bones. Yet, it does so while always remaining within a perspective: it proceeds by adumbrations, and it never reveals the overall identity of the thing. It manifests repeatedly the thing's side, but every time while removing into absence the sides that have already been grasped. It is thus unthinkable that any object can give itself in a concluded perception in all its sides according to the totality of its aspects. And yet one must acknowledge that in its being perspectival, perception is intentionally aimed at one same object: it lives this or that side of the thing in the original, yet at the same time it cointends other sides that are not given in the original, that are only possible, and it refers all of them to the same thing.

We can repeat ourselves analogously and consider the immanent "lived experiences" [*vissuto*] of perception. In this case, we will again address a processuality that goes from the past to the present and from the present to the past, from the past perception to the one that now occurs and from this to the memorial gathering of a whole. Yet this whole, the proper identity of the thing, what in itself links the various aspects into a unity, is never given to me as such. It will be brought to be an idea, but in itself, in its unifying unity, it is never experienced. Yet it is asserted and, precisely, cointended in any perspectival move.

We find again the Kantian reference of phenomena or appearances to a noumenal identity. In the first edition of the *Critique of Pure Reason*, Kant has precisely written of the noumenon as of "that unity which must be met with in any manifold of knowledge which stands in relation to an object."[6] This is a definition that will come back also in Kant's late essays, like in this incisive passage from the *Opus postumum*: "The thing in itself (*ens per se*) is not another object, but rather another relation (*respectus*) between the representation and the same object so as to think the latter not analytically but rather synthetically as the knot (*complexus*) of intuitive representations as phenomena."[7] What is the value of this noumenal identity, and why call it the "thing in itself"? How is its assertion possible if only the sides and aspects of the thing that are perceived time after time can really be asserted? Kant's writing is not in this respect without difficulty as much so that it enables contestation of an idealistic kind. How can one, in fact, assert that of which one has properly no experience, that which is not at all given in the perceptive process, and that belongs, according to the letter of the *Critique*, only to an intellectual representation? Phenomenology, as put to work by Kant, and the declared alterity of intellectual life with respect to the data of the sensible intuition,[8] seem to prevent overcoming the objection. Yet, a nonsecondary passage in Kant's text offers a way out, and this precisely in relation to the succession of the perceptive process. Kant writes, "Immediately I perceive [*wahrnehme*] or assume [*voraus annehme*] that in this succession there is a relation to the preceding state, from which the representation follows in conformity with a rule, I represent something as an event, as something that happens."[9] If we develop this suggestion, we come to say that in the flux *in the present* of perceptive life what is given is not a discontinuous series of perspectives, but rather a succession and a mutual connection of perspectives: a self-dilation of the perceptive flux through manifestations that fade away, but that retain, at the same time that they fade away and pass into new manifestations, what has just disappeared. In sum, what is given is a presentifying [*presentificante*] *continuum*, on the thread of a unity of presences and retentions. One could think, for example, of the flux of a melody or a polyphonic piece. A sound resonates incisively and then fades away in its sonority, but it is always the same sound, and the perception that follows it preserves and distinguishes its sonority through a series of presences and retentions. This sound is not alone, but rather contemporary to other sounds. Also, the fusion of sounds itself changes with the fading away of one sound or the other. Yet, in this fusion, past sounds remain retentively linked with the other sounds and with those that emerge until the whole musical piece disappears. Analogously, and still as an example, I can speak of the vision of a house. I only grasp one aspect of it in perspective. And yet, in the very perception of the fading away perspective, a reference to and a sort of anticipation of other aspects is given to me. Presence, retention, anticipation and, then, remembering of the sides that have disappeared give me the identity of the same house, even though this is never given to me in its entirety, and even less in the invisible principle of its connections. This phenomenological given brings us to recuperate the sense of Kant's noumenon with a decisive distinction: the identity *in itself* of the thing remains in any event subtracted to the sequences of perspectives that refer to it, and yet the reality of that *in itself* is *asserted* legitimately. In itself, the *in itself*, understood as the very principle of the connection, is in fact other than the multiplicity and differences it connects and in which it expresses itself. Precisely because it expresses and manifests itself in that multiplicity, however, it remains nevertheless declarable as real. Scholastic language used to say, *operatio sequitur esse* [action follows being]. We could translate this expression by saying that the *esse* [being] of something manifests itself only in its *operationes* [actions]. In and by itself, it could not be identified. And yet, the somewhat unitary experience of the *operationes* speaks for its operating reality.

The paradox of perception lies thus in its proceeding only by perspectives and adumbrations, though intending always the same object. This sameness or identity, although asserted, remains however *in itself* forbidden to perception. It remains ultimately invisible like an indication that will remain empty out of principles. And yet this emptiness, this X, as Husserl remarks, is not nothing. It is instead like a frame in which the data of perception are enframed; they take part in it.[10] Although it is as such unreachable, the *in itself* of the thing counts thus as a real reference without which the perception process itself would be impossible. One of Kant's passages finds its confirmation here, and it reveals itself as more than a simple reference to, or a simple necessity of the intellect: "If appearances were things in themselves, then since we have to deal solely with our representations, we could never determine from the succession of the representations how their manifold may be connected in the object."[11]

If this is the conclusion to which a correct phenomenological reflection leads, we must then acknowledge that, already in its most elementary and still passive levels, the process of the life of consciousness brings within itself a real *meta-physical tension:* time and again, it lives in a *reference to the invisible that, although always remaining such, nevertheless constitutes the necessary and real presupposition of its orientation.* Of course, at this level the term "meta-physics" does not retain the load that tradition has assigned to it, nor does it have a theological value. Yet, this first, as it were, simpler conclusion counts as a constitutive ground to go deeper into our theme. Let us proceed gradually and still on the thread of a transcendental recognition.

The Perceptive Constellation

For reasons of simplicity I have so far considered the perceptive movement in almost molecular terms. In truth, no perception stands on its own, as no finite reality stands on its own. Although it stands and moves in its own identity, anything is at the same time by virtue of its other. It is, in some way, its other, because the alterity that overcomes and surrounds it differently participates in its constitution. Perception, which intentions this or that object in perspective, could not be given without being at the same time coperception of a background or a constellation of data and events in which the focus of its attention gets determined. Thus, when we move from the perceptive flux, from its passive self-constitution between part and whole of being, to the question of the meaning of this and that, we sense that the answer could be given only while recognizing the whole and, ultimately, only within the depths of the nexus that grants and gathers everything in the reciprocity of constitutions.

One can specify this conclusion by following the tension of the perceptive flux from another side. We noticed how, while it little by little binds itself to a specific perspective on reality, the whole process is at the same time led by an empty intention, by a reference to a thing that is not given in bones and flesh, that is, for perception, still a nonbeing, and that nevertheless looms within the limit and reciprocity of the perceived sides. The perception of the negative, of the insufficiency, of one's own conditionedness is thus coessential with the perceptive process itself. It constitutes its movement and guides toward the being that the perception itself is not. And yet, as I remarked earlier, this reference is not a reference to nothingness and not even to a pure need of the mind, which could not occur without a real condition of possibility for it. Nonbeing is thus not nothingness, but rather is *heteron*, the other than being that in its alterity, in its absence recalls and orients the cognitive flux, retrieves and frees the insufficiency of perception from contradiction and nonsense. If we consider again the perceptive unity within the constellation of possible perceptions, we must acknowledge that the entire cognitive movement is led by *the subtended presupposition of a fullness of being as source of adequation and meaning*. If, in fact, the last step of the cognitive reference were to stop at nonbeing, we should say that at the origin of the process and, at the same time, at the origin of the constellation of being is properly nothingness. We would be in the contradiction that forbids the identity of being and nonbeing.

Conditioned and Unconditioned

Naturally, and it should be remarked immediately, the conclusion we have reached has a reflective character, and it answers the question of the conditions of possibility of the perceptive movement. It corresponds to a thematization that has transcended the passive spontaneity of perception. Perception becomes effectively knowledge, is effectively exposed to the assertion of the truth, when it is elevated to the active height of judgment, the only place where, as we know from Aristotle,[12] the distinction between truth and falsity is given. Nevertheless, moving from perception was necessary not only to retrace the life of thought in its elementary and thus always recurrent constitutions, but also and consequently to warn that the passive presupposition of perceptive stream constitutes the essential passivity of any cognitive process. To clarify this undoubtedly essential aspect, let us try better to thematize or give shape to what has been said so far.

Perspective transgression is moved, as I said, by the subtended evidence that if held in and by itself, any perspective, any determination would amount to a nonsense. Perception of insufficiency is thus in itself relative to some sufficiency. In Kantian terms, we could say that at the same time that cognition of the conditioned is given, cognition of the unconditioned, that is, the relation to the unconditioned, is also given. Which is the *primum* [the first] in this relation? If we consider the cognitive process, the *primum* is with no doubt the conditioned or, in perceptual terms, the perspective side, the determination of this or that temporal presence. However, if we wonder about the logic and ontological structure of cognition, and then about the referent itself of cognition, we must then say that the *primum* is with no doubt the unconditioned.[13] We find here the conclusion Descartes reached in his third *Meditation*:

> I clearly understand that there is more reality in an infinite substance than in a finite one. Thus the perception of the infinite is somehow prior in me to the perception of the finite (*priorem* quodammodo *in me esse perceptionem infiniti quam finiti*), that is, my perception of God is prior to my perception of myself. For how would I understand that I doubt and that I desire, that is, that I lack something and that I am not wholly perfect, unless there were some idea in me of a more perfect being, by comparison with which I might recognize my defects?[14]

As one can see, this conclusion is also achieved on the thread of the transcendental question of the conditions of possibility of thought. Emphasizing it further is not necessary. I would rather pause on two significantly revelatory passages: the first, in which the assertion of the priority of the unconditioned is made with a reservation, that of considering the notion of the infinite as primary but only "somehow" [*quodammodo*]; the second, in which the analysis of the life of consciousness is extended to the whole of human experience: what is questioned is not only the doubt of the mind, but also the desire of the heart. Without some perception of the infinite how could I perceive, Descartes asks, "that I doubt and desire?"

The first issue, with that *quodammodo*, is certainly essential because it states, and this time in a general sense, the *metaphysical* condition of thought. Whether one considers the determinateness of perceptive life or, at a higher level, the delimitation of our judgments (*determinatio est negatio* [determination is negation], Spinoza will claim), we encounter in any event the insurmountable finitude of our life of consciousness. The reference to the infinite, to the unconditioned, is thus a reference to reality, since without the absoluteness of being no determination could be given. But it is, at the same time, a reference that by itself could not adequate its own object. This becomes even clearer if we consider more closely the place where, time and again, it is actually thematized that any determination stands by virtue of its other, that any being is at the same time itself and other than itself. This happens precisely when a noun or a sequence of nouns are gathered in the unity of a judgment, in the predication of this or that attribute, in sum, in the *conjunction in one of the differents*. As Aristotle again teaches us,[15] it is then the copula that sanctions the cobelonging and the unity of the differents: the "is" of the copula precisely as the place of meaning and truth in which the being of the thing becomes visible. And yet, despite the fact that at first it appears paradoxical, we should also say that the copula is also the place for a metaphysical reference, the mark or the subtended presence of the invisible. In fact, if the constitution of a being is given in the cobelonging, in the ontological nexus between a subject and one or more predicates, one must then acknowledge that among what is given in a union there is a reciprocal congruence, a certain identity of being, which moreover does not annul but rather preserves and makes possible the difference of the conjoined elements. In other words, we could say that any compound being gives itself as an analogical constellation, as a unity that is a bearer of differences. The importance of this phenomenological observation is of great relevance: *it makes us suppose that a sameness of being partakes itself differently in the identity of a being.*

This conclusion must be extended as to its comprehensiveness once one takes up the general assertion according to which a being does not stand on its own, but only thanks to a cobelonging involving its singularity. From this perspective, we consider not only the internal cobelonging of one or more predicates in a subject, but also the cobelonging of a being and other beings, each of which in its own way lets others be, constitutes others. If we turn, therefore, to consider this cosmic constellation of beings, then we must again suppose that it is possible because of the differing of a same substance.

The ultimate roots of the many is in this sameness, the reality of which, however, can only be induced. In itself, it is not given to us because the world of phenomena gives itself immediately through difference. I will say something more extensively about this difficulty shortly. For now, let us notice that the examination of the mind, which this time occurs at a superior and more active level, where only one can speak of truth and false,[16] brings us again to recognize that the entire process of thinking is structurally oriented by an ultimate transcendence. At the same time, this constitutes and overcomes thought that, however, inhabits it, even when it is not thematized, even when it is contested, even when human beings, to say it with Heraclitus's ancient words, "are at odds with the *logos*, with which above all they are in continuous contact, and the things they meet every day appear strange to them."[17] Of this originary *logos*, and starting from the basic data of the mind, Plato speaks analogically, resorting to the event of light. In *Republic*, we in fact read that although we have sight and things have colors, we could see nothing without light. Light is therefore the transcendent condition of vision. At a higher level, that which precisely concerns intelligence of the truth, there is the assertion of the ultimate condition of thinking: that metaphysical light that "gives truth to the things known and the power to know to the knower."[18] We are exactly at the assertion of the absolute, the idea of the Good that "produces both light and its source in the visible world, and that in the intelligible realm . . . controls and provides truth and understanding."[19]

The reference to the root of being, intended in the idea of the Good, enables us now to dilate our phenomenology to the world of consciousness. We can thus take up Descartes's second passage, which in the precognition of the infinite linked the events of doubt and desire. One should recall, moreover, Descartes's definition of the *cogito*: "A thing that thinks. What is that? A thing that doubts, understands, affirms, denies, wills, refuses, and that also imagines and senses."[20] In what sense, though, is desire properly human? Often the term is uttered as equivalent to "need." This is a confusion that seems legitimate at least for one aspect because in both instances it is a matter of a striving [*tensione*] toward what is missing. Yet, between desire and need, there is a relevant difference. Need, in fact, is geared [*teso*] toward a determined lack, and is always with reference to some vital, primary necessity; it is thus need for food, air, warmth, or any other factor necessary for survival. On the contrary, although it is also driven by some existential necessity, desire is extended [*disteso*] in indetermination, in the polyvalency of its goals, and for this reason it is less certain of its boundaries and destinations. The etymology itself of the word suggests so much. As its derivation from *sidus* [star] reveals, "desire" could be understood, on the one hand, as an "awaiting from the stars" and, on the other, as a "loss of the constellation that was leading us," and thus also as "an uncertainty that feels and mourns a loss, and that orients itself with difficulty." This weakness of desire is at the same time a mark of an unlimited powerfulness, of a superiority specific to human beings. Plato has splendidly grasped this when retracing the myth of *Eros*, the son of Penia and Poros, of poverty and acquisition, of aporetic ignorance and the wise god:[21] *Eros* as desire for the beautiful. It is known that beauty is truly such only when it lives in relation, *in proportione debita*, as the old Scholastics would say. It is concordant harmony of elements, but at the same time harmony that inscribes itself in a whole, in a totality of being of which it is part and evocation. One can even contest, in its degrees, the ladder of desire Plato designs in *Symposium*. What in that dialogue remains uncontestable, however, is that desire for corporeal beauty is more authentic the more it can situate itself in and regard the perspective of the many, lastly in the light of the whole and the one. *Eros* thus appears as desire and name for the whole.[22] And again as it has occurred when reflecting on the metaphor of light, Plato remarks on the originary and participated sense of this tension [*tensione*], so that it acts also passively, even when one does not seem to have clear consciousness of it. It is not, in fact, only the pleasure of bodies (as we read in *Symposium*) that brings together lovers with such passion; it is also obvious that "the soul of each is wishing for something else that it cannot express, only divining and darkly hinting what it wishes."[23] I would say that exactly in this being carried by what one cannot say but only hint, exactly in this passivity of love, or in its being a "passion," is the decisive indication. Had desire been brought to thematization, it would be acknowledged as being recalled by an ontological memory. That strong passage from *Phaedrus* is essential here, wherein one reads that the vision of earthly beauty brings with itself memory of true Beauty. This memory is pierced by a divine madness, so that for earthly human beings the one who is possessed by it appears as if he or she had gone out of his or her mind.[24] He who finds himself in remembrance of that time, in remembrance of the origin, as we read still in *Phaedrus* in a fine phenomenological remark, "when he sees a godlike face or form which is a good image of beauty, shudders at first . . . then, as he gazes, he reveres the beautiful one as a god, and if he did not fear to be thought stark mad, he would offer sacrifice to his beloved as to an idol or a god."[25] The anxiety of desire lies thus in the search for the place where the *plain of truth* [*pianura della verità*] is.[26] It lies in perceiving, in the beloved face, the *traces* or the *image of one's god*: the god of the origin toward whom memory pushes.[27]

The Invisible and its Traces

With this reference to the "plain of truth," a circle seems to have been concluded. We started with an analysis of cognitive processes and then moved to the sphere of feelings. Yet, now these too are revealed as a path of metaphysical cognition. One would even be tempted to say—as a well-known French scholar has done—that it is not perception that arouses desire, but on the contrary it is desire that arouses perception: *thumos* as source and rule for *nous*.[28] There is something true in this conclusion, but only if in desire one recognizes the dynamic factor of any movement of consciousness, be it intellect or reason, perception or feeling and love. In the various movements, we still always find the same labor of the negative and the same paradox that, in perspective, is simultaneously intention of the whole: in the end, intention of the absolute because only then would desire be appeased. The utopia of desire lies in its own death. It is an impossible utopia because in any event the condition holding us in perspective, in the partiality of phenomena, remains insurmountable.

This conclusion could be written through another paradox that, in several manners, was already transparent in the course of these analyses. We said that cognition of the negative, of the conditioned, of the finite would not be possible without the subtended reference to an absolute, an unconditioned, an infinite. And yet, it necessarily happens that, while they are at the beginning and foundation of finite perception, in themselves these comprehensive ways of being are marked only in a negative form, as the absolutely other in relation to the world of phenomena. This is not by chance. In fact, we cannot seem to exit the circle of phenomenality if it is true that we are always bound to the perspectival condition of consciousness. Precisely because it is at the origin, in the way of the unconditioned, the absolute that on reflection we had to acknowledge as originary reference for any form of cognition remains as real as it is unknowable in and for itself. Reflection brings us to the assertion of its *daß*, but it does not let us enter its *proprium*, its *was*. Kant writes, "The unconditioned is not to be met with in things, so far as we know them, that is, so far as they are given to us, but only so far as we do not know them, that is, so far as they are things in themselves."[29] Yet, how do we exactly say, in what we know, what we cannot know? Or, still to use Kant's terminology, how do we *think* and say what we cannot know? At this point, the conclusion Wittgenstein drew at the end of the *Tractatus* seems to be imperative: "What we cannot talk about we must pass over in silence."[30] We know, however, that it was precisely Wittgenstein who reiterated a sentence by Augustine, from which we too could start: "*Aut quid dicis aliquid cum de te dicit? Et vae tacentibus de te, quoniam loquaces muti sunt* [What does any man succeed in saying when he attempts to speak of you? Yet woe to those who do not speak of you at all, when those who speak most say nothing]."[31]

Which language remains possible without having the correct invitation to silence fade away? In my previous writings, I thought I could indicate a way out within the horizon of the analogy. If in fact any being is constituted in a participatory relation with the whole of being, if any being in the end gives itself as the differing of an originary sameness, then it is legitimate to say that any being is in its own way a trace of that origin. Any being can come to language by itself, but also by the infinite that goes across and transcends it. From this perspective, I have been able to indicate in the metaphorical character of symbolic language the most adequate horizon for the word of the sacred. The expressive value and strength of metaphor rests in fact, as we know already from Aristotle, in the conjunction of similes, in the overcoming of the definitions, and in never properly being a definition, but rather an expression of the subtended and operating identity in differences.[32] Earlier I said that the dimension of the sacred can emerge precisely there where in the copulation of differences one is ultimately referred to an originary sameness, effusive of itself. In its expressive climaxes, the language of symbols and metaphors, such as that given in musical fluid, thus seems the most apt to manifest the sacred. The history of religions is mainly a confirmation of this.

Addressing here a reflection to which I have amply devoted myself in previous years is not possible for me. Let me instead declare its limitation: a limitation that would open up the very question of symbolic language on another side. Everything started with a reflection on the essential modes of thought. Through various stages, we have identified a metaphysical orientation in the life of consciousness, and through various stages we have reached the assertion of a sameness immanent in the multiplicity of being: a radicality of meaning that is nevertheless unreachable in its identity and thus in its innermost transcendence. If one considers it carefully, precisely because such a radicality of meaning announces itself only through its effusiveness, only as a necessary nexus in the multiplicity of experience, that the language of the sacred may go beyond the chant of assonances and attributes, moving from the news of the sacred and the divine to the determination of the divine in a subject, now seems impossible. With respect to this, Jean Nabert has written that God does not precede but rather follows the criteriology of the divine, which is implied in the plots of consciousness; what follows must be entrusted to historical experience and to the faith that such an experience brings with itself.[33] One could say that Christian consciousness itself has gone through this distinction. We can sense this by recalling one of Augustine's penetrating remarks on Exodus 3:14–15, a remark that Edith Stein has also taken up with special care. The matter was that of sending Moses to the Israelites, Augustine writes. And then God said:

> I AM WHO AM, and *Thus shall you say to the children of Israel, HE WHO IS has sent me to you.* But because it was difficult for the human mind to take in the concept of absolute being, and a man was being sent to other men and women (though not by a man), God immediately tempered his glory. . . . So he continued, *Go and tell the children of Israel, the God of Abraham, the God of Isaac, and the God of Jacob has sent me to you. This is my name for ever.* . . . When I said *I AM WHO AM*, it was true, but you could not understand it. Yet when I say, *I am the God of Abraham, the God of Isaac, and the God of Jacob,* that too is true but you can take it in. The name *I AM WHO AM* is suitable to me, but the name *the God of Abraham, the God of Isaac, and the God of Jacob* is adjusted to your comprehension.[34]

On the one hand, then, is the annunciation of an indefectible presence and meanwhile the prohibition of the name; on the other hand, is the delivery of this mystery to particular events in history. On this side the experience of historical faith opens up, the one which, for Christians, brought to recognize the particular icon of God in the event of the Resurrected Christ.[35]

The transcendental scheme I have tried to unfold did not allow the reaching of such a point, even if it may constitute an indispensable premise without which not even historical faith can do.

Notes

1. Immanuel Kant, *Critique of Pure Reason*, trans. N. K. Smith (New York: St. Martin's Press, 1965), p. 21.

2. Ibid., p. 22.

3. As far as Kant is concerned, allow me to refer to Virgilio Melchiorre, *Analogia e analisi trascendentale, Linee per una nuova lettura di Kant* (Milan: Mursia, 1991).

4. This distinction implies, as we will see, a metaphysical opening against all forms of idealism. In this respect the warning formulated, on the wake of Descartes, by Emmanuel Levinas in *Totality and Infinity*, trans. A. Lingis (Pittsburgh, PA: Duquesne University Press, 1969), pp. 48–49, holds true: the access to the question of meaning implies that the horizon of the *cogito* gives itself as a *chronological priority*, and that thus the cognition of meaning and the infinite are an *a posteriori*; yet, the *logical priority* of the process of consciousness implies, on the contrary, *memory* of an a priori, the infinite as a priori. The rest of my discourse moves in this direction.

5. Edmund Husserl, *Analyses Concerning Passive and Active Synthesis*, trans. A. Steinbock (Dordrecht: Kluwer, 2001), pp. 39, 129ff.

6. Kant, *Critique of Pure Reason*, p. 137.

7. Immanuel Kant, *Opus postumum*, in *Gesammelte Schriften* (Berlin: de Gruyter, 1938), Bd. XXII, p. 26. Trans. note: This passage is not contained in the English selection, Immanuel Kant, *Opus Postumum*, trans. E. Förster and M. Rosen (New York: Cambridge University Press, 1993).

8. A passage like the following might be determinant in this respect:

> the combination (*conjunctio*) of a manifold in general can never come to us through the senses, and cannot, therefore, be already contained in the pure form of sensible intuition. For it is an act of spontaneity of the faculty of representation; and since this faculty, to distinguish it from sensibility, must be entitled understanding—be we conscious of it or not, be it a combination of the manifold of intuition, empirical or non-empirical, or of various concepts—is an act of the understanding (Kant, *Critique of Pure Reason*, p. 151).

For a thorough analysis of this quotation, refer to Melchiorre, *Analogia e analisi trascendentale*, pp. 94–99.

9. Kant, *Critique of Pure Reason*, pp. 224–25.

10. Husserl, *Analyses Concerning Passive and Active Synthesis*, pp. 41–44. Among Husserl's many phenomenological outlines, one could quote the following as particularly meaningful:

> The object then shows itself from a variety of sides. What was pictorially suggested from one side, becomes confirmed in full perception from another; what was merely adumbrated or given indirectly and subsidiarily as background, from one side, at least receives a portrait-sketch from another, it appears perspectivally foreshortened and projected, only to appear "just as it is" from another side. All perceiving and imagining is, on our view, a web of partial intentions, fused together in the unity of a single total inten-

tion. The correlate of this last intention is the thing, while the correlate of its partial intentions are *the thing's parts and aspects*. Edmund Husserl, *Logical Investigations*, trans. J. N. Findlay (New York: Humanities Press, 1970), vol. II, p. 701.

11. Kant, *Critique of Pure Reason*, p. 220.

12. Aristotle, *On Interpretation* 4, 17; *Metaphysics* E 4, 1027b16–28; Z 12, 1027b16–28; Θ 10, 1051a34–1051b2–5.

13. See n. 4.

14. René Descartes, *Meditations on First Philosophy*, Meditation 3. With a somewhat Platonic undertone, this quotation will be retrieved almost literally by Malebranche: *"Je crois qu'il n'y a point de substance puramente intelligible, que celle de Dieu; qu'on ne peut rien découvrir avec évidence, que dans sa lumière"* (*Recherche de la Vérité*, P. I. L. III, chap. I, I).

15. Aristotle, *On Interpretation* 5, 17a8–10. See 10, 19b12.

16. Still Aristotle reminds us that true and false are not in things, but only in thought. See Aristotle, *Metaphysics* E, 4, 1027b16–28.

17. Heraclitus, fr. 72; see also fr. 1.

18. Plato, *Republic* VI, 508e.

19. *Republic* VII, 517c.

20. Descartes, *Meditations*, Meditation 2.

21. Playing with words, Plato says precisely that Penia is in the aporetic need of Poros: *dia ten autes aporian* (*Symposium* 203b).

22. *Symposium*, 205d.

23. *Symposium*, 192c–d.

24. Plato, *Phaedrus*, 249c–d.

25. *Phaedrus*, 251a.

26. *Phaedrus*, 248b.

27. *Phaedrus*, 252e–253b.

28. Nicolas Grimaldi, *Le désir et le temps* (Paris: Vrin, 1992), pp. 80–81.

29. Kant, *Critique of Pure Reason*, p. 24.

30. Ludwig Wittgenstein, *Tractatus Logico-Philosophicus* (London: Routledge and Kegan, 1961), p. 7. That Wittgenstein loved Augustine's *Confessions* as "the most important book ever written" and that he used to quote the abovementioned expression is something I learned from R. Monk, *L. W.: The Duty of Genius* (London: Cape, 1990).

31. Augustine, *Confessions*, I, 4. I have discussed this contrast in an essay from some years ago, *Metafore del sacro* (1986), now in Virgilio Melchiorre, *Essere e Parola* (Milan: Vita e Pensiero, 1993).

32. For an analytic examination of the language of symbols and metaphors, see Virgilio Melchiorre, *La via analogica* (Milan: Vita e Pensiero, 1996), which also includes an essay on Aristotle.

33. With respect to this, consider Nabert's essay, "Le divin et Dieu," *Etudes Philosophiques* 3 (1959), which has been followed by many lines of development. These have been posthumously published under the title *Le désir de Dieu* (Paris: Éditions du Cerf, 1996). Nabert's perspective, according to which the reference to a transcendent principle would be in contradiction with a structural analysis of the *cogito* and not simply underivable from this, remains however debatable.

34. Augustine, *Expositions of the Psalms 121–150*, trans. M. Boulding, O.S.B., in *The Works of Saint Augustine*, ed. B. Ramsey (Hyde Park, NY: New City Press, 2004), pt. III, vol. 20, pp. 195–96. The passage is taken up by Edith Stein, *Endliches und Ewiges Sein* (Freiburg im Brisgau: Herder, 1952), p. 98.

35. 2 Corinthians 4:4.

Chapter 7

The Truth of Existence and the Sacred (*ethos anthropo daimon*)

MARIO RUGGENINI

The Transcendence of the True

The truth that is necessary to think—the truth that summons existence— is the truth that announces and at the same time hides itself in human speech. That is, *the truth that eventuates itself in language* keeps human beings in conversation and therefore makes them exist. It is neither the truth of the immutable nor is it the truth of a being that is first of all in itself, beyond language, and to which thought should conform to let the truth appear as it is, in a discourse capable of not betraying it. Whatever the form in which it is reproposed, the myth of conformity [*adeguazione*] in fact does not survive the circle in which it collapses as soon as it is thought because it presupposes an already known truth as the measure of the relation that should institute it. It imagines a reciprocal exteriority of being and saying, which is contra-dicted (*aufgehoben*, Hegel would say) as soon as one assumes that words may say things as they are. But which things are, and how are they? And how can we know this if being stands in itself, is indifferent, and saying and being— but, concretely, our experience—supervene accidentally to things, at least to their indifferent natural consistency? When conceived as subsistent by itself, nature decays to mere material, exterior presence; human beings have not produced it; they become aware of it through work and study, which ap-proach nature with difficulty in its immediate exteriority to conform them-selves to nature, and thus bend it to their own needs. The more exterior the

This chapter continues the discourse I developed in Mario Ruggenini, *Il Dio assente. La filosofia e l'esperienza del divino* (Milan: Bruno Mondadori, 1997), and in other following works, in particular "La verità dell'evento. L'ermeneutica tra la filosofia e la fede," in *Studia Patavina* 3 (1998): 159–77; "L'esperienza del sacro nell'età della tecnica," in *Ars Interpretandi* 4 (1999): 61–92 (parts of this work have been reworked in the central paragraphs); "La trascendenza del vero," in *Studia Patavina* 1 (2000): 59–75; "Il dominio, la parola, il sacro," in *Terza Navigazione* (Milan: Mondadori, 2002).

relation as it happens in the passage from the medieval to the modern epoch, the more the relation of conformity changes into the violent appropriation of that which to human beings first appears as separate and opposed. Human beings posit themselves as subjects of the relation, and nature is reduced to objectivity available for their needs. The world of natural realities is replaced by the world of objects. However, as soon as they assume their own consistency, these very objects and all artifacts get estranged from the constitutive relation with their maker if they are considered as entities present at hand (*vorhanden*), independent in their being, and yet prodigiously available to our own conforming strategies. This is not to deny that our mind effectively adapts itself through the hand to the utensil that it finds ready at hand or to the forms that nature seems to have predisposed by virtue of some mysterious and providential demiurgical ability of its own. That is, this is not to deny that in our daily practices something may happen resembling what comes to our mind when we think we can grasp, in the conformity to a reality seemingly exterior and independent, the feature defining the truth we are looking for. The search for the truth would thus correspond to a fundamental need for conformity. Thus the truth is indeed conceived of as relation—and not already resolved in the immediate being of the thing completely defined in itself for what it is—however, without questioning how a relation can take place between elements as heterogeneous as the word and its meaning on the one side, and the thing as reproduced as meaning in human discourse on the other. The truer, then, is what is the more exact and stable. Yet, how can it be that the meaning of a word in discourse can conform to the being of the thing because they are presupposed as separate dimensions of being? Does one not think, in fact, of having to do with separate spheres of being, the psychic aspect [*psichicità*] of meaning on the one hand, the physicality of real things on the other? Or is it instead not true that we do not know anything either of the word or of the thing if not by virtue of the event in which they are both produced together in their distinction? Things are the things of our experience as speakers. They are always already such insofar as we encounter them in the world, which is always and already open as a world of discourses to any existence occurring in it.[1] Likewise, words are the words of things, even when they fail them, even when they are idle and do not find anything because they have always already found something that induces them to try further, to try other ways of experience, in which they may get lost or find something else they did not expect. *Error and truth.* We are beginning to orient our thoughts toward an experience of truth and error that understands both where they occur, that is, in our discourses, or better stated, *in our experience of the world as experience of speakers.*

The discourse on truth, on the contrary, presents itself as a discourse without a future if truth remains established in itself, in the presumed self-sufficiency of independent entities, and if that which a new revelation comes to announce exists beforehand, steady in its inexorable fixation. It becomes substantially a discourse that, to be true, must sublate itself as such. It must suppress the contingent characters that always make of it only *a* discourse, never *the* discourse, to fixate itself in a repetition of the same that is nevertheless impossible to think. Truth, on the contrary, gives itself to thought only because it lets itself be said. It thus produces or denies itself in conversation, putting itself at stake for the very fact that it makes human beings speak. It must therefore be conceived as *the truth of existence*, because as truth it "is" not; it neither stands nor is it given once and for all. Rather, it comes to existence. Truth occurs [*av-viene*] because existence speaks. Its speaking, however, is not a self-production of discourse; rather, it is an entering the conversation in response to the fundamental, unavoidable appeal resonating, for everybody in the words of others as the *appeal of the other*. One must thus think a *transcendence of the true* that does not mean its preexistence to or independence from discourse, and thus its indifference to its being said or not. *The transcendence of the true is, on the contrary, its difference.* In other words, it is its irreducibility to the power of any speaker, who is always in conversation with others, not as the one who has discourse but instead as the one who has been invited to an already occurring conversation, wherein each interlocutor tries to answer to the truth that addresses him or her. This means that truth unveils its possibilities and determines its needs every time in relation to the answer that each is able to give. However, while it multiplies itself in the exchanges occurring among the interlocutors—questions and answers in which it puts itself at stake—every time the truth circumscribes the eventual space where differences can come to reciprocal confrontation and self-recognition as such.

The event of language thus produces itself as an *irreducible multiplicity of events*, which truth keeps together, insofar as it does not let itself be identified, but rather makes itself be sought, thereby inviting the different experiences it provokes to a conversation. To the intransigent truth of the same, which is destined to reveal itself as the fetish of truth, and to the obscurity of its illusory transparency, a hermeneutic consideration of the truth opposes the *necessary plurality*, the enigma of the truth that can be experienced in many languages through its multiple revelations. It is the truth of many forms of knowledge, which nourish the conversation of existences precisely because no one exhausts it; rather, they all often lose sight of it. It is the truth of thoughts pursuing it with questions. It is the truth of the wonder with which human beings acknowledge its happening when this produces itself in a discourse or an experience. It is the truth of the anguish in front of the enigma, which takes away the courage to confront it and its tenacious resistance. To this ungraspable yet unavoidable truth, religions give a name, in different ways. Some turn it into the God of a revelation carrying with itself the promise of a privileged initiation to the enigma of existence, or even of its resolution. Exactly in this promise, however, is the tragic ambiguity of any religious experience when in a more or less surreptitious way it turns from a revelation of the mystery of the world into the certainty, for those who adhere to it, of having the word, the method, the way—the terms become synonyms—enabling its unveiling. The revelation that compromises itself with all too human premises perverts its relation with the sacred, and turns itself into an insurance strategy for existence and the domination over the world.

Truth and Enigma

The hermeneutic experience of discourse is the experience of a taking part understood as a having to respond, even when the speaker is aware of daring a word that has never been tried before. Those who say in a responsible way, exposing themselves to the risk of what they say, obey the instance of truth moving them to speak. They do not produce a truth that they have in themselves, and which they can use as tool for domination. They interpret the truth that may happen in their own words, or withdraw from them, and that produces itself in the words of the direct interlocutor or in some others to which their attempt at saying is nevertheless referred and in which they recognize the anticipations of the truth they await or the traces of the truth that has already revealed itself and motivates their quest and awaiting. *Human beings speak insofar as the truth has come toward them from the beginning*, but in a way such that its revelation is always also its hiding, and what has already been announced nourishes the quest for something else that always remains to be said. For this reason, the instance of truth that governs the discourse of existences and that is at the origin of the very power to lie is nothing voluntaristic or ideal as one thinks in modern times. Rather, it arises from the fact that *the truth has always already been said in human speech*. In speech, it is not only preserved, but it has also always faded away. No human word is ever simply word of truth because each word only says with limitations; it says and it does not say, and therefore can always be equivocated, also because truth does not stand complete in itself first, to come to discourse later. It makes itself, rather, within discourse. Thus, it searches and loses itself, that is, puts itself at stake in the speech in which it lets itself be said. This *finite truth*, which is not preconstituted but *eventual*, is the truth of which we have an experience, the one we can live, despite the proven tendency of thought to deny its own finitude and to search for a stable truth beyond discourse. Only such a truth would be able to solve any often tragic ambiguity and obscurity that human speech gathers around the uncertain light by which it is nevertheless able to enlighten the being of things and of the very existences themselves. The absolute truth is nothing else than a myth that thought builds for itself illusorily to free itself of the limitations of discourse. Thought can in fact ask for the path to exit discourse only from within discourse itself, from the reserves of meaning that discourse makes available to it, from the possibilities of moving among them that discourse unveils to it. Yet, although apparently condescending, in reality discourse does not let itself be duped or transcended. Rather, patiently and yet inexorably, it awaits for thought to abandon its metaphysical dreams and to discover that the only transcendence with which it deals is that of truth within language, not beyond it.

Even in its most updated versions, metaphysical thought is very far from taking on itself the paradox on which it rests, although only by virtue of a type of, albeit abused, conjuring trick. It allows itself the easy conviction that, as thought, it can benefit from the authorization to speak every time while dictating to language, which it claims it is simply using, a definition of meanings that ignores the insaturability of the semantic field opened by any discourse. The task that a hermeneutic thinking has not finished completing is, on the contrary, that of a loyalty to discourse to the limits of language in which any discourse is formulated—a loyalty that does not lose sight of the multifarious but always binding experience of the truth situated at the origin of the conversation of existences in the various languages in which the conversation unfolds. Those who speak with truth respond to the truth that wants to become speech in their words. This is so thanks to the responsibility they assume in relation to the discourses they have already heard and that make them capable of new hearing. Their response interprets *the necessity of the true*, the need of the true to reveal itself. This is nothing else than *the need of truth for which we speak*. Those who know that by speaking they also respond, also understand that no response, no matter how elaborate and complex, can get hold of the truth, tearing it away once and for all from its hiding. The integral true is not somewhere busy preparing its own triumphal *parousia*, its revelation unobscured by shadows and unconstrained by limits after the partial revelations in which it would have given sign of itself only enigmatically. *The enigma belongs rather to the destiny of the truth that comes to existence and cannot be solved by any parousia.* Truth in fact makes existences speak insofar as it is gathered in the memory of language, and from here announces its need to happen always anew in any speech that says the being in the world of humans and their need to exist. Thus the truth that comes to language is not afraid of time; rather, it is *the truth of time*, which is for existence *the time of the word*.

Truth as *Aletheia*

Existence speaks because the manifestation of the being of things occurs in speech. Existence is always preceded by this need of the world to open, in existence, the space for the manifestation of all entities and events. This means that no one decides to speak by oneself; rather, everyone is assumed from the beginning in the service of the need of the world to become speech. One corresponds to this need that makes one be insofar as one assumes the responsibility of guarding what one has heard and of translating it into the speech through which one takes part in the conversation of existences. *Everyone thus speaks to tell the truth, that is, to interpret and thereby reveal the being of things.* Exactly for this reason, exactly because it speaks, existence can also conceal the truth it has interpreted, lying, keeping silence, confusing others' search. Yet, the concealment is not a somewhat extrinsic consequence of the destiny of the truth; it is not consequent only to the speaker's indolence, to his or her smallness in relation to the burden with which the truth loads existence. On the contrary, the truth that unfolds in speech opens up this space of play between disclosure and concealment, the former being necessary to the latter, in the same way as the manifestation of something always refers to something else that remains hidden, whereas we think of what we still need to search only starting from what of it has come to light. The truth of what is hidden, its revelation, brings with itself the necessity that what becomes manifest always produces a new concealment of what any manifestation necessarily conceals. This remains unthought and unspoken until a new word, a new revelation, comes to solicit the questioning and the explicit experience of it, although it was already at stake and secretly influencing what was of concern in the conversation. It thus happens that what was first revealed takes on a different meaning: sometimes it may appear as a more complete truth, at other times it is understood as a correction or even a denial of what was taken to be true. Nothing in what has become manifest once can be given to a light without sunset. Rather, its decline is often the necessary condition for the emergence of a new truth. The revelation of what is hidden is thus, at the same time, the concealment of something else that remains to be sought. Likewise, it produces a sort of unavoidable forgetfulness, or at least obscuring, of what had already been brought to full light.

Heidegger has changed the name for this experience of truth and has unveiled how much the speech we employ hides the essence of that of which one speaks. It is not a truth that is or is kept still; rather, it is a revealing that hides and a hiding that reveals. No longer *veritas*, then, but rather *aletheia*, as the Greeks always said even if in the course of their history they have lost the deep sense of an understanding to which one must listen anew when wondering about the relation between truth and existence. When the issue is that of understanding the human experience of the truth, which is fundamentally *the experience of one's own finitude*, the indication coming from the ancient word is much more enlightening than any triumphalistic discourse on the immutable being of the true, which speaks of something inaccessible for human beings even if such a discourse holds true as an expression of their vain desire. Which truth in fact answers for this desire (or too-human need?) for permanence and indefectibility [*indefettibilità*] in front of the continuous fading away or staggering in the course of the days as well as in the succession of generations and epochs of what promises stability, solidity, security, and comfort? Which truth justifies the need for the transcendent protection to which the metaphysical-theological history of the West has consigned itself if not the violence and the urgency of need itself?

What Heidegger has not been able to attain with the necessary clarity, though, is the consideration that what makes the comprehension of the truth as *aletheia* unavoidable is finite existence's very destination to the word. We should thus say, and, moreover, think that *aletheia is necessarily the truth of language*. This is the only truth that we can experience as finite intelligences. Meanwhile, this is the truth that no revelation can take away from us because the condition of finitude is not, first of all, the despicable cause of our necessary erring. Rather, finitude is opening to the truth that destines itself to human beings as speakers. Belonging to language, being destined to discourse defines, and that means delimits, the finitude that gives the chance to exist to a certain kind of living entities—that means, it gives them the paradoxical responsibility for their being born and having to die. Existence is not simply given by virtue of the fact of living between birth and death. Existence is not a fact, but rather a possibility that is disclosed in the destiny of having to speak. In this sense, only human existence is finite because it alone must bear responsibility for birth and death. It is as speakers that human beings experience that the truth of any word reveals and veils at the same time because no discourse says everything. Rather, it says not only by virtue of what it says, but also of what it keeps silent and can only be kept silent. For this reason, any word says at the same time more and less than what it means in relation to the context of discourse and intelligence in which it inserts itself, in relation to the willingness to listen that welcomes it, in relation to the ability of interpretation that replies to its announcement. *The truth of conversation*, the one that questions and makes the interlocutors speak beyond their expectations and intentions, takes advantage of these light and shade effects, which produce the speeches that speakers exchange. Do we not all have the experience of often understanding others' words according to our own interests in a way incongruous with the intention the speaker makes manifest to us? Yet, for us, such a misunderstanding may have a meaning of truth that questions and solicits us beyond any philological concern toward a text, or beyond the due respect for the interlocutor, when in the direct exchange his or her discourses open up ways that are unforeseen or unshared by him or her. Analogously, can we know how one will understand the words that we try to formulate at times with the greatest clarity and care for the definition of their meaning at times when we discuss with specific interlocutors, at times when we write for readers destined to remain anonymous? The destiny of speech always fulfills itself beyond or on this side of the best or worst intentions because it is not exclusively the destiny of each individual speaker; it is also the destiny of the truth that produces itself in the *conversation of the world*.

No one has this destiny at one's own disposal. On the contrary, it reaches us insofar as it challenges our responsibility toward the truth that summons everyone in a conversation with others. The truth of our as well as of others' words does not belong to any individual speaker. It is in fact the *truth of language* as event, as "the other" that makes any existence speak. It is thus the truth's need that makes human beings speak, not human need that makes the truth that is convenient for them be. *Language's need for truth* is the need to open up to the world the possibility of revealing itself in human speech as "the other" that makes humans be. In this way, language offers to its speakers possibilities of existence that restore to the world further possibilities of becoming an event in the conversation to which it invites them. The truth of language as *aletheia* is the truth of the world. Only as such does it produce itself as the truth to which and for which existence answers. In no way is existence in control of the truth. Likewise, it is not in control either of language or of the world. Therefore, *the transcendence of the truth* should be understood not as the selfsameness [*inseità*] of something, which remains what it is regardless of human discourses—something to which the intelligence of discourse should only conform. Rather, it should be under-stood as the self-producing of the truth in the words human beings exchange without its reduction thereby to the disposition of each speaker. The truth thus adjudicates the discourses of the individuals based on the judgment each of them passes on the discourse of others. Yet it never coincides with any of the formulations achieved by the confrontation among speakers. The truth confronts the discourse of one with that of others to produce ever new possibilities of discourse. It does not hold as the verdict conclusive of dis-course, to which nothing can be added or subtracted except for the authori-tative commentary imposing disciplinary obedience. *The ver-dict of the truth*[2] is instead the one that, thanks to the twilight glow it casts, repeatedly re-opens discourse to new possibilities of intelligence, which human beings need to remain in a mutual conversation. In language, that is, *in human discourse*, what is at stake is the possibility of a world enabling humans to exist, that is, a world allowing to find in each others' words the truth that by keeping them together in a conversation calls on each interlocutor to answer for his or her own difference while respecting others' differences. This means that the *destiny of human language*, of human discourses, remains *the truth of the world*, that is, its revelation protecting its enigma. The repeated specification aims at reacting against the equivocation, according to which to insist on the alterity of language means to produce some sort of hypo-statization, rather than understanding that when taken away from human control language becomes the evocation of what is human and of everything that humans are called to interpret—nature and history, gods and demons, good and evil, justice and grace. It is not language that belongs to humans, but humans that belong to language, as well as is the case for nature, the gods, and everything that time lets us encounter in the opening of the world.

In the world, we find ourselves existing with others, *but starting from* "*the other*": not only in the sense of the needs for which nature assists, but

even beforehand, insofar as it is from the world that the words calling existence to be come to it. *The world is the world of others.* We enter a relation
with it as human beings in the existential sense of the term, not because we
"have" words, but because words are given to us. Thus, what is given to us
is the responsibility to keep up with the discourse of others. *This is the
discourse of the world.* Human beings are the beings of responsibility because
they are the beings of speech in the sense that they are in any event the ones
who must answer. The speech each addresses to the other is not simply
information, signaling of the current rule of use, or banal description of states
of things. When, according to its essential destiny, it resounds as appeal from
one existence to another, speech is always more than the word that one
human being addresses to another. It is *the speech of the world,* to which one,
namely the addressee, has to answer for the being one has received, trying
to discern, among the possibilities that meet one, those that open one to
one's worldly destiny of faithfulness to the earth and those that close one in
obstinate affirmation, haughty in one's own being: against others, against "the
other" calling one to be oneself beyond oneself. *The world is "the other" calling
each existence to answer for one's own finitude.*

Logos: Language and the Sacred

The language coming to existence as the very self-disclosing of the world
that calls and welcomes existence *opens the dimension of the sacred.* Existence
belongs to it on the ground of the relation to "the other" that constitutes it.
*Existence is the event of "the other" than human beings precisely because it is called
to speak.* In the beginning was *logos.* In its light, nature, the gods, and the
goods and evils of the world come to human beings. The great experience of
the word, developed through the Jewish tradition and posed at the origin of
the Christian tradition, finds perhaps its highest expression in the beginning
of the Prologue to John's Gospel: *En arche en ho logos* [In the beginning was
the Word].

The experience of discourse announces itself through these words of
ancient wisdom as the experience of the divine that grounds not only human
experience, but also the opening of all realities thanks to the event of the
word. *Logos* is at the beginning; *logos* governs them. The reference to *logos*,
however, does not have by itself the character of an explanation making
everything clear and manageable for human reason. Nor does it configure that
omnipotent reassurance of existence that will be perfected by the following
Christian theological elaboration. This is certainly not the case for Heraclitus,
for whom "nature loves to hide" (fr. 123), and who refers to the hidden
harmony as stronger and better than the disclosed one (fr. 54). This does not
seem to be the basic thinking of the Prologue either, which enacts the drama
of the contraposition between the generating and enlightening power of *logos*
and the tenacious, even overwhelming resistance of the darkness. Thus, the

true light is not recognized: *ho kosmos auton ouk egno* [the world knew him not]. *Logos* is not welcome by all those who nevertheless belong to it. If the fundamental message of the Prologue is that *logos* becomes flesh to reveal God's truth in the earthly vicissitude of a man, Jesus, and thus to make itself word in human discourse, this is the message of the revelation of a God who manifests himself insofar as he reveals himself. The conclusion of the Prologue says this with an extraordinary power: "No one has ever seen God; the only Son, who is in the bosom of the Father, he has made him known" (John 1:18). The invisible God is the God of mystery, whom no gaze can penetrate and about whom no word ends speaking, not even the word of the Son. *Ekeinos exegesato* [he was made known]: the revelation of God's mystery in the man Jesus is the annunciation of the enigma in which the being of any person is wrapped. The individual is called to welcome and interpret in his or her own words the "exegesis" of such an enigma that the Revealer has given in his own words and life. There is no other truth in the Christian God than the one guarded in this enigmatic revelation.

For any experience of the divine, however, does any possible truth exist other than the one that entrusts itself to human language? In the silence of the mystery surrounding the earth and any existence, its words resound as the voice of "*the other*," and not simply of other human beings, when such words gather the speakers to share the destiny of finitude that joins them and makes them witnesses, the ones for the others, of the nameless power of language calling them to discourse. Is it not an extraordinary mark of the enigma for which "we are a conversation, and we can hear the ones from the others,"[3] according to the poet's precious expression, that the *incipit* to the Prologue utters the word *logos* before the word God, only then to bring *logos* back to God as the highest? Or better, is this not the only possibility of speaking of the mystery of God's being? Were God not *logos*, what relation would we have with the divine, and what could we say, think, or expect of it? With what would we nourish the respect inspired by his revelation? God—the divine—reveals himself—cannot but reveal himself—because he is word, whereas human beings can exist because the generating word invests them. It manifests itself as the word of God insofar as it makes human beings speak.

The enigma of revelation—of *any* revelation—is the enigma of human finitude insofar as it is not closed on itself; it is instituted, rather, in its being by the relation with the "*the other*" announced to it via its dependence on language. This is an unavoidable, even if mistaken, dependence. Without claiming that the Prologue speaks directly about this, what is said in the passage we mentioned earlier is quite meaningful for the set of considerations we are making here. The presence of the life and light of *logos* is not recognized by those who are enlivened and enlightened by it, who owe their own possibility of being to language, who thus belong to language, rather than being themselves the holders of language. *Logos* is the divine breath of "*the other*" giving them the freedom to be as finite beings. *Human beings are finite because they have to speak.* All beings, the determinable entity of which is founded in the event of the word, and which thus have a relation with human existence, are finite. Is this so also for the one who announces oneself as a god?

Even though asking about God's finitude may seem scandalous, even absurd, we will have to come back to this fundamental question, which the experience of language raises. With respect to this, we should emphasize the consideration that exactly because such an experience institutes *the relation of alterity that makes human beings "ek-sist," it opens them to the experience of the sacred while it calls them to speak.* This should not be mistaken with any experience of dependence, or with a (too vague?) sense of the "infinite" hovering over humanity, or with the (too obscure?) sense of the "numinous" exposing us in fear and trembling to the revelation of a tremendous and fascinating majesty. These experiences are not excluded. Yet, they are delivered from their vague indeterminacy insofar as they are raised and qualified to the level of a speech relation between the alterity of the world and finite human beings. *The sacred of the word* is the experience of alterity rendering human beings different, the only living beings called to interpret the mystery of the surrounding reality and of their being in it. If existence perceives the transcendence of such a word, despite the fact that *only* the words of others can give voice to it; if it nevertheless perceives it coming from the unsurpassable distance of an abysmal silence, still it is the word that destines human beings to answer for themselves to the earth they must inhabit. This is the revelation of a mystery that does not consign us to the powerlessness and vanity of our own being, but rather awakens us to the responsibility of being in the world, we who are called to a task that has been entrusted only to us, which no one else can take up, and from which in any event nobody can alleviate us. This is the task for which each existence is irreplaceable. The being in the world of each existence is its being for the world, for the only world to which we belong and to which we are related beyond the multiple "worlds" in which each individual life unfolds. It is to the mystery of this solitude, which is yet dominated by the reference to the alterity that makes us be, that *we are referred by the experience of the sacred that comes to us enigmatically, where we perceive the ungraspable proximity of a god.*

Near and far is the god, according to the word of the poet.[4] The god is near in the call that reaches any existence at its roots, when the—often most silent, less showy—word that imposes itself to be listened to provokes everyone to decide of one's own being, without escape. Yet the god is far, ungraspable, because the word of "*the other*" has no ascertainable provenance. It is, in a deep sense, *no one's word.* For this reason, it exposes the being of existence to the enigma of its finitude. It does not root it in any ground because it reveals that the roots of its being sink in the mystery of the earth, which it is called to protect while inhabiting it. Is the earth itself not perceived

as divine by the most ancient religious experience because it is the earth of
our birth but also of our death, as well as of the resources that nature makes
available for our needs? "She, the greatest of gods, the earth/ageless she is,
and unwearied," is sung in the first stanza of *Antigone*'s chorus.[5] Guardians of
the sacredness of the Earth, we are thus confronted with the enigma of the
relation to the divine that makes us be. The measure of our existence becomes our faithfulness to the relation of finitude that consigns us to the
earthly dimension of our own having to be without possibilities for an evasion toward other worlds if not in the form of vainly consoling illusions.
Religions taint themselves with unfaithfulness toward the earth when they
indulge in mythologies that promise humanity redemption from its worldly
finitude. Usually, in a more or less programmatic manner, they make use of
metaphysical doctrines that cultivate their own intolerance toward that
belonging to the world that makes human beings be the beings of the word.[6]
In these religious and metaphysical doctrines of redemption, the common
feature consists in the *loss of the sacred of the word*. The word makes the earth
liveable since it celebrates its divine mystery. The word commemorates it,
the word questions it, the word sings it. At the origin of religions the word
happens as poetry and myth of the relations between the gods and humans.
As such, it makes itself tradition in its interpretative and normative aspects
of conduct of existence and of interrogation and symbolization of the enigmas of the world. Only because human beings speak to one another has
supplying sufficient resources to grant survival to the weakest of the living
species been possible. Moreover, in the discourse of the ones with the others
are the roots of the community of existences, which can have "understanding of good and evil, of just and unjust" only through the word.

This strong claim comes from Aristotle. It follows from the premise
according to which "language serves to declare what is advantageous and
what is the reverse, and it therefore serves to declare what is just and what
is unjust."[7] Analogously, within the already mentioned context, Sophocles
claims that we learned civil impulses together with the word and the aerial
thought; thus, together with the danger of being banned from it, we learned
the possibility of becoming famous in the city.[8] If the lymph nourishing the
life of the city is justice, the root transmitting and attaining it from the
divine resources of the earth is *logos*. Following Aristotle, we can say that
logos is the manifestation of the divinity of nature by means of the difference
of human beings, of their being destined to the word. Well before being
established as the domain of the logical calculation of thoughts and their
grounds, Aristotle's *logos* is the foundation of the human as belonging to the
sacred domain of *phusis*. We are no longer able to understand that, perhaps
precisely for this reason, the rigor of logic, in general of calculative reason
is not necessarily opposed to the experience of the sacred. At least this is not
so for Aristotle. For him, *logos* means the order of thoughts as much as of the
occurances of nature. For this reason, only the *logos* of shared discourse

instructs humanity about the order of the *polis* and the measure it dictates to human life. In the *Politics*, it is said that nature, which does nothing in vain, gave human beings *logos*. Nature, however, is nothing else than the god, as is written in *On the Heavens*: "*ho theos kai he phusis ouden maten poiousin* (divine nature does nothing in vain)."[9] In human language, the divinity of the world is sought and hidden. Heraclitus's perhaps most enigmatic, certainly least understood, saying states that to live by the divine belongs to human beings: *ethos anthropo daimon*.[10] What is proper to humans is to dwell in the mystery.

Greek metaphysics hesitates, however, because in its Platonic inspiration it has become diffident toward language. On the contrary, the Christian thought of the origins provides the extraordinary indication concerning *logos* as the generative principle of everything that is. *Logos* makes the world full of every kind of beings because it gives life and light. *Logos* reveals. *Logos* opens up the space of the world for the encounter between existence and the sacred. Is this not the *freedom of the sacred*, no longer restrained within the limits of ritual practices and prescribed foods, gestures, or places, which is inaugurated by Jesus' word? The Gospel according to John is the propagandist of this in the most explicit way: "If you continue in my word [*en toi logoi toi emoi*], . . . you will know the truth, and the truth will make you free."[11] *The truth of the word is the truth that frees the sacred*. The sacred is such insofar as it is the sacred of the truth. Thus, the truth that claims to relinquish its relation with the sacred loses its mystery and its own transcendence. It loses itself as truth.

The Sacred at the Origin of the Relation between Gods and Human Beings

Despite Christianity's falling back into a prescriptive understanding of the sacred, philosophy owes its own need to think the experience of the sacred as experience of freedom to Christianity or at least to its originary power of announcement. Actually, the Christian theological tradition remains too metaphysical to be able to think that *the divinity of the Logos can simply realize itself in the conversation in which the human world takes shape*. That is, that it can realize itself as the word that calls humans to existence, the word to which we must answer for our being born and our having to die. *The sacred of existence and of the world* produces itself nowhere else than in this event, in the responsibility we take up in front of any birth as well as any death, whether our own or others.' For this reason, birth and death are never merely biological facts; rather, they mark the terms of the possibility of being-in-conversation-among one another. Existence, in fact, is not finite first of all because it has a beginning and awaits its end. It is finite because in birth and death it finds the double seal of a finitude that is such because it depends on the word calling everyone to be part of the worldwide discourse of human beings.

At this point, to understand the sacred of the conversation of existences as the paradoxical dimension of the *polemos* that makes everyone other
for the other, trying the enigmatic way of Heraclitus's wisdom, from which
we have already taken more than one indication, is once again helpful.
According to a famous fragment, *polemos* is in fact recognized as having the
originary power to distinguish what at the same time remains joined precisely
thanks to the tension that it develops among the opponents: "*Polemos* is the
father of all and king of all, and some he shows as gods, others as human;
some he makes slaves, others free."[12] Here Heraclitus names something that
is not a thing; it is a dimension, an event, the uncircumscribable open in
which humans and gods meet. It is unlike them because it generates them
in the deep sense of revealing (*edeixe*, according to the Greek text) their
respective nature in the relation: that is, as one relative to the other. Maybe
for this reason, another, already mentioned fragment speaks of the ambiguous divinity of the One, the only *sophon* ("*hen to sophon mounon*"), which
"does not and does consent to be called by the name of Zeus,"[13] almost as if
to warn that the event that opens the region of differences is not one of
them. That which reveals that the human is human because it is not a god,
and that a god is divine, not human—this fecund principle of differences and
opposites is not a god. Rather, it is in some sense greater, more welcoming,
more generous, but also more impenetrable than any god. And yet, this
"*divine alterity*" does not completely disdain the name of the supreme god
because of its character as principle of all things in the enigmatic sense that
it contains and governs all.

*The divine as alterity, the divinity of the world is what we must think of as
the sacred.* It generates and protects differences. It makes it such that gods
and humans, slaves and free are together. It calls them to fulfill their respective task insofar as it asks from each of the mortals that they come together
in the common conversation and that each takes up, in the confrontation
with others, responsibility for one's own existence. On the other hand, *the
task of any god* in approaching humans is that of announcing *the differing
alterity of the principle* that calls them into a conversation, its being and not
being nameable. As such, the sacred has no proper name; it is not this rather
than that. Although it can manifest itself anywhere, it is the god of no place,
condition, or status that differentiates humans through their dignity. Insofar
as it is the sacred of the word, it frees existence from any bond and from any
servitude that is not its faithfulness to the earth, that is, its faithfulness to the
relation of finitude referring it to the mystery of the "*other principle*" that
makes it be. The names we use to think the sacred are thus those that,
derived from the experience of worldly events, are solicited to say what
cannot be said in a determined way. This is evident in Heraclitus's very need
of approaching the enigma of the sacred through a plurality of designations,
each of them improper, each of them fit, if anything, to remove any definitional
pretension. One should think of the designations we are encountering such

as *polemos, kosmos, logos, to sophon, hen.* But one should also think of the need to think of the divine god through the attribution of contrary predicates: "god is day night, winter summer, war peace, satiety hunger; he undergoes alteration in the way that fire, when it is mixed with spices, is named according to the scent of each of them."[14] It is the versatility of the divine that escapes any determination, but that thus propitiates the encounter of humans and god, their eventual correspondence, in the relation that makes them differ from each other.

In its various manifestations, the sacred is not reduced to a mere projection of the human; rather, it comes to humans from the *divine alterity* that makes them be only if the word that announces it is itself divine. The word of a divine god is *the revelation of the sacred of the world,* of the mystery that assigns to humans no less than to the gods it evokes the role they must sustain within the relation that makes *both of them* be. As we read and tried to think in the words of the more ancient wisdom, *the sacred of the world* is the generator of the mutual differing of humans and gods, which come to an encounter only by the mutual preserving by the ones of the mystery of the others' being. If human beings are human only by not closing themselves to the mystery of "the other," the god is a god only if he abstains himself from any form of domination over humans so as to disclose to them with no motion of envy the sacred space within which humans can live their finitude [*esistere la propria finitezza*]. Perhaps this is possible next to the god of healthy difference, a god who does not overcome humans, but who rather frees them for the responsibility that the god entrusts to them. Once again, *ethos anthropo daimon,* but in the sense that when humans exist as humans, they inhabit the propitious *absence of the god.*

The Sacred and Religions

The divine god must be thought of as an *eventual god.* He must reveal himself first of all as *a god of the world,* who in the world, in the open of its originary event, comes toward humanity that is destined to it as its part. Like humans, gods too are subject to the sacred destiny that makes it such that they have to realize a certain manifestation of the divine. The canonical tradition interpreting Jesus's mission says this clearly when it has Jesus declare that he has not come to do his own will, but rather the will of the one who has sent him. He confesses that the one who sent him is greater than himself.[15] Human beings find themselves in the world and recognize themselves as humans by conversing. In such a way, they answer one another for their mutual differences, as peoples and as individuals. What differentiates them as existences is in fact the way in which they sustain the revelation of the mystery of the world occurring in their discourses. If the event of the world is thus the clearing [*l'aperto*] of any possible manifestation, every god shapes the destiny of a certain humanity in relation to that experience of the divine of the world to which the god calls such humanity to respond. The earth is thus inhabited by human beings as the earth that belongs to many gods or to many manifestations of the divine.

This polytheism historically has been the ground for an uncompromising refusal on the side of metaphysical reason, particularly in its monotheistic variation, historically bound to an onticorealistic understanding of unity. For metaphysical monotheism, unity is such only if it is realized, according to a substantialistic paradigm, as the absolute identity of a supreme being, which contains in its being the causal, productive ground for all things. The conception of unity it imposes determines unity as a definable entity to which philosophy and theology can give a dogmatic expression so that such unity can be represented even in the visibility of the people or of the "sacred" institution. The uncontainable mystery of the invisible god is thus circumscribed within the precise limits of a controllable manifestation through the prescribed discipline of ritual and dogmatic formulae. The word proclaimed as divine revelation is preserved by institutional theology, thirsty for visibility as the fiat of the supreme being, which orders the historical realization of the unity of faith and does not tolerate the multiplicity of the experiences of the divine characterizing, on the contrary, human history. This means that the God of mystery is reputed credible only if it requires and produces the positive, ascertainable unification of religions, that is, the manifest, declared conversion of the many errors to the truth that is claimed to be one. In this way, the dogmatic conception of revelation expresses and also strengthens the metaphysical conception of the truth as substantial identity. The theology that expresses it withdraws horrified when confronting the thought that the truth can only produce itself in the conversation in which existences necessarily come together yet differ in an irreducible manner by virtue of their finitude. Yet, although repressed, this unavoidable experience of the truth presses and disturbs inexorably any honest philosophical and theological reflection that is not distorted by apologetic prejudices, that is minimally touched by the memory of the tragic history of conflicts, scissions, coerced conversions, and the tenacious resistance of ancients faiths. With respect to these, the dogmatic intransigency of the one and only truth has not been able to find, for the most part, any other resolutory argument than violence.

In the fields of both philosophy and religious experience, *the conversation of the truth* is realized, on the contrary, in the multiplicity of discourses in which truth is not dispersed, but allows itself to be sought. The fact that no one of the participants can rightly vindicate the title of exclusive warden of the postulated identity of the truth does not precipitate the quest for that other nondogmatic truth, which existence does not cease needing, into the relativism of the indifference of each to the others' reasons. On the contrary, the secret matrix of any relativism clearly appears to be sought nowhere else than in the dogmatic conception of the truth. The freedom of the sacred from all restrictive and constrictive forms characterizing its history comes from the experience of the truth that makes itself in speech. *The one and only truth is such only if it is the truth of finite existences*: not the one that they tend to shape according to their own needs, but rather the one they know they must obey when it reveals itself or they sense to withdraw when they act in the obscurity and silence of the word. But when the possibly enlightening word is late or missing, exactly then existence senses that it awaits life from the word. In this sense, the abandoning as well as the assisting word, to which existence gladly entrusts its destiny, discloses to it the dimension of the sacred, of the granted or denied grace. *Existence is in search of the truth of life in the sacred of the word.*

The sacred word does not come toward us if not as human speech in which the saving truth is and is not said, speaking but in an enigmatic way, exposing the listener to the risk of his or her own life. Like the word of the Delphic lord, it neither says nor hides, but rather hints.[16] Since the most ancient times, the mark of the sacred thus is its ambiguity, which is often tragically resolved in blood, as we should never forget. The sacred in fact announces an enigmatic promise of salvation, which nonetheless can never dissolve the not less enigmatic possibility of destruction. If the eventual god is the one who, approaching human beings, refers them to the mystery of their being in the world, this mystery towers above them in the time of joy as well as in the time of restlessness and in the time of destitution. The sacred is such because it lets existence be within the limits assigned by birth and death. It is not the prodigious power absolving it from its finitude. The god announcing it is not only the one that human beings sense close in the decisive steps of their path, but also the god they miss, *the god who makes the weight of his absence felt*. Both when they are sustained by the necessary strength to overcome the test and when, on the contrary, they feel they are succumbing, left to their own impotence, human beings live of this enigmatic relation with the sacred, since at the limits of its own finitude existence meets *"the other" testing it*. What in everyone's life becomes event, starting from birth and in view of death, that is, the decision through which existence puts itself at stake; the happy meeting as well as the irremediable loss; the deep pain as well as the exulting joy that change the meaning of the days together with the small habits supporting confidence in life, but also the sudden anxiety suspending existence over the abyss—all these announce the sacred dimension of human beings beyond any calculation of reason, be it theological-metaphysical or philosophical-scientific. We need to understand that not only theology, but also philosophy itself lose any reason for their thinking if they do not find again the experience of the sacred at the origin of their questions as well as of their claims, that is, if they do not find the experience of *the relation with "the other"* that founds human existence in the unjustifiability of its being. *"The other" remains other because it gives no reason for itself*. Only in this way can it support the interpretation that, trying to walk the path of the necessary relation with the religious history of humankind, dares to qualify it as the divine, which however withdraws itself in the ambiguous sense of Heraclitus's fragment from any direct identification with any god. What may profane *the revelation of "the other"* supporting the conversation of existences is, on the side of the religious traditions and of the theologies that have shaped them, the anxiety for self-confirmation, rather than for letting themselves be questioned by every new announcement of "the other's" difference. *"The other" remains other only if it does not cease to announce itself*, both with its word and with its silence, as the crisis of any established certainty. The immediate translation of its alterity into the conception of the divine established by theologies and churches always runs the risk of the radical equivocation that, in the sacred, looks for the sanction of the existent rather than for the revelation of the enigma that it preserves.

On the contrary, *the experience of the sacred as relation with the divine alterity* can return its mystery to the divine only on the condition that it destroys the persistent idolatry that has turned all gods into the all-too-human expression of human needs and projects. This does not mean that the divine sacred, which rejects the measures through which reason claims to verify its transcendence, throws humankind into the darkness of an unrestrained irrationality. On the contrary, this means that the experience of the sacred can give rise to *another reason*, one capable of recognizing and respecting the mystery of existence, beside the reason that, after the illusion of being able to dissolve with its own light the darkness thickening around human existence, has ended up trapped in the net of its own superstitions. The reason that questions the mystery is the one that knows how to listen, in the words of the others, to *the silent voice of an "other," another voice* that has the power to bind one's existence beyond what is allowed and possible for any human power. The sacred of one's truth questions others' existence if, and insofar as, one's truth is not one's private truth, but rather reveals itself as the truth of *logos*. The reason encountering the mystery of the word in the word of others recognizes the privileged place of the manifestation of the mystery of the world in the conversation of existences, that is, in the fact that human beings exist insofar as they speak to one another. It also experiences the truth that makes the existence of others sacred to anyone. *The sacred truth of the word* is the one that withholds the hand that would like to rise violently against others' convictions to break their stubborn resistance. But it is also the one that reveals how the god of the word can be only *an absent god*, even when he seems to manifest his mystery most brightly. In any event, the "evidence of the mystery" can only be its self-denial to any resolutory unveiling regardless how authoritative and authorized.

The Enigma of the Absent God

The question to which these reflections try to give an answer concerns the possibility of the experience of the sacred in the time of the "death of God."

This is, at the same time, the time when the bloody violence of the sacred has become intolerable, and yet it is far from being exhausted; it is even strengthened in an exponential manner by the technological apparatus in its service. Is the unstoppable history of this violence perhaps not also an argument against the gods to whom humankind has offered its sacrifices? After the excess of presence and positivity of the god, of the many gods humankind has known, especially of the warrior-gods of too many "revelations," the issue is thus that of thinking and protecting *the absence of the god*. This absence is propitious to human existence, against the intrusiveness and aggressiveness of the metaphysical god, or better, of the multiple divinities that a violent religiosity has created for itself, and that the refined metaphysics of the West has not been able to refuse. Rather, it has even armed such a god with the claim of absoluteness. Under the mask of a falsified and abused sacrality, *the gods of omnipotence* have proliferated, often the very same god self-divided and lined up on both sides of the same battlefield, a god in reality made on the scale of what human beings are content with being. This is a fetish god in the service of a desire for power that is always frustrated and that thus is transferred onto something other than the human as its supreme legitimation; it only seems to come to rest in the domination by the powerful over other human beings: the enemy, the stranger, the savage, the slave or subject, the misbeliever, the different one, the weaker one. It is a limitless god, the infinite god whom human beings have needed to erase their finitude, the god of all miracles, omnipotent lord but actually made on a human scale, the god who detains all answers and thus is authorized to all abuses, being always capable of self-justification. Against this falsely protective, in truth deeply hostile divinity, through which human beings have realized only the maximum of violence against themselves, nature, and the earth, perhaps the "piety of thought"[17] must find again and protect *the secret god of all revelations*, of all prophets, and of all masters the world has known and revered. Such a god has been repeatedly forgotten and overwhelmed by his anthropomorphic counterfeit as the god of promises, of covenants, of sacrifices, of nations against other nations. The god of armies and blood has overshadowed the god or gods of the strife for a truth that unifies and gives life insofar as it wants to be sought and loves confrontation, rather than a truth that divides and kills because it claims an unchangeable identity for itself and practices authoritarian imposition. This other and almost secret god, who in fact loves to hide, not to be put aside, but instead to make human beings part of his enigmatic destiny, has nevertheless continued to speak with the deep and patient voice of the truth that human beings search, for and of which they speak. This is the truth that does not let itself be reduced to a human scale; rather, it continues, as long as it is truth, to spur human beings beyond their being human. It is thus not like the god of the sacred who bans and destroys. Rather, it is like the god who welcomes and gathers the differences he gives rise to in the reciprocity he protects, in mutual respect for the neighbor as well as for the stranger, because any neighbor is in fact a stranger, needy of attention and care. Likewise, any stranger is a neighbor, involved in the conversation that we are, capable of bringing us the word we have not yet heard, and of asking us for the one we still owe to him or her. *This is the sacred of the event of the other.* This has been prophesized by all prophetic voices that human beings will never stop waiting and looking for as they are reminded by the power of words of truth and life that cannot be suffocated even by the blood and suffering they have cost. "Jerusalem, who kills the prophets." This will be so at least until human beings each live off *the desire for the differing other,* that is, off *the experience of the divine* that any encounter with others can disclose; when the alterity of the other existence (the mystery of the other inhabiting the other's being and rendering it sacred, inviolable for us) reveals itself in such a deep and ineludible way as to refer us to the discovery of the other in ourselves, the other than ourselves, by whom we exist, whether we know it or not, for ourselves and for others. *Ethos anthropo daimon:* the archaic word can perhaps be translated as such: "the divine is the dwelling place of the human."

The divine god of the sacred who unifies without oppression, who gathers without confusion or reduction to a coerced identity, whose differing opens itself up as the divine of differences in human existence: is this perhaps the extreme experimentation with the divine that is allowed for human beings? Is or can this be recognized as the "last god" thought of by Heidegger? Or is this instead to be thought and awaited as a new god? Yet, still a god, one more god? Have we not known enough of them? Are we not done with gods? In truth, the absent god is the divine god that has always been in the sense that such a godhead has made its mystery present always again at the bottom of any revelation and religious experience. Its continuity has nothing in it of a simple, fixed presence, of the immobility of a presumed permanent being. On the contrary, it is the recognition that the ancient experience of the divine finds in the novelty of the always differing interpretations it provokes. Such interpretations are yet capable of referring one to the other, be it among difficulties and contrasts. Nor can such continuity fix once and for all at least the general traits of the face of the god we would like to revere or of the divine by which we would like to be loved and welcome. We would like to make sure that its mystery does not obfuscate its goodness, that the iniquity of history is conquered by its justice. Yet what is goodness, and what is justice? We know that the possibility of existence for which we must answer is realized by taking part in the revelation of his mystery in mutual conversation. This is the divine we experience in the days of life that are allotted to us. Therefore, we must live [*esistere*] the propitious absence of the godhead that has no face because it has all the faces with which it discloses itself every time at the appropriate time (the time of *kairos*), yet without letting itself be identified by any. It "is" not with its own definable identity, yet it "comes and goes" as the divine of all experiences in which the wonderful and tremendous truth of the possibility of existing in "the other" is announced to human beings. "God is day night, winter summer, war peace, satiety hunger; he undergoes alteration in the way that fire, when it is mixed with spices, is named according to the scent of each of them." We have already heard this word about the god of opposite predicates, yet it must come back in the conclusion. It reminds us that the god of *polemos*, father and lord of different destinies, is the god of the event that marks for human beings the sacred time of the revelation of being that has been entrusted to us. Yet, the truth of good and evil, of which one is called on to decide, remains inexorably hidden to all in the depth of its secret. This is the truth of a destiny that fulfills itself beyond one's knowledge because one cannot know of it but that which is revealed. The rest is in the hands of the eventual god, who perhaps reveals it to others while keeping hidden from them further revelations that are not destined to them.

Notes

1. Trans. note: The author uses the term "existence" (*esistenza*), as well as its plural, "existences" (*esistenze*), to evoke what Heidegger would capture in the term "*Dasein*."

2. Trans. note: By hyphenating the word "ver-dict" (*ver-detto*) the author is playing on the double meaning of the term (which results from the two roots *verum* and *dictum*) as both verdict and truth (*ver*)-saying (*detto*).

3. Friedrich Hölderlin, *Friedensfeier*, second draft, vv. 73–74.

4. Friedrich Hölderlin, *Patmos*, vv. 1–2: "*Nah ist / und schwer zu fassen der Gott.*"

5. Sophocles, *Antigone*, vv. 337–39.

6. The effort of Bonhoeffer's extreme theology, that of the letters from prison in *Letters from Prison*, trans. R. Fuller (New York: MacMillan, 1967), consists in the attempt to free Christianity from its historical destiny as *Erlösungsreligion*. I refer to Mario Ruggenini, "Assenza di Dio? La crisi della teologia da Nietzsche a Bonhoeffer," in *Bonhoeffer e la comunità del cuore*, ed. R. Panattoni (Padua: Il Poligrafo, 1999), pp. 53–78.

7. Aristotle, *Politics* 1253a14–18.

8. Sophocles, *Antigone*, vv. 353–55, 364–71.

9. Aristotle, *Politics* 1253a9–10; *On the Heavens* I, 4, 271a33.

10. Heraclitus, fr. 119.

11. John 8:31–33.

12. Heraclitus, fr. 53.

13. Heraclitus, fr. 32.

14. Heraclitus, fr. 67.

15. John 6:38–39; 8:26–28; 12:44–50; 14:10, 29.

16. Heraclitus, fr. 93.

17. "*Die Frömmigkeit des Denkens*" [the piety of thought] is Heidegger's felicitous expression. See Martin Heidegger, "The Question Concerning Technology," in *The Question Concerning Technology and Other Essays*, trans. W. Lovitt (New York: Harper and Row, 1977), p. 35.

Chapter 8

Transcendental Without Illusion

Or, The Absence of the Third Person

Marco Maria Olivetti

A t first, I had thought I would devote my chapter to a theme that could
have been aptly titled "The Rationality of the Third Person." In this
chapter, I think I have addressed the theme I had in mind. I thought it
would be more appropriate, however, to present my considerations under the
current title. Despite the equivocal genitive, a title such as "The Rationality
of the Third Person," might have led one to think of an "unarguable" transcendental: a transcendental that would enable the I (the "I-think") to place
itself in the position of the judge and of the thirdness by definition characterizing such a position, thereby playing on two tables and acting simultaneously as part and judge, first and third person.

The title I finally chose for my considerations may sound a bit discon-
solate. In truth, it only wishes to invite a giving up of philosophy as consolation, a giving up of the perversion of the *melete thanatou* [practice of death][1]
into tranquillizer and analgesic. Precisely this has been, instead, for the most
part and in actuality, the function played by transcendental thinking.

To renounce philosophy as consolation does not at all mean to renounce the consolation of philosophy, even the edification of philosophy.
Perhaps it does not even mean to renounce the transcendental. However, if
philosophy can and must be a minister of consolation, that is, if it must
ad-minister but, even prior to this, if it must have such a *munus*—in both
senses of the word: this gift to give, but, even before, this duty to fulfill—if
philosophy must have this *munus* of consolation and edification, this is only
because philosophy *responds* to an ought. It does not have the first word—
proto-logia—but rather it is response. It responds with a word that literally
"puts protology into place," not by dissolving it (far from it!) but by inscrib-
ing it and by showing its grammatical character (*gramme*). It inscribes it into
a nonencompassable anteriority. One could also say, it inscribes it *between* a
nonencompassable anteriority and posteriority. It inscribes it, in sum, in an

interim that paradoxically gives protology an interim, interlocutory character (as we shall see, in the sense of both provisionality and interlocution).

This means to renounce the transcendental as an illusion, in addition to renouncing the "transcendental illusion" of Kantian resonance because this latter illusion—the *transzendentale Schein*—follows directly from the former. The transcendental as illusion is the thought of a transcendental apperception that directly intends, contains, conceives, and maybe constitutes the object: the aimed-at object, the object of *theorein*.

Of course, the term "transcendental" is a *pollachos legomenon* [a term used in many ways] (as, on the other hand, all human words are). This word "transcendental" has been uttered repeatedly in the context of a philosophy of being, a philosophy of the subject, and, recently, even a philosophy of linguistic communication (the "synthesis of communication" as transformation of the "synthesis of the apperception," according to Apel's program of *Transformation der Philosophie*). However, even in the latter case, that is, even in the case of the synthesis of communication, one does not escape the illusion of the transcendental by which the I (*ego*; *Ich*) anticipates the third: the I anticipates the third and its rationality infinitely, *unbegrenzt* (think of Apel's *unbegrenzte Kommunikationsgemeinschaft* [unlimited community of communication]), playing on two tables simultaneously and arrogating thirdness for itself: arrogating instead of really asking, better, instead of responding.

"Transcendental without illusion" means the radically responsive and responsible character of the subject—or the I, or the person, to use *pollachos legomena* that will have to be resemanticized within the context of the discourse I wish to advance. It is so radical a responsibility that it can be stated only through the expression "responsibility for responsibility." One is responsible not so much, and not in the first place, for something, but for someone. That means for those who are responsible, in place of those who are responsible, and so that *there may be* those who are responsible.

In its formalizing, universalizing, increasing, and multiplying reduplication, responsibility for responsibility may well be said to be "transcendental," as long as this does not induce the illusion of a subject-object structure having a theoretical, content-wise encompassing, conceiving, and grasping character. One should rather think of a subject-subject structure, of intersubjectivity—to use words that, however, once again will have to be resemanticized, freeing them of the illusion of which they have been charged in the tradition of an analgesic philosophy.

The first resematicization would be that of immediately connecting intersubjectivity—and the term "intersubjectivity"—to theology. To be able to think of God, one must think of intersubjectivity, and to think of intersubjectivity, one must think of God. This is the thesis that subtends all my present considerations.

I have purposefully employed the indirect and nontechnical expression "to think of" ("to think of intersubjectivity," "to think of God"), rather than the direct technical expression in which the verb "to think" is followed by the direct object ("to think intersubjectivity," "to think God"). The latter is a mode of expression more apt for an objective scientific discourse, which one should rightly expect here, but which, in the terms of direct thinking, would risk not being sufficiently critical and criticistic.

The "I think," the *cogito*, the *ich denke* thinks directly and objectively: *ego cogito cogitata* [I think thoughts]. Like King Midas, who turned into gold everything he touched, the thinking subject—the modern subject, the "subject" according to the modern resemanticization of the term—thematizes, objectifies—it "thinks," precisely in the technical sense, everything *about which* it thinks.

Yet, if some *cogitata* [thoughts] escape or cannot be grasped in and by thinking as "I think," these are precisely intersubjectivity and God. *Pros-logion*, *con-fession*: the intersubjective, better interlocutory and praying character of what, from Kant on, has been called the "ontological argument" has been forgotten in the same way in which its transcendentality without illusion has been forgotten. "*Ergo Domine non solum es quo maius cogitari nequit, sed es quiddam maius quam cogitari possit* [Therefore o Lord, *you are* not only that than which a greater cannot be thought, but *you are* also a being greater than can be thought]."² *You are*—you are—greater than what can be thought. To think of, to address oneself to, does not mean to think, to conceive, to catch that good "*quo melius cogitari nequit* [than which a better cannot be thought]" (where the declination into *melius* [better], which is present also in Anselm and, even before, in Augustine's *Confessions*, better marks the transcendental limit beyond which one thinks of an absolute, that is, a qualitative, and not quantitative-extensive transcendence). Not to be able to think anything greater or better does not mean that you can be thought: "but you are *quiddam maius quam cogitari possit*" [a being greater than can be thought].

Intersubjectivity and God are ungraspable not only, and certainly not in the *first* place, because they are *thought* of as ungraspable. This is only a consequence, a "wretched" consequence. It is only a wretched consequence because richness is neither in the *ousia*, that is, in substances that one can possess—as the collective singular indicates in Greek—nor in the substantiality that one claims as "proper" [*propria*].³ Richness is in the nonpossession of that to which one is attracted, in its attraction escaping the essencing [*essenziante*] grasp and pretense of thought: *epekeina tes ousias* [beyond being]. To think of, to address oneself to, does not reach that which attracts, does not constitute it by intentioning it. Rather, it is constituted by the attraction exerted by that which transcends it.

That which attracts and transcends "thinking of" is not properly "that which," but "the one who" attracts and transcends it. It does not respond to the question "what?" (the metaphysical *ti esti* [what is it?]), and, in a way, it does not respond, but rather elicits and provokes the question "who?" One should perhaps say: *tis ei* (who are you)? With respect to this phrase, two remarks can be made, one regarding the voice of the verb "to be" that resonates in this question, and the other regarding the "second person" that would seem to resonate as this very voice.

The voice of the verb "to be" that is used in the eventuation of the question "who?" should not be overestimated. Unlike the *ti esti* of ontological metaphysics, what matters in this nonmetaphysical-ontological question—in this question that responds to the appeal—is not the verb "to be" but rather the interrogative pronoun "who?": an interrogative, and not *simply* a personal pronoun like the "I" of the transcendental subject. It is a personal interrogative pronoun, of course, yet it is not subordinate to the "what?" as a specification of the kind "thing," which would enjoy the privilege of being *first* genus and then also species. It is a pronoun—"who?"—whose standing in place of a noun should not be interpreted in the first place as a request for information regarding essence, as a curious need or desire for a designation and duplication of the *res* [object] through a *nomen* [name]. In the pronoun "who?" the standing in place of a noun is interrogative: a nonstanding, an instability, a not having an *ubi consistam* [place where to stand], and it should be understood first of all or, better, beforehand—before any protology— as a *request* for essence, *essance*, and standing.

It is a noncurious need; it is rather a literally alimentary need (it seems that King Midas actually had alimentary problems). It is a need for "alimentation" in the ordinary sense of nourishment and in the sense of the passive form *ali*, "to be sustained" and "raised," and sustained *insofar* as one is augmented. This latter sense, however, is neither different from that of everyday bread or maternal milk (is maternal milk a "what" or a "who?") nor more abstract than they, but only more general. Or better: it is the "full" sense, which vivifies the "literal" sense, and makes the literal sense be not "abstract" and, therewith, dead, even killed: human beings live not only by bread alone, but by every word that comes out of the mouth of . . . whom? The question, as one can see, does not respond to a mere curiosity. It is pressing: life is at stake in it.

The question "who?" does not express a curiosity. It is pretheoretical, anterior to *thaumazein* [wondering] as protology. It is anterior of an anteriority that, if it is well expressed in the usual adverb of the transcendental lexicon "always already," nevertheless does not indicate—in the *first* place—a need for information, but rather—beforehand—a need for authorization in all senses: in the ordinary sense of "being authorized by . . . ," "being authorized to . . . ," "being authorized with. . . ." Yet, all this is precisely in the full, vital, and not only literal, that is, essentially killed sense. It is a need for authorization as authorization for one's own very existence, a need for authorization of existence in itself and as one's own, existence as need and lack, that is, need for *augeri*, for being augmented by an *auctoritas* [authority] insofar as one is legitimized by it. And one is legitimized to exist insofar as one receives a law from the *auctoritas*, which is *auctoritas* insofar as it dictates laws. It commands, it gives a mandate, insofar as it sends [*manda*]. It sends to others: to augment others and to provide aliments to others. It sends as aliment for the others.

Being, that is, the voice of the verb "to be," matters only as personalized, I would like to say "personed," that is, made to resonate in the inter-locution, unfolded by the inter-locution, that is, folded in this *inter-*, in this in-between. In fact, despite all appearance and all *transzendentale Schein* [transcendental appearing] of a representational-visual-theoretical-synoptical kind, the interval of the interlocution is an *interim*: a diachrony, an interval that is nonspatializable-representable-synchronizable-graspable by a look that the inevitable transcendental illusion and the inevitable illusion of the transcendental make appear as launched from "nowhere."

As there would not and could not be, therefore, *res cogitans* [a thinking thing] if not in the first person—insofar as *cogito*—analogously, there would not and could not be "who?" if not in the person and—dare I say—in the "personation" [*personazione*] of the voice.

The voice of the verb "to be" that resounds in the eventuation of the question "who?" should not be overestimated because what truly counts, what matters in truth—what is "worth" and is *fragwürdig* [uncertain]—is "who?" (it is very well possible that the specialists might want to find a reprehensible nihilistic *déjà vu* in my discourse so far. This does not seem to be the case to me, though).

If "who?" gives itself only in person—in and to the question in which it eventuates itself and for the "first" time comes to being—we must return to ask ourselves in which person the voice of the verb "to be" will resound in the eventuating question—will resound "in truth." Maybe will it resound, as we were saying, in the "second person" ("who are you?")? But it is not so simple; the issue is undoubtedly more com-plicated.

Once we have moved or, if we want, regressed from the *cogito* to the *loquor* [I speak]—from the principle of *cogito* to the fact of *loquor*—presence is no longer the presumably simple presence of the *cogitata* to the *cogito* and of the *cogito* to itself as *sum*. In the fact of speaking, presence is essentially diachronic. Presence is essentially diachronic of a diachrony that cannot be synchronized in transcendental consciousness and cannot even be made symmetrical in the communicative transcendental. Presence is in fact essentially diachronic also and first of all in the instant of the event, that is, in the instant of the question "who?," of the request for alimentation and authorization.

The "instant" is thus by antiphrasis, and the instant is as antiphrasis. It is an instant that properly does not stay and that does not stand properly on its own; rather, it turns, and moreover, turns itself toward the other. Of course, the question "who?" turns itself toward something other—*aliud*—as the other—*alter, alter ego, alter loquens* [other speaker]. This is so precisely insofar as it turns [si volge] on its turn; it ad-dresses [si ri-volge] and responds. Yet, this does not signify the stability of a personal identity. It does not indicate a similarity subsequent to one's own identity and to identity as one's own. This would be an initiating and protological identity that would enable mirroring oneself in the *alter ego* by looking in his or her face, by seeing oneself in the idea, that is, the idea of oneself. Even less does the turning of the question "who?" toward the other mean the stability of two personal identities, different yet assimilated to each other through the transcendental, synchronizing look, which is cast from nowhere according to that symmetry of the communicative transcendental for which—as some have remarked—the *ego* is the *alter ego* of the *alter*. As response, "who?" is a need for a *sponsio* [promise, commitment] that literally "embodies itself" as question: a question that responds to the *sponsio*, to the ob-liging covenant that is knotted by the appeal.

In the fact of speaking, therefore, there is a complication and a co-implication of persons that is "essentially" and "literally" in-explicable, that is, nonsimplifiable (*sine plica*) because in the co-implication the persons essence themselves [si *essenziano*], and in such a co-implication the very scene of being, that is, of interlocution, unfolds, explicates [*dispiega*], that is, implicates [*implica*] itself.

Of course, "grammatically" the person giving voice to the question and personifying the question addresses the "who?" as a second person ("who *are* *you*?"). Yet this essential grammaticality signals exactly the secondariness of the question of being. "Essential grammaticality" means, of course, not speculative grammar, but rather ironical grammar, although in a peculiar sense that does not exclude seriousness. Rather, it demands the extreme sole seriousness: true seriousness, the seriousness of truth. "Essential grammaticality" means the deuteronomic, always already grammatical and obedient character of the essence ("it is written").

The responding (*re-spondere*), that is, obedient (*ob-audire*) question "who?" is not a simple and impertinent "who are you?" This initial, obligationless question would not be a response: it would not respond to anyone and would be irresponsible. It would, once again, be the protological, theoretical question, in which the questioning "I" mirrors itself: a suppository question that, by supposing the stability of the I, maybe thinks, but does not speak because it has no need; that is, it has no need to speak.

The obedient question is instead a response. It is "itself" thus complicated and implicated. It is not simple in its "own" identity—in its sameness and its ipseity. Only in such a coimplication, "who?" is, it essences itself [si *essenzia*]: both question and response at the same time, in a complication that is, precisely, the diachrony of presence, of the same time.

True response, response that "in truth" listens to the appeal, would not be that which subordinates obedience to the exhibition of ontologically sufficient and satisfactory—satisfying, *satis*—credentials. That is, it would not be that which obeys on the condition that, first, the appeal obeys the impertinence

and supposition of the ontological and protological question "who are you?"
The response is an unconditioned surrender to the appeal. It is restitution
without residual of what the appeal gives, that is, of "who?" that is instituted
through the obligation and as obligation by the self-giving of the *sponsio*.

In the obedience to the obligation that is instituted by the *sponsio*, in
listening, turning toward the other, "who?" essences itself [*si essenzia*] and
consists for the first time. It is an ally, we could say an accomplice (*cum-
plica*), of the instituting *sponsio*. It stands insofar as it dis-poses itself [*si dis-
pone*] completely, in its own person, personed by the appeal, re-sponding
with a second word and existing in truth only as this response and unconditioned surrender.

If the surrender is however unconditioned—"here I am!" (Exodus 3:4), and
not "who are you?"—where does the interrogative character of what is "truly"
worth and "in truth" *fragwürdig* come from? Why would the response that
listens to an appeal be a question if such a *responsio* essentializes itself as
unconditioned surrender and thus is interrogative neither with respect to the
respondent, who makes himself or herself available, nor with respect to the
auctoritas, which gives disposition [*disposizione*]?

Were the complication of presence simply the interval between two
persons, the response could not be at the same time a question. And "the
same time" would not truly be diachrony, truth of presence, but would only,
better simply (*sine plica*) be the two I's objective copresence to the transcendental, synchronizing and symmetry-making look that comes from nowhere.
"Who?" is *fragwürdig* and worthwhile, that is, the response is at the same
time the question because the third is always present in the *interim* of the
interlocution. The *interim* thus is not *Zwiefalt*, duplicity, but rather *Dreifältigkeit*
[trinity] and triplicity. The third to whom the authoritative appeal sends is
present as absent, is "essentially" present as absent.

A different *ergo* is implied in the fact of *loquor*. It is an implication not
simply different from the egoic-ontological implication of the *sum*, which
synchronically coincides with the *cogito*—or anyway is different from the
implication of the transcendental apperception as horizon of presence. It is
an implication that is different also diachronically: deferment and difference,
which, in truth, is complication of presence and co-implication of three
persons. Such a co-implication is anterior to the being it defers, anterior to
the grammar that literally is inscribed in it. The transcendental without
illusion would be more a complicated fold than a synthesis. The different
ergo of the *loquor* might perhaps resound in the referential metonymy *sum?*—
praees—*abest* [Am I?—You direct—it is absent].

The eventuating-transcendental question "who?" personifies itself as
response to the mandate that sends [*manda*] the I to the third, and because
of this, the response is a question. One's making oneself available, "here I
am," is at the same time "who am I?" (Exodus 3:11: "Who am I that I should

go to the Pharaoh, and bring the children of Israel out of Egypt?"). Not "who are you?" and which ontological credentials do you show to the supposing and supposed "I," but rather "who am I?"

Who am I to be? Who am I to speak words of truth to the third person (whoever is he or she? Who are the absent, those who are not?)? Who am I to make myself a neighbor to "who?" reaching as far as the third person, alimenting him or her, giving him or her being?

In sum, at this point temporalization imposes itself: who am I to be able to say "I will be"? Temporalization imposes itself: the anterior appeal—anterior to being, *epekeina tes ousias*, immemorially anterior to being and to transcendental consciousness, *unvordenklich*—calls myself to being by sending me. The authority of my word (objective genitive), the sustenance that renders it present to the third making it persevere—persevere in being and truth: persevere yet as an aliment, and yet aliment that does not end, aliment for the third person, food of eternal life—this authority is not in me—who am I?—but rather outside of me, in the exteriority or radical anteriority from where the call to being, the anterior appeal comes, to which I reply "I am present." Outside of me, prior to me, and yet by me: "I will be with you" (Exodus 3:12). Temporalization imposes itself. The anterior *sponsio* gives itself. It gives itself as warrantee and promise to the response-question that it itself provokes. The commandment that sends to the third is a covenant.

Not "who are you?" but rather "who am I?" Similarly, not "who is the third?" but rather, "what will I respond to the third when the third asks me who sends me?" (See Exodus 3:13.)

Not "who is the third?" Indeed the third is absent, and I do not know who he or she is. Neither can I summon the third onto the scene of interlocution—summon "who?" Nor can I make the third present by calling him or her to being: who am I to have such a power? I can look at the third in his or her face (and mirror myself there, speculate) as little as I can see in its face the anteriority from where the appeal comes. In this, the third to whom I am sent is similar to the command. In fact, the third is the *content* of the command (on the other hand, how could a command without content be given or how could it be?). The similarity is not that of a face one can see (as in the objectifying synchrony or in the theoretical mirroring of the *ego* into the *alter*). The similarity—the true similarity, the veri-similarity, the similarity as truth[4]—is precisely in this impossibility to see the face.

As the obedient question—the question that is response and making oneself available—does not ask "who are you?" but rather "who am I?"; *similarly* the obedient question does not ask "who is the third?" but rather "what will I respond to the third?"

The temporalizing anticipation of myself as response is still a question: "what will I respond?" This anticipatory question, however, is not an anticipation of *my* question. Rather, it is anticipation of the question of the third, who asks by whom I have been sent. It is care for the third; it is question that obeys the command. What is in question ("what will I respond?") is once again my authorization: "what will I respond to the third when he or she will ask me about the name of the one who sends me?"

The request of the third thus interrogatively anticipated—is it a "what" or a "who"? The request is the request of the authoritative name: not a name that doubles the thing by making it "common" or by "rigidly designating it," but rather a name as being, and essence, and *essance* of the sender, a sender who is anticipated as third on the scene on which the third is anticipated as interlocutor and questioner to whom I must respond ("which is the name of the one who sends you?"). It is a perfect and fulfilled similarity between the form and the content of the command (*cum-mandare*).

The surrender to the appeal is not conditioned by the exhibition of ontological credentials on the part of the imperative call; the exhibition of ontological credentials is nevertheless a condition to have the authority to speak to the third person, that is, to aliment the third person, that is, to be (being = aliment).

The eventuation of "Who?" is neither "who are you?" nor "who is it?" nor "who *am* I?" if this question has to be understood in the sense of a precedence or priority of being with respect to the person to whom being would give essence. It is not even "who am I?" (in this sense) because I *will* only *be*. Better put, I will be *if* I will be: I will be on condition that I make myself without conditions, on condition that I make myself available as nourishment. I will be if I relinquish *my* life.

"I will be with you" is the response to the question "who am I?"—a response that repeats the *sponsio* of the question and gives itself as promise. Similarly, the response to the question that anticipates the request of the third—"what will I respond?"—repeats the *sponsio* and gives it as a name, that is, it gives it for the third.

The name, in fact, is not—"essentially" it is not—for me or for you who speak to each other and look into each other's face. Essentially—in essence—the name is for the third and of the third, who does not interlocute, and yet is always present as absent (how could one speak without names?). The name is for the third so that he or she can call. It is of the third so that he or she can be called.

The repetition of the *sponsio* as a promise for and of (objective genitive) the third gives itself as name, gives itself as essence. Immersion in being, baptism in spirit and truth.

The self-giving of "Who?" as name—"I am who I am," or however one should translate it—is not *spekulativer Satz* (the Hegelian "speculative proposition" in which subject and predicate, particular and universal *convertuntur* [converge]). It is in the first person, and it is a name, or rather, a proper name. The proper name is the promise for the third, and the promise of the third. It is giving oneself as essence; it is making oneself neighbor to the absent; it is aliment to the third; it is writing, flesh, living letter.

But this is theology, not philosophy, some will say. I would rather say that the name is response. The question, and precisely the astonished (*thaumazein*) and metaphysical—but not metaphysical-ontological—question "who?" is appropriate (*ad-propriare, zu-eignen*) to philosophy.

One can certainly distrust this question that mimics the *ti esti* of ontological metaphysics by echoing it through a personal pronoun (echoing it? What, however, is the echo of whom?). One can distrust this question that is expressed through a personal, interrogative, interlocutory, interim pronoun, which is furthermore emptied of the verb "to be." It is a personal pronoun that may seem to imply a "personal ascription" (as Anglophone philosophy, following Strawson, likes to say). And one may admit that it implies this, as long as the ascription is understood in a precategorial sense. The interlocution is not apophasis. "Who?" is not *ti esti*. "Personal ascription" is an expression that discounts the grammar in which the speaker is always already inscribed. In a grammared (and thus meaningful) way, it projects writing—*ad-scribes*—beyond the scene that is appropriate to it and within which alone meaning is proper/one's own.

One can certainly distrust these considerations on the personal, interrogative pronoun "who?" These considerations are expressed through what one might come to call "grammatical metaphors," yet after all speculative grammar has been dissolved. Actually, the affirmation of the precedence of the deponent form *loquor* over the active *cogito* amounts to the radical dissolution of the possibility of relying on the transcendental character of grammar at the same time as such affirmation prevents reference to metaphors in the traditional meaning of the term "metaphor," which implies the proper and original connotation of the employed terms.

One may distrust. Nevertheless, "Who?" is a precise question. It is the question of a questioning subject, who is itself in question. Such a subject is not the subject of the *cogito* and of *theoria*, but of response and responsibility.

The subject that responds and is responsible responds to someone ("someone": personal, indefinite pronoun) and is responsible in front of someone before being responsible for something. But also: before being responsible for something, the responsible subject is responsible for someone ("indefinite" personal pro-noun, so indefinite that the name is missing). Responsibility for responsibility. Transcendental responsibility. Apparently—*scheinbar*—empty responsibility, and, on the contrary, itself without illusion, without transcendental *Schein*.

To ask the question *ti esti* is already an act of high responsibility—a putting responsibility into being as one's own—in the same way as it is, later, the possible response to this question. To ask the question *ti esti* is already a way of responding to "Who?" and of being responsible in front of "Who?"

Yet- it is certainly an insufficient way when it remains trapped in protology. Protology is always already inscribed ("always already": this beautiful adverb from the transcendental tradition is apparently, *scheinbar*, a *lucus a non lucendo* [dark grove]). Protology is itself always already response. An always insufficient response, always *schuldig* [guilty], always unable to extinguish its debt. "Who?" will save us from the insufficiency of the response?

Despite the appearance, the *Schein*, the question "Who?" is thus a very precise question that, however, despite the inevitable transcendental illusion, should not be mistaken for the question "who is my neighbor?" This is a very similar question, if similarity and image are ever given. Yet it cannot be mistaken, if one does not want to fall into the transcendental illusion and into the transcendental as illusion. "Who?" is not the subject of *Paarung*, of "peering," not even of an "analogic" kind (to use Husserl's famous expression), until it eventuates itself as an appeal. In the question "who is my neighbor?" predication, that is, the concept, is already functioning (the universal "my neighbor": universal that is empty, on the ground of its reference to me, that is, to the utterer; thus, the answer that is appropriate to the question radicalizes the pragmatic and "opaque" character of the question, making it retrace the parabola at the end of which there is the I that, in the eventuation, makes itself a neighbor to "Who?"). Such a functioning of predication already shows the presence of the ontological *ti esti*; it is, I hope, a concerned and responsible presence; yet, possibly, it is irresponsible and tempting. In this latter case, it is the *diaballein* [slander, perversion] that always already presupposes that which it perverts. Although it is not to be mistaken with the question "Who?," nevertheless, prior to any possible perversion, the concerned and responsible question "Who is my neighbor?" represents the parabola of the former that makes the latter understandable.

Despite the appearance, the *Schein*, the question "Who?" is a very precise question. Actually, the very problem of appearing presents itself in it: an appearing that is always already intersubjective, so to speak, because the responsible subject, in whose consciousness all appearing appears, is subject to "Who?"

Notes

1. *Phadeo* 84a.
2. Anselm, *Proslogion*, XV.
3. Trans. note: The term "proprio," which we have rendered as "proper," refers both to propriety and to property.
4. Trans. note: The author is here playing with the words *vero/verisimile/verità*.

Chapter 9

Finitude and Responsibility

For an Ethics of the Finite in the Time of Risk

SALVATORE NATOLI

The Magnificent and Progressive Destinies

Technics is not something external to human beings; it is rather their distinctive mark, their *originary and original* feature. The human species has not become extinct because it has adapted to the environment; but unlike other animal species, it has adapted the environment to itself, modifying it to its own advantage. This constitutes a sufficient reason to say, the human being is an *artificial* animal par excellence or, more exactly, is the artificial being *by nature*. It has, in fact, selected itself as a species by forcing nature *with its own hands*; it has manipulated it in the etymological sense of the term, bending it to its own needs. Anaxagoras said it well at the beginning of philosophy when he wrote: "The human being is the wisest of the living beings *because it has hands*." That human beings force nature is demonstrated by the pure and simple fact that they draw from it beings, objects, and things that nature would have never produced by itself. Technics is thus that kind of *making* that we generally define as *producing*. And because it coincides with "putting into being" something that nature by itself would never generate, the *artificial* is precisely opposed to the natural. Through technics, human beings have slowly emancipated themselves from the constrictions of necessity. From this perspective, technics is really the offspring of need, and therefore, ever since the beginning, presents itself as "expedient," as "discovery."

The human being has thus always and *by nature* been an artificial being. Indeed, our civilization would not be what it is without technics. What does it mean then when one speaks of the age of technics if technics characterizes more or less any epoch of humankind and humankind in general as a species? We have had many world epochs, but never before had

161

technics so deeply characterized the spirit of the time, never had it marked an epoch as in the two past centuries. What are the reasons for this?

In the course of the nineteenth century, the successes of technics began to be widely observed. During that period, however, technics was associated directly with science, and it was almost entirely absorbed by the latter. The binomial "science and technics" was inseparable, and the naming of many museums proves it. The formulation was clearly of Enlightenment derivation, where the apology of science as "true knowledge" rested on technics understood as the moment of its simple application. During the Enlightenment the metaphor of light was dominant; science as true knowledge had the task of dissipating the darkness of ignorance through critique, of enlightening to attain undebatable and well-grounded truth. Between the nineteenth and twentieth centuries things quickly changed, however: the "realizations of science," that is to say the increasingly and in certain respects impetuous unfolding of its applicative aspects—that is, the results that were visible also for the one who was not a scientist—progressively shadowed the sublime and intellectualistic metaphor of light in favor of the celebration, in some cases even rhetorical, of the *actual enlightenment*: gas and electricity, concrete realizations, perceivable by everybody and thus mark and symbol of the nineteenth century. Technics has rendered science prosaic at the very moment when it has transformed it into a world. Meanwhile, as "practical power," it has become *destiny*. From here comes the inevitable retreating of the image of science as "critical knowledge"—of Enlightenment matrix—in favor of technics as "manipulative-imposing" power. By virtue of its own results, technics has turned into *mythical mask* of science. In the popular imagination, it slowly configures itself as an unconditioned power of manipulation, and therefore as domination without conditions on human beings and things. As with any power, it is good or bad according to circumstances.

From here derives the implant of a misunderstanding: the naïve fascination with the effects has given place to a kind of *technological imaginary* linking salvation and terror. This masking has nourished naïve hopes, and meanwhile has favored general and superficial demonizations. In any event, it has diverted attention from science as effective practice, as investigative exercise of a correct rationality. Obscuring the humility of science—which only knows little, no matter how much it knows—in the eyes of many, technics has increasingly manifested itself as an impersonal and blind power, capable of manipulating the world without limits. Technics is not such, but every story contains some truth. By virtue of its increasing power, technics has brought civilization under its sign, has become the measure thereof. Held within such a power, the epoch understands and defines itself as the "age of technics."

According to Heidegger, technics consists in *imposition*. The dangers that it brings, however, depend not so much on machines and devices, but rather on the fact that technics affects the human being in its essence. "The rule of Enframing threatens man with the possibility that it could be denied to him to enter into a more original revealing and hence to experience the call of a more primal truth."[1] I intend to discuss neither Heidegger's position, nor what he means by "more original." Rather, I only intend to indicate "under which conditions" technics, forever and simply known as applied science and transformative ability, has changed itself into *epoch*.

In the course of the nineteenth century science had already begun to manifest itself as an increasing power of manipulation. These mutations, especially when opposed to the Romantic past, already retained a character of prodigy. The nineteenth century is the age of glass and cast iron—two among the most recent technological conquests—and with them, of the blazing of light: "Aside from the great quantity of lights maintained by the merchants."[2]

With its unforeseeable successes, science was definitely bringing to an end the world of spirit or, to say it with Nietzsche, spirit as the "behind-the-world." At the same time, science was rendering the heaviest matter spiritual: intelligence takes up a body in the machine, and the spiritual embodies itself in things, animates them. This epochal change does not escape Walter Benjamin when he remarks on a notation by Meyer with relation to the construction of the Eiffel Tower: "Thus the plastic shaping power abdicates here *in favor of a colossal span of spiritual energy, which channels the inorganic material energy into the smallest, most efficient forms* and conjoins these forms in the most effective manner . . . (A. G. Meyer, *Eisenbauten*, p. 93)."[3]

As spiritual, technics is anticipation and project; it is thereby innovation by excellence. In its results, it constitutes "novelty." Together with the indubitable advantages that it brings, however, it produces unavoidable inconveniences. This is an uneasiness that between the end of the nineteenth century and the beginning of the twentieth century still appeared only to few, but that slowly shapes a collective preoccupation. Human beings entrust themselves to technics to gain greater safety; paradoxically, they find themselves among devices that develop counterfinalities. For us today, the discoveries of technics do not present themselves any longer the way they did in the nineteenth century. They are no longer marks of *progress*. On the contrary, the successes of technics are largely taken for granted, appearing even too few with regard to the never satisfied wishes of the present. There is instead a new, different perception: we are more easily tempted to associate the discoveries of technics with the dangers that it induces, and thus we fear and meanwhile love such discoveries. No one in fact is able to resist the benefits deriving from it. Hence, one encounters an unavoidable, inextricable vicious circle.

The Ruling of the Improbable

Given such coordinates, a formulation such as "age of technics" seems to me to be already underdetermined to identify our contemporaneity, to describe the phenomena characterizing it. The formulation that better defines the present is "age of risk." In the course of modernity technics has been usually associated with progress. Today, this is an idea that is definitely passé and with it is the perception of technics as factor and motor of human emancipation. The idea of *progress* has become *epoch* and has characterized the path of modernity in its complexity only when the various human experiences have been ideally and forcedly channeled into one direction, the different vectors of temporality have been oriented toward a single and final goal: *humankind as freed*, if not from death, then at least from precariousness and need; evidently from evil and, perhaps, from pain. Especially in its last stage, the ideology of progress has increasingly identified itself with technics: a power that, at first sight, is "neutral," that is refuted by no one; indeed, it is considered by many to be irrefutable. For this reason it is considered the most powerful and can indifferently be associated with communism as well as with the consumeristic society with the logic of justice as well as with that of opulence. Today technics, which in the nineteenth century was associated with the idea of progress, determines itself completely differently and combines itself more exactly and better with the notion of *catastrophe*. This occurs in several ways for the simple reason that the term "catastrophe" has a wide semantics covering different meanings.

"Catastrophe" can be understood at least in two ways. The current meaning is that of "ruin." It is a precipitating into disaster, a falling into nothingness or, at least, a dissolving and resolving oneself into nothing that can be used. In Greek, however, the verb *katastrepho* means "to unfold until the end," "to terminate." Of course, one can end by extenuation or upsetting, and the result is dissolution. Yet the term "catastrophe," understood as the unfolding of something until the end, also has a different and not less precise meaning: it is indeed an upheaval, yet in the sense of a "change of direction," a *turn*. In this case, it does not at all coincide with a passage into nothingness; it is least of all a total annihilation of what was before. It is rather the synonym of an irreversible *transformation*. In it something reaches its definitive end, and something else instead begins. A metamorphosis thus takes place in which some of what is maintains itself because it is capable of configuring itself differently, of taking up another shape, of corresponding to the indeterminate that comes forth. Change and indetermination: it is a law in nature and even more so in the human being.

With respect to this, Alexander Woodcock and Monte Davis write that the catastrophic transition "is discontinuous not because there are no intervening states or pathways, but because none of them is stable: the passage from the initial state or pathway to the final one is likely to be brief in comparison to the time spent in stable states."[4] Taking this dynamic model as a paradigm, one can imagine that any form or structure can find itself in a stage of greater or smaller equilibrium. Where the equilibrium is less, it gravitates around a point of indetermination or *catastrophe* that will be inevitably followed by a change in form. The transformation does not coincide at all with a precipitation from order to pure disorder; rather, it is to be understood as an "order by fluctuation,"[5] from which, time after time, emerges what in a broad sense we like to call the new. Keeping with the analogy with natural dynamics, we can say that if an *epoch* coincides with "a peculiar gathering of time in itself" to gain quality, then it can modify itself within itself, or even flake away. When an epoch reaches a high stage of instability it exits from itself, but it does not fall into emptiness. If one then speaks of "end of modernity," one means that understanding history in terms of progress is no longer possible; but this does not at all abolish time or even history. If anything, the conditions for a different experience of temporality, different ways of combining past, present, and future emerge.

Today technics generates evident counterfinalities. Were the benefits no longer able to compensate the damages adequately, technics would no longer look like the royal way to solve problems, but rather it would configure itself as itself a problem. We are not yet at this stage, but we are moving indeed from technics as definition of an epoch, to the *epoch of risk*. The— given or expected—counterfinalities of technics challenge precisely "that unstoppability of employment" that in 1953 Heidegger named as the unsurpassable horizon of the present.[6] The risk imposes new and unprecedented questions. In the 1953 conference, Heidegger paused for a long time on Hölderlin's famous lines: "*Wo aber Gefar ist, wächst/Das Rettende auch.*"[7]

I know neither whether there is salvation, nor the sense in which one can still talk of it. I definitely know that technics does not provide it; rather, it limits itself to provide well-being, as much as it can. It is, however, a commonsensical remark that with its progressive growth technics really increases danger. Yet, if technics is born out of need and it has made itself plausible only because it has disclosed itself capable of providing solutions, will it ever be able to continue to maintain its plausibility if it introduces dangers at the very moment when it provides solutions? Technics is no longer in question—we are already there. What at each moment we are called to confront and solve, rather, are the questions that technics imposes on us. And these are not small. It is no longer a matter of confronting ourselves with the question of technics. Conversely, it is technics that, out of its very irrevocability, must instead find its own measure. Technics needs therefore to be measured. But who can give it such a measure? I would be guilty of being humanistically pathetic [*patetismo umanistico*] were I to answer: the human being. I think, however, that I move in the right direction if I say that technics finds measure and limit in its own very improbabilities. In fact, with respect to the solutions it provides, it introduces problems in a more or less alarming way. For this reason, it constantly brings itself beyond itself; it relativizes itself at the same pace with which it progresses. It is thus not human beings that limit technics; rather, its failures are indeed its measure.

Now, the human being—but which human being?—may no longer be the primary end of science, but science is actually more teleological than what one thinks. To discriminate between successes and failures, one must elect ends beforehand. In the selection of the ends, human advantages are not an irrelevant variable. It is trivially humanistic to think that there is technics in the service of human beings, conceiving of the human being as a separate and independent essence. Yet, if there is no *faber* that is not a human being, then *only the human being* is *faber*. One may say, though, that the human being is not only *faber*, it is also other things. But let us pass on this. For now, if technics enters the definition of the human being *ab origine*, then the human being inevitably enters the definition of technics. From one epoch to the other, they redefine each other mutually. Within this framework, to speak of technics only in terms of an epochal question amounts to reducing an important question to a general question. To say technics [singular] means in fact to say "many technics [plural]," to define determined problems, to identify the risks.

Heidegger wrote, "when we consider the essence of technology, then we experience *Enframing* as a destining of revealing."[8] How does the world manifest itself, though? What colors does it assume in the time of risk? This questioning links technics and apocalypse. Now, apocalypse is not synonymous with destruction. It carries that connotation, but its most proper meaning is that of *revelation*. In the history of religions and in its most properly theological meaning, however, the apocalyptic revelation alludes certainly to a final unveiling, though in the sense of a fulfilled, definitive unveiling. After the apocalypse history no longer exists. It does not know of a beyond because it is the discriminating event between the end—the definitive past—and perfection. In the epoch of risk, technics has somehow to do with the end. On the one hand, in fact, technics realizes it; on the other, it indicates it.

Mesotes: The Temptation of the Excess and the Rediscovery of the "Just Mean"

The epoch of risk somehow realizes an end in the sense that it archives technics as epoch. The epoch of technics is by now fulfilled; it is something that is historically acquired, archived, irreversible. A return to the pretechnological is impossible. Technics can only move forward, no one can stop it. What technics cannot do, however, is to abolish the limit. It can infinitely push it away, but it cannot annihilate it. Technics cannot become God; it can never be the actuality of everything that is possible, least of all the *complexio oppositorum*, omnipotence. As a proof thereof, considering how the achievements of technics immediately change into new problems, how they confront one with alternatives among which choosing is not easy, is sufficient. Once, discoveries were an occasion for triumph, and the damages they introduced were greatly balanced by the advantages. But today the risk lies there where the best shines. When human beings discovered fire, deciding whether continuing to freeze or getting warm was better most likely did not take much time. In societies with low complexity, technics has developed without problems and with limited dilemmas. In highly complex societies, any solution reformulates itself as a problem.

If things are considered from this perspective, one realizes that technics is in some way displaced by its results and that it inevitably posits itself beyond itself. To use an older terminology, one could say that in its *essence* technics is characterized by its never being completed. But whereas it is opening toward new possibilities, what cannot be concluded may also disclose itself as inconclusive. Such a tension is not new. On the contrary, it appears already at the beginning of modernity. It occurs precisely in Pascal, a modern man and yet a believer. He had well understood how, when faced with the unlimited progressing of time, progress was something irrelevant, especially for the human being taken in its singularity. Until now progress has not triumphed over death. Therefore, the one who dies cannot measure its success. For this reason, the access to the infinite is impossible in time.

When modernity is concluded, technics remains as the last goddess. Yet, what is the meaning of emphasizing technics if, no matter how great progress is, human beings in flesh and blood still die and will most likely continue to do so? One may say, so what? So, nothing. There is, nevertheless, something unsurpassable that technics always leaves behind itself, regardless how far it advances. History is too full of scum to be able easily to sing victory. No matter what stage it reaches, the advancement of technics will not be able to liberate human beings from their *finitude*. On the contrary, it will always and every time reconsign them to it. Technics cannot transform the finite into the infinite. Yet it can—and this is good—always reformulate anew the condition of finitude within which human beings and forms are constituted. If human beings were not ontologically constituted as finitude, they would not even be *faber* [maker], and technics would be completely inessential to their existence. They would become such if, in a mental experiment, one were to imagine a *homo felix atque immortalis* [happy and immortal human being]. Were such humans able to be produced, technics would delegitimize itself at the very same time. This reasoning helps to show how and why technics reconsigns the human being to its limit.

We must take our own burden on ourselves, and consciously: without question we have become more powerful, but not thereby all-powerful. Expecting the accomplishments of technics is completely normal. What characterizes it today, however, is the fact that technics appears inextricably linked to danger. The difference between modern and contemporary is given precisely by the perception of the imponderable, which is indeed what comes from the outside, but, even more so, what depends on our decisions. In this lies the true discontinuity. What is open in front of us is no longer the ad/vent [*l'ad/venire*] of progress, but rather the "without limit" of the future: the *indetermination*. This without-limit forces contemporary human beings to continuous *moves at the limit*. One never touches the ground. A world with variable coordinates is, however, constitutively at risk. Human beings have always found themselves in situations of uncertainty with respect to the future. Yet this does not mean that they have always faced it in terms of risk. One starts talking about *risk* beginning with "the transitional period between the late Middle Ages and the early modern era. The etymology of the word is unknown. Some suspect it to be Arabic in origin."[9] In any event, in the course of modernity the idea of risk is formulated with relation to gambling, and from there it finds a vast field of application with respect to trading and sea traveling.[10] "Maritime insurance is an early instance of planned risk control."[11]

The notion of risk arises in association with the idea that some advantages cannot be obtained if not through taking risks. In its practical and not psychological definition, gambling is exemplary in this sense: one plays to win. Of course one risks losing, but one also stands to gain much more. The structure of taking risk is organized on the basis of the forecast of what one can gain. The calculation is given in terms of costs/benefits.

The logic of risk changes in relation to the increasing power of humanity. Briefly, the difference between gambling and the construction of a nuclear power plant is given by the fact that in the former case I can lose everything, but I know more or less what I lose. In the latter, I can gain very much, but I am not in the condition of forecasting the damages that may follow my decision. They might be such that they not only nullify the initial conditions—no gain—but also pull them back—regression (for example, irreversible destruction of the environment, damages to the present and future populations).

The more humans learn to dominate nature, the more easily they avoid the damages that may come from nature. Meanwhile, however, human beings *introduce* risks in nature. Once, the logic of risk found its limit in one's own safety: is it worth risking or not? Today, it is in many ways risky not to face risks, the cost being the previous discarding of opportunities, a renunciation to growth that amounts to regression. In a logic of defense one could avoid taking risks, but in a logic of development taking risks is, in many ways, an obligation. This does not mean that we are condemned to risk, and yet, we cannot subtract ourselves from it more than some. Today, humanity is called to risk its own finitude at multiple, diversified, as well as improbable levels. To face such situations, one needs something other than a weak thought, unless by weak one means simply mobile, open.[12] Risk has become the current measure of responsibility. Human beings—and, more in general, society—must decide always and every time, at the bifurcation between their own possibilities and impossibilities. For this reason, the task of humans is no longer to direct history, but rather to dominate the contingent. It is no longer a matter of going along with the cryptofinalism of tendencies, but rather of electing ends that can be pursued, starting from the situation in which one is.

Since the beginning, modernity had discovered that human beings are not an end. Contemporaneity challenges human beings as those who can and must give themselves ends and, even if the world may not have a meaning, it is precisely human beings who have appeared to confer one to it. On this issue, Nietzsche has categorical words: "*Greatness means giving direction.*—No river is great and abundant of itself: it is the fact that it receives and bears onward so many tributaries that makes it so. Thus it is too with all great men of the spirit. *All that matters is that one supplies the direction* which many flowing tributaries then have to follow, not whether one is poorly or richly gifted from the beginning."[13] Finding goals in the unlimited is impossible when it is taken rigorously; the goal for the human being lies then in knowing how to transit, in knowing how to inhabit its own transiting. One must know how to camp in what passes and what puts every nihilism out of the game. Nihilism is also the other face of the emphasis on the absolute. To be able to dominate contingency, one must possess *conjecturality*; developing a "counterfactual" logic of the kind: "how is my situation going to change if I introduce a variation X with respect to the one already given?" is necessary.

I do not intend to explore here such a vast epistemological horizon. I limit myself to indicate my philosophy—which I like to define as an "ethics of the finite," or as neopaganism—as a proposal that is congruous with the acosmism [*acosmismo*][14] of our civilization and that is adequate to face and take upon itself the challenges of the present.[15] In this context, the famous line by Horace, *carpe diem* [seize the day], becomes timely again, although with a different meaning. When it is uttered now, it means something different as well as deeper. It should be translated differently: "dominate contingency, face chance."

The domination of contingency has nothing to do with an intoxication with the moment, but rather with the feeling of one's own exposure. In this sense, it is an opening to the future; it calls the future forth. In the pure present, humans can only immerse themselves in it and perish, burn their life. Living, however, is inevitably involved with time, and time with *responsibility*: today for tomorrow, and every day for the following. At the moment in which the diffraction of temporality has definalized history, to confront its indeterminacy successfully the human being must somehow anticipate the future, and this not so much to conquer it, but rather to be able to maintain oneself in it, to be able to imagine it as one's own. Every life as life wants a future for itself. When it reserves it for itself, every individual contributes, even if not intentionally, to the future of everybody, to the care for the world as such.

Rather than unfolding in front of human beings the possibility of an irreversible and unlimited progressing, risk imposes the conscious assumption of the limit to everyone of us, and to society as a whole. In ancient times, human beings suffered from the limit, suffered from it as from a subjection. Today, the very breadth of opportunities presents itself as continuous provocation, hence new and unknown dangers. And yet, human beings, and "only" they, are called to decide such dangers. There is no one else to whom the burden can be passed—not even a God to obey, a good old alibi for one's own

inability to decide. Not haughtiness of intelligence, but rather much rationality and *mesotes*. In this context, Protagoras's saying that the human being is the
measure of all experiences sounds more timely than ever. Yet humans can be
the criterion and measure for values only if they give themselves a measure, if
they restrain themselves. If they trespass, they cannot delimit boundaries, least
of all can they assign destinies. Humans have become moral because of measure. Nietzsche writes, "Perhaps all the morality of mankind has its origin in
the tremendous inner excitement which seized on primeval men when they
discovered measure and measuring, scales and weighing (the word 'Mensch,'
indeed, means the measurer, he desired to name himself after his greatest
discovery!)."[16] Yet, what is measure when one wants to understand it as a
moral quality? Again, to cite Nietzsche: "*Measure.*—When thought and inquiry have become decisive—when, that is to say, free-spiritedness has become
a quality of the character—action tends to moderation: for thought and inquiry weaken covetousness, draw much of the available energy to themselves
for the promotion of spiritual objectives, and reveal the merely half-usefulness
or the total uselessness and perilousness of all sudden changes."[17]

Haste is often nothing else than superficiality. In some cases, it is
longing for immediate results in the complete ignorance of the consequences.
One says *measure*. It seems easy: neither too much, nor too little, neither . . .
nor . . . but. . . . Identifying that which is to be excluded is often easier than
identifying that which is to be chosen, toward which to orient oneself, or
toward which to direct. Aristotle already knew well that the just mean is not
at all comparable to the medium of a segment of which one knows the
extremes. Rather, it is the medium of an unlimited. For this reason, finding
the medium means above all to guess the moment, to understand what one
should do every time. The just mean is a temporal middleness (*medietà*), and
the better one finds it the more experience one has of things: the enumera-
tion of cases, a story of stories, and finally, the ability to read the detail, to
discern, to suspect. The ethics of the finite implies a great practice of the
world, a strenuous and continuous work on oneself. General terms are needed
to identify things, but they do not always give account of reality in its
specificities and differences. The escape into abstractions—*middleness* herein
included—is an *escamotage* to avoid the impact with the real hardness of
things and events. For this reason, I am not concerned with reasoning abstractly but with writing about life, specifically about philosophical life. I
write therefore of pain and its forms, of happiness, and thus of the ways of
being of human beings, of their living and their self-appreciation. I write
about ideas—that is, about philosophies—by describing the situations from
which they emerge, the procedures that formalize them. The ethics of the
finite is not, nor ever can be, a formula; it must concretize itself in a real
crossing through finitude. For this reason, in my philosophizing I reason
about vices and virtues, both public and private, about virtues that have
passed and those to be retrieved, about that underlie the very vices, about

that which turn into vices because of their presumption of perfection. Wisdom works on passions. It does not inhibit but modulates them. It is curious attention as well as temporizing. It is—why not?—*skepsis*.

By the Greeks, all this was common conviction:

> our wisdom is not of the intellect, not
> in presuming too high for human thought.
> Life is short. A man who pursues immense
> speculations may find, for today's expense,
> he has nothing in cash. To me, such a man is mad,
> who will not reckon with time—his planning, bad.[18]

These lines are by Euripides, a tragedian who belongs to a relatively recent epoch of Greek civilization, but in them echoes a wisdom that is much older, shrewder, and paradoxically more than ever useful for us today. We aim more or less—beyond any conscious thought on our side—at grasping all what we can in the shortest possible time, ignoring, or at least giving little thought to the consequences of our indigestible voraciousness, of our haughty self-sufficiency. We live in a civilization that demands and simultaneously fears too much. If and when it thinks about it, civilization fears itself more than anything.

In the passing of time, there are constellations that never fade, eternal voices. Euripides, in fact, obsessively asserts over and over to us something that was obvious already to the Greeks and that nevertheless, beyond all evidence, remains strangely unthought. He invites us to ponder about the historical reiteration of a singular, identical circumstance: with royal unawareness, human beings fall continuously back into the same mistakes that condemn them, even if sooner or later they pay the price for it—in their heritage, in the species if in nothing else. The reiteration of such a behavior through time has transformed it, to use a term here out of context, into *original guilt*, into something in itself indelible, unavoidable. Too great a self-presumption is in fact a very old vice, *hubris* being an immemorial temptation for the species that resurfaces epoch after epoch in various disguises. For this reason, every epoch is called to reformulate, *always and anew*, an ethics capable of containing, limiting, and defeating our original haughtiness in its various reappearances. It is then a matter of starting all over. To us contemporaries falls the task of analyzing the conditions of the "here" and "now" in which we are situated, of determining the parameters of behavior adequate to our civilization, of elaborating an *ethics of the finite* that is commensurate with the dilemmas and the needs of the present, that prepares a favorable future for those whom we bring to the world. *As we love them so much*, the future cannot but worry us, even if it is never going to be ours. It is a future with which we entrust them, but, equally inexorably—and I would say almost *destinally*—which we also assign to them.

Notes

1. Martin Heidegger, "The Question Concerning Technology," in *The Question Concerning Technology and Other Essays*, trans. W. Lovitt (New York: Harper and Row, 1977), p. 28.

2. Walter Benjamin, *The Arcades Project*, trans. H. Eiland and K. McLaughlin (Cambridge, MA: Harvard University Press, 1999), p. 151. Benjamin remarks, "the quote is probably referring to the *Galerie de l'Opéra*. J. A Dulaure, *Histoire de Paris . . . depuis 1821 jusqu'à nos jours*, vol. 2 (Paris, 1835), p. 29."

3. Ibid., pp. 160–61 (emphasis added).

4. Alexander Woodcock and Monte Davis, *Catastrophe Theory* (New York: Dutton, 1978), p. 32.

5. On this issue, see Ilya Prigogine and Isabelle Stengers, "Order through Fluctuations," in Ilya Prigogine and Isabelle Stengers, *Order Out of Chaos* (Toronto: Bantam, 1984), pp. 177–212.

6. The "Question Concerning Technology" was a conference Heidegger held November 18, 1953, in the Auditorium Maximum of the Technische Hochschule in Munich, Germany.

7. Heidegger, "The Question Concerning Technology," p. 28.

8. Ibid., p. 25.

9. Niklas Luhmann, *Risk: A Sociological Theory*, trans. R. Barrett (New York: De Gruyter, 1993), p. 9.

10. Ibid., pp. 8–14.

11. Ibid., p. 9.

12. Trans. note: The reference is to the hypothesis advanced by Pier Aldo Rovatti and Gianni Vattimo, *Il pensiero debole* (Milan: Feltrinelli, 1983). See also their chapters herein.

13. Friedrich Nietzsche, *Human All Too Human*, trans. R. J. Hollingdale (Cambridge: Cambridge University Press, 1986), p. 512 (emphasis added).

14. Trans. note: This term derives from the Greek *a-comos*, lack of a cosmos, that is, lack of an orderly, directional universe.

15. On this issue, see Salvatore Natoli, *I nuovi pagani*, and Salvatore Natoli, *Dizionario dei vizi e delle virtù* (Milan: Feltrinelli, 1996). This essay retrieves and discusses ancient virtues to indicate a behavior that is congruous with an ethics of the finite.

16. Nietzsche, *Human All Too Human*, p. 310.

17. Ibid., p. 169. Trans. note: The German term "*Maaß*," which Hollingdale's translation renders as "moderation," has been changed to "measure" to remain closer to the Italian.

18. Euripides, *The Bacchae*, trans. D. Sutherland (Lincoln: University of Nebraska Press, 1968), p. 19, vv. 395–402.

Chapter 10

Praise of Modesty

PIER ALDO ROVATTI

Ethics as Weakening of Philosophy

Out of the present reality, out of that zone of consciousness in which we are situated time and again, an appeal is addressed to philosophy. This appeal, whose symptoms we see reproduced in everydayness, for example, in newspaper pages, in the recurrent (not only induced) demand for "philosophical opinions," takes up the form of a self-entrusting, of a need for trust. One turns to philosophy as if philosophy were still capable of representing a *strong* instance: in sum, as if it could maintain the claim or could still be invested with the claim of "unifying," "totalizing," giving a "sense" to the dispersion of phenomena. One wonders whether philosophy has lost its "public" character or at least what transformations this character has undergone, which of its survivals maintain legitimacy. Whatever the answer at the theoretical level, and regardless of the ways and qualitative levels of the practical replies, the demand for philosophy seems to differ from other cultural demands because of a peculiar advantage assigned to it: a supposed privilege, which has to do with the nature of philosophy itself, and with the imaginary projection *into* philosophy of a demand belonging to the structure of our common subjective experience. Saying that philosophy *cannot* answer this demand and that this cannot give itself explicitly today in the form of an unwillingness, in the sense that currently philosophy *has set for itself* a disenchantment, an effect of *disillusion* with regard to the totalizing claim, will not suffice. In fact, philosophy will have to ask itself whether it has something to say with regard to this strong claim of subjectivity, the imaginary projection of a strong self, or whether it must give in completely to the psychoanalytic interpretation or to other "explanations."

This work first appeared as Pier Aldo Rovatti, "Elogio del pudore," in Alessandro Dal Lago and Pier Aldo Rovatti, *Elogio del pudore* (Milan: Feltrinelli, 1989), pp. 23-47.

In other words, we are aware of the nihilistic curvature that philosophy assumed after Nietzsche. For contemporary thought, truth as interpretation means exactly the "destruction" of the philosophical illusion or claim. Within such a curve, Freud warns us of the feature of "defense" implicit in this illusion. Yet, what critical distance can there be between the Nietzschean gesture and our consciousness, the consciousness of those—in sum—who try to question the meaning of philosophy after Heidegger? Nietzsche appears to us as a philosopher whose decisive gesture (decisive for our consciousness) is still animated by an illusion that escapes nihilism. This is the illusion of being able to accomplish a transvaluation of the will to power, briefly, of being able to dissolve the claim while actually doubling it. Heidegger (rightly considered the greatest interpreter of Nietzsche) lets us see in Nietzsche a symptomatic repetition of "metaphysics."

The distance between Nietzsche and us may consist in a deepening of nihilism: in the awareness that the strong instance of philosophy cannot be simply dissolved (because philosophy is not *simply* an illusion); that the issue, rather, concerns the contradictory and paradoxical character of the unrenounceable movement of our subjectivity. Only for a short stretch does the path of *weakening* coincide with that of the *dissolution* of the philosophical claim because the gesture of weakening turns out to be oriented differently. It aims to produce critical effects the main target of which may become precisely the illusion that the "strong" character of thought can be erased, removed, or unworked through the renewed "power" of a philosophical, although radically transgressive, consciousness.

I would like to recall the interpretative core of the image of weakening that Gianni Vattimo proposed.[1] It is an interpretation of nihilism through Heidegger and precisely through the reconsideration of the notion of *Verwindung*. According to Vattimo, this notion opens a semantic constellation: recovery-distortion-acceptance (of metaphysics). Weakening (which for Vattimo is the "truth" of hermeneutics) is both *a repetition* and *a distortion*; in no way does it amount to a destruction-cancellation. From this it follows that hermeneutic truth and truth as adequation are not mutually exclusive, opposite poles. Not only do they imply each other, but also the manner of their inclusion is not simply a variation of the common image of logical inclusion by superimposition, belonging, contiguity, and so forth. The way of this nonexclusion is as little granted as the very movement of weakening is problematic. The "distortion" has to do with a radical redefinition of hermeneutic "opening." In this crucial area of his reflection, Vattimo also acknowledges that because it differs from any possible translation in terms of simple pluralization of the ways of thinking, or in the consequent terms of cultural relativism (of the kind one can read in Richard Rorty), the idea of truth as opening does not and cannot have the status of a pure and simple notion, nor, *a fortiori*, the status, which remains however stable, of a concept.

I believe that Vattimo's interpretation plays itself out in this risky zone, wherein the hermeneutic circle encounters in fact its own paradoxical character, and philosophical thought is exposed to the risk of its own distortion. It is not a matter of "explaining." But neither is it a matter of replacing explaining with "understanding" (which is equally truth related [*veritativo*]), nor of trying to describe a mixed paradigm in which, within the horizon of hermeneutic understanding, epistemological explanations may have a relative autonomy. On the contrary, it is a matter of a change of register characterized by the impossibility of giving an account of truth as opening [*apertura*] in simply cognitive terms. The effect of philosophical distortion can be seen as condensed in this remark by Vattimo: "The truth of the opening seems to be thinkable only on the ground of the metaphor of dwelling."[2] Thinking and thought are linked to the metaphorical resources of language. Between knowing and "dwelling" a gap has become necessary. A movement of distortion-weakening has precisely happened and of this we can perceive a double tonality: a linguistic tonality (to weaken means to resort to metaphorical resources) and an ethical tonality (to weaken means "to distort" knowing into dwelling).

The paradox can be dwelt in. In the metaphor of dwelling is the possibility of the "opening," of being within the contradiction, of a "belonging" as a play between fiction and reference. In brief, the metaphorical gap opens up an "other" relation with oneself in which the predominance of "seeing" is weakened in the direction of a "listening." Vattimo appears extremely cautious in moving within this horizon, as if he fears taking too risky a step. Dwelling is, for him, "an interpretative belonging": the story in which the metaphor is unfolded is that of "staying within a tradition" in a manner analogous to how one dwells in a library. "The truth of dwelling," Vattimo emphasizes, "is rather the competence of the librarian who does not entirely possess, in a punctual act of transparent comprehension, the totality of the contents of the books among which he lives, nor the first principles on which such books depend."[3] One is reminded of Aby Warburg, whose library is not organized according to a *nomos* but on the criterion of "good neighborhood." The librarian is the one who has interiorized Warburg's principle and who thus "knows" where to find the books and how to construct a path without possessing comprehensive analytic knowledge.

To dwell in the world does not equate living in a library, however, and the "practical knowledge" of the librarian is nothing else than a limiting example in comparison to the opening, to the change of attitude that the movement of weakening of the truth indicates to us. Dwelling may suggest the idea of a practical knowledge, but the latter does not seem to lead us back to dwelling as to an experience in which the claim of philosophy is hosted and deviated: the movement of this "distortion" does not seem to be given back from "interpretative belonging"; rather, it seems to be softened, urbanized.

Again, it would not seem that there is a coincidence between the weakening and this hermeneutic movement that softens the metaphysical violence of the truth into a "knowledge" of tradition. Weakening can only put subjectivity at risk. Its ethical tonality has the pathos of rift and risk; it exposes itself to the splitting of the self and even loss; it introduces to the condition of paradox as the normal condition of subjectivity. Metaphor does not have the function of softening; it is rather, first of all, disorienting. Dwelling, as metaphor, is a distortion of the "being in": one can no longer speak of a self that dwells in a place, is still the "lord" of that place, *knows* how to orient itself, is in *its* place. What has weakened? In "dwelling" as a declination of knowledge, the self takes *distance from itself*. The tonality of experience that delineates itself is that of disorientation[4] and passivity. It is a matter of breaking up the idea of proximity, of standing-by, as mastery. This breaking up is the possibility of experiencing the paradox of the distance from oneself. Interpretative belonging is already a reorganization of proximity; it is already an experience of repatriation.

One could object: Is not in fact our experience, phenomenologically, precisely a continuous play of repatriations and adjustments to the self's own mastery? Is there an experience that is only exile and not also repatriation? It does not exist; and because of this the philosophies of alterity can turn into the opposite of what they promise. Yet, if experience also is a play of repatriations, we can think of a way of "dwelling" in this very experience that time and again "preserves" an interval, that arranges itself in the attitude of the one who moves up the stream and deviates the claim thereof. We can "think" such a way of dwelling; however, it will be a proceeding *against* the habit of thought that asks for a circumscribable and representable object and for an identifiable and powerful subject.

The weakening of the philosophical claim, which we can describe through the metaphor of dwelling, configures a discretion, a *modesty* of theory. The figure of modesty enables us perhaps to start to describe this counter-movement. At stake is especially the predominance of the gnoseological paradigm. That is to say, the relation we can establish with the "truth," the distancing to which I have hinted, is neither translatable nor describable in terms of a theory of knowledge because truth can no longer be an object to be assumed, and the subject can no longer be only a disinterested spectator or a possessor of rules, methods, or criteria to apply to things. I term "ethics"—well aware of the numerous meanings and the circuit of mental habits in which this term can be absorbed and preempted—the sliding outside or on this side of the cognitive paradigm, that "distortion" accompanying repetition. "Ethics" can be characterized, then, as the function of weakening with respect to the philosophical claim: function that has nothing to do with norms. It is indicated by the figure, or by the series of figures, capable of describing the paradoxicality of the movement of distancing of the subject from its claim.

When understood in this way, that is, as disempowerment of philoso-phy, ethics certainly cannot have a special content of its own. It is not knowledge, and thus it does not avail itself of normative knowledges, no matter how minimal, to be affirmed and universalized. This ethics is not "rational" and does not legitimate any "public philosophy." Not only does it distance itself from any rational ethics of a Kantian descent, but it also opposes itself to it. Better still, it assumes rational ethics as a presupposition, a philosophical "given" that belongs to the overall claim of philosophy that is to be "worked on": to be eroded precisely in its claim to universality, in its only affirmative appeal to the proximity and transparency of dwelling, in its "direct" use of the truth.

If, understood in this manner, ethics does not produce any knowl-edge, and if, when considered from the perspective of the cognitive claim, it can really look like an "almost nothing," this apparent inconsistency may be for us determinant because of the simple fact that it orients experience, it comes into play in any acting. The attitude, furthermore, that it configures has its own specificity, which is as "precise" as its effects on acting are determinant. The figure of modesty, which I will now try to delineate better, cannot be confused with simple critical distance, with pulling one-self out of situations, with the viewpoint of the external observer. This confusion would be so misleading (and I am thinking especially of the equivocations that might arise out of the phenomenological attitude to which I will return later) that we would mistake modesty as risk precisely for that from which it means to distance itself. As we now well know, this is not only the immodest coincidence with the object, with the consequent and evident disappearance of subjectivity turned into scientific criterion, but it is also the contemplative and disinterested attitude of a subject that measures its mastery in terms of detachment and that is, in the end, no less immodest in such an illusion.

Full and Empty

To summarize the features of the hypothesis I am trying to delineate: We can think that modesty is the figure, the metaphor, that indicates the movement of weakening. This movement is not a literal moving from one place to the other. What "moves" is subjectivity, by which I mean the entire subjective experience of each of us, not only self-consciousness. Although it holds onto consciousness, this movement tries to go beyond, to reach on this side of the already constituted consciousness; it tries to oppose a resistance to the spur of the self toward its self-affirmation, that spur that philosophy gathers, for example, under the term "will to power." Weakening appears as the attempt at slowing down this impulse, at unbalancing its claim. One can say, in brief, that modesty is a pause; yet, it is a pause that to be realized requires the setting into motion of the entire experience. It requires an attitude such that the privileged and mastering zone of subjectivity is moved a little from its center, is distanced, made relative.

What I have just summarized with a thingly and inadequate vocabulary is not a small gesture. What is at stake is actually the overall character the style of experience. In a certain way, it is an upheaval, an upsetting of subjectivity. The term "ethics" would indicate this *possibility* we have to upset the inertia of the I. This is a possibility we employ, without naming it, in certain moments of our existing, which poetry, novels, and art have often narrated to us, and which we are at least able to "imagine." Is philosophical thought really condemned to be blind in front of it? Or is there a possibility, for philosophy itself, to open up an empty space, a disempowerment within itself so that the ideal claim is decentered and a space of describability of what we have here called "weakening" is made free? According to my way of looking at it, this is what is at stake in weak thought.

To proceed to such an "emptying," first of all philosophical thought must give up the claim of encountering things, of adhering to reality; that is, ultimately it must give up the *fullness* of its word. The picture then splits. One cannot avoid proceeding simultaneously on two levels: first, the level at which we say that weakening is a real experience, a movement of subjectivity, and so forth, the level at which also the reference to modesty has a literal connection with the feeling of modesty we have experienced or can experience in certain situations; second, the level at which weakening concerns language and warns us that we have no words philosophically to describe the emptying of the I. Here modesty takes up the physiognomy of a "fictional" word that does not want to give, but rather to take away meaning. If this second level were not at work, the erosion would be a joke, or better, a simple assertion. Yet, its presence cannot be constant, complete. It is rather intermittent, partial, and so weak thought is not only the indicator of an oscillating experience, but also finds itself continuously in an oscillation, and, again, at each moment, is exposed to the claims of philosophical truth.

There is recognizability, however; one can indicate features, draw distinctions. Modesty, we said, has to do with an emptying. At stake is fullness. Full and empty refer to a spatial and thingly paradigm. Literally, they are alien to the "movement" we want to describe. Yet they help us, in their metaphorical variation, to draw a picture. In this picture, we have an initial fact: the idea of a "too much," a too full, hypertrophy of fullness, occupation of space, draining of the interstices, the idea of a saturated block. Is the reality in which we live not such or increasingly similar to this? But then, are the meaning and value we are prone to give to our identity also not ever more similar to this? We introduce therefore a second feature into the picture: *to be in a situation like this*, one must loosen the "too much," open up interstices, create zones of nothingness and emptiness. In everyday language, in instrumental language, Heidegger saw a similar hypertrophy: the poetic word should have acted on the philosophical word as a "minus." This picture, however, can be a picture of subjectivity. Where is the meaningful and paradoxical point? It is in that a decrease may produce meaning in a horizon that leans toward hypertrophy of meaning and thus toward meaninglessness. In that it is even necessary to dismantle the fullness of our subjectivity, to produce within us zones of emptiness, silence, shadow, alienness; or, more precisely, to make ourselves once again able to recognize them. The paradox is the fact that one must try to dismantle something compact and "functioning" to give rise to a much less controllable play of levels and differences within subjectivity itself to be in a situation like this. We could also say in order to "dwell" in a situation like this.

If we bring emptiness back into subjectivity, then identity oscillates. Each of us would recognize himself or herself no longer as a full identity, but rather as a multilevel, multivocal process. The search for alterity, differences, and internal oppositions within ourselves could even be the way toward ungrounding false recognition. Ricoeur means something similar when he speaks of "narrative identity," that is, bringing the dispersion of temporality, the plurality of stories and their plots, within ourselves, dismantling the *idem* we think we are and we want to be. This emptying, which makes dwelling mean being in a tensional [*tensionale*] plurality of levels, modifies also the idea of intersubjectivity that we normally have. In fact, recognition through fullness loses value, whereas that through which there can be recognition acts at the level of weakening. The other will be like me if I recognize in him or her an analogous movement from self-transparency to self-opacity, an analogous opening to the other who is within him or her. I will not recognize another as "equal" on the basis of an idea, albeit enlarged, of shared human essence. I will perceive instead that he or she is involved in a movement of opening comparable to mine.

This last consideration, which introduces a "distortion" in the phenomenological model of intersubjectivity, could perhaps dissolve some equivocations having to do with pluralism. "Weak thought" is manifestly a radical criticism of any reduction to the same. The problem, it seems, does not arise at this preliminary level of *tolerance* toward differences. Weak thought is even a thought of difference, or better, of differences in its very hermeneutic tonality according to which dwelling in the truth amounts to an interpretative belonging: plurality of interpretations, viewpoints, types of subjectivity. The problem seems to arise when the boomerang effects of relativism are perceived, that is, when one asks the inverted question of the indifference toward any viewpoint, and consequently the request for a criterion arises again. Hence, as I have mentioned, come many of the, as it were, "political" doubts about weak thought. One could easily reply to these doubts by applying hermeneutics to itself, and thus by delineating a horizon marked by the nearer or farther closeness to the recognition of truth in a hermeneutic sense: a horizon in which diversities by principles, oppositions of substantialistic, "strong" truths or identities have no longer value.

The equivocation, however, could hide in the idea itself of pluralism, in that initial tolerance. Differences might simply be apparent. Could each viewpoint, each identity be nothing other than the differentiated replication of a superindividual criterion? What ensures that the play of differences is not simply fictitious? That tolerance is not a disguised assimilation? That a *merely philosophical* idea of community and intersubjectivity is not continuing to act? With respect to what does difference measure and decline itself? I think that the play of differences can be attended to only by a putting into question of identity *within* subjectivity itself. We can talk of subjects in the plural form only if we do not simply stop at the legitimation of the plurality of viewpoints and if we succeed in naming the movement thanks to which plurality is constituted as opening and, simultaneously, as risk within the subject itself. An "external" plurality can very well be the pluralization of "full" identities, have nothing to do with the movement of modesty, even be opposed to weakening. By reducing the "fullness" of the I, dislocating and relativizing its ideality supported by the philosophical category of subject and by all everyday applications of such a "claim," alterity and difference come to be part of an experience of subjectivity the critical movement of which consists in the attempt at *withdrawing* exactly the projection outward of what is not "full," compact, identical. From this perspective, the assertion of pluralism *outside* us could also simply be a mask.

It is a matter, then, of gaining an empty zone in the fullness of subjectivity, in the "too full" image of ourselves we have. This gain—it is worth repeating—is not granted by any rational morality. The movement of modesty cannot be learned through a "normative" knowledge, through some "science" of subjectivity and its behaviors. Nor, it seems, can we proceed very far on the path that chooses to erase the issue of subjectivity as a false issue, philosophically already completely compromised. I do not deny that this path—which is, in the end, the one trod by Heidegger himself—may produce, by dislocation, important outcomes of thought. Between these outcomes and the individual attitudes, however, one will then have to build bridges, otherwise one risks that the possible transformation of the claim of the I remains out of the issue and out of the scene.

We can only attempt to retrace and describe this "paradoxical" experience. The language of such description will have to maintain within itself the oscillating and unstable character of the movement through which subjectivity weakens. The insistence on the ambivalence of the symbol, however, on the need for a "poetical" suspension within the language of philosophy, the insistence on the unsolvable tensionality of metaphor, on the "mythical" as well as rational character of the figurative image identify a by now very wide and articulated horizon within contemporary thought and especially within the current debate. The attempt at a description is thus situated within an already widely prefigured territory. It is not the case of sporadic and isolated episodes, but rather of a "form" of thought that is delineating itself or that can be delineated. All this—it is almost superfluous to mention—has nothing to do with "irrationalism"; the problems this latter [concept] has raised seem completely irrelevant and certainly misleading in comparison with the issue of thinkability that is here at stake.

Shadow-Zone

As I show in the following paragraphs, where the main points of reference will be Heidegger and Husserl, the central scene of contemporary philosophy can provide us with the features of the figure of modesty as disorienting movement of weakening. At least one reference to psychoanalysis is however opportune. The "emptiness" we can carve out in the hypertrophy of the I has to do very closely with that zone of subjectivity that, from Freud on, has been called "the unconscious." Literally, it is an unrepresentable part of us, that is, it cannot be described through the cognitive modality of truth-object. Let us think of the problems connected with the "meaning" of dreams. The unconscious that exhibits itself in dreams is not comparable to a simple object for knowledge. It implies a distancing, a transformation, a rhetoric, a narrative play.

Freud's *The Interpretation of Dreams* is the benchmark for these issues. What is important for us is the fact that, out of it, we do not get a theoretical translation, but rather an aporetic tension. As if by trying to make sense of the "oneiric work" supervising the gap between manifest and latent dimension of the dream, Freud finds himself time and again in the condition of *not* being able to erase this gap that he would nevertheless like to close; rather, he identifies precisely in the gap the zone where to test thought. Freud seems to oscillate between the preoccupation that here, in this zone, thought loosens (that is, it comes up short of its rational task) and the perception that exactly here, in this loosening up (figural, metaphorical, seeming to mean a "loss"), what is at stake are the specific effects of the unconscious on thinking, on self-consciousness to which thinking is intimately related. Let us think about the unsatisfactory way with which Freud deals with the oneiric symbol (a representative for something else and thus translatable), and let us ask ourselves: Is a reading of *The Interpretation of Dreams* that takes Jung's perspective into account possible, that is, a reading that takes into account the tensive character of symbol, a thematic accentuation on the unrepresentable? I recall this hypothesis of a "Jungian reading" of the unconscious Freud discovered and first described in the great work of 1900 because I believe that through this way one can interpret "censorship" (which Freud emphasizes and which for Jung is the obstacle to be removed) precisely in terms of "modesty" and of the ethical tonality that is proper to the movement of weakening.

The term "shadow" has a double peculiarity: it indicates the unrepresentable zone, and it indicates it metaphorically, thus warning us that no "name" will be able to identify it. The term is Jungian, and Jung uses it to characterize the personal unconscious; yet, it can have for us a broader meaning: for example, it characterizes as well that zone that Freudian censorship protects and defends, a disquieting and threatening place that the perceptive relaxation of dreams puts in contact with the luminous place of our subjectivity and that precisely the oneiric censorship (transfiguring its features) undertakes to filter, preventing its invading us with its anxiety effects. The ciphered character of dreams is thus, for Freud, the effect of a defense mechanism. Ultimately, it would be the masking of what we cannot see with a direct look and, as it were, with a naked eye. It is already a modesty, but its effect is more in the order of closure than of opening. This goes along for Freud with the prevailing of the light-shadow paradigm in its gnoseological value. What prevails is the positivity of seeing, whereas the zone of shadow is what remains—negatively—outside of visibility, what opposes it, what resists to it. Through Jung, however, we have a distortion of the paradigm: the shadow is no longer a defectiveness of light, and thus it is no longer only or mainly a threat.[5] In this manner, the shadow reconquers precisely its metaphorical character. It is metaphor that is not translatable into "absence of light," cannot be resolved into a specific content, does not depend on a defense mechanism, and, for all these reasons, is no longer functional to a gnoseological paradigm. Thus Jung can claim that insofar as it jeopardizes the luminosity of our consciousness, our relation with the shadow has a fundamentally *moral* stake. Freud's greatness, on the other hand, lies in the fact that he proceeds against the stream of his very project: an aporetic reading of *The Interpretation of Dreams* is possible precisely by virtue of the contradictory oscillations and tensions within the Freudian thought.

I think that the move from censorship to modesty can be measured precisely through the emergence of the ethical tonality. This passage, which can be observed in the interpretation of dreams, has then to do with the "nature" of the overall (and complex) relations that link consciousness and the unconscious, the I and its shadow.[6] We can understand, then, why Jung stresses the "moral character" of the dream out of the hypothesis that, for him, "the shadow is a moral problem that challenges the whole ego-personality."[7] The I is a little island surrounded by a vast archipelago; thus there is always—there cannot not be—a shadow zone around us, in us. First of all, there is a *measure* to be kept: one must defend of course the survival of the little island because the archipelago could absorb it; but, moreover, one must guard oneself from the possible *inflation* of the I. There is no doubt that, for Jung, this swelling is the "psychic sickness" of our present. The measure to be kept is then, ultimately, the safeguard of the shadow, and modesty consists precisely in opposing the cannibalism of the I, its phagocytizing will, the whirlpool that it provokes toward everything that is other than its self-image. Ethics is thus the always repeated, never truly carried out move through which we *succeed* in embanking the I within its relative and partial constitution. It is the move, in sum, with which we succeed in living our I as if it truly were a little island within an immense archipelago, the uneven stretch of the Self of which the shadow constitutes the trace, one could say.

This whirlpool is always already at work in language, as well as in the very term "shadow." Jung oscillates in turn: the "inferior," "low," and "secondary" are inertially associated with the shadow. Yet, the shadow, the inferior zone, is such only from the standpoint of the "superiority" that the zone of light, the I, claims for itself. It is the "low" zone exactly because it is the part of us we do not want to accept, which generally we expel to the outside, project onto the world (things and persons) that surrounds us. What is at stake is precisely this "superiority," and the hierarchy of values that depends on it. The task of the metaphor is to operate a suspension and a margin in the "naturalness" of literal values.[8] The "moral" test of which Jung speaks is the bifurcation in front of which we go on finding ourselves: either we safeguard the scission by defending the partiality of the zone of light as if it were a whole, or we start on the path of "compensation," which is the way of retreat, retreat of projections and retreat toward an identification of ourselves as unstable and contradictory amalgama of light and shadow. This is the operational meaning that Jung gives to the symbol:[9] an unstable coincidence of opposites. And because according to Jung the dream aims at realizing such a process of compensation, a symbolic "life" of this kind, the dream can be called "moral."

In conclusion, I want to emphasize this point, which seems symptomatic of the possibility of an overall "reading" of psychoanalysis: [what can be called] "moral" is the process, never fully realized, through which the I operates an upheaval (not only a becoming aware) of its own attitude that consists in the weakening of its own power (which is recognized, among other things, as pathogenic), the undermining of its own fullness, the widening of its own limited borders, and the acceptance of the shadow zone as such as an essential part of itself. The unconscious is not an epistemological object, a new territory to be added to knowledge, but rather the crisis in the inflation of the I, a need for a turning around of experience, the experience of the necessary retreat of the will to power. In this perspective, the language of the unconscious is one and the same with the need to introduce some modesty into language as is testified by the obliqueness of the oneiric metaphor with its unresolved play of references. The ethical instance, I repeat, can be recognized in the difference between a metaphorics that can be resolved in a hidden meaning (and which is, rather, a pseudo-metaphorics) and a metaphorics that reintroduces meaning exactly by weakening the ownership of *a* meaning.

The Philosopher Warms Himself by the Oven

Heidegger addresses the anecdote I recall now in the "Letter on Human-ism."[10] It concerns Heraclitus, and Aristotle has told and handed down the tale to us. Foreign visitors take the great thinker by surprise while he is warming himself next to a bread-baking oven. It is a trivial and everyday scene. More than surprising Heraclitus, though, the visitors are themselves surprised and disappointed. We can imagine that these tourists, who wanted to see a true philosopher at least once in their lifetime, had planned their visit, making sure that Heraclitus would let himself be seen by them, had faced expenses and sacrifices, a long trip; and that, in the not short period of these preparations, their expectation had grown, and the already somewhat mythical idea of the philosopher, which they had in mind at the beginning, had become increasingly mythical and unreal. And here they are, finally, entering the austere threshold of the house of thought. The great Heraclitus cannot be the very average character who is warming himself by the oven!

A lesson in humility. This anecdote seems to be the other side of another, more famous one, which has as its main characters Thales of Miletus and a Thracian maid and on which Hans Blumenberg has built one of his most fascinating researches on the history of metaphor.[11] Completely ab-sorbed in the sky he is searching—as Plato has it in *Theaetetus*—Thales does not look where he puts his feet; faced with the scene of the fall of the philosopher, the maid from Thrace cannot resist laughing. Perhaps Heraclitus's visitors expected him to be absorbed in the questioning of the blue depths of the sky with no care for the trivial businesses of the earth. And probably, in a circumstance similar to Thales's, they would have pretended not to see and would have cast a severe look at the impertinent and somewhat blasphemous maid. Yet it is not simply the case of a lesson in humility. In fact, Heraclitus, having become aware of the puzzlement of his guests, rewards them for their trip with this sentence, "Here too the gods are present."

We do not know what the visitors thought when they went back: whether they were simply gratified by the fact that the philosopher had reserved for them a few somewhat enigmatic words (to relate to friends as a confirmation of the commonplace opinion that philosophers are weird and unpredictable), or whether they were enlightened and therefore a little bit deflated by Heraclitus's sentence aimed at striking their very surprise. In retelling the story, Heidegger forces us to reconsider such a state of mind and warns us that what is at stake is that something we persist in calling "ethics." Ethics comes from *ethos*, and Heidegger translates this Greek word not so much with "feature proper to humans," but with "abode," "place where one dwells," "open region within which humans dwell." And he interprets Heraclitus's fragment in which one reads *ethos anthropo daimon* as "man dwells . . . in the nearness of god." This interpretation coincides with the words of the anecdote: "Here too the gods are present."[12]

Ethics is dwelling, "poetic dwelling," as Heidegger continually states recalling a verse by Hölderlin. This, however, puts into question his whole thought after *Being and Time*; finding direct references to ethics in Heidegger is rare, but when there are some—as in this case—they prove to be decisive. Dwelling is in fact the figure of being for human experience.[13] This enables us helpfully and legitimately to build a bridge between Heidegger and Levinas, who by emphasizing ethics, nevertheless seems to us to be very far from and even averse to one who had been one of his philosophical teachers. And it enables us to connect Heidegger and Jankélévitch, who has always been clearly anti-Heideggerian.

The condition that, by rethinking Heraclitus's word, Heidegger considers to be of "nearness to the gods" is separated from our usual, "inauthentic" condition by a very thin veil: actually, an "almost nothing"—to use an expression by Jankélévitch—distinguishes Heraclitus's attitude in the anecdote from an anonymous and unqualified practice. The *nearness*, in the spatial and obvious sense of the terms, and the *proximity* to things exemplified by Heraclitus are different only because of an ethical tonality. Yet this small, almost imperceptible difference brings with itself a radical modification in look and attitude. This is precisely the tonality that we may indicate with the term "modesty." Levinas speaks of "patience" (and "passivity") in front of the "other." For Jankélévitch, who constantly returns to the theme of modesty, it is "respect for a mystery." For Heidegger, dwelling in the world as a way of being modest toward things is a safeguarding, a protecting, an awaiting, a self-entrusting. One can see well how, although it is a completely everyday fact and exhausts itself in its "appearance," Heraclitus's proximity to the oven at which he warms himself constitutes a relation *non*measurable with the measure of our habitual knowledges and not even with that of philosophical "professionalism." Yet, Heidegger emphasizes, it is a *measure*; it is even *what gives measure* to human beings.

The bridge that may connect Heidegger with Levinas and Jankélévitch, hypothesizing a path not granted in philosophical contemporaneity, enables us to reconsider Heidegger within the movement of weakening. How can we interpret today the *daimon* Heraclitus mentioned when he takes leave from his guests? And in what sense is the "proximity" of this dwelling not an adding but a taking away? To answer these questions, we can indeed make reference to Levinasian patience and to Jankélévitch's "almost nothing." Both experiences describe a halt, a suspension, a pause that interrupts the "simple presence-at-hand" of things, pause that, however, enables us to come closer to the shadows. Are the shadow (of which we spoke in the previous section) and the *daimon*, the divinities of Heidegger's "fourfold," truly opposite dimensions? In the pause, what is created is not only an awaiting, but also an inversion: the pause interrupts the movement of a subject that arranges itself with respect to the world and can give room precisely to what Heidegger calls "releasement." Dwelling is the experience of "letting be."

The activity of this experience is measured precisely through the opening up to the passivity that disturbs the notion itself of a subject. There is, then, never a dwelling in the sense of a "*staying*," of a rest. This experience of "place" constitutes itself in time: the stretched as well as pulsating time of a distancing from oneself.

To entrust oneself to things is to keep oneself on the side. Literality cannot account for this paradox. Here is the "almost nothing," the ethical gap, the *daimon*. It is to recognize the priority of the event; to respect, in things, the dimension of what is not knowable (exactly the divinities in Heidegger's language); it is a nearing that paradoxically amounts to a keeping distance. The upheaval that this "almost nothing" entails is the ability "to suspend" our habitual way of being within the everyday experience, a way that is characterized by the opposite of modesty, that is, by the mastery we think we have on things or even only by the unaware prevailing of a relation of knowledge and usability. If knowledge and mastery through knowledges already orient (without our need to project such an orientation) our average experience, the ethical upheaval will not be another knowledge to line up with the one already functioning; rather, it will be the possibility to tarnish and suspend mastery. In sum, the matter is that of a relaxation of the network of knowledges within which we are always already caught. This does not mean to deny the efficiency and the importance of knowledges, but rather to reclaim a precedence and a difference for our "dwelling." From this perspective, Heidegger, Levinas, and Jankélévitch move along the same path.

In the same "Letter on Humanism," we can find precious indications with respect to this. One worth emphasizing above all is when Heidegger says how we must not ascend but rather *descend* toward proximity. The descent of which he speaks is much less easy than the ascent because it has to do with a *minus*. Heraclitus who warms himself, rather than cogitate as Descartes would do, realizes a risky diminution. What may it mean? We may understand it if we think that modesty, the step backward, the introduction of a "minus" take upon themselves the risk of taking away legitimacy from the ascending and progressive chain to gain a distance-displacement in which another idea of human being (and this, beyond any equivocation, is Heidegger's goal) that is not the effect or the repetition of the same chain can be recognized. Bergson had perceived this art of the "minus" with respect to the quantification of the psyche, and the Bergsonian Levinas and Jankélévitch have then nourished an ethics of diminution. Heidegger's modesty, we might add, pushes itself to being suspicious of ethics itself, which can immediately become a privileged form of knowledge. It limits itself to saying "dwelling" and to indicating a sort of metaphorical space in which the very notion of "being" will not properly be at home.

The Figure of Withdrawal

A significant part of twentieth-century thought offers us a philosophical gesture that is a way of inhabiting experience. We can think not only of Heidegger, Levinas, Jankélévitch (and Bergson), but also of Hannah Arendt and Simone Weil, Deleuze's taking up of Nietzsche, and, of course, we can think of the phenomenological line Husserl-Ricoeur. Within these philosophies, despite their apparent differences, we shall not circumscribe a particular section, the special place of ethics; rather, we shall observe how each of them aims at an experience of thinking that, as exercise, involves the whole of subjectivity and attempts to erode the predominance of the will to power. The ethical movement of weakening, which obviously traverses from one side to the other as well as the horizon of current hermeneutics, cannot then be treated as if it were a local and secondary path in the contemporary philosophical debate. On the contrary, it seems to represent an epochal feature that perhaps allows to delineate a physiognomy in a philosophical scenario that appears fragmented, plural, void of a specific "historicity."

If Husserl's phenomenology is a variation of the Cartesian *cogito*, and Heidegger's thought is a reconsideration of ontology, with the name "ethics" we can try to mark a border or a line that identifies the overall attitude with which these philosophies take leave from the traditional concepts of truth and knowledge. Ethics thus comes to indicate the dominating tonality, a shifting in the way of thinking. If we want to try to describe this shifting, it will be useless to look for concepts, rules, Humanity and its imperatives, values, in sum, a Morality. We will first have to grasp a movement of thought within and even against itself. Not to betray it immediately, we may try to give a *figure* to such a movement. This image or figure can no longer be that of a dash: a dashing forward, a progressing, a self-planning ahead, a self-projecting. Certainly the figure of the "beyond" repeats itself in contemporary thought in Heidegger and Husserl themselves. But which torsion or metamorphosis can we discern in repetition? It is no longer or only a going beyond, a widening, a transcending: it is not only a crossing, a proceeding; it is no longer a grasping, a taking possession. It is not even only an approximating, an attempting at adhering to things. It is rather the figure of the withdrawal, of the self-withdrawal: the diminution, the suspension, the step backward, the withholding, the inhabiting the distance.

The audacity of this gesture, as it were, consists precisely in its modesty. It is not a gesture of mastery: I do not stop, I do not step back to interpose a safety distance, to have time better to "see" the object and thus better to grasp it, to catch it within the concept. The withdrawal upsets the seeing as well as the grasping, and essentially puts in danger the pair "subject-object." Through this movement, the subjects *declines*; in a certain way, it explodes and exposes itself, finding again its own experience, but as the experience of its own paradoxicality. This risk is not treated by the contemporary thought to which I refer to as an engulfment, a destruction, a tragic nihilism; it is, rather, a possible recovery, the possibility we have to bring ourselves back in a continuous, swinging movement to the uncertain and ambivalent place that is the place of our experience. The ethical experience, the exercise, consists in knowing how to stay within this movement comprised of withdrawal and oscillation, whose intermittent withdrawal has no halting place, whose place is not a place but again a movement, a going back and forth, a pendulum, and whose language, finally, can no longer be a code, a rigid exchange between things and words; rather, it will have to open up on its own turn to mobility and oscillation.

Let us start with Levinas, who has spoken of "retroscendence." The experience, the patience of passivity—as Levinas understands it—is precisely a movement of withdrawal, a stepping back from the "luminosity" of being toward the twilight of the *il y a*, of existence.[14] In fact, if we observe how, in his intellectual biography, Levinas comes to the primacy of ethics (a wisdom that, for him, comes "before" philosophy), we discover that the path is given by the siphoning [*risucchiante*] ambivalence of the *il y a*. One can think of the themes of his works from the 1940s, which are often intertwined with Blanchot's analogous themes: insomnia, night, the murmur of the impersonal existence, eros, death. In truth, if we look at the genesis, we realize that for Levinas himself ethics does not constitute itself as a content of wisdom (in his case, Judaism), but rather as the fatigue and the risk of bringing oneself back to a standpoint before the light of preconstituted knowledge: to an identity that is an alterity. The exercise that opens up to ethics requires the *neutralization* of the existent that gives itself as already codified in an "ontology" essentially violent.

Is this not precisely the dominating tonality of the phenomenological exercise? Is Husserl's suspension, *epoché* truly, as Levinas would have it, the organ that presides to the modern philosophy of light? Or is it, rather, an exercise in distancing, not from the world of things, but from a phenomenon with no enigmas, from an image of the world where subject and object mutually offer each other the mirror, and finally—but primarily—from the very notion of the subject as something full and already given? The abstention from the worldly—the key of the phenomenological "method"—is an ethical gesture Husserl acknowledges as an *immer wieder* [again and again] exercise, an exercise of life, not a technique with which to think better, a resistance to the enframing of the real, a fight against the "psychologism" that would want the I to be simply a piece of this real.

In one of its astronomical meanings, the term "*epoché*" originally denoted the light arrest in the lunar eclipsis; in sum, it was a measure of shadow.[15] The exercise of the *epoché*, which Husserl claims to be legitimated by a secularized warranty (in comparison with the Cartesian doubt), reveals itself to Husserl himself as an exercise with no net, with no bottom. In section 53 in the *Crisis of European Sciences*, we read that the "fate [of phenomenology] . . . is to become involved again and again in paradoxes."[16] The modesty of *epoché* as an exercise in withdrawal, a measure of shadow, can only result in the paradox of subjectivity. An I that is at the same time and contradictorily both servant and master, that is consuming its own mastery and can find itself only by staying in the paradox, in a balance in which it is no longer substance, is no longer object, and not even identical pole of its own acts. Where then does it find itself? In the exercise itself, in the practice itself of distancing, which then is no longer simply a way to reach a goal (an egology, for example); rather, it is already the landing place. Literally, the path leads nowhere: meaning and "rationality" ultimately play themselves out in this running across, in the continuous upheaval which, for Husserl, is precisely a "revolution" in the way of thinking.

Levinas's refusal of the *epoché*, which occurs precisely when he describes the exercise of thinking as a withdrawing, certainly has Heideggerian roots. In his Marburg lectures from the 1920s, and then in *Being and Time*, Heidegger had in fact erased the *epoché* as the organ of transcendental subjectivity, and thus of modern metaphysics. Yet, Heidegger's later thinking will focus around *Gelassenheit*, or releasement. The dominating tonality will become the "letting be," and its leading themes will be proximity as distance, the dimming of light (*Lichtung*), the measure of experience to be found in the instable play of the fourfold (*Geviert*), of the event (*Ereignis*). One should practice the *art of lessening*, Heidegger will say: one has to fight the "overfull eye"[17] that prevents us from "seeing" something that instead reveals itself only through a dimming, a withdrawal, a self-withdrawing. As we have remarked earlier, the difference between a house present-at-hand and a poetic dwelling cannot be established through a conceptual identification, that is, through a beam of light that circumscribes and thus defines the entity that is lit up. This decisive difference, which I have called ethical tonality and have indicated with the movement of modesty, is *literally* invisible. Yet, this almost nothing determines our thinking and our entire existing.

How is perceiving the invisible possible? The modesty of Heraclitus, who warms himself by the oven, is for Heidegger emblematic of an attitude that is not the simple "use" of things; it is not willing power, grasping with the hands and the mind. It is rather a nearing distance, a displacement in the direction of ourselves, a dis-estrangement. What accompanies this—as Heidegger constantly emphasizes—are the features of "meekness," "tenderness," and the entire semantic constellation characterizing the "weakness" of weakening. There is a shift in register here, exactly as in Husserl's *epoché*. The step backward, by which Heidegger reproposes and unknowingly reinterprets the less striking meaning of *epoché*, is such a shift in register: from knowing to dwelling, from seeing to a "listening" that is "another light."

I think that Heidegger and Husserl's indications must be taken up with this breadth and in their entire aporetic aspects, even beyond the somewhat unilateral "seriousness" with which both keep treating the attitude they are clearly indicating to us.

In the conclusion of *Time and Narrative*, Ricoeur remarks on the set-back Husserl encounters when he realizes that philosophical language is no longer literally capable of expressing what the *epoché* lets one see:[18] phenomenological transcendentalism is thus crossed from side to side by a metaphorics that is polarized around the image of the "flux." On the one hand, according to Ricoeur, this metaphorics is the first sign of the nonmastery on the side of the constituting consciousness. The metaphor introduces distance, and distance necessarily goes along with something illusory; the metaphor, in its withdrawing, is accompanied by irony. The nonmastery, the dismissal of the pretense entails an ironic gap. On the other hand, for Jankélévitch, modesty borders with irony. The withdrawal, which affects the mastery of knowledge and the mastery of the subject's knowledge of itself, or which, at any rate, for a moment allows one to see things in a different light, is at the same time a self-entrusting to a mobile and risky zone. The fictitious and ironical feature of the metaphor expresses this instability. It is as though—through the movement of modesty—we are to perceive the almost nothing that differentiates a gray scenario from a scenario "inhabited by the gods," but then, precisely because of this, we are to find ourselves acting with a further caution: the caution of not turning into something "serious" and stable a condition that rather resembles a (never fixable) moment of unbalance.

Notes

1. I refer to Gianni Vattimo, *The End of Modernity*, trans. J. Snyder (Baltimore: Johns Hopkins University Press, 1988); "Ontology of Actuality," in this volume, pp. 89–107 ; *The Transparent Society*, trans. D. Webb (Baltimore, MD: Johns Hopkins University Press, 1992); but especially "La verità dell'ermeneutica," in *Filosofia 88* (Bari: Laterza, 1989), pp. 227–49.

2. Vattimo, "La verità dell'ermeneutica," p. 234.

3. Ibid., p. 235.

4. See Gianni Vattimo, "Art and Oscillation," in *The Transparent Society*, pp. 45–61.

5. For a clarification of this point, refer to Pier Aldo Rovatti, "Riflessioni sull'ombra," *aut aut* 229–30 (1989): 99–110.

6. See Carl Gustav Jung, "The Relation between the Ego and the Unconscious," in *Two Essays in Analytical Psychology*, vol. 7, trans. R. F. C. Hull, *The Collected Works of C. G. Jung* (Princeton, NJ: Princeton University Press, 1978), pp. 123–244.

7. Carl Gustav Jung, *Aion: Researches into the Phenomenology of the Self*, vol. 9, part 2, trans. R. F. C. Hull, *The Collected Works of C. G. Jung*, p. 8.

8. With respect to the critique of literality, see James Hillman, *Re-visioning Psychology* (New York: Harper and Row, 1975).

9. See Umberto Galimberti, *La terra senza il male: Jung dall'inconscio al simbolo* (Milan: Feltrinelli, 1984), and Mario Trevi, *Metafore del simbolo* (Milan: Cortina, 1986).

10. Martin Heidegger, "Letter on Humanism," in *Basic Writings*, ed. D. F. Krell (New York: Harper and Row, 1977), pp. 193–242.

11. See Hans Blumenberg, *Das Lachen der Thrakerin: Eine Urgeschichte der Theorie* (Frankfurt: Suhrkamp, 1987).

12. Heidegger, "Letter on Humanism," pp. 233–34.

13. See Martin Heidegger, "Building, Dwelling, Thinking," trans. A. Hofstadter, in *Poetry, Language, Thought* (New York: Harper and Row, 1971), pp. 143–62.

14. See Emmanuel Levinas, *Existence and Existents*, trans. A. Lingis (The Hague: Nijhoff, 1978), and *Time and the Other*, trans. R. Cohen (Pittsburgh, PA: Duquesne University Press, 1987). For the remarks on this theme, refer to Pier Aldo Rovatti, *Intorno a Levinas* (Milan: Unicopli, 1987).

15. For a discussion of these ideas, see Pier Aldo Rovatti, "L'enigma dell' 'epoché,'" in *Filosofia* 88, pp. 127–38.

16. Edmund Husserl, *The Crisis of European Sciences*, trans. D. Carr (Evanston: Northwestern University Press, 1970), p. 181.

17. On this, see the remarks on Heidegger and metaphor developed in the first part of Pier Aldo Rovatti, *Il declino della luce* (Genoa: Marietti, 1988).

18. See Paul Ricoeur, *Time and Narrative*, vol. III, trans. K. McLaughlin and D. Pellauer (Chicago: University of Chicago Press, 184–88), pp. 267–68.

Part 3

Opening the Borders

The Appeal of the World

The chapters in Part 3 welcome the indication widely advanced in Part 2 that the themes of ethics, the finitude of existence, and human subjectivity constitute the meaning of philosophy in the present age and the response to the current philosophical situation and engage in a theoretical meditation on more concrete issues that present themselves to philosophy once it has accepted its declination into ethics. The following meditations on the nature of passions and rationality, on the embodied nature of subjectivity and of sexual difference, on the concept of justice in the time of globalization, and on the very concept of globalization open wider the borders of ethics toward a redefinition of its intersection with religion and, especially, with politics.

The first chapters in Part 3, "Logics of Delusion," is by Remo Bodei (Università di Pisa). Bodei's philosophical interests have focused on German classical philosophy, on utopian thinking in the nineteenth and twentieth centuries, and on contemporary political philosophy, extending later to include the Greek and Roman worlds, Augustine, and the notions of individuality and passion with special attention devoted to the theme of desire, that is, to the role of passions in attaining better life conditions. According to Bodei, the passions traditionally have been considered a threat and a cause of incertitude for the serenity of the mind and the firmness of character. The passions appear as rendering humans enslaved to external powers so that when one falls prey to them, one is said to be outside of oneself—to fall prey to the passions means not to be free. Thus, Bodei concludes, reason is traditionally opposed to the passions. On the one hand, there is logic, and on the other there is the absence of logic; on one side there is order, and on the other is disorder. What Bodei's chapter shows is not only that the passions, explored through the concept of delusion, have their own logics, but also that they need to be taken into consideration as far as moral behavior is concerned; moreover, they do not constitute at all a "cancer in reason," as for Kant. According to Bodei, new spaces open up then in the folds of rationality.

The opening up of new spaces for philosophical discourse is also the topic of the second chapter, "Toward a Symbolic of Sexual Difference," by Luisa Muraro (Università di Verona). Educated in the metaphysical, neo-scholastic tradition of the Università Cattolica del Sacro Cuore in Milan, Muraro was heavily influenced by the metaphysician Gustavo Bontadini. From the start, Muraro's work has been tied to feminism; she is among the founders of the Milan feminist bookstore and publisher *La Libreria delle Donne*, and of the philosophical community *Diotima*, which has developed and dif-fused the thinking of difference until it became an undeniable reality in contemporary Italian philosophy. Written in a very personal style that con-sciously resists the temptation of abstract theorization without giving up the rigor of speculation, Muraro's chapter begins with a consideration of the fundamental historicity of human beings and hence of the historical charac-ter of the ethics in which they engage. Muraro then argues for an ethics of sexual difference, the meaning of which she explores, starting not with a vindication of rights and equality (that is, with a politics of justice), but rather with the linguistic formulation of the meanings and desires that being man and woman assume. In the end, for Muraro, an ethics of difference amounts to a symbolic of difference, and she concludes with a call to a symbolic revolution that redesigns the borders between being man and being woman, between culture and nature.

The opening of the borders from ethics toward other dimensions, more specifically toward religion and politics, is at the center of Emanuele Severino's chapter, "On Virtue." Severino, who taught for many years at the Università di Venezia, was educated at the Università di Pavia under the guidance of Bontadini, with whom he clamorously broke relations while they were teach-ing together at the Università Cattolica del Sacro Cuore in Milan in 1970. This break, which originated in a dispute regarding Bontadini's analysis of becoming and also took the feature of a geographical move to the Università di Venezia, marked the beginning of the development of Severino's own original thinking, which has been named "neoparmenidism." According to Severino, whose philosophical position develops in sustained conversation with Nietzsche, Heidegger, and Marx, the Western world is dominated by a nihilistic will to power, to domination, to abuse, and to the devastation of nature, which is the consequence of the folly of placing trust in the notion of becoming. The will to power, ultimately displayed in the technological attitude, is in fact based on the conviction that things and humans are destructible, modifiable, and manipulable because they are exposed to nullification due to the process of becoming. Against the "folly of becoming," Severino suggests a return to Parmenides that does not deny the multiplicity of beings, but rather asserts the immutability of Being. Through his original Parmenidean ontology, Severino reads the entire history of metaphysics as the alteration and forgetfulness of the authentic meaning of being. In his chapter, Severino intertwines his metaphysical position with considerations

related to the spheres of ethics, politics, and religion. In its originary meaning, Severino argues, virtue means strength or power. Within the Western
tradition, ethics and politics confer to human beings and to the *polis*, respec-
tively, the greatest power, because they connect them to the absolute power
of God. In this sense, Christian theology speaks of cardinal and theological
virtues. The physical and psychic power of human actions (wherever it unfolds,
whether in ethics, politics, religion, economics, law, art, and so on) is successful only when it is inscribed in the "true" power, that is, only if it
presupposes some opening to the meaning of the truth. The advent of philosophy consists in such an opening. Later, Severino remarks, Christianity
has attributed to the faith in Jesus those features that for the Greeks were
possessed by the truth, namely, incontrovertibility, conclusiveness, indubita-
bility, totality. Yet, he argues, in our epoch thought has brought to an end
the truth of Western tradition—God is dead. The power and strength of
virtue can no longer be based on true power. The various forms of virtue
become mutually conflictual. Virtue is no longer defined by its truth, only by
its power to annihilate the antagonist powers. Today the supreme virtue,
capable of subordinating to itself the goals of any other form of virtue, is
technics guided by modern science—technics that in its deepest meaning is
irreducible to the scientific, physical, and technical conception of technics.
The ground of the faith in virtue that supports the entire history of the West,
and by now of the world, is for Severino the way in which Greek philosophy
has understood power ever since its beginning: as the ability not only to
make things and events of the world become other, but also to make them
become that absolutely other which is their existence (being) and nonexistence. The inhabitants of the Western world are the inhabitants of supreme
virtue, and they do not even suspect, Severino concludes, that their faith is
the supreme violence, the extreme folly.

The political theme in relation to the current world situation power-
fully dominates the next chapter, "Two Concepts of Utopia and the Idea of
Global Justice," by Salvatore Veca (Università di Pavia). Veca studied at the
Università Statale di Milano, where he worked under the guidance of Enzo
Paci and Ludovico Geymonat, first on issues of theories of knowledge and
epistemology later focusing on themes of economics and social and political
theories, both in relation to Marx and to the wider international scene.
Influenced by the Anglo-Saxon perspective and the tradition of normative
political theorizing, Veca has introduced the debates on theories of justice
into the Italian political discussion and has oriented his research interests
toward the problem of the relation between normative and political theory
with a specific concern for the question of pluralism as a fact and as a value
in democracies and in theories of international justice. In his chapter, Veca
starts with the consideration that the major challenge for normative political
theory is that of delineating an idea of global justice. Those who aim at
pursuing such a goal, he argues, are bound to run into several kinds of

objections, among which are those deriving from political realism and maintaining that the goal of a theory of global justice is unachievable unless one falls into the fatal mistake of a negative utopia, as well as those deriving from contextual or communitarian theories maintaining that the criteria or principles of justice are inevitably local and situated and that no universalistic perspective can be achieved with some hope for success. Against both, and through a conversation with Rawls and Habermas, Veca argues for and develops several notions salient for a theory of global justice that is capable of withstanding the resistances of political realism and of various versions of communitarianism or contextualism in ethics and politics.

The horizon of globalization constitutes the background of Giacomo Marramao's chapter, "The World and the West Today." Marramao (Università di Roma Tre) studied at the historicist school of Eugenio Garin in Florence and in the tradition of critical theory as developed by the Frankfurt school. After having addressed the themes of the revision and crisis of Italian and European Marxism by focusing on the philosophical status of the notion of *praxis*, Marramao has increasingly been concerned with two issues: the theme of power and the question of time. With respect to the first issue, Marramao's philosophy delineates a theory of power centered on a rigorous genealogical reconstruction of the presuppositions of Western rationalism; as for the second, he has attempted a radical reconfiguration of the problem of time that, against Bergsonian and Heideggerian theories of authentic temporality, emphasizes the inextricability of the nexus between time and space. In his chapter, Marramao genealogically retraces the set of phenomena generally labeled "globalization" back to the "hit" (*urto*) between the world and the West, which marks the entire event of modernity. Such phenomena call for a reinterpretation of the main conceptual pairs inherited by the tradition, such as identity/difference, redistribution/recognition, necessity/contingence, universal/singular. A crucial testing field is constituted precisely by the pair global/local. According to Marramao, because the "local" is neither resistance nor delay, but rather the interface of a "global" that can no longer be conceived according to linear schematics such as progress-regress, modernity-tradition, center-periphery, it follows that the phenomenon of the "glo-cal" is destined to affect deeply our way of understanding the logic of identity. Thus, far from resulting into a Westernization of the world, globalization presents itself with the features of what Marramao defines as a problematic "West passage" (*passaggio a occidente*) destined to transform not only the "other" cultures, but also our democratic civilization itself. Marramao concludes by formulating a universalist politics of difference grounded on a critical reexamination of the typically Western categories of democracy and philosophy.

The theme of the global is indirectly at the center also of the concluding chapter in Part 3, "Names of Place: Border," by Massimo Cacciari (Università San Raffaele), in which the need arising from the political contemporary scenario to cross and intersect borders, whether disciplinary or geographical, is explicitly thematized. Before taking his current position, Cacciari taught for a long time at the Università di Venezia. He was educated in the politically active tradition of the Università di Padua, where he participated in the 1968 student protests and was (and is still) involved in various leftist parties and political movements. At the center of his philosophical meditation is the crisis of modern rationality, which has revealed itself as being incapable of grasping the ultimate meaning of reality and has abandoned the quest for the foundations of knowledge. Moving from a study of "negative thought" between Schopenhauer and Nietzsche, whose connections with twentieth-century literary, artistic, and scientific culture he analyzes, and constantly conversing with Heidegger, Cacciari intertwines philosophical and theological questions and revisits the entire history of philosophy and Heidegger's own interpretative paradigm to retrace the presuppositions of negative thought in some aspects of Western philosophical thinking and religious tradition. In his chapter, on the wave of those crucial positions that identify in Aristotle's *Physics* some of the richest and most meaningful parts of Aristotle's *corpus*, Cacciari begins with an original analysis of the meaning of Aristotle's concept of *topos*-place. *Topos* ultimately means, Cacciari argues, not a statically circumscribed place, but rather the extreme of the body, the place that the body achieves in its movement, and thus its extreme limit, that is, its border. Yet according to Cacciari's interpretation, the border can be defined only as the place of contact—of the contact of the body, which has reached its extreme, with what is other than itself. Thus, the place can only be defined through its relation with the other because what "borders" the place is nothing else than the place where place touches the other and is touched by it. These philosophical aporias, Cacciari remarks, can cast new light on the contemporary political processes. Cacciari's concern is that the elimination of borders might mean not at all a liberation from barriers, but rather the creation of an undifferentiated space-time where no body exists in its singularity and where thus no relationship can occur. Against such a possibility, he argues that it is not the border that needs to be eliminated, but rather its isolating-segregating notion, which contradicts the very concept of *topos*-place. Cacciari concludes his chapter with an invitation to Europe to become the place where Aristotle's ancient notion of *topos*-place becomes once again possible. Thus, again as in Plato's beginning, with which Part 1 in this volume opened, philosophy colors itself with the political, but a notion of the political that has accepted the challenge of a different ethics and that will thus yield to different religious configurations.

Chapter 11

Logics of Delusion

Remo Bodei

Delusion represents an exceptional test case for the principal categories of common sense and philosophical thought: "reason," "truth," and "reality." Through an engagement with Freud's legacy and the most considered results of twentieth-century psychiatry, this chapter analyzes its paradoxical forms and sheds light on the logics that underlie and orient its specific modalities of temporalization, conceptualization, and argumentation.

Whereas in English one may use frequently the term "delusion" instead of "delirium" to indicate what in the Romance languages we call "*delirio*" or "*délire*," the etymology of this term is significant. Its origin lies in a peasant metaphor, in the act of *de-lirare*, of overstepping the *lira*, the portion of ground bounded by two furrows. The idea of moving beyond the area of sown ground also has connotations of sterility and excess. Like Odysseus, who feigned madness by plowing the sand, the one who is deluded struggles vainly to cultivate soil that will not bear fruit, turning his back on the fertile fields of reason. Delusion, then, has traditionally been presented as synonymous with irrationality (absurdity, groundlessness, error, chaos), whereas by contrast its mirror image, reason, has been defined in terms of evidence, demonstrability, truth, and order. Over time, the two concepts have become complementary.

Aside from any play on words, why should one evoke the "logics of delusion"? The first step toward convincing oneself that it is not a matter of a baroque paradox consists in not allowing oneself to be unduly influenced by the seriousness that terms such as *logos* and "logic" have acquired because *legein* refers to the work of gathering, sifting, and ordering. If that is so, nothing prevents us from speaking of one or more logics of delusion, by which we mean specific modes—however anomalous—of articulating perceptions, images, thoughts, beliefs, affects, and moods according to principles

---

An earlier version of this chapter appeared as "Logics of Delusion," in *History of Psychiatry* 16 (2005): 61–72. This version of the essay was translated by David Webb and revised by Brian Schroeder.

of their own that do not conform to the criteria of argumentation and expression a determinate society shares.

One might object that such logics are not within the scope of our
reason, precisely because it rejects them; or else that one should resist the
temptation—as Roger Caillois has said in relation to dreams—of regarding
delusion as any more significant than the designs found on the wings of
butterflies or what appear to be the outlines of cities and of clouds on stones
such as agates.[1]

Yet the simple alternative between delusion and logic, on the pretext
of their incompatibility, makes sense only from the point of view of a restricted, defensive, and self-referential rationality. Without annulling the
difference in level between the two terms or in any way renouncing our
critical faculties, I show how a hospitable and expansive reason—more humble,
but no less rigorous—may be capable of recognizing the nuclei of truth, the
typicality, and the rich variety of delusions. Its welcoming approach is not
based on conceit, on mere "logical charity" (on the desire to align oneself
with psychical suffering to alleviate it) or on the intent of exorcising what
one does not understand with a superstitious, "Be gone!" Rationality of this
kind tends to take on the contradictions and paradoxes of delusion without
allowing itself to be fascinated, caught, and held by it. In fact, such rationality is aware of an asymmetry that works to its advantage: it can comprehend
delusion, whereas delusion cannot comprehend it. It is thereby able to account simultaneously for its own truth and its apparent negation (such as the
theory of heliocentrism, which explains how we continue inevitably to see
the sun move around the earth).

With the adoption of this perspective, the utter irreconcilability of
logic and delusion becomes less plausible, and diffidence in the face of what
is unknown or hard to recognize evaporates. But the hardest task is still
ahead of us: to identify and describe the forms in which delusion is organized
according to intentionality and horizons of meaning that are irreducible to
the natural character of the marks on the wings of butterflies. Without ide-
alizing delusion, we can see that it constrains lazy or timid reason to look
into its own folds, to recognize itself not as monolithic, but as a family of
procedures that refer to a common origin and that to evolve must accept
continual challenges.

The question that I tacitly pose—approaching the issue against the
grain from the opposite direction to that generally taken—is not so much
why delusion occurs, as why for the most part we continue to reason normally. With this inquiry I am continuing a program of research that began
with a study of the passions and of those phenomena—such as political
ideologies—in which rationality does not appear to enjoy the right of citizenship. Such a project is justified in my eyes because I am convinced that
perhaps the most noted trend of modern philosophy, the introduction of so-
called rationalism into common sense, in seeking to imitate the successes of

the mathematical and physical sciences, has adopted a model that is strictly inappropriate to the human world. Unable to find anything corresponding with this model within its own boundaries, it has abandoned large and crucial areas of individual and social existence to the thorns and thickets of ignorance. It has thereby handed the task of establishing order to political and religious power, to history, traditions, habits, and fate. To paraphrase Lévi-Strauss (who speaks of *pensée sauvage*, meaning thought that is untamed, spontaneous, uncultivated),[2] I would call the *vie sauvage* that whole area of human experience—including our passions, fantasies, beliefs, and delusions—that is left to the mercy of the "irrational."

It therefore seems indispensable today that we begin a long and exhaustive process aiming at the collective recognition of these terrains, their reintegration into the intellect and cultivated life, and their conversion into the seedbeds for the production and reproduction of meaning.

I begin with the hypothesis, mentioned in passing by Freud in a letter to Fleiss dated December 6, 1896 (and then later abandoned),[3] according to which our psychic mechanisms are not given once and for all and do not develop in a continuous and cumulative manner. They are constructed, rather, from overlapping layers whose congruence is normally ensured by the periodic rearrangement of and repositioning of ideas and memories. Each reordering of the past produces differing versions of the history of an individual whose existence never unfolds in a straight line by successive and constant additions, but instead proceeds by way of leaps and discontinuities. One's existence is split into different "epochs of life," homogeneous spaces of psychic time separated by *cesurae*. After each break in the development of individual existence, there is a "return to base," a retranslation, a regiving of meaning to the "psychic material," and in particular to the mnemonic traces of the preceding phase within the cognitive and emotive horizon of the most recent epoch of life that has been lived through.

As the body "transliterates" its earlier breaks, absorbing them in new forms that conserve traces of the world even as they annul them, so the psychic apparatus reintegrates its material in more or less coherent forms. In all ages of life, suffering that exceeds a certain threshold produces—"almost always"—disturbances of thought that prohibit the processes of translation. This is particularly true of the earliest epoch in which the procedures of symbolization are not yet established. But there are traumatic experiences that by virtue of the suffering they produce resist every translation into the language of successive ages of life. The past thereby manifests itself in two ways: either as dissolved in its recodification within a new system of signs or as encapsulated in the space carved out by the traumatic event. In the first case, it undergoes a metamorphosis into a present that advances and that is able to look on the past as already behind it. In the second, a blank in memory takes the form of a mold, of a receptacle subsequently filled by actions, dreams, fantasies, or delusions. The past and the present are therefore inseparable because the past refuses to give way to a present on which it continues to bear (in the sense both that it "presses" and that it is of "concern").

Each individual is "divided"—a "dividual"—traversed by fault lines and cracks. To pursue the metaphor of writing, the individual is like a palimpsest continually scraped clean and recovered in new layers of signs, until—as long as he remains alive—an *editio princeps* no longer exists. Everyone's biography is in this way studded by areas of darkness, covered with secret wounds that have never completely closed, its temporal structure a complex curve, broken at various points, full of revisions and second thoughts.

When the work of transcription fails adequately to connect the different epochs of life, a part of the subject is excluded and rendered incompatible with the rest. The focal point of suffering is isolated, at the price, however, of establishing an *enclave* within a psychic province subject to laws that are suppressed elsewhere and where psychic materials follow procedures judged *a posteriori* as archaic.

Delusion begins to take the form of a generally failed attempt to translate itself into the present. Grafting itself onto a past that has not been worked through, a real trauma serves to detonate deeper psychic charges that bring incomprehensible remains of what has already been crashing to the surface. These turn out to be just as incomprehensible when combined with new fragments of lived experience. In delusion one is caught in the middle of a tangle of logics that have each structured the experience open to them at different times and that cannot now account for the con-fusion of all the material before them. Caught in this vicelike grip, deluded individuals must shape for themselves a personality and a reality that is synchronized intermittently with the shifting equilibrium reached in the struggle between these logics. Their mind becomes the matrix of further translations that are inappropriate, absurd, and bizarre, yet in conformity with the new world in which they wrap them.

When different levels of "epochs of life" intersect and impede one another, one's awareness of the logical, perceptual, and affective present is dulled. The old wounds bleed and in delusion one seeks areas of compensation that are "extraterritorial" with respect to the interests and preoccupations of the present. The usual temporal parameters are altered. The future, as a simple prolongation of an unacceptable present, is negated and blocked. A kind of sickness of hope occurs, a weakening of the vital force, a loss of interest in oneself and the world. From this moment the life of deluded individuals is closed: each of their projections into the future and into the world of the sane is denied to them. The future closes like a shutter and they are trapped in a time that presses on them until in the end it flattens them. Many of us may, in moments of extreme unease, have had the impression that the future is barred, that life is finished before the inexorable approach of death. For most people, this is no more than a momentary occlusion of the future, of the effort of somehow giving order to the chaos in which an existence thought to have no way out may fall. Delusion arises when it becomes permanent and unavoidable. As Eugène Minkowski writes: "The specific form of the delusional idea is nothing but the attempt of thought, which remains untouched by madness, to establish a logical connection between the different stones of the building in ruins."[4]

In delusion, the past is also modified insofar as it merges with and modifies the present. Moreover, as we see in *Thoughts for the Times on War and Death* (1915), psychic time has a particular constitution for Freud. Against common sense and the whole philosophical tradition, Freud states that coexistence and succession are interlaced. The thesis is not as banal as it might at first seem. To bring out its originality, one need only think of Leibniz (as a point of contrast), for whom time represents the order of succession, whereas space configures the order of coexistence.[5] In Freud, by contrast, time takes on simultaneously the twofold nature of Leibnizian time and space, insofar as "succession implies also coexistence." This initially obscure formula indicates that the past lives on with the present and the immobile (or that which moves more slowly) stands alongside what flows, such that psychic time ends up as precisely the coexistence of coexistence and succession.

From the point of view of the perception of physical space, the copresence of past and present is just as unimaginable as ancient and modern buildings in Rome standing together, whole, in the same place. In our psychic apparatus, however, this kind of miraculous copenetration of stages is real—all the more so because Freud trusts (in accordance with the physiology of his time) that "in psychic life nothing can perish once it has been formed and everything is in some way conserved," such that in the right circumstances "everything can come back to light." In this way, disturbances in thought and affectivity derive from an inability to distinguish and order the various stages of succession within coexistence; that is, from the disarticulation of time as coexistence and as succession.

What happens to someone who cannot translate the suffering encapsulated in the past (reawoken and redoubled by traumas in the present) into an acceptance of their state or an effective will to change it?

I put forward the hypothesis that psychoses arise when the suffering caused by what has been repressed provokes psychic tensions so unbearable that they cannot be made manifest as localized symptoms of compromise, when their translation into the language of the present fails completely. Delusion is therefore the result of a rupture between different stages of existence that is very difficult to overcome. It is the result of an earthquake that wrecks the layers of personality that had been carefully laid one on the other. A trauma, stress, or a life event (or any quite ordinary, perhaps even joyous, matter that intimately involves the existence of the individual:

marriage, divorce, the birth or death of family members, moving homes, changing professions, unexpected financial gains or losses) may reopen wounds that had never completely healed; reactivate unsatisfied desires; renew old fears, feelings of guilt, or misunderstandings, uncovering and aggravating latent cracks and old failings in the logico-affective delimitation of the internal and external worlds.

In the delusional individual, the old world not only vacillates, but it is also set aside and replaced by another one. However, its loss is counterbalanced and made good by the "creation of a new and different reality" that does not present "the same impediments" to the satisfaction of desires. This is not a partial privation of reality: the whole universe as previously perceived, imagined, or thought as wrapped all around in passions and desires, seems suddenly to give way; it must therefore be rebuilt as soon as possible. This is how the contents of delusions appear: like shreds or rags found— however and wherever—to plug the cracks in the relation between the world and I. The fear of seeing one's own life sink increases with the recognition that the tears are concentrated where the dividing wall between the subject and the object is thinnest and most fragile.

The deluded individual breaks the agreement (by no means tacit; in fact annoyingly repeated and disseminated in innumerable localized versions) that demands of everyone that they conform to reality. In all these cases the concept of "reality" must be understood in a sense that is more prescriptive than descriptive. In fact, it indicates an obligation to be faithful to reality as the guarantor of the survival both of the species and of the individual. It indicates the discipline that has been and still is necessary to maintain a shared world and to bring each human being into tune with it, limiting the range of conceptual, perceptual, and affective variation allowed.

Psychoses take the place of reality, reshaping and remodeling the world via hallucinations and delusions, which thereby appear as modalities of a forced *adaequatio*: it is "external" reality that must at all costs conform to "internal" reality, hence the endless attempts to reformulate the perceptual, ideational, and affective present in such a way as to nurture and strengthen the mind's newborn reality. This is, in its own way, a demiurgic work of remodeling the universe, analogous to artistic creation or to "the work of dreams" or to a meticulous activity that is closer to the capillary character of the Roman colonization than it is to devastations from barbarian invasions. Delusion is paradoxically a project of the foundation of the unfoundable, an attempt on the part of one who is lost to make oneself at home in a strange world, the search for an elsewhere to make one's own.

Delusion, in its reconstructive form, is not simply falsity, absence of reason, or error of judgment; rather, it is, paradoxically, overcompensated truth, which—having been repressed, fought, and denied for so long—bursts out like a coiled spring, expanding so powerfully and excessively as to break into areas of sense regarded subjectively as contiguous. One errs, or precisely one becomes "extra-vagant" (moving outside of the *lira*, the sown ground), because due recognition has not been given to a truth that, in its way, just keeps on going: the truth enclosed in the nucleus of experience from preceding epochs of life so terrible that it could not become conscious. The recognition of this truth of delusion cannot occur without there initially being a pain more horrendous than the delusion itself. For it to be overcome, truth must prove preferable to the "compensations" of unreality: it must lead not just to the resigned acceptance of what one has always tried to ignore, but to its positive welcome.

In delusion, it is not that logic proves defective or that the reality test has failed: it is the content gathered there that obeys a different logic. What logics can we be speaking of here? Already in 1956 Gregory Bateson and a group of his colleagues attributed schizophrenia (and delusion) to the effect of "double binds," that is, to messages that cancel each other out or to orders that cannot be followed. When a mother claims to love her child, but does not want to let him grow up as an independent person, in reality "she desires the child for herself, and does not love him for what he is: he must satisfy her profound need for wholeness, purity and affection (being loved). He is not allowed to reject the function imposed on him; above all, he must not grow too much, he must not become autonomous." The child is in this way sent conflicting messages of the type: "I (don't) love you / I (don't) love me." The paradoxical character of messages such as this can be summed up in the command: "Be who you are not!"—the exact opposite of the classic precept (which Pindar, Aristotle, and Nietzsche formulated) "Become who you are!" The "sender" of this message, in this instance the mother, is in the grip of narcissism, but a torn and unhappy narcissism (in which love and hate are turned toward the self and others all at the same time). It thereby transmits to the "recipient" ambiguous signals of manipulation [connivance] and conflict. Clearly hypocritical, it gives to the other a promise of love and freedom, yet also means by this passivity and dependence. And so arise "relational traps," unilateral demands that ultimately become reciprocal and close both parties in a cage with no way out. The demand made on the weakest thereby takes the form of a game of power in which the one who submits effectively says, "I'll become what you want me to become as long as you take care of me."

In technical terms, Bateson and his group develop, at the level of distorted communication, the idea of a deviance with respect to Russell's theory of logical types. "The central thesis of this theory is that there exists a discontinuity between a class and its elements. The class cannot be an element of itself, since the term used for the class is of a different level of abstraction (of a different logical type) to the terms used for the elements." The schizophrenic transgresses this rule of discontinuity and, for this reason, cannot discriminate between different modes of communicating with him or herself or with others, "We advance the hypothesis that whenever an individual finds himself in a situation of a double-bind, his ability to discriminate between logical types suffers a collapse."[6]

In delusion, what changes is the way that the logical mechanisms shared by a determinate community function in the sense either of conceptual formation or of discursive development.

The theses of the psychiatrist Goldstein on the "concreteness" of schizophrenic thought, or its inability to generalize, have for the most part been refuted today.[7] If anything, the opposing thesis prevails, emphasizing marked tendency toward abstraction in schizophrenia, as though in more comprehensive concepts it sought a guarantee against the dissipation, confusion, and the flight of ideas. The idea of overinclusion, proposed for the first time by Cameron in 1944, is thus especially worthy of attention, even if it stands in need of partial correction.[8] The overinclusive idea, common in acute schizophrenia, consists in the inability to choose the elements belonging to a concept, eliminating those less relevant or completely unrelated. To give a simple example, it constitutes an overinclusion to place "Saint Joseph" in the category "furniture" because he is a carpenter. Its complementary opposite is underinclusive thought, which can be found in cases of chronic schizophrenia, and where by contrast the conceptual range is restricted, such that the category "furniture" is applied to tables, but not to wardrobes or to chests of drawers. The apparent concreteness of schizophrenic thought, as Goldstein observed, and the prevalence in it of Cameron's overinclusive model, indicate phenomena that may not be incompatible with one another. I believe that these positions—reformulated and placed in relation with another thesis, that of Frith—may combine to form a new theory capable of connecting and explaining a greater number of phenomena.

According to Frith, overinclusion derives, paradoxically, from the hyperawareness of delusional individuals.[9] They are not able to filter and thereby work through the enormous flux of information reaching them from the external and internal world, nor, above all, the surplus lying beneath the threshold of consciousness in the clinically sane that, if it breaks through, is immediately eliminated and ruled out. Such a position is diametrically opposed to the hypothesis—which Jung took from Pierre Janet, transforming it in the process—according to which in schizophrenia we find an *abaissement du niveau mental* [a lowering of the level of consciousness] to a "fatal level" at the moment in which individuals enter into contact with the archetypes or the symbols of the collective unconscious whose "tide" washes over them.

In Frith's view, delusions are not the products of a troubled consciousness, but the outcome of a failed attempt to interpret coherently the incoming harvest of data. I amend this hypothesis by adding that the flux is not completely without filters. The filter changes: consciousness is awake and ready to gather much of what is normally considered insignificant, but this surplus of data is nearly always assimilated according to other criteria, which may be loose or vague but are nevertheless significant. One could even say that the logics of delusion are modeled on these filters that select lived and thought meanings and let them pass through the bottleneck of consciousness.

In this respect, the "concrete" nature of schizophrenic thought may be nothing but the emphasis given to inappropriate elements within overinclusion to that which has flooded into the field of consciousness, placing itself "illegitimately" under the umbrella of a given concept without having been sifted or ruled out in advance. This explains why the patient finds significance in what others would not even have given any consideration, such as the color of all the ties worn by those attending a party. The abnormal heightening of awareness in mental processes produces a redundancy of information that the deluded individual is unable to catalogue or categorize adequately according to normal standards. This prevents him from ascertaining that the fluxes of conscious become capillary and from working through complex information. The streamlining filter Frith postulated involves a blockage, a turbulence of thoughts and images that form combinations that are bizarre, yet not without meaning.

Overinclusion implies that the concept takes on a broader extension than that commonly accepted, yet also that, within the concept, supplementary or inappropriate connotations are treated as relevant. The two processes are complementary. If we hold the key to the specificity of the deluded individuals' lived experience and to the relevant features of their culture, we are also well placed to understand how the elementary associative chain that generated overinclusion was formed: furniture/carpenter/Saint Joseph. In this case they employ—literally—a metaphor, or rather a "displacement" of meanings that leads, in our Christian-based civilization, from furniture to Joseph. In normal reasoning this association, were it ever to come to mind, would be ignored as without influence or as misleading with respect to the ends of normal communication (although it may conceivably be of use in some witty remark). The deluded individuals are in this respect highly metaphorical, for by means of analogical and subjective intentions they cross-pollinate and hybridize ideas and images that are remote from one another, sometimes inadvertently producing poetic effects, but more often producing associations that are strange and absurd.

Let us now try to extend the validity of this modified notion of overinclusion from the sphere of conceptualization to other fields, and in particular to that of discursive or syllogistic reasoning, which involves the intersection between categories and the corresponding contamination between regions of experience normally thought to be distant and unrelated to one another.

For Von Domarus, the most striking anomaly of schizophrenic thought lies in the presence within it of a logic founded on the identity of the predicates of propositions rather than the subjects.[10] Dogs and tables are placed together by virtue of the fact that they share the property of having four legs. A logic of this kind, traced back to the modus operandi of "primitive thought," assumes that delusions are a form of regression to phases philogenetically and culturally surpassed, to "paleological" thought. Arieti, who shares this view, illustrates it by way of the following example, "A patient believed that she was the Virgin Mary. The process of her reasoning was this: 'The Virgin Mary was a virgin: I am a virgin: I am the Virgin Mary.' "[11]

Von Domarus's theses have been subject to justified criticism for comparing delusional thought to primitive thought, and it has been shown how in delusion one is dealing not with a simple turning back of the mind, but rather with the break up of an already developed structure. The views of Von Domarus and Arieti can still be seen in what Matte Blanco has called the "symmetrization" of a restricted class in a wider class: "a patient who stated that a man was very rich, when asked why he stated this replied: 'Because he is very tall.' Both were subsets of the wider set of those who have something to a high degree. The symmetrization leads to: 'very tall = very rich.' "[12] Like dreams and other unconscious phenomena, delusion is for Matte Blanco attributable to such "symmetric" logic, which is moreover present in all of us alongside "normal" ("asymmetric" or "heterogenic") logic. In the latter it is correct to say that "all cats are feline," but not that "all felines are cats," that "A is the father of B," but not that "B is the father of A." In "symmetric" logic, by contrast, such equivalences are the rule (precisely because what is said is reversible, the subject turning into a predicate and vice versa, thereby canceling the asymmetry of relations). Human thinking and feeling are thereby antinomic by nature. Both logics coexist there, incompatible with each other yet each in competition to assert its own truth. A cohabitation of this kind does not imply their being founded in a higher order structure. "They are like nitrogen and oxygen in the air: together, yet nonetheless separate, never combining to form nitrogen dioxide."[13]

I will not dwell any longer on the solution I have offered to the question of the deluded reasoning as based on the conflict between different logics and temporal orders (to say nothing of the conflict between affects). I end with a few remarks of an existential nature and with an ancient appeal to wisdom.

In its banality and strangeness, delusion reveals the latent fragility of everyone's experience, its reliance on assumptions that are uncorroborated, unanalyzed, or simply forgotten. One trusts in these invisible linchpins around which we have automatically made our thought and our life turn for so long: at least until they crack, dragging down the trust that we had in ourselves and in others as they give way. The desertlike polar solitude in which the deluded individuals close themselves in the company only of their fantasies of persecution, jealousy, and greatness; the visions and the voices; the anomalies in conceptualization and reasoning; the feelings of guilt, shame, or emptiness; the suspicion or the garrulous rush; the ruin, loss, separation, or release from what one loves; all this cannot but drive them further from the path of common experience. Delusion is disturbing and feared precisely because it threatens and puts shockingly into question the world of each and every one of us in all its supposed obviousness.

Should we therefore ignore it, consigning its pure absurdity to an un-inhabited land? The frequency with which madness strikes precisely those individuals whose minds are alert, sharp, and agile did not escape Montaigne. Hence his provocative and disturbing proposal, launched against those who wished to immunize themselves completely against delusion to live within the horizons of a lazy and bureaucratic rationality: "Do you want a healthy man, do you want him well ordered and in a stable and safe condition? Wrap him in darkness, sloth and torpor. We must render ourselves stupid in order to become wise, and dazzle ourselves in order that we may know how to find our way."[14]

Notes

1. Roger Callois, *L'incertitude qui vient des rêves* (Paris: Gallimard, 1956), and *The Writing of Stones* (Charlottesville: University of Virginia Press, 1985).

2. Claude Lévi-Strauss, *The Savage Mind* (Chicago: Chicago University Press, 1966).

3. Sigmund Freud, *Thoughts for the Times on War and Death*, in *The Standard Edition of the Complete Psychological Works of Sigmund Freud*, ed. J. Strachey (London: Hogarth Press, 1961).

4. Eugène Minkoswki, "Etude psychologique et analyse phénoménologique d'un cas de mélancolie schizophrenique," *Journal de psychologie normale et pathologique* 20 (1923): 543–60.

5. G. W. F. Leibniz, *Réplique au troisième écrit Anglois*, vol. VII, in *Streitschriften zwischen Leibniz und Clarke, Philosophische Schriften*, ed. C. J. Gerhardt (Berlin: Weidmannsche Buchhandlung, 1890).

6. G. Bateson, D. D. Jackson, J. Haley, J. W. Weakland, "Towards a Theory of Schizophrenia," *Behavioral Science* 1 (1956): 251–64.

7. Kurt Goldstein, *Language and Language Disturbances* (New York: Grune and Stratton, 1948).

8. Norman Cameron, "Experimental Analysis of Schizophrenic Thinking," in *Language and Thought in Schizophrenia*, ed. J. S. Kasanin (Berkeley: University of California Press, 1944), pp. 50–64.

9. Christopher Frith, "Consciousness, Information Processing, and Schizo-phrenia," *British Journal of Psychiatry* 134 (1979): 225–35.

10. Alexander Von Domarus, "The Specific Laws of Logic in Schizophrenia," in *Language and Thought in Schizophrenia*, pp. 104–14.

11. Silvano Arieti, *Interpretation of Schizophrenia* (New York: Basic Books, 1974).

12. Ignacio Matte Blanco, *The Unconscious as Infinite Sets: An Essay in Bi-Logic* (London: Duckworth Press, 1975), p. 54.

13. Ibid., p. 118.

14. Michel de Montaigne, *Essais*, vol. II, XII, in *Oeuvres completes*, ed. A. Thiboudet and M. Rat (Paris: Gallimard, 1962).

Chapter 12

Toward a Symbolic of Sexual Difference

LUISA MURARO

A n ethics of sexual difference is a formulation we do not find in the philosophical tradition. To begin with, we want to know what it is. There is no one who can tell us, however, because on its side the tradition is mute with respect to this, and on our side we are only at the beginning. We must hope that the definition we lack comes from an exchange among us when we are aided by the work of language. It is a matter of coming to know what the expression ["ethics of sexual difference"] means, and our words do not come to us without the language's agreement and cooperation.

We immediately notice how the language we speak does not ignore the fact of sexual difference. It has two grammatical genders that are termed masculine and feminine,[1] like the sexual genders. Moreover, in it also the names of inanimate or abstract things are masculine or feminine, and this seems to make us perceive the whole world as gendered, from sun to moon, from truth to homeland, up to the legs of tables. I do not know. It is a matter of linguistic facts that lend themselves to different interpretations. They all agree, however, on the recognition of the significance that the fact of sexuality has or has had for us human beings. And this is so even before the fact was linked to procreation.

We could almost see here the beginning of an ethics. This is so because language creates the first symbolic order in relation to which any other order, including logic, finds itself secondary. Yet, in itself, language is neither logical nor right nor true: this is so not because of any indifference or shortcoming as some presumptuous one might think. Oh no! This is so due to language's extraordinary ability to embrace anything and its contrary with their mysterious consistency; this is an ability only poetry attains.

This work has been published as "Verso un'etica della differenza sessuale," in *Introduzione all'etica*, ed. C. Vigna (Milan: Vita e Pensiero), pp. 211–29.

211

Language does not exonerate us from our personal commitment to judgment because language itself does not judge, does not discriminate, and is good for everything and everyone, like the sun or the rain. Ethics, on the contrary, is a qualified and selective symbolic order; that is, it is oriented in one direction rather than another, in the direction of good, just, happiness, and so on, according to different doctrines.

What language does on its own is simply to make the biological given of sexuation sayable, and thereby human, thus exposing it to all the complications of our humanity. Among these, we must include also the silence of the philosophical tradition with respect to the theme that concerns us; we are forced, therefore, to leave it and walk other paths.

Uccio's Difference

After the birth of my brother Uccio, something, maybe the name or the use of the masculine ("*el xé così bon!* [he is so good!]"), warned me that he was not like us, that is, like my sister Giuliana and myself, who were like our mother. I lived in a world populated as well by men, some with a uniform (during the German occupation), some without, and the issue gave me nothing more to think than the existence of animals; like the latter, the former too were different from us, and one could tell it easily. Yet, not Uccio: he had just been born, he looked like Giuliana, and he had very intimate relations with my mother.

"Mom, I asked her, how could you know that Uccio is not a baby girl?" When translated into Italian, this was my question. Notice its precise formulation, which did not allow for storylike escapes. I did not ask a why, I did not discuss the fact; I only asked about its knowability. But through this path, I clearly aimed at the fact of difference, which was there, endowed with a mysterious evidence, in front of my eyes without my noticing anything.

If we stick to the form of the question, strictly speaking we could not say that we are outside the philosophical tradition, unknown scholastically but in some way formally present to that questioning little girl. We are already outside of it, however, because of the maternal authority called into picture, which the Western philosophical tradition does not ignore, but does not recognize as such. We will see shortly the effects of distortion due to this missed recognition.

How do you know what you know? How have you made what you have made (someone different from us)? This is what I was asking my mother. I addressed her without attributing to her the decision of Uccio's different gender, but rather with the certainty that she, and she alone, had the acuteness and the authority to assess the true. The question was well posed, but there was a problem, or rather, two problems, connected between them. I immediately intuited the first; but the second, I (we) have been thinking about all these years.

I knew that, besides being the best informed, my mother was also someone reliable who did not tease children, as other adults often did. I was also certain that she had no problem in putting together words and reality, but in this I was wrong, as I discovered at that very moment. The daughter of an elementary school teacher, she was convinced that, religion aside, the truth had to be sought in what is stated by the positive sciences. But what of issues of sex and sexuality? Not exactly, because in this field she had partly remained very attached to an archaic culture of sexual mysteries, together with the help and disturbance, at the same time, of the imperatives of Catholic sexual morality.

As soon as I asked, I realized that perhaps it would have been better not to have asked, so that I accepted the answer without persistence, although it was not at all clear to me. "*Dal pipì*," my mother answered, thus succeeding in being positivist and sibylline at the same time. In the language we spoke, which we had learned from her, one said *la pipì*, that is, in the feminine, and this was what doctors called "the urine." The concept, well supported by corporeal needs and experiences, was clear to us. On the other hand, there were no words for the genitalia. That strange masculine form, *il pipì*, employed by my mother, made me think, as a consequence, that sexual difference was in the urine, though not in an evident manner (I knew Uccio's peepee), but rather in a way that could be found through special procedures, such as lab analysis (of which I had some idea because of a recently experienced illness).

I was silent and did not draw conclusions, and when, on the occasion of a childish and mixed game, at the end of the garden, behind an edge of wild herbs, I could admire our different genitalia, I did not think at all that that was the meaning of the famous answer. It could not be because the answer was dry and serious, whereas the spectacle we offered ourselves was luxurious and, moreover, comic. In fact we laughed, like the goddess Demeter in front of the nudity of the affectionate Baubo,[2] and like Abraham and Sarah when they discovered themselves pregnant.

When I became a grown up in my turn, I thought that my mother had been guarding a door behind which was nothing left to be guarded because everything had been demolished or carried away along paths she did not know, for example, women's emancipation.

Now, I do not think that any longer, and I think that her poor answer was truthful both for what it said and for what it did not say. The question remained as an ear open to words that perhaps were never uttered, that perhaps were lost or made inaudible. But this was in fact a too much suffered knowledge, written entirely in the bodies ever since who knows how long, so that my mother, her generous goodwill notwithstanding, could make up an answer for me, an answer that could be, what, clear and distinct? No, alive and speaking like the stuffed dolls she used to sew when she had an hour's time. She tried, without succeeding; she should have torn her flesh and given it to me to read.

In this way, through the narrowing between telling the truth and there not being words for it, I was reached, not only with the insufficiency of positive sciences, but also by the sense of a story different from any of the others for which words were not lacking—fables, family stories, memories of war. My mother had been through two world wars, and she liked to narrate. What kind of story was this other one, which left such a dear and capable narrator speechless?

This is the second of the problems I mentioned earlier: the historicity of sexual difference, that is, the fact that our being women and men enters, does not enter, and how it enters into the stories we tell ourselves or we write for other men and women.

If I have to write, and if all who are here want to reflect on the ethics of sexual difference, we cannot neglect the problem of a mother who is found to be speechless on this topic. And found by whom? By her little daughter.

"Ethics" is a word that concerns human beings: neither God nor dinosaurs, but us. And we are inseparable from historicity, that is, from the fact that, while we come from the perfect, unmoved, and musical silences of organic and nonorganic life, once we are brought to the world the past of the world, step by step, becomes ours, and we become its, for good and for bad, with some joy, sorrows as hard as stones, and all the rest we know of. It goes well; that is, it goes. It goes because we are brought to and put in the world by a mother who, between that most high silence and this low, noisy, sharp-edged (and living) world, interposes her own flesh, her own voice, her own smell, like a bridge, to make us come to this side. And she speaks to us and makes us speak not to let us go back to the other side, until, around age four or five, memory springs up in us, which embraces centuries and millennia of human history.

She liked going to school (I am talking of the child I have been), but this did not make her learn the story hidden behind the maternal reticence; and, after some attempt, she gave up. She in fact realized that at school, neither the books nor the teachers knew anything of what was happening at her home and in real life. Nothing was known at school of the light of summer when the cicadas scream in it in full voice, nothing of the trips to the Guá in whose waters, between banks with no holding places, two or perhaps three mythical boys of her town had drowned, nothing of the way in which one dies when one dies of tetanus, nothing of the meetings around a clandestine candle in the space under the stairs that smelled like mold, not to speak of the collection and sale of *boasse*[3] that was aimed at financing the purchase of a real doll—a project of her older sister.

As for history books, she liked these too, but in them were only men and some goddess (who, however, was not history). They were men of the average kind, that is, those who had been forever different, all similar among themselves and busy with boring things, forced to this by their own ineptitude regarding pleasant things and by their ignorance of life. Not all of them, to be sure. She came across some attractive ones, among them, for example, Frederick II of Swabia, who warmed her almost more than a game would. But secretly. He burnt in a nonscholastic place, she knew it, a place unknown to the books as well as to the professors and to her very notebooks, and it was better this way.

She did not wonder why no women were in the school books; the matter seemed obvious to her, since women were, by their own nature, beings made of flesh whom one comes across live, like her mother, who was so important and so outside of the ordinary that, honestly speaking, she could not occur in a regular history book.

In the Theater of History and Science

"But why are women not in history? Or better: why do they not appear in it if not marginally?," Gianna Pomata, a professional and feminist historian, asks in the opening pages of her most famous essay, "La storia delle donne: Una questione di confine" [Women's History. A Border Question].[4]

In the 1970s the first thought of beginning feminist historiography was not the historicity of sexual difference, but rather the history of women. The reconstruction of the past, as Pomata writes, is a space of social representation, resembling a theater in which some things are brought to the front, and others remain, go back to the background, or go outside the scene. Theater of the past but staged in the present, and thus also a mirror of the present.

In the 1970s, together with the feminist movement involving all the industrialized countries of the globe, a historiography determined to narrate women's past began. Professional and amateur historians began a hunt for documents in archives and libraries with an energy that has not weakened yet.

I found myself in the Casa della Magnifica Comunità at Poschiavo, in an alpine valley on the way to St. Moritz, reading the minutes from dozens and dozens of witchcraft trials in the sixteenth through the eighteenth centuries. I touched and read those pages as if they were revelations of my mother's secret story. I quickly learned to decipher the notaries' writing; my tears functioned as a lens. I was also helped by the archival work being done, with real *pietas*, by a local scholar, Judge G. Olgiati. I thought I was working with a brother. At the Biblioteca Ambrosiana in Milan, when I asked whether they had material pertinent to the hunt for witches, the librarian came back with a wheelbarrow full of scattered papers. Precisely that, a wheelbarrow. Such was the status of the matter; I do not mean in relation to the hunt for witches, which has always been a topic for research, but with respect to women's history.

Now it is no longer so in the sense that women's history is no longer offered in chaotic wheelbarrows. Today it is a scientific discipline, and it is rightly respected. It does not correspond, however, to what one had expected. It should have been a change of scenery in the historical theater; instead, what came out is a minor history and a specialization.

Paola Di Cori, a professional historian who, from the first, chose to devote herself to women's history, has recently drawn this balance of her discipline:

> On the one hand, it is at the forefront of research; on the other, it still has to fight so that the most basic rights of citizenship are recognized to it. For example, it is evident that in the majority of the actual developments of historiography, from political to economic history, to the history of culture and of everyday life, there is no sign, if not in a minimal way, either of women as an object for study or of the women who professionally concern themselves with history, or of the feminists who are engaged in women's history.[5]

What happens to women scholars is what has already happened to women, as if there were the same symbolic device that goes on functioning, even through the great changes separating us from the past, and decrees women's marginality in the theater of history.

As soon as they realized the turn that the project was taking, some women authoritatively proposed to thematize the historicity of sexual difference, and conduct research privileging the work of sexual difference within history: sexual difference as a historical operator.

> To emphasize the need to do "women's history" has no other goal than that of making the sexed character of any history appear as a simple given, which we could consider as trivial. Women's history is done from the perspective of the particular only in order to be more convincing regarding its inscription in general history.

Thus writes Geneviève Fraisse, philosopher and scholar of the history of feminism.[6]

Although meaningful and acute, the plan has not worked. Between the researching subject (the women historians) and the object (women) a very fecund hermeneutic circle has been generated; the scientific production, qualitatively as well as quantitatively, testifies to this, yet without an interaction with history in general. History resists the insertion of women's history and women's difference. Or vice versa. They do not interact between each other, unlike what happened for the history of social classes, which has modified and enriched entire chapters of general history.

Failure reveals itself to be a result, sometimes. This is also the case here, I think.

By failure I mean that we do not know whether and how the fact of sexual difference works. Nor do we know what, in women's history, resists its translatability onto so-called general history. The easy answer is that it is only a matter of time; let time run its course, and so on. This, however, does not have so much power, or, better, it does not have this kind of power, which would amount to substituting itself for us in knowing the contradiction and drawing conclusions. With time one gets used to the issue to the point of not seeing it any more; time can do this until someone comes along who on the contrary can see it.

What is there, then, to be seen? That one cannot see everything, that there is history outside of history, that there is a transcendence of history inscribed in history itself, like a silence and an enigma, like a silenced word, or like a separateness. And thus, that history spills out of itself, like flour that has been put in a bag with holes. The so-called general history is not, cannot be a general history. There is something other, and the issue is not solved by labeling it "minor." There is something other than our theaters, including the scientific one, so that we must admit that history exceeds itself or that it is not everything, although everything presents itself to us historically. We must admit, I mean, not the fact in itself, as if it were the conclusion of a reasoning, but our perception of it, inseparable from the perception of that which, instead, lets itself be seen. With respect to this, Simone Weil spoke of the hidden face of the cube, invisible but embodied in our visual perception; otherwise, we could not see what we see.

To speak of something other we must speak allegorically, as the ancients and the medievals knew. Allegory in fact signifies that which does not let itself be com-prehended, and it signifies it precisely through that which veils it. And, the scholars of rhetoric say, allegory is a figure that finds us moderns to be deaf because it has been replaced for many poetical and scientific effects with metaphor. Will this be true, however? Or will it not be that, for the comparison, we turn to an already dead allegory (the "dark forest"),[7] and ignore our resources, neglecting, together with our symbolic needs, also our experiences? Take, for example, Emily Dickinson's poetry. Or the stuffed dolls that Maria Brunello used to make and give as gifts to her daughters when she had a worn-out pillowcase and two hours of time.

Let us be clear: if women's history escapes so-called general history and if we exclude, sensibly, its consideration as a minor history, it remains nevertheless that it does not become an other and unsayable history. And vice versa: if a mother does not find the words to explain sexual difference to her child, it will not be a human science that will be able to do this for her. The *allos* [other] of allegory is a leap, a scansion in our very experience that may always happen as soon as we stop forcing things because of our wanting to understand everything that occurs to us. Similar to a *lapsus* [slip], although superior to it in the same way that L'infinito[8] is when compared to a *calembour* [pun], allegory is the hole in the edge that gives charm to any supposedly enclosed space.

My discourse on allegory does not refer to a metahistorical or ahistorical alterity. It refers to the more or less perceptible gap that occurs between what we say, thanks to the symbolic devices available to us (language, forms of knowledge, powers, social situation, and memory among others), and what on the other hand affects us, matters to us—simultaneously the closest and the farthest—one cannot say whether from inside or outside, from an outside in, when we suffer, enjoy, desire. And when we love. When I say "there is something other," I think of the opening on the other side of the edge. I do not like to offer definitions, as I said in the beginning, or to provide theories because these must be concluded and coherent, and that is their charm, and I am sensitive to it; yet, when it is my turn, they become a constraining obstacle. Although this may be insufficient, I prefer to write on what matters to me and nothing else, and not jump over the facts that protrude from the roundness of theories.

What is striking about human reality is that it never rests in itself, not even when it sleeps, and that it seeks and toils constantly without, however, ever completely losing its desire to enjoy and be free. Ethics and historicity are different names (there are others) for this so common and so extraordinary *quest for something other* that perhaps coincides with the only possible quest for oneself. To this we are spurred on by a *lack of being*. The formula is absurd: how can a being lack being? It would not be a being but rather a nonbeing. This, however, is the formula to which the philosophy of our time has resorted to signify the human condition, and it looks like this is the only thing that is left to us after centuries of quest for the true, the good, and the just (penicillin, atomic fission, optical fibers, and other like things aside). These would be the words of our portion of possible experience (as long as we accept the verdict) at the end of a millenary quest. So little, even nothing? No, it is quite a lot. We are the heirs of nothing, this is true, but the nothingness of our heritage is given to us in very promising words: we must start everything all over again, yet we have the certainty it will not be a repetition.

The challenge is that, by starting all over again, we may gain (or gain back) our heritage, both women and men.

I return to the initial question: why do women appear marginally in history? And why does women's history remain a secondary discipline? Perhaps simply because they are at the margins of what history is in the scientific and theatrical sense of the word, far from this center and *close to another*. But why do I say "because"? From where they are, decentered, as one says of the foci of an ellipsis, what women and their historians ask us to think is not an explanation or a correction of their decenteredness, but rather other geometries, other histories, and open boundaries.

Beyond Equality

From here an ethics of sexual difference can begin with the realization of the *asymmetry* that exists between the two sexes as they present themselves to us on the theatre of history: men for the most part at the center, and women for the most part at the margins. It can start from here on the condition that we suspend all value judgments that history itself suggests with its hierarchies, its criteria of measurement, and with what we could call its topology, which is notoriously androcentric. However, one must also suspend (and this can be harder) corrective counterjudgments uttered on behalf of an ideal justice that imputes women's marginality to men's domination. That is, one should be able to see the historical asymmetry of the two sexes without interpreting and without correcting it, to see it in all that it contains of unbalancing and decentering for our conventional vision of the world. Personally, I do not know of any other opening to the sense of sexual difference than this upsetting of any possible concluded order.

If there were nothing else, that is, if absolute historicism were true, for which not only everything is history but also history is everything, then the sense of the difference between the sexes would be recapitulated in the dialectic between center and periphery, superior and inferior, master and slave. There is something other, however, and thus one can think of another symbolic order. I do not mean an order alternative to the dialectical one (which, in its partiality, I consider to be valid), but rather one that is other insofar as open to other and, therefore, unconcluded. Such is the symbolic order of the mother, thanks to which we receive a body and learn to speak, word and body in a plot unique and exclusive to every child who comes to the world, every time with its risks and uncertainties. It is thanks to this *open* symbolic order, an order that is at the same time powerful and precarious, as everyone who has tried and thought about it knows (every man and every woman, in some sense, because all men and women are born of a woman), that we can acknowledge the significance of sexual difference. By this I mean its irreducibility and thus its inexhaustible ability to be a sign and to signify. In a book we will consider shortly, Luce Irigaray writes that "the most obvious symbol, that closest to hand and also most easily forgotten, is the *living symbol* of sexual difference."[9]

An important step toward an ethics of difference was taken, I think, by Carla Lonzi (1931–1982) in a text with a violent title, *Sputiamo su Hegel* [*We Spit on Hegel*]. She writes, "Hegel's relation of slave and master is a relationship internal to the human world." And then, "Woman is not in a dialectical relation with the male world. The needs she unfolds do not imply an antithesis, but rather a movement on a different level. This is the point about which it will be the most difficult for us to be understood, but it is essential that we do not fail to emphasize it." And then again, with one of those hyperbolic abbreviations that give an adamantine feature to her language, "Woman's difference is millennia of absence from history. Let us take advantage of the difference."[10]

In other words, an ethics of sexual difference does *not* start with doing justice to women in relation to men. It starts neither with rights nor with a politics of rights. Lonzi writes, "the equality that is today available is not philosophical, it is political: do we like, after millennia, to insert ourselves in this manner in the world planned by others?" The same idea appears, in not very dissimilar words, in a book written in a calm and reasoning language, *Composing a Life*, by Mary Catherine Bateson, daughter of the semiologist Gregory Bateson and the famous anthropologist Margaret Mead. Of herself and of some friends, the author writes, "To different degrees, each of the five of us has been discriminated against because we are women; we have all sometimes been treated as less than equal. But each of us seeks out relationships of difference, a little puzzled by the necessary political thrust toward equality." Necessary because any difference is quickly transformed into an inequality, and the only ethical answer to injustice ends up being equality, together with the promotion of symmetrical relations at all costs, including "creating the illusion of symmetry."[11]

An ethics of difference thus starts in terms that we could call, paradoxically, unpolitical and unjust. Let us say it better: unbalanced. The reason for this is not difficult to intuit if we consider that, as the traditional view of history is androcentric, so are our rights unilateral. In fact, they have been thought by adult males to regulate their relations without excluding the whole of social relations, of course, but on the basis of their own experience and of their own symbolic necessities.

To do justice to women in relation to men would be a recentering of the world around man. To this extent, then, let us keep the injustice—so has been written by a feminist.[12] An ethics of difference starts, to use not new words, with becoming aware that man is not the center of the universe—neither of this world, nor of its history, nor of himself. One arrives to this world moving through a relation of dependence that we can even close, disown, or forget, but not without an indelible scar. Its mark in fact dominates, in full sight, on the summit of our bellies, to remind us that both sexes are born from the female one. Primary asymmetry that has given prehistoric humankind much to think.[13] All inequalities and injustices that have burdened women historically can perhaps be brought back to it.

Is eliminating the latter and saving the former possible? By saving the living mark of difference with its ability to make us desire and think at the same time? Can we go beyond the need for equality, beyond (not against) justice? Can we live and act the lack of being in the relations with other women and men, at the same time increasing enjoyment and freedom?

Perhaps a way exists. It must be sought in the invention, invention and fight at the same time, of a free sense of sexual difference. This refers not only to the relation between one sex and the other, but also, in the most autonomous manner, to the relations between individuals of the same sex: women with women, men with men. Let us think that sexual difference does not run any longer between two sexes, each endowed with its own social identity, rigidly imposed to women and to men, more to women than to men. My being a woman no longer corresponds to a gender identity as it may be constructed and imposed by a certain culture in a certain society for its own goals. Today a sexual difference of this kind still exists, socially defined and translated into roles, obligations, and stereotypes, but it is diminishing, and it is probably destined to disappear. The (my) woman's difference is primarily of me from me because of an alterity that runs through me with uncertain effects, from schizophrenia to the need for exchange. Above all, it is up to me to interpret it. It is not confined in the two and it cannot end up in the three because the two has already decomposed me from inside, and it interposes itself in any coincidence of me with me. There are neither social roles, nor mirrors, nor codes that can heal this decomposition. Only the word exchanged with the other, insideoutside [*dentrofuori*] me, can do it.

In View of Something Other

Discussion about sexual difference begins with the 1984 publication in France of *The Ethics of Sexual Difference*, by Luce Irigaray, perhaps the most famous name within the panorama of feminist philosophy the past thirty years. The book opens with an often-quoted affirmation, "Sexual difference is one of the major philosophical issues, if not the issue, of our age."[14] According to Heidegger, Irigaray explains, every epoch has one issue to think about; well, for us, it is this.

We thus return to the silence of the philosophical tradition on the theme that concerns us.

Ethics constitutes of course an important chapter in philosophical research, from Aristotle to our day, almost without interruption. Does this mean that until now philosophers have thought of ethics without considering that human beings are men and women? Not exactly. Philosophers do not ignore the reality of sexual difference, but neither do they have a thought of sexual difference. They consider it an empirical fact (as a fact, in this world human beings are women or men), without assuming it as a feature characterizing their condition as thinkers. One can notice this when comparing it with the reflection on death. Philosophers do not say: as a fact, we die; but rather: we are mortals; sexual difference remains instead within empirical factuality, which is indeed recorded, but as something that is not accounted for by the thought that wants to gain access to the standpoint of the universal (exceptions, at least in part, as Irigaray acknowledges, are Hegel and the Romantic culture of his time).

What happens consequently is that philosophy develops as a thought influenced by the male condition but without an awareness thereof and without the necessary mediations when it (also) comes to the other sex.

This attitude of the philosophers—to ignore male difference, not to seek mediations with the other than oneself, and to claim, despite this, to be talking from a universal standpoint—does nothing else but reproduce a typically male and patriarchal attitude, which men have practiced and considered as practicable insofar as it was integrated by an enormous and misrecognized work of mediation operated, by love or force, by women.

"Dasein is in such a way that it exists *for the sake of itself*," Heidegger writes. As we know, Dasein is the name for that being which in philosophy is traditionally called "man." The world, he explains, is not a being itself, but rather "that for the sake of which Dasein exists." We find no contradiction between the two claims because the world is part of the maturing of the very self of Dasein (of its *ipseity*).

The one who writes these words ignores several things about how the world functions, starting with how human beings come to it. The maternal relation, in fact, establishes itself by virtue of an originary being for the sake of the other, seeing and hearing the other, and this is true also of the amorous relation, as well as any relation that is not instrumental but has its own end in itself. It is not so much an issue of egoism or altruism, and with respect to this the philosopher is right ("The statement: *Dasein exists for the sake of itself*, does not contain the positing of an egoistic or ontic end for some blind narcissism on the part of the factical human being in each case"), but rather a matter of *there-being* in the relation with the other. Heidegger establishes a sequence ("Selfhood is the presupposition for the possibility of being of an 'I,' the latter only ever being disclosed in the 'you.'") that means to have the features of a Kantian *a priori*, and that actually corresponds to the stages of a man's possible exit from a state of tenacious narcissism (man as male, I mean; there are other experiences and other ways of being in the world, in fact). The conclusion that follows, therefore, in the great philosopher's scholastically complicated prose, seems to me to be the portrait of one of those men whom, in my childhood, I used to see as existing on their own and with no joy: "Never, however, is selfhood relative to a 'you,' but rather—because it first makes all this possible—is neutral with respect to being an 'I' and being a 'you,' and above all with respect to such things as 'sexuality.'" What follows is a claim based on authority, which is not such because this is the matter at stake, "All statements of essence in an ontological analytic of the Dasein in the human being take this being from the outset in such neutrality."[15]

It is true that, historically, there is this assumption of neutrality, but it concerns only men, not women. Women, in fact, are marked by sexual difference, so much so that difference itself is signified and recognized mainly as female difference. The language we speak also testifies to this; in it, "woman" is the human being who is different from "man," whereas "man" means both the male human being and the neuter human being, according to the contexts or, not rarely, indifferently, as for the famous "primitive man" in our school books, who did everything himself, except for nursing the babies and sewing the skins. We should note that this kind of occupation, abusive of the universal by the male, is an effect of linguistic usage because, rigorously speaking, in Latin (as well as in ancient Greek) there were different nouns for human being (*homo*) and for the male human being (*vir*). The usage, however, has erased not so much the difference between the two, but rather the need to signify it, and has thus rendered superfluous the second noun, *vir* (the root of which has on the other hand remained lively and noticeable).

The result is an inverted translation of the primordial asymmetry, the one according to which everybody, women and men, are born of a woman. In the mirror of language, on the opposite, women are included in the term "man." The move from nature to culture shows here an interesting feature: the first thought is an afterthought, the first universal is unilateral, the science of life starts out as a nonscience. Attributing the features of a simple overturning to this extraordinary move would be wrong; in fact, there is not an originary natural situation, which can be perceived as such and which would then be overturned. The human begins with the afterthought, with unilaterality, with the science of the nonscience, that is, in the most arbitrary manner. In the passage from nature to culture, the primordial asymmetry of the sexes presents itself again, at first, as an "injustice."

With all this, I do not exclude the hypothesis of a historical or, better, prehistorical moment for the more or less violent constitution of patriarchal power. Actually, we can find precise historical traces of this, for example, in the mythology of ancient Greece. What I cannot imagine, simply said, is an originary state of innocence and a golden age. If it is true, as the French anthropologist Françoise Héritier teaches us in *Masculin/féminin*,[16] that sexual difference gave primitive humankind something to think about, then the first thought that imposed itself was a unilateral and "unjust" thought whose only difference in relation to the previous stage, the so-called state of nature is the loss of that innocence that other beasts have maintained instead, as well as children in the very first years of their life.

I suggest one should read in this light that extraordinary philosophical and mystical novel which is Clarice Lispector's *The Passion According to G. H.* It narrates her sliding (provoked by the involuntary stepping on a cockroach, in which the story of an abortion could be hidden) toward the beginnings of life, a sliding that, step after step, turns into a trip culminating in the hopeful and ecstatic arrival at life. In the end, this is expressed with words that (incidentally stated) significantly contrast with those by Heidegger quoted earlier, "The world interdepended with me—that was the confidence I had reached: the world interdepended with me, and I am not understanding what I say, never! never again shall I understand what I say. For how will I be able to speak except timidly, like this: life is itself for me. Life is itself for me, and I don't understand what I am saying. And, therefore, I adore . . . "[17]

For a "Symbolic" of Difference

The silence of the philosophical tradition could be explained by considering that, when nothing else is in sight, sexual difference is nothing else than nature's blind decree, or chance's throw of the dice, where there are some who win and some who lose, but without freedom for anyone.

As we know, philosophy and, in its aftermath, the sciences, separate and oppose nature and culture to each other, and this is not without good arguments (which are fought with a still uncertain result by the author of *Toward an Ecology of the Mind*). Sexual difference is rent asunder by that separation: thought and subject on one side, body and "sexuality" (the quotation marks are Heidegger's) on the other.

It is interesting to know that on this issue of the cultural translation of the asymmetry between the sexes, feminist thought is internally divided and battled. (It is the problem that underlies the opposition between feminism of equality and of difference, an opposition that would be otherwise rather easy to overcome.) The conflict is between those who think that the asymmetry is not translatable into free forms and that the only possible break with sexist domination begins with equality, and those who think that equality without free signification of sexual difference yields, for women, a mutilated and conditional freedom as emancipated individuals, and that one must therefore strive to conjugate difference with freedom.

Is this truly possible, however? In the relations between sexes and in the relations among human beings in general, when sexual desire comes in, everything passes and happens—hatred, love, children, honor, power, business, sense of duty, pity, money and despair; as for freedom, though, there is always very little or nothing. In relation to this, psychoanalysis from Freud to Lacan and world literature have said things that are difficult to remove. Patriarchy is over, but this neither means that all domination imposed or suffered because of sex is over, nor that difference gives way to a free exchange.

A contract has never existed between nature and culture and, I think, there is no possibility to establish it. Precisely for this reason, sexual difference does not have a meaning on which we can agree.

In a well-documented book on the "dissonant" relations between feminist thought and contemporary philosophy, I read, "It may be that the deepest source of dissonance is the fact that men and women in question do not agree as to the theoretical significance of their respective differences. As if they were so great as to prevent all dialogue: we do indeed differ about our differences."[18] We differ about and in our differences: the primordial asymmetry does nothing else than present itself again, and never in an innocent state. It in fact reappears as prevarication, mutism, comedy of equivocations, deceptions, and self-deceptions, in university classrooms as well as in bedrooms, on sidewalks as well as in poems or trade union managements.

Yet, something passes between nature and culture, and this is language. And this is what is at stake primarily: the meaning that the fact of being born a woman or man can take up, lose, or change in the stories we tell ourselves. Ethics or the "symbolic" of difference.[19] It is a matter of situating ourselves in that arbitrary and immemorial leap that, from inorganic and organic life, makes us end up in a world full of history, stories, words, and problems. It is a leap, indeed, but it is also a passage because we *learn* how to speak. This is not the learning one does at school, where one learns a lot of things, certainly, but all according to only one version because all words already have their meaning (if you do not know them, there is the dictionary). In the livelihood of the maternal relation, in the first exchange of life and gestures, nothing is already signified because everything is still a signifier and what one learns is the free play between words and things.

Let us start, then, with giving to words the helplessness that our institutions lack, the burst with respect to which our desires are deficient, the light that gives company, the opening that would give life to our sciences. Let us start with a symbolic revolution.

Notes

1. Trans. note: This is true of most, if not all, romance languages; certainly this is the case for the Italian language.

2. See Carl Kerényi, *The Gods of the Greeks*, trans. N. Cameron (London: Thames and Hudson, 1951), pp. 243–44.

3. This is the name, in my dialect, for bovine excrement. I do not know the term in Italian, assuming that it exists.

4. Gianna Pomata, "La storia delle donne: Una questione di confine," in *Il mondo contemporaneo*, vol. 10, part II, ed. N. Tranfaglia, in *Gli strumenti della ricerca* (Florence: Nuova Italia, 1983), pp. 1434–69.

5. Paola Di Cori, ed. *Altre storie. La critica femminista alla storia* (Bologna: Clueb, 1996), p. 16.

6. Geneviève Fraisse, *La difference des sexes* (Paris: PUF, 1996), p. 44.

7. Trans. note: The reference is to the opening verses of Dante's *Divine Comedy*.

8. Trans. note: The allusion is to a famous poem by the Italian poet Giacomo Leopardi.

9. Luce Irigaray, *An Ethics of Sexual Difference*, trans. C. Burke and G. Gill (Ithaca: Cornell University Press, 1993), p. 113 (emphasis in original).

10. Carla Lonzi, *Sputiamo su Hegel: Scritti di Rivolta Femminile 1* (Milan: Gammalibri, 1970), pp. 6, 32, 4.

11. Mary Catherine Bateson, *Composing a Life* (New York: Atlantic Monthly Press, 1989), p. 105.

12. A. Bocchetti, "Bisogno d'ingiustizia," in *Via Dogana 2* (Milan: Libreria delle donne, 1991), pp. 5–6.

13. See Françoise Héritier, *Masculin/feminine: La pensée de la difference* (Paris: Jacob, 1996).

14. Irigaray, *An Ethics of Sexual Difference*, p. 5.

15. Martin Heidegger, "On the Essence of Ground," in *Pathmarks*, trans. W. McNeill (Cambridge: Cambridge University Press, 1998), pp. 121–22.

16. See note 13.

17. Clarice Lispector, *The Passion According to* G. H. (Minneapolis: University of Minnesota Press, 1988), p. 173.

18. Rosi Braidotti, *Patterns of Dissonance*, trans. E. Guild (New York: Routledge, 1991), p. 146.

19. "Symbolic" is a term coined, years ago, by Adriana Cavarero in the context of the events of *Diotima*, the philosophical community.

Chapter 13

On Virtue

EMANUELE SEVERINO

The deep and troubling corruption of Italian society has been surfacing for some time. It looks like an eclipse of the virtue of citizenship comparable to the one in postwar Italy has occurred very rarely, at least in our kind of societies. This is a record for which, it is safe to say, other peoples do not envy us.

Today we do not limit ourselves to the acknowledgment of the moral failures of a people. We know that they negatively affect the good functioning of society (as it is indeed happening to us), and thus the level and quality of economic production. It is now openly recognized that the production of any richness, or better the production of forms of power, demands a certain degree of morality in its producers. This is a plausible discourse, but precisely in relation to the interests of richness and power. Otherwise, it loses sight of the fact that to be moral in order to produce richness (or, in general, power), to be good in order to be rich means not to be moral and not to be good. The meaning of an action is in fact determined by its goal. If this changes— and, for example, the goal of an action is no longer moral goodness, but rather richness and power—only apparently does the action remain what it was. In reality, it has become something essentially different.

The production of richness also is a virtue of citizenship. This even mobilizes and involves all others because it is the condition of their existence. The production of richness, or in general of power, coincides with the production of survival, that is, of that without which one could not even practice all the other virtues.

To produce richness to live virtuously—to be rich and powerful to be good according to what is proposed by our cultural tradition—is an action fundamentally different from the production of richness as goal of the other forms of virtue. This means that, among these other forms, we see a tendency

With the exception of pp. 238–39, this chapter is from Emanuele Severino, La buona fede (Milan: Rizzoli, 1999).

toward the production of conflict, which our cultural tradition has tried to avoid by thinking the multiple virtues as different forms *of* virtue in terms of that sole virtue that comprehends within itself individual and civic virtues and that consists in the will to pursue the common good of society, the good of the *polis*. "Political virtue" is the unitary totality of virtue, of which the other virtues are but specifications. Montesquieu defines it as "love of the laws and of our country," which "requires a constant preference of public to private interest," and which "is the source of all private virtues," which "are nothing more than this very preference itself."[1] "Public interest" is what in the language of the Aristotelian tradition, taken up also by the Catholic Church, is called "common good." From this perspective, no particular virtue is the goal of the others; rather, each is a specific way of practicing the universal virtue that pursues the "common good" of society as its goal. The virtues of citizenship are the same virtues of the individual insofar as they have the common good of society as their goal.

Yet, if universal virtue becomes unthinkable and impossible to carry out—as happens in the development of Western culture and customs—the conflict among virtues opens again; the values pursued by them appear to be incompatible, so that, for example, to be good in order to be rich (where the determining value, the goal, is richness) becomes incompatible with being rich in order to be good (where the dominating value is goodness).

If in a society the production of richness is the production of the survival of that society, the production of survival is simultaneously in its concrete meaning the production of the *force*, that is, of the *power* that enables such a society to prevail on both internal and external enemies threatening its existence. That is, force, or fortitude—the availability of economic goods being an essential component thereof—is the civic virtue that holds as a condition of all others.

In its oldest meaning, the Latin term *virtus* (hence, virtue) means "force," "powerfulness," "ability." *Virtue is force*, and when it is referred to human beings, it means force and the ability to realize the goal that they intend for themselves. The same meaning belongs to the Greek word *arete*, which corresponds to *virtus*. Language indicates the reference of *virtus* and *arete* to force or fortitude. Both the Latin and the Greek words are construed on roots that can be brought back to the root *art*, which is the root of the noun *ars*, "art." In its originary meaning, art is the ability, the power, or the force to coordinate means to achieve goals. Art is technics. The root *art* can be brought back also to the word "fortitude": the *virt*-uous is the *forc*-eful [*fort*-e].

That the word "virtue" ended up indicating a specific form of art—the art that enables being happy, the art of happiness—is an analogous fact to that by which the Greek word *poiesis*, which means "production," has ended up indicating that specific form of production that is poetic production, *poetry*. The specification does not erase the specified dimension. When one thinks that virtue is the opposite of force—as in the Christian virtue of love—one properly opposes virtue not to *force*, but to *a certain* kind of force, for example, brute or evil force (which ultimately proves to be a weakness) because for the Christian, love is infinitely more forceful and powerful than any other force and power because it even enables one to achieve the kingdom of heaven as well as eternal life and happiness.

In *Tusculan Disputations*, Cicero writes, "*Appellata est enim ex viro virtus; viri autem propria maxime est fortitudo.* (It is from the word for man [*vir*] that the word 'virtue' [*virtus*] is derived; but man's peculiar virtue is fortitude [*fortitudo*])."[2] In Spinoza, the identity between virtue and powerfulness is still explicitly present: "*Per virtutem et potentiam idem intelligo; hoc est virtus, quatenus ad hominem refertur, est ipsa hominis essentia seu natura, quatenus potestatem habet quaedam efficiendi quae per solas ipsius naturae leges possunt intelligi* [By virtue and power I mean the same thing; that is, virtue, insofar as it is related to man, is man's very essence, or nature, insofar as he has power to bring about that which can be understood solely through the laws of his own nature]."[3] By asserting that originary and supreme virtue is the *conatus sese conservandi*, "the *conatus* to preserve oneself,"[4] Spinoza makes explicit the fundamental meaning that virtue possesses in the entire Western thought. Virtue is powerfulness that enables *being*, that is, that enables maintaining oneself outside of *nothingness*. For Christianity, it makes human beings enter eternal life. With the help of grace, virtue conquers the demon, the deadly enemy of human beings.

Kant is already very far from conceiving virtue as force through which one reaches the goal of prevailing on one's enemies. Virtue is obedience to the moral law, and such obedience is authentic only insofar as it has no other goals. One is not virtuous so as to be happy. Yet, for Kant, virtue makes one *merit* happiness. Because it does not mean to be a means with respect to an end, virtue is the decisive means that enables one to reach human beings' essential goal, that is, happiness.

Kant continues to conceive of virtue as force: moral force, *fortitudo moralis*: "the capacity (*Vermögen*) and considered resolve to withstand a strong but unjust opponent is *fortitude* (*fortitudo*) and, with respect to what opposes the moral disposition *within us, virtue* (*virtus, fortitudo moralis*)."[5] Here virtue is courage (*Tapferkeit*), that is, the force (*Vermögen*) and the firm proposal with which one fights an enemy threatening not only the existence of a homeland, but rather the existence of virtue itself, that is, of what for Kant is the deepest root of any homeland and any authentic existence. Also for Kant, as for the entire Western thought, the supreme virtue is *fortitudo*, the powerfulness that opposes the enemy threatening the existence of humanity's "supreme good," which for Kant is the moral conscience and the possibility of listening to it (hence the specificity of Kant's discourse, which can substantially be brought back to the Christian notion of good will). However, even when it dissents from the way in which Kant determines the supreme good, the entirety of Western thought is in agreement in its conception of virtue as *fortitudo* that defends, against annihilation, the *being* of what time after time is considered to be humanity's supreme good.

When in its development Western thought comes to the conclusion that there cannot exist a supreme good that holds unconditionally and immutably for everyone and forever, the individual forces of the human world identify themselves with the supreme good. In their eyes, the supreme virtue is their very longing to be and self-preservation. That is, the will to power that, in individuals, societies, and States defends itself against its enemies—which, by definition, are therefore always "unjust enemies."

From the individual's perspective, the will to survival is above all civic virtues; whereas from the perspective of the social ensemble, the authentic civic virtues are the *fortitudines* by which it is defended. The State in service of the individual is a central demand of the modern world. When one realizes, however, that there cannot be a supreme good capable of unifying and subordinating to itself all individual goods and virtues, it is unavoidable that, in the conflict between different goods and virtues, the good of the State constitutes itself as something heterogeneous with relation to the good of the individual, and that it prevails on it. And, in name of the "*raison d'Etat,*" the subordination of the individual to the State demands the sacrifice of the virtues in whose name the individual is opposed to the State, and even the sacrifice of the individual life itself.

If the overwhelming *fortitudo* of the social ensemble makes it such that individual virtues are subordinated to civic virtues, such subordination prefigures the subordination to *technics* brought about by the great forces that in our civilization delude themselves about the use of technics to prevail on one another. If the State is the means through which every individual defends himself or herself from other individuals, it is inevitable that to each individual the force of the State appears as something unrenounceable, which must not be weakened, and therefore must not be subordinated to individual goals and virtues.

To assume something as a means is always to weaken such a force with respect to the strengthening of the goal, that is, with respect to the force that constitutes the realization of the goal. When the means must not be weakened by the pursuit of the goal—because, as is the case with social relations, the survival of the individual depends on the survival and the force of the State—it is inevitable that the means becomes the goal and that, as far as the relations are concerned, the good and the virtues of the individual are subordinated to the good and the virtue of the State. Private virtues are subordinated to civic virtues.

Within this context, one can also understand that dominating feature of our century, which has been the conflict between the capitalistic-democratic system and real socialism. Together with the fascist and the national-socialist States, these are the two fundamental configurations of the State in our century. Today, one tends to forget that, for both sides, it was a matter of a *deadly* contrast, and that therefore, on both sides, any possible means to prevail on the opponent had been adopted: to the point, on the one hand, of organizing a system of offense-defense centered on a nuclear weaponry that, when put in motion, would have destroyed the Earth; and, on the other hand, so resistant to the wear due to the waiting time of the cold war to be able to survive indefinitely to the ideological motivations that had determined its origin.

In the contrast between democratic-capitalistic system and real socialism, each of the two opponents considered the possibility of destroying the Earth so as to prevail. The *fortitudo*, that is, the *virtus* of each opposing system, organized the possibility of destroying itself, together with the destruction of the Earth, to the end of prevailing and destroying the *fortitudo* and the *virtus* of the opponent. In each of the opposing systems the *conatus essendi*, the will to be organized its own *non-being*, its own annihilation, precisely to realize its *being*. Once atomic energy became available, avoiding such a *contradiction* was no longer possible. If, in each of the opponents, the will to power and existence had renounced the military use of atomic energy, and thus the contradiction provoked by its effective use at the military level, the will to power and existence would have surrendered to the opponent, would have let itself be destroyed. It was inevitable that, in each of the two opponents, the *virtus* would organize the death of the Earth and itself to save itself.

Because such a contradiction made the actual atomic conflict impractical, one had to employ all ways and means that would consent not to lose ground in front of the enemy, which was identified with supreme "injustice."

Only from the outside, and even in a state of reckless distraction, has public opinion perceived the character of the conflict between capitalism and communism, which was not only epochal, but moreover cosmic (it was in fact the destiny of the *cosmos* that was and still is at stake). Meanwhile, however, the conflict had bent the shape of society to its demands and had configured it. This is a process that had to take place in all States belonging to the two opposed blocks and, first of all, in the two superpowers. Thus, it had to take place also in Italy with a specific intensity due to the presence of the strongest communist party in the Western world and to the weakness of Italian democracy and capitalism.

One is scandalized today by the seriousness of the corruption of Italian society, and one even considers the possibility of a genetic predisposition of Italians to moral corruption. Correlatively, one believes that, through the appropriate use of judiciary means, one can bring Italian society back to health. In both cases, one loses sight of the world context that has rendered corruption possible—and not only in Italy.

Even in the most mature democracies in the capitalistic Western world, the efficacy of the organization of the fight against communism has required the *secrecy* of such an organization. To be efficacious, democratic-capitalistic *virtus* or *fortitudo* had to remove itself from the eye of external and internal enemies; it had to hide itself, that is, hide the greatest part of its practice from the public domain, not only with respect to military plans, but also with respect to any other plan and initiative aimed at contrasting the opponent on the internal and external levels. Because the public character of the decisions pertaining to the State, however, belongs to the essence itself of democracy, what has happened is that to defend itself, the real democracy of our time has had to deny and damage itself. To survive, parliamentary democracy has had to renounce most of itself. The fundamental civic virtue, that is, the defense of the system, has been forced to give up some of its essential features, and thereby a great part of the system that was defended by it. The defense of democratic legality has had to adopt illegal practices. And, even if in a less traumatic manner, the legality of capitalistic relations has in turn defended itself with procedures that are illegal from its own very perspective.

For the democratic-capitalistic system, the need to deny itself to survive has been a further *contradiction*. Together with the one considered earlier in the chapter, this has formed the soil of radical uncertainty and loss of identity of the system, in which individual dishonesty could take root. If, to survive, the very democratic-capitalistic system has had to deny and damage itself (somewhat similar considerations can be developed with respect to the means used by real socialism, which aimed at eliminating social injustices with violence), this damage has been the opening enabling the passage of the forms of corruption geared toward the achievement of individual advantages and that have determined a further damage to the health of the system.

Moral corruption—the eclipse of *virtus*—is not a pathological phenomenon attacking the democratic-capitalistic system from the outside. Rather, it belongs to its *physiology* because it would have given up its own force and would have let itself be destroyed by the opponent if it had not acted against the forms of legality, which it itself bore in the name of efficaciousness and thus of the secrecy of the defensive-offensive plan against the deadly enemy. In our times the fundamental civic virtue of the democratic-capitalistic system has been and will go on being forced to act in a nonvirtuous way (also from the perspective of individual virtues). For Italy, because of the presence of the Italian Communist Party (PCI), the danger of exiting the democratic-capitalistic system and moving toward the area of real socialism has been greater than elsewhere. One can maintain, therefore, that this process has been more intense than anywhere else. In it, political illegality, which democratic-capitalistic legality has had to practice to survive, has had illegality and private corruption as a subproduct.

To the illegality whose absence would have resulted in the destruction of the system, forms of illegality were added whose absence would have produced,

or one thought they would have produced, serious damages to its good health—
especially if, like in Italy, the system found itself more in danger than elsewhere. The issue is that of the illicit financing of anticommunist parties and
of the practices, extremely onerous for the State, through which the system
has bought for itself the electoral consensus of the citizens. ("Consocia-
tivism"—through which the system has taken into consideration some fundamental demands of the working class led by the PCI—has been the price
the system had to pay as a consequence of the "block of the alternation," in
turn due to the impossibility that, during the conflict East-West, the PCI
became a party in power). This is the alliance between democratic-capitalistic
legality and the big forms of international criminality. By bringing to an
extreme the capitalistic will to profit, they also bring to an extreme the
anticommunist attitude, and thus they have been (and still are) considered
to be greatly reliable in the fight against communism. Especially in Italy, the
matter is that of the phenomenon of terrorism during the 1970–1980s, which,
no matter the color of its presentation, by terrorizing the electoral body had
the task of preventing it from choosing new ways in a situation wherein the
PCI substantially proposed the new way.

Illicit financing to anticommunist parties, abnormal expansion of the
public debt, the alliance with big international criminality of certain anticommunist belief, and the terrorism of the 1970s and 1980s have thus
been the forms of the fundamental civic virtue of the democratic-capitalistic
society, that is, of its will to survive in Italy. They are also the forms that
such a society had to inflict on itself to survive. The opening that was
created has authorized the damages inflicted to the social system out of
personal advantages. Not only have these damages been the subproducts of
the anticommunist fight, but they have also been considered to have a
positive function because many believed that those with an interest in
practicing civic virtues could strengthen more efficaciously the existence of
these virtues (and thus strengthen the system) if they gained, through
behaviors that effectively weakened the deadly enemy, personal interests
definitely superior to those the system would legally lavish on its supporters
and functionaries.

Claiming that corruption can be eradicated through judiciary means is
naïve. It belongs to the physiology of the social system that has been victorious in the fight against communism. Additonally, believing that, after the
victory, the winning system lets itself be weakened beyond a certain limit or
even be destroyed by those who would like to free it from corruption using
judiciary procedures that seem to be inspired by the principle *fiat iustitia et
pereat mundus* [let there be justice, even should the world perish] is also
naïve. This is an even greater naïveté if one compares it with the fact that,
in immediate postwar Italy, the Communist Party avoided starting the judiciary incrimination of the fascist society—which, insofar as it was an illiberal
society, could have been considered entirely illegal—that had nevertheless
been defeated in the fight against democracies.

The judiciary activity might possibly unhook the low-profile corruption simply aiming at personal advantage from high-profile corruption, whose goal is instead the survival of the system—and which, even today, despite the end of real socialism, has serious reasons not to step aside. However, because the boundaries between these two forms of corruption are not sharp, any judiciary cleansing—which precisely in this period we see to be in a crisis in Italy—will be able, at best, to reach a compromise in which what remains unaffected are the forms of illegality that are already too deeply rooted in the will to the survival of the system—that is, in the fundamental civic virtue—to be uprooted from it.

These remarks are in no way a justification of the eclipse of virtue in the Western world and in Italy. They simply indicate the consequences of the way in which the West conceives virtue.

When confronted with the possibility that the State perish, and thus, concretely, that the democratic-capitalistic order perish, not only does the supreme virtue suited to this order organize the destruction of the Earth and sacrifice some of its own essential features, but it also sacrifices any other civic virtue—harmony, prudence, justice, tolerance, freedom, and so forth—whose practice may put in danger the safety and survival of the system.

To those who reply that the traditional conception of virtue asserts the interconnection of all virtues and that none can be sacrificed to the others, one can reply, among other things, that even the Catholic Church (which is one of the most relevant expressions of the Western tradition) has considered the death penalty to be legitimate when the common good and the survival of the society were at stake. If, for the Church, the virtue that respects life can be suspended in principle for the superior good of the community, all the other civic virtues and also those more properly individual can be suspended or subordinated with even better reasons for the safeguarding of such a good. For example, once one admits the principle of the admissibility of death penalty for the sake of the common good (a principle that, for the Church, is still valid, even if today the Church thinks that society can defend itself more efficaciously with other means), the Church must accept in principle also that which it refuses to accept at the level of demographic control: for the survival of humankind all forms of demographic control today available must be adopted, and therefore, as the virtue of respect for life has been subordinated to the common good, so the virtue of chastity as it is conceived of today by the official doctrine of the Church must be subordinated also to the common good of humanity.

It is illusory to think that the problem of virtue may be resolved through *exhortation*. Westerners have always been exhorted to virtue, but rarely the exhortation has been heard.

What makes the exhortation a failure is the conviction, which inspires it, that the exhortee is *free* to accept or refuse it; that is, that the exercise of virtue is a free act. Yet, either virtue is an act of freedom, and then one decides to be virtuous not because one is exhorted to, but because one freely wants virtue, and thus the exhortation fails in its intention of producing virtue; or the exhortation succeeds, but then virtue is no longer a free act, but rather something that is necessarily determined by the exhortation. It is not possible to exhort to freedom because freedom is such only insofar as it is negation of all dependency on something else.

If one wants to claim that freedom is not blind but instead motivated, and that exhortation aims at proposing the authentic motivations, then the defendants of exhortation to free virtue must also recognize that the motivation cannot be absolute and indisputable because in that case the will would find itself faced with an evidence, and thus it would not be free either to accept or to refuse it. If an absolute and indisputable motivation for a free decision cannot exist, what *ultimately* determines the authentically free decision is the decision itself apart from all external conditioning, and therefore from all motivation and exhortation. Exhortation is determining and succeeds in its task of producing virtue insofar as its listener is not free, that is, insofar as the virtue that it produces is not virtue—it is not from the same logical perspective on which the exhortation is grounded.

Human beings cannot *be made free*. If they were made free, their freedom—their free decision—would be the effect of a cause different from freedom. It would not therefore be freedom (their decision would not be free). If the intensity of the exhortation were to determine the inclinations or propensity toward a certain decision, the one who was truly free would know the absence or the smaller intensity of the opposite exhortation, and thus would restore the balance that has been altered by the inclination and propensity provoked by the prevailing exhortation. That is, one would suspend such an exhortation. On the contrary, if the intensity of a certain exhortation determines a certain inclination or propensity wherein the absence or smaller presence of the opposite exhortation is not taken into account, the prevailing exhortation is not suspended, but rather *makes* the one who decides *free* by considering such exhortation. Thus, one is *not* free, and the exhortation does *not* make one free.

In the philosophical tradition of the West, virtue is not only the means that must be firmly possessed—so too must be "custom," *ethos, habitus*—to achieve happiness and the good, but such a means is effective, appropriate to this task, because it is the acting that is commensurate and adapts itself to the immutable order of reality, that is, to the sense and immutable configuration of the Whole, which philosophical knowledge, as first and indisputable knowledge (*episteme*), claims to be able to unveil. The immutable order is the divine order of the universe, the law to which human beings have to subject themselves, and which the Greeks call *Dike*, divine "Justice."

Supreme virtue and human justice consist in the adaptation to such an order, that is, in wanting what is in conformity with it and what develops it through time. The multiplicity of virtues is the way in which the adaptation to the immutable unfolds. The immutable and divine Order is the denial of nonmeaning [non-senso], it is Meaning [Senso], objective rationality, truth unveiled by human reason. As true Meaning, whose features cannot be incompatible among themselves, it guarantees that the multiplicity of virtues adequate to it is not realized as a state of conflict, but rather as a unitary and harmonious system. Virtue is a unitary articulation, wherein individual virtues cannot expand themselves to the point of rendering the others impossible.

Expressing the attitude of the whole philosophical tradition, Malebranche writes, "love of Order," that is, of the immutable Order of reality, "is not only the principal of the moral virtues; it is the unique virtue. It is the virtue of virtues, fundamental and universal, the virtue which alone makes virtuous the habits or dispositions of minds."[6] The "median" character that Aristotle attributes to each moral virtue expresses precisely their belonging to a total context that prevents their exorbitance. For just this reason, virtues are interdependent; individual virtues cannot exist independently from civic virtues and vice versa. None can realize itself if the State is not virtuous, that is, if the human community has not given itself laws that command the adaptation to the Order and true Meaning of reality.

Christianity preserves the meaning that was given to the divine Order by Greek thought, yet it superimposes on it the meaning that is given to the divine within the Old and New Testaments. Truth becomes Christian truth, and virtue becomes Christian virtue. Cardinal virtues are linked to theological virtues. The laws of the state are true laws, that is, they command the adaptation to the true Order of the world only if they do not conflict with but rather favor Christian truth and virtue, and instead contrast any behavior that is in conflict with the revelation of Christ. The principle that the State must conform itself to revelation, banning anything that opposes it, belongs to the essence of this revelation. In the doctrine of the Catholic Church, the absolutist power of Christianity becomes completely transparent.

This absolutism is connected to the conviction, which belongs to the entire Western tradition, that, on the one hand, there is access to the vision of the truth on the side of human beings; and, on the other hand, that there is action, through which human beings can realize their essence and become happy only by a self-adaptation to the truth that they can access, only by the realization of a form of society and State from which the denial of the truth is completely banned. If ethics, as *ethos*, is the site wherein the truth enlightens human action, then politics, as the action of the *polis*, is inseparable from ethics, and ethics has its climax and fullest reality in politics, that is, in the dimension in which individual virtues are joined with civic virtues.

Our time realizes, albeit through a path crossed by deep shadows, that an immutable truth, overarching the becoming of the world, is impossible, and that there is no human beings' access to the truth. There is, therefore, no immutable Order to which human beings must conform themselves through virtuous actions; there is no ground that guarantees that the entirety of virtues is not a conflicting multiplicity.

Already in the modern period, the unity of ethics and politics toward which Christian conscience aims undergoes a progressive fragmentation. First, ethics and politics regain autonomy in relation to the Christian conception of the world, and virtue can again present itself as virtue, even when it is not Christian. Politics separates itself from ethics, and ethics itself divides itself into an ethics of intention and an ethics of responsibility, an ethics of the individual and an ethics of the citizenry. In our time, both ethics and politics separate themselves from any absolute truth and any categorical imperative, and authority too separates itself from truth. If in the tradition of the West each law is authentic only when it is produced in the light of the truth—so that authority itself is authentic only as incarnation of the truth—of each law one must say today what Hobbes said of the law of the state: *auctoritas, not veritas facit legem* [authority, not truth makes the law].

In the time of the disappearance of any immutable Order overarching becoming, the individual and opposed forces of becoming move forth as only possible protagonists of action. *Virtus* becomes the will to survival and power inspiring each of them. In our century, the great forces of absolutism and democracy, capitalism and communism, have fought against each other. After the end of the common enemy, the conflict between capitalism, democracy, and the Catholic Church has opened again. After the collapse of the Soviet Union, the Catholic Church has remained as the only one great institution wherein the traditional relation between truth, virtue, ethics, and politics survives. Such a relation has, on the contrary, entered a crisis within capitalism and democracy, which tend evermore decisively to conceive of themselves no longer as absolute and immutable orders, but rather as a pure will to survival and power, whose values are not guaranteed by any absolute ground.

In a more or less pervasive and explicit manner, each of those forces has meant to *use technics* when fighting the others. That is, each has posited itself in relation to technics (led by modern science), assuming it as the most appropriate tool for the realization of the values of which each is a bearer. Yet, once ends and values no longer have an absolute foundation, the means that produce them are no longer definitely tied to their nature of means. Likewise, the contents of the values and ends are no longer definitively tied to their being ends and values. The content of the means (that is, what functions as a means) can become end and value, and the content of the ends can become means.

This is not a pure possibility because this reversal of ends and means belongs to the fundamental tendency of our time. Totalitarianism, democracy, capitalism, real socialism, Christian conscience—the great forces that intend to assume technics as means for the realization of their opposed goals—have not and do not realize that this form of their relation to technics is already becoming an *illusion* because technics itself is a force. It is a force that in its ability to dispense with naïvely scientistic and technicistic inter-pretations of its essence, frees itself in an increasingly peremptory way from its subordination to other forces. That is, it frees itself from its nature as means and prepares to subordinate to itself the forces that intend to use it.

This is an inevitable reversal because the conflict among the forces driven by such an intention forces them not to weaken the scientific-technological apparatus that is available to them since this is the decisive and irreplaceable device through which forces can in the end prevail over one another. The necessity not to weaken such an apparatus is already their subordination to a goal different from the one each of them intends to pursue. In fact, it is their subordination to the will, by which they are them-selves led, to make such an apparatus ever more competitive and powerful. Because of their subordination to the power of the scientific-technological apparatus, they strengthen the goal to which such an apparatus is geared *by itself* (that is, beyond the goals that such forces would like to assign to it): the indefinite increase in the ability to realize goals.

There exists a giant *inclined plane* along which the great forms of the Western tradition and also the forces—capitalism, democracy, Christianity—that have been victorious against real socialism are sliding toward their end. For thirty years I have been intimating the reasons that ground such a thesis and that have enabled me to foresee decades ahead of time the impossibility of a nuclear conflict between the United States and the USSR, the end of the USSR, the nearing between the East and the West, the moving of the planetary conflictuality from the axis East-West to the axis North-South, and the plausibility that the nuclear arsenals of the North are used against the pressure exerted by the Third World on rich countries.

More than twenty years ago, for example, I wrote, "The continuation of the current equilibrium does not exclude that the Soviet society may develop in a democratic direction, and that the American society may push to its fullest the process of mass participation in businesses' profit."[7] And, about fifteen years ago: "Today one considers to be 'realistic' the possibility of a total nuclear clash between the USA and the USSR. Yet, this 'realism' is a naïveté in relation to the forecast that the privileged countries of the Earth use their power not for mutual destruction, but for their survival in a world that is becoming increasingly uninhabitable."[8]

It is not a matter of boasting of such forecasts, yet it is foolish not to take into account the conceptual structure that made them possible and that today with Islamic integralism in action enables one to forecast what Islam, in its entirety, is running into. Briefly, it is inevitable that the *inclined plane* that is making all forms of our civilization collapse will also make Islam slide and collapse, leading it to its end. What inclines that plane is, at one end, the heart of modernity, that is, the philosophical thought of the last 200 years, which shows the inevitability and indisputability of the "death of

God." At the other, it is technics guided by modern science. Beyond the scientistic-technicistic conception of technics, the authentic dimension of technics is the unity of these two sides. The *inclined plane* leads such a dimension to domination over the world.

The forces today that intend to use technics are in fact *destined* to serve it. They must not hinder its functioning, and thus it is inevitable that the power of technics becomes their goal and they become the means so that such a goal increases in power. Along the *inclined plane*, we are moving toward an epoch when technics no longer functions to realize profit, democracy, and Christianity. Profit, democracy, and Christianity (as well as real socialism) serve to augment the power of technics.

Islam also intends to make use of technics. It intends to use scientific-technological rationality, typical child of our civilization, to safeguard and strengthen its own values (this has a much deeper meaning than the circumstance, terrible and yet banal, that Islamic integralists use products from Western industries to strike the West). The affinity between Christianity and Islam is also accentuated by the common philosophical ground. For the Catholic Church, Thomas Aquinas remains the principle reference, yet Thomas is extremely close to Avicenna, who is among the major Islamic philosophers.

In the West, Christianity has run into an increasingly stringent criticism from the side of modern, philosophical culture. Because of this criticism, which addresses at the same time Christianity's traditional philosophical foundations, in Christianity integralism and intolerance have stepped evermore to the side, or have taken up increasingly less violent forms. Islamic culture, instead, has lacked the experience of modern philosophy. If for Islam there is a "Satan" against whom to fight, it is not Western hedonism, but rather the philosophical thought of the last two centuries, which has shown the inevitability of the "death of God"—whereas "Islam" means "submission to God's will."

The philosophy of our time has not only legitimized life-forms that are intolerable to Islamic conscience; it has also opened up the ground where the will to power of technics is legitimized to project an always increasing domination over the world. If God is dead, then there can be no limit to the will to transform the world. A deep and indissoluble link unites technics and the philosophy of our time. Islam deludes itself into thinking that it can use technics against Western civilization that, even when it ignores it, has its diamond point in the philosophy of our time! Islam deludes itself that it can use the weapon against the hand that is holding it. Technics reflects the "death of God," and thus it is the Trojan horse against anyone who wants to use it so that God's will be done.

In this situation, wherein the conflict among the great forces of our time is the same conflict against the great *virtues* that contemporary human beings can practice, technics presents itself as the supreme force, that is, as the supreme virtue subordinating to itself democratic, capitalistic, communist, and Christian virtues. To the present conscience, these can no longer appear to be grounded on an absolute truth.

The subordination of any virtue to the virtue of technics is in fact an inevitable consequence of the death of the truth. After the death of the truth (which is, at the same time, the death of God), technics is the supreme virtue because it is the site wherein *being*, and thus the human being, wants itself, its own perpetuation, and its own infinite growth more deeply and purely. Therefore, unlike what happens in the ideological administration of technics, which has provoked the conflict between capitalism and communism, it is the site where the planetary virtue of the scientific-technological apparatus has the ability to avoid ideological contradictions, first of all the one for which each of the two opponents had to organize its self-destruction to save itself.

The supreme virtue of technics cannot be hindered by any other form of virtue, which on the contrary can only favor the enactment of the infinite creativity of technics. Technics inherits, in an extreme manner, the infinite creativity of the divine, to which the West had in the past addressed itself. Any other form of virtue becomes a means to realize the technical-scientific creation of the new face of the world.

Because virtue saves humanity from nothingness, the primary duty is that of saving virtue, which is the condition for the salvation of humanity. Since, as the scientific organization of force, technics is now at last the supreme virtue of humanity, such a supreme virtue must first of all save itself, must have itself as goal, must prevent the practice of other forms of virtues (such as the civic and individual virtues of our tradition) from hindering the salvation of what is by now the condition for the salvation of any value and any good of humanity and the world. The other forms of virtue can be only means to favor the self-salvation of technics. By becoming the means and exiting the dimension that must be primarily saved to save humanity from nothingness, these other forms of virtue will inevitably transform themselves and take on a new meaning and a new face. Exactly because of its novelty, such a face waits to be deciphered by our culture.

Civic virtues, meant as forces that produce the "common good" defined in relation to the Immutable Order of reality, are *different* (even if they may have the same name) from the civic virtues that produce a common good that is thought independently of such an Order. They are also different from the civic virtues that are meant as forces whose task is the indefinite empowering of technical virtue (and which are thus only superficially the same). The civic virtues that, in the fight against real socialism, have been subordinated to the survival of the democratic-capitalistic system, thought of as society's supreme good, are something essentially different from the civic virtues that are asserted by the Church's social doctrine and from the civic virtues that have as their goal the strengthening of the scientific-technological apparatus. That is, the social organization varies according to the different goals toward which civic virtues, in whose mobilization such an organization consists, are coordinated. The philosophical-political-religious-ideological organization of society (that is, the traditional organization, determined by the set of virtues promoting the common good, as defined by its relation with the immutable Order of the world) is progressively replaced with the scientific-technological organization of society. In it, technical virtue tends toward the infinite strengthening of itself; it dominates not by unifying the multiplicity of virtues in an organic totality (to which the common good and the immutable Order correspond), but rather by imposing itself on the unrelated multiplicity of virtues that is established when virtues separate from one another and become conflictual because of the loss of the immutable Order and unitary Meaning of the world.

New meanings of civic and individual virtues arise because of the fading away of the meaning that tradition has attributed to truth. If in Western thought virtue is the force by which human beings, provisionally or definitely, save themselves from *nothingness*, such a force transforms human beings while transforming itself. It produces the condition for salvation either by reproducing in time, and thus mirroring, the immutable Order of reality, or by producing a new order, the ground itself of salvation, therein realizing itself as pure creativity.

No type of person is as virtuous as the Westerner because the will to salvation from *nothingness* requires that *nothingness* come to light in consciousness, and only the West begins to have consciousness of nothingness as the extreme danger from which humanity and being itself must save themselves. Western virtue is extreme since, because of the extreme danger, the force that saves one from it must also be extreme. The extreme virtue of the West reaches its own extreme form in technics. In the age of technics (whose advent is due to the philosophical thought of the last two centuries), virtue is not limited to creating the image of the eternal in time. It is pure and absolute creation that does not feel itself limited by anything and that even means to redeem and put the past under its own domination.

The virtue of Western tradition fades and the sense that virtue takes up in the age of technics arises because the very notion of virtue that the West construes—virtue as a force capable of enabling the survival of human beings and of itself amidst the becoming of the world, that is, in the waving in which the things of the world come out of and return to nothingness—demands the nonexistence of any definitive virtue, any absolute, any ground, any immutable, indeed, any "God" that contains already in itself the force that virtue must produce for the salvation of humanity. In opposition to what happens in the Western tradition, where there can be virtue (that is, authentic salvation from nothingness) only if God exists, one realizes that, if God exists, no human virtue could exist. Since virtue exists, there can be no God. First of all, not even that God who is truth (as the place wherein the West has evoked any God and any immutable) can exist. If there were a God—that is, if there existed the place in which all perfections and all events of the world have always and already been present—the force with which human beings act for their salvation would become a simple appearance, an illusory commitment and effort. The force of virtue, whose availability appears as the supreme evidence for Western human beings, demands the death of all gods.

It is at this point that the highest journey of thinking begins. The virtue of technics still has in front of itself a long path, which leads to the *paradise* of technics. It leads to the *praemium virtutis* [the reward of virtue], and thus to the *Angst* that essentially belongs to such a paradise—when, at the climax of happiness, peoples realize that the achieved happiness cannot have *truth* because it is grounded on the hypothetical logic of scientific knowledge, and is therefore exposed to the possibility of a total failure. It will be the time when peoples, and not only individuals, are called to thinking the meaning of truth chorally.

This would be a form of thought itself destined to fail if it did not take into account the circumstance that the entire history of our civilization springs out of the dimension facing the eyes of the West ever since its beginning: the dimension of the force of virtue. It is *force*, of which virtue is constituted, understood as ability to dominate the becoming of the world. What a huge responsibility burdens the shoulders of this *idea*! Everything has depended on it, up to the advent of the paradise of technics. By now, the virtue of the West is the virtue of the whole Earth because the East has become the prehistory of the West.

One can give another reference to the metaphor Walter Benjamin recalled, and say that the West is similar to the angel of history, who proceeds by retreating, turning his shoulders to the direction toward which he moves, and sweeping away everything he has in front of his eyes in his tempestuous gaze. The force of an immense whirlwind, which is at his shoulders, enables him to drawback history. The idea of the force of virtue (the idea of the virtue of force) lies at the ground of the West and carries on its shoulders the responsibility for the process leading from the tradition of the West to the civilization of technics.

The greater the responsibility of the force of virtue, the more indispensable it becomes that the angel of the West, in the end, *turns around* and faces it. The ideas of force and virtue succeed in putting into question the entire Western tradition and enable the most radical practice of a "critical spirit." Such an idea, however, escapes its own critical spirit, and rules uncontested, as the whirlwind behind the angel's shoulders withdraws from the angel's gaze. The clearer it becomes that the whole history of the West depends on the whirlwind of such an idea, the more indispensable it becomes to turn around and look at it: to start challenging it about its uncontested domain and the legitimacy of its domain; to start *questioning* it.

For a long time the West has *become accustomed to* considering the "force that controls becoming" as the supreme evidence. At this point, however, it is precisely this "evidence" that must give account of its own ruling and of its own presence in all thoughts and works of the West. The meaning of virtue does not belong to a chapter of moral philosophy. In the underground of such meaning, the *secret* of the West is hidden. To turn one's gaze toward it, and penetrate it, going beyond all habits of our culture and civilization is necessary.[9]

Notes

1. Montesquieu, *The Spirit of Laws*, trans. T. Nuget (New York: Colonial Press, 1899), IV, 5.

2. Cicero, *Tusculan Disputations*, trans. J. E. King (Cambridge, MA: Harvard University Press, 1927), II, xviii, 43.

3. Baruch Spinoza, *Ethics and Selected Letters*, trans. S. Shirley (Indianapolis: Hackett, 1982), IV, def. 8, p. 156.

4. Ibid., IV, prop. XXII, p. 167.

5. Immanuel Kant, *Metaphysics of Morals*, trans. M. Gregor (Cambridge: Cambridge University Press, 1996), p. 185.

6. Nicolas Malebranche, *Treatise on Ethics*, trans. C. Walton (Dordrecht: Kluwer, 1993), pt. I, p. 53.

7. Emmanuele Severino, *Techne* (Milan: Rizzoli, 1979).

8. Emmanuele Severino, *La tendenza fondamentale del nostro tempo* (Milan: Adelphi, 1988).

9. See Emmanuele Severino, *Essenza del nihilismo* (Milan: Adelphi, 1972).

Chapter 14

Two Concepts of Utopia
and the Idea of Global Justice

SALVATORE VECA

This chapter pertains to ways of thinking about and evaluating politics, of assigning to it goals, roles, and relevance for our lives; ways of interpreting its meaning and identifying what politics is or should be in comparison to other things. This chapter challenges political philosophy and some of its fundamental questions.

The chapter is divided into two sections, the first of which advances some ideas in the form of a balance or a heritage. I wonder "what remains of the day"; I sketch ways of thinking politics that have had a strong hold on observers and participants for a large part of the twentieth century; and I try to delineate the conclusions of a political wisdom *fin de siècle*.

The second section moves from the final balance to outline those that appear as the salient challenges or the main problem for political philosophy for us observers and participants at the beginning of the twenty-first century: the problem of focusing an idea of global justice. The interval between the two sections introduces the notion of a reasonable utopia, a central idea of the *prolegomena* to a theory of global justice. In the first section, the focus is on the idea of utopia in the perfect society. For this reason, my remarks on the different ways of thinking and evaluating politics and its transformation essentially aim at focusing two distinct concepts of utopia in view of a theory of global justice.

A Heritage

We are largely heirs to ways of thinking, evaluating, and judging politics that have assigned to it an intrinsic value and, in any event, a superior or prioritized value in comparison to others. The *priority* of politics over society is the core of the beliefs about politics that have characterized the long twentieth-century season of political constructivism, absolute politics, and politics as an end in itself. This is the long season of political *devotion* and *hope*, a season marked by the idea that political action and choice can and must shape, mold, indeed, build the ways of a time-enduring cohabitation by virtue of the design of a desirable, good, just, or perfect society in light of some criterion of political value.

One should notice that this idea, the fundamental idea of political *constructivism*, has been shared by people who had goals and supported projects of societies and social practices that are very different and conflicting among themselves. We can say that such an idea has nourished the political devotions of a large part of the twentieth century, regardless of articles of faith and sacred texts. In its purest form, the idea of political constructivism lies at the foundation of a utopian, perfect society. This latter is defined by specifying two clauses: the first concerns collective institutions; the second concerns individual motivations.

The first clause tells us that any institutional design is politically possible so as to pursue collective and *impersonal* goals that are deemed worthy of being pursued. Briefly, we will say that, in this perspective, *everything is possible*. The second clause tells us that it is politically possible and dutiful to shape and mold *personal* motivations, individual preferences, and the value orderings of persons in ways deemed worthy. Joining the two clauses, we obtain the utopia of a *perfect society* in its purest form. This is the first of the two concepts of utopia that constitute the center of my remarks on the ways of thinking politics.

Absolute politics receives its value from belief in the utopia of the perfect society because it is political action and choice; it is the use of the authority resource that only can and must shape, mold, and build our ways of cohabiting durably in time. Politics generates the good social order. Often, although not always, such a perspective has been maintained and defended by an appeal to rationality. Some have claimed that political constructivism finds its reasons in the rational choice of its goals or in the deciphering of the rationality of the history that came before and that with inexorable necessity could only lead to such goals. Not to accept political constructivism would imply irrationality.

This strange mixture of hard necessity and Promethean possibility has been the cement of devotions and beliefs concerning the priority of politics over society and of the beliefs that have been nourished by the political hope of most of the twentieth century, certainly by the political hope of that part of the "short century" that, *entre deux guerres* [between two wars], knew the rising of fascist and communist regimes and the big European crisis of democracies.

As the heirs [of that century], we know the outcome of Lagers and Gulags, and we recognize in the Shoah the realized exemplification of absolute evil. As Europeans, in the balance we assay the unsustainable burden in terms of devalue and antivalue of the projects of absolute politics, and of the delirium of omnipotence belonging to political constructivism. At the same time, we must remind those who have considered the burden of the massacre and of European cruelty literally unbearable, those who have thought that after Auschwitz one could no longer do philosophy, or think, and that one should rather adopt the attitude of the leave; we must remind them of the fact that not a banal component of our heritage is the elaboration of criteria to judge barbarity and massacre as barbarity and massacre.

Claus Offe has remarked that the ideal and distinctive European heritage, if there is anything of that sort, can be described as a coincidence, in the same space, of the worst crimes and the most elaborate and explicit criteria for condemnation of those crimes. Throughout its whole history, Europe has given itself the objects on which to exercise an accurate self-criticism. Because of this puzzling *coincidentia oppositorum*, we may perhaps say that the self-critical evaluation of the crimes the Europeans committed during their history and, in particular, during the recent events of the twentieth century, is something specifically European.

Let us then draw two propositions from the heritage: an assertion and a question. First, the European tradition includes both the event of the antivalue as absolute evil generated by politics and the fact of the criticism and moral blame of the antivalue. Second, however, we could also ask ourselves: what remains of the political hope and of the value and goals that is right to assign to politics, once the inherited maxim of wisdom has inexorably shown what the fatal error of the utopia of a perfect society is?

The Utopia of the Perfect Society and the Three Maxims of Political Wisdom

We may answer by clarifying in the first place what precisely constitutes the fatal error of the utopia of a perfect society. The fatal error depends on the *conjunction* of the two clauses. The project of collective institutions must be bound by respect for the individual values of persons. We must think of institutions as they should be, taking seriously human beings as they are. This reduces the space of what is politically possible.

The first maxim of political wisdom will thus be: *not everything is possible*. The second maxim of political wisdom: if you accept that not everything is possible, you should be induced to accept that no social world or form of cohabitation endures in time *without a loss in values*. It is not true that all good things in life, all ideals and possible collective goals can hold together, composing the harmonious *silhouette* of the Platonic temple in which, as Isaiah Berlin has shown, all questions receive only one answer and all values coherently stand together in balance. Nowhere is there a single method to access the answer to the cosmic puzzle. If we want to use probably the most disquieting term of the twentieth century, there is no "final solution." And it is good that it is so. The third maxim of political wisdom suggests in turn that everything or, more precisely, almost everything could have gone *differently*. The reduction of the Promethean plethora of possibilities goes together with the weakening of the strong hold of the appeal to necessity in human events.

The question remains: what is left of political hope and of the value or goals that is right to assign to politics if we accept the heirs' three maxims of wisdom? My answer is this: we can, or perhaps we must, think social institutions and practices, time-enduring forms of cohabitation worthy of praise *within* the space the world concedes to us. The space of the politically *possible* is now a space that has *limits*. Its boundaries are delimited on the one hand by the bond of one's individual motivations and choices and on the other by the axiom according to which not everything is possible and there are no social worlds without a loss in values. This is what defines the goals of a reasonable or, if one prefers, *situated* utopia. There is no good reason to take a leave from the exploration of the politically possible in light of some criterion of justice. The space in which to maneuver, we know it, is not unlimited. Not everything is possible. Yet, the maxim of wisdom that tells us that almost everything could have gone differently preserves the margins of the elusive philosophical *freedom*.

A first provisional, interesting conclusion from the remarks on heritage shows, in the end, that the priority of politics over society is replaced by the priority of society over politics. The thesis of the priority of society over politics holds both in a positive and in a normative sense when we aim at saying how things are as well as when we aim at saying how they should be.

We can recognize, with Robert Nozick, that moral philosophy defines the background and fixes the limits for the best political philosophy. We conclude the first round of remarks by noticing that limited politics requires a praise of *ethics*. It is the responsibility of ethical judgment that comes to the fore with respect to politics, institutions, and social practices when one abandons one's belief in absolute politics and in its value primacy within the variegated domain of what holds for us. It is also natural to ask oneself again at this point: what is the main problem for political philosophy, understood as the search for criteria of ethical judgment and evaluation of social institutions and practices? Which are the salient challenges for us heirs, observers, and participants at the beginning of the twenty-first century?

The Reasonable Utopia

I am convinced that the main issue consists in focusing on a notion of *global* justice in the successful extension of the criteria of justice from the internal side of political communities that have given borders to the international realm, or perhaps better, to say it with Jürgen Habermas, to the postnational constellation. This is, after all, the thesis that is at the center of the *prolegomena* to the theory of global justice I have sketched in the ten lectures in *La bellezza e gli oppressi* [*Beauty and the Oppressed*].[1] I add that a theory of justice without borders has as its focal center a thesis on human rights as fundamental rights of persons, and it requires the adoption of a universalistic viewpoint. Before I address the two salient notions that bring us closer to a theory of global justice that overcomes the many and well-known objections of various kind moved to a similar project, I would like to consider the theme of a *reasonable utopia*, thus introducing in a smooth and natural manner the second notion of utopia.

As John Rawls has remarked, a reasonable or realistic utopia is the one that explores possibilities within the space that the world concedes to us.[2] This means that the one who adopts the evaluative perspective of the realistic utopia is one who aims at testing *extensions* of what is politically viable. Under the condition of its best description, the world binds the array of what is politically possible: human beings as they are and the institutions as they could be, given the bond on the politically possible. The bond reduces the array of viable alternatives and establishes a criterion of accessibility to politically possible worlds, but not without costs and losses. As much as no meal is free, so there is no choice without costs. This has been taught to us by Berlin and his tenacious praise of pluralism.

Claudio Magris has eloquently sketched the attitude I call reasonable utopia in his narrative conjunction of utopia and disenchantment. On the one hand, as he reminds us, utopia means not to surrender to things as they are and fight for things as they should be; utopia means not to forget those anonymous victims, the thousands who died in centuries of unspeakable violent acts and disappeared in forgetfulness, not having been recorded in the annals of universal history. On the other hand, Magris goes on, disenchantment means to know that the *parousia* will not happen, that our eyes will not see the Messiah, that next year we will not be in Jerusalem, that the gods are in exile. In its turn, as Ernst Bloch teaches us, the spirit of utopia suggests that behind any reality there are other possibilities, which have to be freed from imprisonment in what is.

When united with the attitude of utopia, then, the attitude of disenchantment is

> an ironical, melancholic, or passionate form of hope; it moderates its prophetic and generously optimistic *pathos*, which easily underestimates the frightening possibilities of regression, of discontinuity, of barbarous tragedy that are hidden in history . . . behind things as they are there is also a promise, the need for how they should be; there is the possibility of another reality, which presses to come to light, like the butterfly in its chrysalis.[3]

Magris notes very well that the one who believes that enchantment is easy is ready prey of reactive cynicism when the enchantment reveals its rifts or does not show itself. In disenchantment is the awareness that the original sin has been committed, that human beings are not innocent, that Mambrinus's helmet is a small basin, and that the realist Sancho, not the dreaming knight Don Quixote, is right. Magris concludes in this manner: "Disenchantment says that enchantment is not; yet, in the tone and in the way in which it says so, it suggests that, despite everything, it exists and may reappear when one least expects it. A voice says that life has no meaning, yet its deep timbre is the echo of that meaning."[4]

As a note, I add only this remark, which seems to me to be coherent with Magris's suggestions regarding utopia and disenchantment: the one who for a variety of reasons is convinced that exploring the boundaries of what is possible for the *future* is wrong, tends not to acknowledge or remove the fact that in the *past* such boundaries have been overcome and crossed in many cases and important circumstances, fixing time after time *rare* points of no return, points that for us heirs are *exemplary*. The one who commits to the perspective of the reasonable utopia does not accept the strange asymmetry between the look backward and that forward. Even though this person is aware that the points of no return are not only *rather* rare, they are also systematically *rarer* than one usually thinks or hopes. Eduardo Galeano writes, "[The utopia] is on the horizon: I walk two steps, and it moves two steps back. I walk ten steps, and it moves ten steps farther. No matter how far I walk, I will never reach it. Then, what is the utopia for? For this it is: for walking."[5]

The Reasonable Utopia and the Contrast with Political Realism

To understand the concept of reasonable utopia, let us now ask ourselves more analytically, with Thomas Nagel, what properly makes a political theory utopian, in the negative sense of the utopia of a perfect society.[6] Let us reconsider our statement about human beings as they are and the institutions as they could be in a genuinely ethical perspective challenging, on the one side, the twofold orders of a person's personal and impersonal preferences, and on the other side, the double maneuver of justification in normative political theory. This is a maneuver that seems to have to address the person twice: first, the justification must address the person insofar as one holds the *impersonal* perspective; and second, it addresses the very same person insofar as one holds *particular* roles within a system of institutions and social practices that must also be *impersonally* acceptable.

To accept the duality of the orders of preferences and the duality of the justification maneuver of normative political theory inevitably amounts neither to capitulating in front of human weakness or wickedness, nor does it amount to consigning political philosophy to being a hostage to human nature. This is only a necessary recognition of our motivational *complexity*. Conversely, to ignore or neglect the second turn in the justification means to risk utopianism in the worst sense—the utopia of a perfect society. We can therefore claim that within the perspective of the reasonable utopia, to commit oneself to the endeavor that aims at the twofold justification does not mean to give up the primacy of moral justification in political theory. It simply means to acknowledge that personal justifications as well as impersonal justifications do and must have an important part in morality. This simply means that the requirement of a duality of justification is a real ethical requirement.

One should consider that, in cases such as these, saying either that individuals are simply wicked if they cannot behave individually in a manner that would produce an impersonally desirable result, or that given that one cannot legitimately require persons to behave in such a manner, the ideal upheld by political theory should simply be abandoned makes no sense. We should rather both consider the elements generating the dilemma as morally valid, and interpret this as the request to exercise political, social, and psychological *imagination* to mold institutions that will realistically involve individuals in forms of collective life favoring the ideal of our reasonable utopia.

In conclusion, as Nagel maintains, the danger of utopianism, the one leading to the utopia of a perfect society, comes from the familiar and disquieting political tendency to emphasize individual motives too much in the attempt to realize the ideal more fully, or even to try to transcend such personal motives completely perversely aiming at an impersonal transformation of social individuals.

We can conclude that the reasonable utopia rather requires the pursuit of a difficult and probably unstable equilibrium between the elements of moral and *impersonal* equality and the elements of individual and *personal* motivation. One should notice that if we accept such a perspective, we recognize that what is *just* must be *possible*, even if adding a clause is important: our understanding of what is *possible* may be at least in part altered, modified, and shaped by arguments regarding what is *just*.

The clause just introduced requires a remark to emphasize the essential contrast between the favored perspective of the reasonable utopia and the assumptions of reductionism, exemplified by old and new political realism. Before explaining the contrast, however, clarifying a difference between my perspective, that of the reasonable utopia in matters of justice without borders, and the perspectives adopted by globalist philosophers is helpful.

Let us consider Otfried Hoeffe and other globalists' perspectives. They think that it is a *fact* that we are gloriously marching toward a Kantian world republic, and they confirm their beliefs by resorting to a factual theory, for example, based on noticing the transcultural invariance of certain values. Some globalists also seem convinced that political philosophy generates the *Weltrepublik* architecture. A slightly different case is Habermas, who rereads Kant's *On Perpetual Peace* in light of the "undeserved awareness of those to come." Habermas speaks of the transition from "the law of people" to cosmopolitical right. He claims that globalization divides the world, even if it simultaneously forces it—as an endangered community—to communicative action; he remarks that the one who "does not want to deny *a priori* any ability to learn to the international system must place his or her hopes in the objective fact that for a long time now the globalization of dangers has united the world in an involuntary risk community."[7] Habermas seems to be involved in the description of a process or a set of processes. He is convinced that something like a cosmopolitical order is emerging exactly in the turning from the twentieth century to the twenty-first century. For this reason, he maintains the need for a reform of the United Nations and transnational institutions against the background of the metamorphosis of "internal world politics." From this perspective, which seems to me to be characterized by a philosophy of history prone to devotion to necessity or deferent to an obstetric motif in history à la G. A. Cohen,[8] it is clear in which sense one can conclude that cosmopolitical right is nothing more than a development or a *fulfillment* of the idea of the state of right. À la Kant the conclusion is that we must provoke a "cosmopolitical transformation into a state of right of the state of nature among states."[9]

The reasonable utopia is based on Musil's sense of possibility, and it revokes all devotion to necessity. The idea is that we commit ourselves to the exploration of the intricate and nuanced space of possibilities and viable alternatives aiming at testing the conditions of possibility of a just, or less unjust, world. The renunciation of the best possible world is not and must not be, as Edgar Morin has claimed, the renunciation of a better world.

In the third lecture on Kant and the paradigm of justice theories in *La bellezza e gli oppressi*, I have discussed Rawls's realistic utopia of the law of people, and I have clarified in which sense the idea of a realistic utopia establishes that a just social world where the law of people is realized "can exist in some place and at some future time, but its existence is neither necessary nor will it be in the future." After all, it is this idea that gives *meaning* to what we can do, here and now. In Eduardo Galeano's sense, utopia helps to keep walking. This idea is not based on a merely logical possibility; rather, it is linked to tendencies, inclinations, and transformations in the social world. Certainly, the social world does not classify things as tendencies, inclinations, and transformations by itself. We have the responsibility for interpreting and understanding a changing world. We can look at things in *certain* ways.

Philosophy has a limited power to induce us to see things in *certain* ways. Within the space of such a limited power we properly recognize the limits and the relevance of philosophical activity, but meanwhile we test the virtue of the elusive philosophical *freedom*. And here, the essential contrast with political realism is specified: realism functions as a *prima facie* excluding agent of *possible* ways of looking at things. In this sense, political realism exemplifies reductionism. Certainly, the point is not that bonds are imposed on the space of possibilities and alternatives. As we have said, the three maxims of political wisdom suggest the reasonability of bonds: not everything is possible; there are no social worlds without loss of values; everything or almost everything could have gone differently. In *this* sense, the perspective of reasonable utopia does not contrast with political realism: it takes seriously the severe bonds that circumscribe the space the world concedes to us. The perspective from which the reasonable utopia moves is intrinsically *situated*. The essential contrast does not concern, therefore, the fact of the acceptance of bonds.

The essential contrast lies in the refusal and resistance that the reasonable utopia opposes to the reductionistic prohibition realism imposes on the maneuvers of exploration of possibilities within the limits of "not everything is possible." For this reason, we are induced not to give up and to resist the claim of reductionism. We want to go on looking at things in alternative ways that connect us to value. The understanding of things as they are is not independent from the understanding of things as they can be. The just must be *possible*, but the understanding of the possible is not independent, as we have said, from the demonstrations concerning what is *just*.

At this point, let us ask ourselves: what are, after all, *the things* looked at by the one who aims at thinking of possibilities and alternatives? We can answer in this way: the things are simply a state of the world, a landscape where familiar facts are connected with less familiar facts, a Heraclitean world of incessant deformation in which the threshold between certainty and uncertainty is altered for us observers and participants—for us who aim at doing theory. The uncertainty requires theory, and, as I have claimed in the introduction to *La bellezza e gli oppressi*, the fact of globalization upsets the well-ordered discourses of political theory, which is positive and normative. The analysis of the state of the world leads, in the perspective of normative theory, to consider as *exempla* processes and facts that, for us, take up the physiognomy of provisional *signa prognostica*. Where euphoric globalists think they can discover the necessity of transitions and where reductionist realists with the same devotion to necessity find inexorable regularities that translate themselves into theorems of impossibility and prohibition for the thinking of alternatives, those who adopt the Musilian slogan of the sense of possibility find, beyond the boundaries of false necessity, the contingent and uncertain signs of a world that promises justice without borders, and that is all.

Human Development as Freedom

By adopting the perspective of reasonable utopia, I intend to illustrate and reformulate the two salient notions we might employ together with the idea of reasonable utopia in the *prolegomena* to a theory of justice without borders that is capable of overcoming the severe objections of its critics. As we know, the objections are numerous and, moreover, of many kinds. In the sixth lecture in *La bellezza e gli oppressi*, I confront epistemic objections by resorting to the enlightening notion of the richness of reason. I have made it clear, however, that there is at least another kind of objections gravitating around the nature of the object of theory: the space of the contended globe, the Hobbesian arena of persistent anarchy constituting the international community. Thucydides's and Hobbes's severe prohibition is still inscribed in the core of the research program of political realism. Focusing on the concept of reasonable utopia has shown the nature of the essential contrast with reductionism as it is exemplified in political realism. I therefore reformulate the two salient ideas on the background of the criticisms to the first and second kind of objections.

The first idea concerns the criterion of ethical evaluation that theory has to adopt. This criterion must be able to hold, regardless of the different and plural contexts in which it is applied; otherwise, it would fall under objections of the first kind. The criterion of evaluation is more or less the one proposed by Amartya Sen in terms of human development as freedom. My proposal reformulates Sen's thesis on capabilities and introduces the distinction between our dimension as agents and our dimension as moral patients. This is a distinction I have examined at length in *Dell'incertezza* [*On Uncertainty*].[10]

The idea is as follows: we can evaluate social institutions and practices here and there in the world, in the world of differences and inequalities, in the vast and small world in which richness and poverty coexist and the fact of human *oppression* of humans has many faces, by subjecting them to the test of one's functioning and capabilities. When people are reduced to the mere condition of patients because they have without their responsibility a *deficit* in their functioning, then institutions have to be designed in such a way to refund or compensate the disadvantages in terms of functioning. Beyond this threshold, it is a matter of a person's capabilities, of the degrees of their freedom to choose among alternative functioning, their dimension as agents. The criterion of evaluation is not dependent on contexts, cultures, and particular societies because it is sensitive to what for persons in different contexts and cultures is an ideal of the good life, or, if one prefers, of a life worth living.

The remote Aristotelian ideal of *eudaimonia* [happiness] is thus reformulated in terms of a formal schema in the sense that we accept that a life may be chosen as worth living for an essential variety of reasons. The variety of reasons of *choice* will find its roots in the variety of the given *identities*, in the Herderian space of difference. This is a way to account for the richness of reason in a different way. The richness of reason is the resource with which to escape the trap of contextualist criticism.

No matter what the contexts are, we are under the obligation to test the justifiability or lack thereof of social institutions and practices in light of their effect on the compensation for disadvantages in one's functioning and on one's greater or lesser capability to choose among alternative functionings. Thus, one could claim, one's fundamental rights, what is owed to one regardless of the given boundaries and of the communities within which one has a life to live, are ascribed to anyone because all have the same right to shape one's destiny and not to be subjected to or slave to the oppression of unlucky circumstances and cruel and tyrannical institutions. (This remark might be the basis of a justification for the central thesis on fundamental human rights as rights to development as freedom.)

In conclusion, the idea of human development as freedom does not demand that we adhere to only one concept of good life. As we have seen, development as freedom is an idea that goes along with a variety of conceptions of what makes one's life worth living. Therefore, the idea of human development as freedom can be part with full right of the *prolegomena* to a theory of global justice because it escapes the trap of the contextualist objection that gives precedence to identity over choice.

Minimal Procedural Justice

I can now introduce the second salient idea for our *prolegomena*: it coincides with minimal procedural justice. We know that minimal procedural justice must be understood as a virtue of procedures of arbitration, negotiation, deliberation, and judgment: a virtue of social *practices*. Stuart Hampshire has often emphasized the fact that there is a family, which is variegated and heterogeneous in different contexts and in different circumstances in space and time, of practices of arbitrate and deliberation that we are led to recognize as just, thanks to the public properties of some fair procedures that transfer fairness to their outcomes.[11] The space of minimal procedural justice is a space of differences and varieties that corresponds to the pluralism of identities and cultures. It does not coincide with the space of substantial conceptions of justice, the presuppositions of which are in debt toward *beliefs* that exemplify, in different contexts, different interpretations of the sense of justice at work in specific communities.

I am convinced that we should invert the priority of individual beliefs over social practices. In the inaugural language of Plato's great dialogue on justice, we should move from the *polis* and not from the *psyche* because the domain of beliefs is that of the conflict of interpretations over the sense of justice and of substantial conceptions of justice. And here the objection of the contextualists has an easy time.

The axioms of a substantialist theory of justice derive in fact from a specific interpretation, offered by theory, of the sense of justice in a given community. Rawls's pioneering work acknowledges this fact. The thesis of reflective equilibrium confirms that the assumptions of a theory of justice aiming nevertheless at being purely procedural are part of the beliefs constituting a society's public culture. Yet, if we stay with beliefs, it is difficult that the path toward a *step by step* universalism is truly open for a theory of global justice. The others, whom philosophers of language, busy with the dilemmas of a theory of interpretation, would call the *exotic* others, have other beliefs and other interpretations of the beliefs constituting their own inherited vocabularies of politics and morality.

The thesis of minimal procedural justice moves from here and focuses on the features of practices, not beliefs. It aims at possible, not necessary, outcomes of convergence regarding criteria of just and unjust concerning institutions and politics in a Heraclitean world of incessant deformation and conflict between interests and ideals, among the reasons why one's life is worth living. Certainly, the thesis of minimal procedural justice too is not void of assumptions. How could it be differently? Yet, as I have often claimed, its assumptions are austere and thrifty, and can be reduced to the only one axiom expressed in the old legal saying of which Herbert Hart was fond: *audi alteram partem* [listen to the other party].

Let us now consider the interesting inference one can draw from Hart's axiom: in the global space, *fairness* and *unfairness*, just and unjust, will coincide not with canons or criteria of judgment incorporated in some conception of the good, or in some substantial conception of the just and the unjust. Rather, they will coincide with the elementary fact whether the procedures of deliberation and judgment *include* or *exclude participants* from the process. One should notice that, unlike Habermas, I do not think that the principles for inclusion of participants must depend on some transcendental condition that is presupposed to the ways in which people should communicate if they are oriented toward an agreement on the criteria of just and unjust.

In my favorite interpretation, Hart's axiom only demands from us that social practices aiming at fair judgment listen to *all* voices, and that nobody may thus advance the complaint that we can easily recognize as the appropriate complaint for minimal procedural justice: that of having been excluded, of not having participated *with full right* [*a pieno titolo*] to the process of deliberation and judgment on social institutions and practices within which one has a life to live in common with others. The complaint is the memo of the fact that not everyone has been given a *voice* or has been *listened to*. And this is simply *unjust*.

We can thus conclude that the idea of minimal procedural justice confirms itself as a very promising candidate, together with the criterion of evaluation of human development as freedom, to play an important part in the *prolegomena* to a theory of justice without borders. A theory that in the perspective of the reasonable utopia we believe we must explore if and because we are convinced that it is worth neither deserting nor taking leave, but rather continuing testing the *possible* within the *limited* (though not for this less important) arena of politics, within the space that the world concedes to us. The idea of minimal procedural justice takes very seriously realistic criticisms of globalism, and it comes close, in conclusion, to the idea of a background condition of minimal justice functioning as a filter-mechanism for processes of insurgence and projects of construction and design of fair conditions of cohabitation and cooperation for a social world worth living in.

The conclusion holds value for those who are convinced that the space of a utopia having political and moral value is not only occupied by the concept of the utopia of the perfect society with its cruel procession of the consequences of its fatal mistake, but also welcomes the concept of the reasonable utopia, the utopia that suggests jointly the respect for human beings as they are and the exploration of social institutions and practices of time enduring cohabitation as they can be within the space that the world concedes to us.

In this way, we do not renounce loyalty to the value and *beauty* of a possible human world and, at the same time, we do not accept that the fact of multifaceted *oppression* erodes and cancels the promise of justice without borders from the board of the future and of the anticipations of normative validities. Despite its difficulty, as Albert Camus has suggested, in this sense we want to remain loyal to beauty and to those who are oppressed.

Notes

1. Salvatore Veca, *La bellezza e gli oppressi: Dieci lezioni sull'idea di giustizia* (Milan: Feltrinelli, 2002).

2. See John Rawls, *The Law of Peoples* (Cambridge, MA: Harvard University Press, 1999), pp. 6–7, 11–19.

3. Claudio Magris, *Utopia e disincanto* (Milan: Garzanti, 1999), pp. 14–16.

4. Ibid., p. 13.

5. Eduardo Galeano, *Walking Words*, trans. M. Freid (New York: Norton, 1997), translation modified.

6. See Thomas Nagel, "Cosa rende utopica una teoria politica?" in *L'idea di giustizia. La filosofia politica americana contemporanea*, ed. S. Maffettone (Naples: Guida, 1993), pp. 73–94.

7. Jürgen Habermas, *Die Einbeziehung des Anderen* (Frankfurt: Suhrkamp, 1996), p. 217.

8. See Gerald A. Cohen, *If You're Egalitarian, How Come You Are So Rich?* (Cambridge, MA: Harvard University Press, 2000), pp. 58–78. Cohen's idea of the obstetric motif is close to the idea of delivery I have formulated in Salvatore Veca, *La società giusta* (Milan: Il Saggiatore, 1982). An imposing example of persistent intellectual deference toward the obstetric motif can be found in Michael Hardt and Antonio Negri, *Empire* (Cambridge, MA: Harvard University Press, 2001).

9. Habermas, p. 236.

10. See Salvatore Veca, *Dell'incertezza. Tre meditazioni filosofiche* (Milan: Feltrinelli, 1997), pp. 107–17; Amartya K. Sen, *Development as Freedom* (Oxford: Oxford University Press, 1999), p. 18.

11. See Stuart Hampshire, *Innocence and Experience* (Cambridge, MA: Harvard University Press, 1989).

Chapter 15

The World and the West Today

The Problem of a Global Public Sphere

Giacomo Marramao

Introduction

The world and the West. *Not* the West and the world. In its provoking inversion of the order of the terms, the hendiadys closely follows the title of a famous series of conferences: the Reith Lectures given by Arnold Toynbee in 1952 at the invitation of the British Broadcasting Company and published the following year by Oxford University Press (thus published before the conclusion of the monumental *Study of History*, which appeared in ten volumes between 1934 and 1954). Never, as in this case, has the inversion in the order of factors violated the mathematical axiom according to which the product remains unchanged. Here the inversion adumbrates a radical change in meaning and direction, such that it challenges the traditional optical summit that in the philosophy of history as well as in the nineteenth- and twentieth-century social sciences, assigned a privileged position to the West. Toynbee himself anticipates the foreseeable objection to the reversal of terms that he posits:

> Why . . . has the book been called *The World and the West*? Is not the West just another name for as much of the world as has any importance for practical purposes today? And, if the author feels that he must say something about the non-Western rest of the world, why must he put the two words in this order? Why could he not write *The West and the World* instead of writing *The World and the West*? He might at least have put the West first.[1]

The answer is so radical and sharp as to cast light on the interpretative viewpoint underlying the comparative approach to civilizations that is taken in such a vast and ambitious work, comparable in its kind only to that of

Fernand Braudel. We can drastically summarize such an interpretative viewpoint in three cardinal theses: First, not only has the West "never been all
of the world that matters," but also it has not been "the only actor on the
stage of modern history even at the peak of the West's power (and this peak
has perhaps now already been passed)." Second, in the encounter between
the world and the West that has been going on now for four or five centuries,
the part that has had "the significant experience" has been up to now not *the
West* but *the Rest*—the rest of the world. Third, in the "hit" [*urto*] between
the West and *the Rest*, it is not the West to have been hit by the world, but
rather "it is the world that has been hit—and hit hard—by the West."[2]

Toynbee's theory of the "hit" confronts us with the *long duration*, with
the historical-structural depth of that set of events today gathered under the
ubiquitous headword "globalization": an intertwining of events that can be
understood only by going to the roots of that "expansion of the West over
the world"[3] that, if it certainly has its *turning point* at the end of the fifteenth
century with the opening up of the seas and the conquest of the New World,
nevertheless finds a meaningful referent in the Greek and Roman history of
the fourth century BCE with the advent of the Alexandrian empire.
Alexander's march across Asia "made as revolutionary a change in the balance of power in the world as the voyages of De Gama and Columbus."[4] It
cannot be doubted that, by turning the earth into a circumnavigable sphere,
the conquest of America marks the beginning of modern globalization; nevertheless, it is not less true that in the second century BCE, due to the
conquest of India up to Bengal by the Greeks and of the Atlantic frontier
represented by the Iberian peninsula and the British island by the Romans,
the Western—that is, Greco-Roman—civilization of the time could boast of
having penetrated, thanks to the radiation of its conquering culture, those
that then appeared as the extreme edges of a planet whose shape and dimension had more or less been already calculated. The hit by the West had thus
caused the world before the advent of Christianity "as sharp a shock as the
impact of our modern Western culture has been giving it since the fifteenth
century of our era."[5]

And yet, in the movement of the radiating center of Western technology and culture from the Greek and Roman hegemony to the hegemony of
modern Europe (which cannot be understood, according to Toynbee, without that scientific revolution to whose incubation the Islamic civilization
contributed fundamentally) and from Europe to the current U.S. supremacy
and to the "extreme West" represented by the Pacific area, what changes is
not only the idea of the West (with a paradoxical effect of "orientalization"
of the once-dominating centers), but also the nature and the configuration
of the "clash" between the West and the world. When one revisits it today,
half a century later, Toynbee's comparative approach appears—although inevitably conditioned by the assets of the bipolar world—not only anticipatory of our present age in many aspects, but also a precious corrective to

many philosophical genealogies in their claims to reduce current global conflicts to a domination by the technology that is inscribed in the Greek matrix of the West since its origins. If one adopts such a reductivist scheme, one loses sight not only of the spurious genesis of "Western" culture out of the civilizations of the near and far "East," as the most accredited studies on "orientalism" have documented (let me just mention here Jean Bottero's *Mesopotamia*, which starts with an introduction aptly titled "The Birth of the West")[6]; one also loses sight of the totally Western character of the dualism "East/West," which goes back to the polarity Greek/barbarians introduced by Herodotus in the *incipit* to his *Histories*. Furthermore, one loses sight not only of the sliding westward of that oppositional couple, so that, as a consequence of the identification of the West with the Franco-Germanic area, Greece has ended up being part of the "empire of the East," whereas today Europe is treated as an ambiguous and indecipherable entity by the West *par excellence* represented by the United States. More important, one also loses sight of the changes in the form and structure of the world that are subsequently produced by the various stages of the "hit."

It is only with the modern epoch, marked—to say it with Carlo Cipolla—by the lethal combination of the sailing ship with the cannon,[7] that Western civilization deterritorializes itself by going around Asia's terrestrial empires via the sea. This turning point, however, in which technics becomes autonomous and gives rise to an unheard-of intertwining of industrial take-off, military power, and commercial expansion, is understood by Toynbee through the resort to a binary scheme entirely similar to those which he himself had otherwise sharply criticized. The hit between the world and the West caused by modern Europe's planetary expansionism would be nothing else than a *technological Westernization* imposing itself with the retaliation of a *spiritual de-Westernization*, "the present encounter between the world and the West is now moving off the technological plane on to the spiritual plane."[8]

Such an outcome—which seems to echo, albeit with rather different tones and modulations, a famous saying of the great "culture of the European crisis" in the twentieth century—depends, when carefully considered, on the presence of an unresolved tension running through the entire structure of the analysis. Despite the initial exhortation "to slip out of [one's] native Western skin and look at the encounter between the world and the West through the eyes of the great non-Western majority of mankind,"[9] Toynbee is in truth incapable of taking leave of the prejudice underlying European comparative approaches and continues to consider Europe and the West as the center of *radiation* of global dynamics.

Today the theoretical perspectives opened up by cultural and postcolonial studies push European intellectuals and political elites to a courageous relativization of the role to which the modern concept of history had destined them in the course of the last two centuries. The provocative invitation to "provincialize Europe," which was sent to the Western social sciences by a representative of subaltern studies such as Dipesh Chakrabarty,[10] challenges not only the traditional "narratives" of philosophy of history, which postulated the Old Continent as the cradle of *humanitas* and the propelling center of universalizing dynamics, but also the comparative approaches, which under the assumption of European exceptionality turned Europe into the radiation point of a modernity destined to spread to the totality of the globe—a modernity in front of which any movement or trend for change coming from extra-European or non-Western areas is interpreted as a mere "reactive" manifestation to the expansionist processes of modernization.

Out of the just-delineated background, I will now try to offer a reading of the "hit wave" crossing the current global world that, on the one hand, is capable of capitalizing on the work of "deconstruction" and *location* of the European-Western civilization brought about by postcolonial studies, and on the other, is capable of addressing the problem of a possible *re-location* of the European region *after the disenchantment*. This chapter questions the (real or virtual) existence of a public global sphere, which is a more plausible (and analytically viable) question than the theses according to which there already exists, albeit *in nuce*, a "global civil society" (Ulrich Beck's *globale Zivilgesellschaft*, which would take the place of the classical *bürgerliche Gesellschaft* and its Hegelian–Marxian flavor).

To ask such a question, however, implies a double operation: (1) to establish a critique of communication, and (2) to start with becoming aware of the existence in the globalized world of a plurality of "diasporic public spheres" (Arjun Appadurai),[11] which escape the territorial logic of the sovereignty of the nation-states as well as the way in which sociology has up to now understood, starting with Roland Robertson, the phenomenon of the *glo-cal* (or of *glocalization*).[12]

The first operation is made accessible through some recent revisions of the optimistic prognosis of the global village made by the theoreticians of electronic multimedia. For them, rather than producing one sole sphere, the network has given rise to a multiplicity of centrifugal spheres. The second operation calls onto the scene the problematic relation between the two dimensions of the conflict of interests (or better, of the conflict of preferences, given the complexity, after the seventeenth and eighteenth centuries, of the notion of interest that is not at all reducible to the strictly economic-utilitarian environment) and the conflict of identities.

Such a relation, which can be summarized in the pair redistribution-recognition (which has been at the center in recent years of an interesting confrontation between Nancy Fraser and Axel Honneth), can be understood today only in light of a radical redefinition of the concept of public sphere as sharply marked out from the Rawlsian procedural as well as the Habermasian critical-communicative meaning. On the one hand, the political public sphere cannot be simply considered as the space of an overlapping consensus functional to the negotiation of procedural rules of justice that put into bracket the conflict of the "overall conceptions" of the good. On the other hand, it cannot be understood either as a mere communicative exchange of rational value arguments functional to a wider and more inclusive *Verständigung*; rather, it must be understood as an encounter-confrontation of "narratives," which relate to the organization of the global society and come from different contexts of experience and life-worlds.

An additional complication arises from the circumstance that, because of their self-justifying and self-legitimizing potential (which is not inferior to that produced by the schemes of rational argumentation of values), narrations must be taken up in their *contingency*. From here comes a double exigency: (1) to overcome the notion of tolerance with that of reciprocal respect among identities and cultures (a "respect" that, on the one hand, takes into consideration Derrida's appeal to *responsibility* understood as a responding-to rather than a responding-of, that is, as an availability to be put into question by the other, and, on the other hand, does not exclude contamination, confrontation, and in the last analysis conflict itself); and (2) to subtract the category of recognition from the patronizing-supremacist as well as relativistic temptations.

Such an argumentative move implies first of all a sharp distinction between *cultural relativism* (the relevant acquisition and point of no return of the great anthropology of the twentieth century) and *ethical relativism*; and second, a dissociation of the notions—often mistaken or improperly assimilated—of *incommensurability* and *incomparability* between hierarchies of different values. Briefly, the fact that no unique parameter of commensurability exists among symbolic-cultural contexts (as Isaiah Berlin has taught) does not mean eo ipso that they are incomparable among themselves.

A public sphere built around such premises must abide the criterion of a *universalist politics of difference*, sharply marked out, on the one hand, from the universalist identity politics of the Enlightenment kind (which finds its noblest declination in Kant), and on the other hand from the antiuniversalist politics of differences (which are advanced in North America by the communitarians and by some versions of multiculturalism, and in Europe by the "security oriented" ethnopolitics of various localisms and Lega-like movements [*leghismi*]).[13] The thesis announced here is based on ten argumentative passages, through which I take up and develop the interpretative reading of the global world I have tried to propose in a recent work of mine, *Passaggio a Occidente. Filosofia e globalizzazione*.[14]

Global Age: Opportunities and Risks

The title of the book, *Passaggio a Occidente* [*West Passage*],[15] carries the core of the thesis within itself. The heterogeneous set of phenomena we are accustomed to gather in the *passpartout* slogan "globalization" cannot be understood in my opinion either in terms of universal homologation under "one thought alone" (Francis Fukuyama), that is, of the "Westernization of the world" (Serge Latouche),[16] or in terms of the "clash of civilizations" (Samuel Huntington),[17] but rather in terms of a West passage. "Passage" should be understood in the dual meaning of "journey" and "change," of "risk" and "opportunity." The process that, starting at the end of the 1980s, is occurring in front of our eyes is in the last analysis nothing else than an impervious *North-West passage* of all culture—a perilous transit toward modernity destined to produce deep transformations in the economies, societies, and lifestyles not only of the "others," but also of Western civilization itself. In the title is deposited the thesis that guides the multiple "circumnavigations" of the book. In a sense, it carries *in nuce* my philosophical thematization of that set of often "heterologous" phenomena, which is usually summarized in the German and Anglo-Saxon areas under the label "globalization" and in the cultural-linguistic romance area, common to neo-Latin countries, under the name "*mundialization*."

Postmodernity or World-Modernity [*modernità-mondo*]?

In what sense can one discern a difference in two lemmas usually employed as synonyms? "Mundialization" is a term loaded with the symbolic, even more than semantic implications of the Latin *mundus* in its inevitable reference to the idea of "mundanization," and thus of "secularization." Expressions such as "worldly" [*mondiale*] and "mundane" [*mondano*] contain an inevitable reference to the notion of *saeculum* and consequently to the field of tension between transcendence and immanence, heaven and earth. Globalization carries within itself rather the idea of the spatial completeness of such a process, the idea of a world that has become a finally circumnavigable globe—this is an idea, however, that has been declined in the most various and controversial manners. Many (Martin Albrow first of all) claim that globalization is a postmodern phenomenon, a new movie with a script *toto coelo* [entirely] different from all other movies seen so far. It is as if they were to tell us: the movie of modernity is over; now the global one starts. I do not share this position for the simple but decisive reason that in history stages and epochs do not follow one another giving rise to absolute ends or beginnings. As there are not movies that begin and movies that end, likewise one cannot say that up to a certain point (World War I? World War II? The fall of the Berlin wall?) there has been a modern space, whereas today an entirely new space that would be the global has started. I mean that between the two epochs or, if one prefers, between the two spatial orderings is neither an absolute threshold nor a longitudinal rupture. In sum, one must understand that in its genesis and structure, the global space is not conceivable if not as *consequence of modernity* (Anthony Giddens).[18] Clearly maintaining such a claim does not amount to saying that there are not or cannot be break points. It simply means that to grasp the actual aspects of novelty of the global space, we must consider it in close connection with the modern process of secularization. From its being endogenous, that is, internal to the developed Western countries of Judeo-Christian matrix, the dynamic of such a process has become exogenous to the point of affecting the most remote sociocultural realities and religious experiences. In this sense, rather than the advent of "the postmodern condition" (announced in a homonymous pamphlet by Jean-François Lyotard in 1979), globalization seems to mark a problematic and accident-paved transit from the nation-modernity [modernità-nazione] into the world-modernity.

Standardization and Differentiation

Avoiding the paradigmatic alternative according to which globalization is either total homologation or the clash of civilizations is necessary. I am convinced that standardization and differentiation are two sides of a same process—two lines of tendency that simultaneously integrate and refute each other. When observing things from this perspective, the opposed theses of Fukuyama (universal homologation under the sign of competitive individualism) and Huntington (the post–cold war world as the stage of a planetary intercultural conflict) appear not so much as drastic alternatives but rather as two half-truths. On the one hand, globalization is techno-economic and financial-mercantile standardization with the consequent phenomena of deterritorialization and increasing interdependency among the various areas of the planet; on the other hand, it is an equally accelerated trend of differentiation and reterritorialization of identities, of relocation of the processes of symbolic identification. Between the two aspects, which the sociological lexicon tends to summarize in the oxymoron of the *glocal*, there is an interfacial relation. At the same time, however, a dangerous short circuit may arise with paralyzing effects.

The Short Circuit of the "Glocal": A Philosophical-Political Reading

What is specifically the phenomenon of the short circuit? The short circuit is produced by the break of the intermediary link in the international modern order that arose out of the slaughter of the civil religious wars between Catholics and Protestants, which was sanctioned with the Peace of Westfalia in the mid-seventeenth century. This is the link represented by the nation-state and by the structure supporting it: the isomorphism between people, territory, and sovereignty. Here one should clarify once and for all the issue concerning the long seller on the "crisis of the state" that runs through all the great philosophical and juridical-political disputes from the beginning to the end of the twentieth century. The core of the controversy surrounding themes such as the obsolescence of the nation-state, the erosion of sovereignty, and so forth, cannot be addressed only in a purely sociological site. This is so for the simple reason that the application of the quantitative methods of sociology would provide us with a result diametrically opposed to the diagnosis of the crisis of the state. If one were to analyze the health condition of the state from a numerical perspective and through an exclusive resort to the method of measuring, then the result today would be that of an excellent health because after 1989 the world has observed a real boom in the birth of national and subnational states (today, many more states are part of the United Nations than before the fall of the Berlin wall), and the instances and functions of the state have not at all shrunk but rather expanded. The decline of the state must be read then not in purely sociological and quantitative terms, but rather in political and qualitative terms—by focusing on the *efficaciousness* of the sovereignty of the individual states. The situation of the state within the global world thus returns to us the paradox of a "deadly health," of a *decline while increasing*—of a degree of efficaciousness inversely proportional to the rate of quantitative expansion. The inexorable shrinking of the efficaciousness of territorial sovereign prerogatives determines the "break" in the intermediary function between global and local, a function that during modernity was carried out by the state. The "short circuit" arises because individual sovereign states are too small to confront the challenges of the global market and too big to control the proliferation of the themes, vindications, and conflicts various localisms induced. Hence derives that which in my book I name the "tongs" of globalization. On this issue also dissipating some equivocations is appropriate. Reading the hyphen in "glo-cal" as a mere disjunctive and not also conjunctive dash (thus following the interpretative key advanced by Zygmut Bauman in his nevertheless meritorious essays)—as a simple border line between a cosmopolitism of the rich, seen as the jet-set society indifferent to any border, and a localism of the poor, constrained and enclosed in their increasingly marginal and peripheral sites, would be too simple. If things were truly so, the global condition would be less paradoxical and in the end much more reassuring. What happens instead is the reverse: the paradox with which we have to deal today is a cosmopolitism of the poor in front of a localism of the rich, so much so that the aptest tool for assessing the intensity level of localistic and autonomistic vindications would seem to be the "rich meter." Otherwise, one cannot understand why devolution politics are more present in the rich regions of the planet (from Italian Northeast to the other wealthy regions in Europe, from the countries in Mercosur to those in Southeast Asia), whereas the demand for universalism comes from the poorest regions. This does not mean, however, that the poor are immune to that global virus, to that real "pandemic" I call identity obsession. I simply maintain that the drive toward the invention of a communitarian identity recognizable and characterized *per differentiam* in relation to all others—with the consequent fragmentation of the global society into a plurality of "diasporic public spheres"—constitutes a reactive phenomenon: a mechanism of defense-reply to *this* globalization. This is a globalization that homologizes but does not universalize, compresses but does not unify. Thus, under the false appearance of the "politics of difference," it produces a constant proliferation of logics of identity. All meaningful changes in human history have been preceded by great migratory events: by contaminations of cultures (and, obviously, also by allergic reactions to the increasing synergies). This is exactly what we observe happening today both in Western culture plied with migratory processes and in other cultures that, although dominated by the figure of the nomad or the migrant, nevertheless long for a contamination with the West.

Redistribution/Recognition:
Conflict of Interests and Conflict of Identities

At this point the question inevitably arises concerning the characters of the new dimension of the world-conflict [*conflitto-mondo*]. The nature of the global conflict certainly represents one of the settling issues in our current times. We are moving toward forms of conflict that are very different from the ones to which modernity had accustomed us. In the globalized world, the nature of the conflict is simultaneously postnational and transcultural: it exceeds the boundaries of the nation-state and crosses cultural and linguistic identities. With this I mean that in the globalized world not only cultures but also religions appear as subjects and referents of conflict. Religions, however, complicate and destabilize the geometrical linearity of Huntington's clash of civilizations. If carefully considered, the form of the global conflict appears much closer to the religious wars that preceded the birth of the modern secular states than to a clash of allegedly cultural monoliths. The fact that religions are an important moment in the global conflict appears to me as backlight evidence for the thesis that I have tried to delineate in my book and that I have had the opportunity to discuss, discovering meaningful convergences, with Marc Augé, a great anthropologist and extraordinary analyst of "cultural dynamics," namely, that religions are by definition identity aggregations of a transcultural kind. The great religions never identify themselves with only one civilization. None of the "world religions" can be reduced to a monocultural dimension and latitude. This is certainly so for the Islamic religion, which we Westerners too often tend to identify with the Arab world, whereas it is a fault line that runs from Morocco to Indonesia and spans over very different historical traditions and cultural realities.

We have to take into account that this phenomenon, very often reduced to stereotypical expressions such as a "return of the sacred," carries with itself a radical as well as silent change in the function of religion within the globalized world. We no longer have to do either with the "invisible religion," which a false forecast has too hastily confined to the privacy of the interior forum, or with a "religious" understood as surprising vitality of faith after the death of ideologies; rather, we have to do with religions (in the plural) as factors of symbolic identification and belonging. They are factors of identification and also, for the very same reason, of conflict. This conflict is certainly not reducible to the utilitarian model of rationality of modern individualism; yet, it cannot be understood either by resorting to the pure logic of interest or power. Having said this, one should not think that within such new conflicts the material and strategic component is not present. In any historical stage one can observe an inextricable intertwining of the two dimensions of "contract" and "conversion" (Alessandro Pizzorno), of "redistributive conflict" and "fight for recognition" (Nancy Fraser and Axel Honneth), of interests and identity, of will to power and will to value. As the ethical and identity dimension was present even in the most industrialist and trade unionist class struggles, likewise the dimension of economic interest was far from absent from the religious wars between Catholics and Huguenots in France. Yet, the matter is that of identifying, time after time within the constant aspect of the intertwining, the "dominant feature" impressing its characteristic form to the conflict. In this sense, to characterize the nature of the global conflict, in *Passaggio a Occidente* I have thought that such a dominant feature could be identified in the identity moment. With this I have not at all meant to hypothesize a sort of "baton passing" from the industrialist dominance of the conflict of interests to the postindustrialist dominance of the identity conflict; rather, I have tried to stress how, in the current stage, the identity moment tends to encapsulate also the utilitarian moment within itself. In our world asking the classical question of modern individualism, "What do I want?" without previously asking, "Who am I?" seems to be increasingly difficult. The symbolic interrogation concerning identity thus appears as a *conditio sine qua non* to be able to identify one's own interests and scale of preferences.

Difference—Not Differences

What repercussions might all this have on the level of real politics? In my opinion, it has wide ranging repercussions on theory as well as on practice, on the conceptual constellation as well as on the actual reality of the "political." The new form of the conflict affects at its core the contractualist paradigm of political modernity, which finds its classic symbolic representation in the image of the Leviathan-State as macroconstruct or megamachine. Because of the "isometric" presupposition inherent in contractualism, the procedural technics of the Leviathan-State (not only of the Hobbesian absolute Leviathan, but also of the democratic Leviathan a liberal such as Rawls theorized) is capable of ruling only conflicts of interest but not—and here is the crucial point—conflicts of identity through compensative measures of distributive justice.

To solve in a liberating way the prospectively catastrophic antagonism between the neutralizing universalism of the modern state and the identity fetishism of communitarianism and of certain variations of multiculturalism, I have advanced the proposal of a global public sphere marked by a universalist politics of "difference." I mean "difference" in the singular, not in the plural (the famous "cultural differences," about which all or almost all today speak). To explain it better, I understand "difference" not as particular place, subject, or condition, but rather as "optical summit" capable at the theoretical level of breaking with the distributive and "state-centered" paradigm of politics, and at the practical level of shattering the isometry of democratic institutions structurally incapable of handling the new forms of conflict. Far from being a third way between universalism and differences, liberalism and communitarianism—nineteenth-century cemeteries are paved with third ways, as is well known—my proposal aims at reconstructing the universal based not on the idea of a common denominator, but rather on the *criterion* of difference. The reconstructive principle of the universal therefore can be understood only in terms of a *disjunctive synthesis*—based on the presupposition of the inalienable and inappropriable particular difference of each. In my concept of the universal, the relation can be properly thought only as one between *irreducible and mutually inassimilable singularities*. This is exactly at the antipodes of the conception of a social bond understood as a belonging to a common identity-substance (Community, State, but also Reason, Humankind, Language). By activating the criterion of difference, smashing another equation, that between incommensurability and incomparability of cultures, also becomes possible.

Incommensurability and Incomparability

Incommensurability and incomparability of cultures—other concepts that must be clarified better. Let us proceed with order. One of the most precious results of twentieth-century ethnology has been the acquisition of cultural relativism and the consequent disenchantment concerning the hegemonic and supremacist implications of Western universalism. To take seriously the "Copernican revolution" effected by great nineteenth- and twentieth-century anthropology means, in brief, to take the rigorously contextual (and thus relative) character of cultures and the destitution of any a priori claim to universal validity for our values and lifestyles as the starting points of any analysis and political project. This is what we find to be already genially foreshadowed, within the climate of the religious world and the conquest of the New World, in that extraordinary *ouverture* to modern disenchantment represented by Montaigne's *Essais*: it is easy to say "cannibals." Any culture is a world, a constellation of symbols and values that need to be analyzed first of all *iuxta propria principia* [according to its own principles] without projecting our own cultural parameters on that symbolic universe. All this, I repeat, is indisputable, and it is part of the great acquisitions of the century that lies behind us. Yet two aspects need to be considered, which I now introduce in an interrogative form. First, are we really sure that even, or perhaps precisely, when we revert the traditional supremacist and colonialist optics into the relativist one, up into the extreme of third world ideologies, we are not actually looking at the others "with Western eyes"? Second, who has said that the incommensurability of cultures—that is, the absence of only one standard of evaluation—should necessarily amount to their incomparability and incompositionality? On the contrary, cultural realities or *cosmoi* responding to different "metrics" are sometimes capable of giving rise to creative compositions that last longer than many allegedly homogeneous symbolic forms. At this point, however, one should address another issue, which I simply mention: one of the themes à *l'ordre du jour* is the need for a critique of the concept of culture understood as a close system and insular self-sufficiency, and the assumption of the idea of multiple identity as the only possible way of comparative access to the event of civilizations.

Public Sphere and Rhetoric:
Between Argumentation and Narration

What has been said so far perhaps may be true theoretically speaking. Yet, in practice, how can we arrive at different compositions among incommensurable cultures?

As I mentioned, I do not believe a global civil society is being formed; in the present state of things, what is global is only the market-information mix and the name-brands with which we are constantly bombarded thanks to real time technologies. And I do not believe in a coming advent of the cosmopolitical republic, which Immanuel Kant predicted more than two centuries ago, or of the *civitas maxima* which a jurist such as Hans Kelsen postulated in the last century. Nevertheless, I am convinced that one can work, in a medium-term perspective, at a recomposition of the various "diasporic public spheres" (as they are called by Appadurai, a significant representative of *postcolonial studies*) within a global public sphere marked by the universalism of difference. Such a public sphere (which initially will have to develop from macroregional areas—starting from Europe, but this is only a wish) will not restrict the confrontation among the different groups' *Weltanschauungen*—among visions of life and world—to the negotiation of procedural rules according to the method of intersecting or overlapping consensus as contemplated by political liberalism. Neither shall it limit itself, however, to functioning, as Habermas postulated, as a ground for confrontation—geared to agreement—between argumentative models and schemes geared toward a justification of the different value options. Although it represents an undisputable progress in comparison with strictly procedural versions of democracy, such a proposal nevertheless has the inconvenience of an explicit discrimination between subjects with and without communicative-argumentative competence. Yet, even those subjects who are strongly deficient as to the logic of rational-discursive argumentation can be capable of accounting for their ethical choices or for the consequences that the autonomous or heteronomous assumption of certain norms and lifestyles entails for their own existence.

The relational-communicative dimension put into being by the public sphere cannot be argumentative only; it must also be narrative. There may be subjects who, although not capable of producing an argumentative justification for their values, culture, and vision of the world, are nevertheless capable of narrating the experience of those very values that they make daily—an experience, in all evidence, which is not only rational but also emotive. An Islamic young woman living in Paris *banlieu*—to make the most obvious, but also dramatically closest example—may not be capable of arguing for her (more or less free) choice of wearing the veil, but not because of this she will be unable to narrate the *emotive-rational experience of the value* that such a decision entails and its existential implications. In the public sphere, the right of citizenship belongs neither to formal procedures of right (which are certainly essential and inalienable, because without them we could not call ourselves truly free) nor to the logic of argumentation alone. The space of the Cosmopolis, of the global city must—contravening Plato's interdict—extend the rights of citizenship also to rhetoric, to the narration of oneself, to the experience of narrating voices. However, this does not authorize—and this must be emphasized strongly—accepting narrations without reservations. Nothing grants, in fact, that a narrative strategy may not have self-justifying and self-apologetic implications exactly like an argumentative strategy of an ideological kind. In the inevitable mix of reason and experience, argumentation and narration, which marks the relations among the different human groups within the "glocalized" world, a democratic public sphere can indeed accept rhetoric; but only, as Carlo Ginzburg has aptly remarked, on condition that it is a matter of *rhetorics with proofs*, not of rhetorics without proofs. This is the step to make if we want to leave behind us the ethnocentric version of universalism as well as the nihilistic drifts of that historical materialism that considers as an a priori the forms of self-understanding of each particular culture, thus rendering incommensurability a synonym of incomparability and incompositionability.

To face the "global risks" linked to the current interim between the no-longer of the old interstate order and the not-yet of the new transnational order that has difficulties delineating itself, there is only one way: to engage in a reconstruction of the pattern of Enlightenment universalism based on the *criterion*, the discriminating factor, and the optical summit of difference. In other words, the issue is that of delineating a universalist politics of difference by tracing a double line of demarcation: on the one hand, with respect to the universalist politics of identity, which has its noblest expression in Kant's ethico-transcendental program; on the other, with respect to the antiuniversalist politics of differences, which in North America is carried out by the communitarians and in Europe by the ethnopolitics of the various regionalisms and league-like movements. Of course, this is not a solution, but rather . . . a provisional morality. Yet, as I have tried to explain in my book, in this transitional stage of a "West passage," which is destined to last still a while, we will have to write with one hand "universality," and with the other "difference," and avoid the temptation to write them both with the same hand because in any event it would be the wrong hand.

East/West: A Specular Mythologema

East and West are increasingly often identified as the two extremes of what is now defined as a "clash of civilizations." Yet, going beyond the two specular myths of the East and the West is necessary. The fundamental contradiction of the global world is not given, as Huntington hypothesizes, by the clash of the West and Islam, but rather by the confrontation with the Asian giant. I do not mean by this to deny or downplay the extent of the danger represented by Islamic terrorism in the short to medium-range, especially as long as that breeding ground of conflict that is the Palestinian question remains open. Just as fundamentalist tendencies are a sign of identity frustration, likewise terrorist exasperation is a symptom of powerlessness and not of strength within the Islamic world. Despite its atrocity, the global terror of September 11, 2001 (and March 11, 2004) is a desperate reaction against the process of modernization and secularization. It is a reaction the intensity of which is inversely proportional to the ability of the Muslim multiverse [*multiverso*] to configure a real global alternative to the West. Thanks to the originary relation with technics inscribed in the genetic code of its civilization, and thanks to its ability to appropriate Western technologies and innovate them deeply, China instead is able to delineate the profile of *another globalization* by promoting a capitalist productive economy based not on individualist-competitive but rather on patronizing-communitarian grounds.

The fact that, in all probability, the twenty-first century will be marked by the challenge between two concurrent versions of the global—the American individualist version and the Asian communitarian one—based on the shared ground of accelerated technological productivity and innovation leads one to revise radically some famous diagnoses and prognoses Western science elaborated in the course of the last two centuries. I am referring especially to the substantially dismissive judgment of Confucian ethics uttered in the past in Max Weber's *Sociology of Religion*, which still today is the most important comparative picture of cultures. For Weber, Confucianism is a morality of obedience and adaptation to the world that is dysfunctional to the creation of a conduct of practical-active life, and thus of a productive and dynamic socioeconomic system. As I have tried to bring out in my book, the optical distortion of Weber's forecast depends on the assumption of Puritan Protestantism's lifestyle—simultaneously ascetic and secularly oriented—as the prototype of capitalist ethics and, at the same time, as the parameter for the comparison between different "world religions." Weber's judgment of Confucianism is thus vitiated by the assumption of "intramundane asceticism" as the optimal way of realization for a productive society. The features that Weber identifies as passive, adaptive, and nonproductive within Confucianism are not by chance producing an alternative model of globalization, which—let me be clear—I am far from defending. We should not forget that the so-called Asian values advertised by the elites of China and the countries belonging to the macroregion of Southeast Asia call with no hesitations for the subordination of the individual to the state authority, the submission of the individual rights to the collective. However, underestimating the efficaciousness of some aspects of that message—for example, the need to maintain harmony in the relation between generations—when compared to the marginalization of the elderly and the isolation of the individuals characterizing the "great cold" of our Western civilizations would be wrong.

Regardless, this is a challenge that cannot be faced if one does not critique the traditional stereotypes of the East created by our culture. As Karl Jaspers declares, the dualism "East-West" is a typical product of Western thinking and is unknown to Asian civilizations. (Is it by chance that it is a philosopher of the European crisis such as Jaspers who foreshadows the postcolonial criticism of binary schemes—civil/barbarian, colonizer/colonized, racism/antiracism—as forms of stigmatization of alterity that are functional, even in their specular reversals, to the continuation of the hierarchy?). At this point, however, for cultural (even before political) Europe to assume the radicalness of the criticism of Western dualisms and the logic of symmetrical oppositions implies an ineludible consequence, which amounts to a peremptory call to the assumption of responsibility in front of global challenges. It is the "call" to play finally the role of global player and delineate its original alternative both to (allegedly) "American" individualism and to (allegedly) "Asian" communitarianism. This implies, however, a work of rigorous deconstruction of the oppositional polarity "East-West" (with the resort to a differentiated analysis capable of identifying the existence of a plurality of "Easts" and "Wests," as Amartya Sen suggested), but it also implies the arduous task of redefining radically both terms of the pair—namely, individual and community—which are too often uncritically subsumed under the binary logic and arbitrarily ascribed to both poles.

Cosmopolis and Philosophy: Toward a Global *Dialégein?*

This is the last step in my argumentative path. Which role can be played today by philosophy in this time suspended between the no-longer of the old interstate order and the not-yet of the new transnational order? Projected on the global scene, philosophy—understood not generally as way to wisdom or vision of the world, but strictly as form of questioning, Socratic knowledge, focused on dialectic and dialogue—is a sort of "business card" with which Europe (the first root of Western civilization) should soberly present itself to the other great cultures of the planet, and confront itself with their specific forms of knowledge, which are different from philosophic knowledge. Only in a general and metaphorical sense can we adopt expressions such as "Indian philosophy," "Chinese philosophy," "African philosophy," and so forth. In the intercultural multiverse of the global, or better, of the glocal, philosophy finds itself stripped of its traditional claims to universality and thereby inevitably relativized. And yet despite the incommensurably wider space in which it is called to operate, philosophy today finds itself, within the globalized world, in a spiritual situation similar to the one in which it found itself at its beginnings with Socrates in the Athenian *polis* of the fifth century. It is in the need to open up a path, a method, a way of questioning capable of escaping the paralyzing alternative between the wise world visions of the first pre-Socratic thinkers (*sophoi*, not *philo-sophoi*, that is, wise, not lovers of wisdom) and the absolute relativism of great sophistry. To renew "the Socratic moment" today, within this Kakania or global Babel, means to escape the jaws, on the one hand, of the normative claims of the great cosmologists and bioscientists, and, on the other hand, the false disenchantment on truth and universality proclaimed by the postmodernists' hyperrelativist *bricolage*.

To play today the Socratic game of *dialégein*, of the dialectical confrontation of viewpoints, is even harder when we think that the addresses and interlocutors of such a game are no longer the Athenian citizens, but rather the nomads and migrants who have come to Cosmopolis from the most various regions, languages, and traditions. Yet it is perhaps more worth today than yesterday to bet on philosophy as on a relational practice that employs the *medium* of language to exercise a displacing, dislocating look on our daily realities. This is a dialogical practice of confrontation-conflict that, by operating in a space made of variable geometries and in a multiverse of dissonances, helps us to see that which we all have in front of our eyes, but which we are not capable of observing from a different perspectival angle, that is, from an angle capable of disclosing to us a new horizon of things, thus liberating us from the unbearable feeling of being caught in a one way or on an eternally premarked path. Only under this condition will the Europe of philosophy (and thus, of right and politics) be able to posit itself as relational and dynamic polarity for a culture of *global constitutionalism* capable of opening welcoming spaces for a multitude of "unexpected guests." Only thus, thanks to a paradoxical inversion in the path of modern philosophy of history, will Europe, through the identity paradox that wants it made of irreducible and inassimilable differences, emerge in a not-too-distant future as *the future of America*.

The new universal of the planetary public sphere we are called to build either will be the result of a relational maieutics, of a real *experimentum* of reciprocal "translation" among different experiences and cultures, or, simply, it will not be.

Notes

1. Arnold Toynbee, *The World and the West* (London: Oxford University Press, 1953), p. 1.

2. Ibid., pp. 1–2.

3. Ibid., p. 85.

4. Ibid., p. 86.

5. Ibid., p. 87.

6. Jean Bottero, *Mesopotamia*, trans. Z. Bahrani and M. Van De Mieroop (Chicago: Chicago University Press, 1992).

7. See Carlo Cipolla, *Guns, Sails and Empires* (New York: Pantheon Books, 1965).

8. Toynbee, *The World and the West*, p. 16.

9. Ibid., p. 2.

10. Dipesh Chakrabarty, *Provincializing Europe: Postcolonial Thought and Historical Difference* (Princeton: Princeton University Press, 2000).

11. See Arjun Appadurai, *Modernity at Large: Cultural Dimensions of Globalization* (Minneapolis: University of Minnesota Press, 1996).

12. See, for example, Roland Robertson, "Glocalization: Time-Space and Homogeneity-Heterogeneity," in *Global Modernities*, ed. M. Featherstone, S. Lash, and R. Robertson (London: Sage, 1995), pp. 25–44.

13. Trans. note: The reference is to the Lega Nord, the Northern League, a right-wing movement and party which advocates, among other items, the separation and separatism of Italy's northern regions from the center and the south of Italy.

14. See Giacomo Marramao, *Passaggio a Occidente. Filosofia e globalizzazione* (Turin: Bollati Boringhieri, 2003); English translation forthcoming (London: Verso).

15. Trans. note: The title of the book evokes the 1940 film *Northwest Passage*.

16. Serge Latouche, *The Westernization of the World* (Cambridge: Polity Press, 1996).

17. Samuel Huntington, *The Clash of Civilizations and the Remaking of the World Order* (New York: Simon and Schuster, 1998).

18. See Anthony Giddens, *The Consequences of Modernity* (Stanford: Stanford University Press, 1991).

Chapter 16

Names of Place

Border

MASSIMO CACCIARI

"Border" can be said in many ways. In general, it seems to indicate the "line" along which two domains touch each other: *cum-finis*. Thus, the border distinguishes while joining. It establishes a distinction while determining an *ad-finitas*. Once the *finis* is fixed (and the same root of *figere* probably resounds in *finis*), a "contact" is "inexorably" established. Yet, before we unfold this essential idea that grows together in our language, what do we mean by "border": *limen* or *limes*? *Limen* is the threshold, which the god Limentinus guards, the *passage* through which one enters or exits a domain. Through the threshold, we are either welcomed, or *e-liminated*. It may turn toward the "center," or it may open up to the *un-limit*, to what has neither shape nor measure, "where" we would fatally get lost.[1]

Limes is the path that surrounds a territory, that encloses its shape. Its line can certainly be oblique (*limus*), irregular; yet, in some way it balances the *danger* that thresholds, passages, *limen* represent. Where is the accentuation when we say "border"; is it on the *continuum* of the *limes*, of the border space, or is it on the "open door" of the *limen*? There can be no border, though, that is not both *limen* and *limes* together. The line (*lyra*) that embraces the town within itself must be so *well fixed*, must represent such a powerful *finis*, that the one who is *e-liminated* from it is condemned to *delirium*. The one who is delirious is the one who does not recognize the border or who cannot be welcomed within it. Nevertheless, the border is never a rigid *boundary*. This is not only because the town must grow (*civitas augescens*), but also because there is no limit which is not "broken open" by *limina*; and there is no border that is not "contact," which does not simultaneously establish also an *ad-finitas*. In sum, the border escapes any attempt to determine it

This chapter first appeared as Massimo Cacciari, "Nomi di luogo: confine," in *aut aut* 299–300 (2000): 73–79.

univocally, to "confine" it into a meaning. What, according to the root of the noun, should appear to us as firmly fixed (such as the *hermes* of the god Terminus at the borders of the fields), in the *end* [*alla* fine] reveals itself to be indeterminate and elusive. And this is very highly so for those "immaterial" borders that put in "touch" conscious and unconscious, memory and forgetfulness.

The difficulty in defining the border cannot halt the need for it. The border cannot be *e-liminated*. Our quest for a place where we can dwell, which a *limes* can guard, seems necessary. We construct-build to correspond to such a necessity. No nomadism can silence it: nomads bring with themselves their place, which is the *carpet* in the richness of its symbolism.[2] They enter the carpet the same way we enter (entered?) the house. Even an object, a talisman, can function as a place, accompany the nomad, and anywhere define nomadic *Lebensraum*. We cannnot supress this need. And yet its satisfaction seems to be an arduous enterprise. We cannot dwell (and thus build), we do not have an *ethos* unless we mark some borders. And yet, defining them rigorously seems impossible.

In Aristotle's *Physics* is perhaps a precious hint that enables us to unfold our aporia. As we have seen, the idea of border in fact refers to the idea of place. The border defines, although problematically, a place. But what is a *place?* Whoever is concerned with *phusis* must necessarily search this notion. "All suppose that things that exist are somewhere (*pou*)" (208a29). It belongs to beings "to reside" in a *topos* [place]. Yet to know what a *topos* is, is a question of the greatest difficulty, is an inquiry covered in "many aporias" (208a32–33). Although it appears that it has some dimension, *topos* is neither matter nor body (209a16–17). Neither is it form (because it is evident that bodies do not take up their form by virtue of the place in which they are), nor is it principle or end of movement. Perhaps beings are in a place as bodies in a vase. Can one represent the relation between beings and place as the relation between a container and what it contains? (209b28–30). Bodies do not "clash" against the place, however, like objects in a vase do. Container and contained are of a quite different nature. Yet this does not seem to be quite the case for the relation between thing and place. Nor can we assert that the place is the interval between the container and the contained (a *diastema* [extension] functioning as a *metaxu* [intermediate, inbetween], 211b7–8) because either this interval does not exist or it is constantly "overcome" by the movement of the thing. There remains, then, only one possible notion of *topos*: it is the limit (*peras*) of the container, but insofar as this *touches* the contained im-mediately (without *diastema-metaxu*, 212a6). That is, the place *is* the extremities themselves in im-mediate contact, *ta eschata* [the extremes, limits, boundaries] (211b8). This implies that defining place without reference to the body is impossible. There is no "uninhabited" *topos* because its notion implies the *eschaton* of the being that stands on it. Thus, one cannot call *topos* a uniform, equivalent, empty extension. One can never mistake *topos* for an a priori idea of space.

How does one conceive of the contact between *eschata*? Is understanding it as an immobile line perhaps possible? We have already seen how the comparison with the vase does not hold true. Beings do not define their border by clashing against it, as if it were an impenetrable wall abstractly separate from them. All beings are certainly enclosed within their limit; yet it is in its movement that this limit, this *extreme or end* of beings touches other extremities. The container is nothing else than the *eschaton* of another being. The place defines itself time after time at the *border* [*con-fine*] of the contact between bodies, where each body is both contained and container, limited and limit. Thus, *topos* looks like another name to say the extreme limit of a being, the line where it enters a relation with the other than itself, where it "gives itself" entirely to a contact with the other.

If this is so, then the place is nothing other than the border itself, the extreme edge of a being, that is, its *shared end* with the other than itself. We cannot define the place other than as the *eschaton* of a being, that is, as its border. The border is the essence of the place. The place is where the thing experiences its own *limes*, the line that contains it and that, by containing it, places it into a relation. The place is where the thing "becomes" contact and relation. Once again, language knows how "to think" this issue. Do we not call *topos* the fundamental theme of a discourse? Do we not call *topoi* those places in a tradition where the tradition seems to concentrate its *ultimate* meaning? Is not *topos* the *eschaton* or the *achme* [apex] of a cultural formation? Analogously, the German noun *Ort* originally designated the spear, the extremity, the edge of an object, or that place, that village situated at the last border of a territory. Place is "where" the place ends, and the place has its *end* there where the beings it contains have reached their limit, present themselves according to their last figure. Therefore, the border does not delimit a place from the outside, as something that contains its beings (precisely as a container, as a vase). The border constitutes the place. The place rests on or consists of its border. It is conceivable, as it were, only *eschatologically*.

Topos is the "where" that is aimed at its own border. Topology cannot be separated then from "tropology." To define place is to describe the movement toward their *eschaton* of the entities wherein "contained," their *conversio* to their extreme limit. *Da-sein*, being-here, means being-for, being-geared toward one's own ultimate limit, being for one's own end. *Topos et tropos convertuntur* [*topos* and *tropos* converge].

The end [*fine*] is the border [*con-fine*], contact with the other. The extreme limit of a being, what greatly defines it, is also the *common*, what it has that is essentially in common with the other than itself. No border can therefore enclose the place. No border can *e-liminate* or exclude the other because it implies it in its very essence. That the name of *topos* is "border" means that it is a relation-term, or better *nomen agentis*: the place is the beings' being geared toward their own *eschaton*. There can be a place when this gearing-toward ends in the *problema* of the other, in the appearing of the other who *touches* us, and whom we cannot avoid in any way, as we cannot avoid the limit of our very body.

Exactly because the place "is" at the border, no place can be abstractly separated. In its being-border, the place becomes *limen*. Were the border to enclose its own threshold, were it to wall its *confinium* in, were it not able to recognize the *con-finis* in the other—that is, what is close by virtue of bordering, the *ad-finis*—then the place would no longer be place. The idea that the place may be defined by exclusion evidently refers to its image as a vase, a container, something separate from the bodies that inhabit it and from their movements. Yet, the place can only be understood as the ultimate edge of such bodies, as the *eschaton* that always subsists even though it always changes their configuration, as the *eschaton* that is in immediate contact with another extreme, with the *tip* of other bodies, necessarily endangered in the relation with them.

The sharper the line of contact—the border—delineates itself, the more is it threshold, *limen*. No body can transgress its own limit, go out of itself. Rather, the border escapes any rigid determination; it is the contact that refuses any univocal meaning. It is not the bodies that transgress, but rather the border that always transgresses. Transgression is the way of being of the border because the border implies *polemos* between what is distinct (according to all the nuances of *polemos*); yet, the border will always reestablish itself precisely because bodies cannot overcome their own *eschaton*. The border cannot be transgressed because it is transgression.

The situation is difficult and paradoxical: we do not have any other way to correspond to that originary need to dwell in one's own place than by conceiving of it *at the limit*, as border. The border is that *through* which relations and conflicts are produced, through which the place is always endangered, that is, is always *set back on its way*. To fix the place by trying to close its border will not save our dwelling from danger, will not constitute any stable *ethos*; it is rather the opposite. To enclose the place is not, in fact, to guard or defend, but rather to annihilate it; it means to violate its very nature and *meaning*; it is not to recognize them. Rather than ensuring the place, all attempts aimed at "fortifying" it will put an end to all dwelling because a place that is defined by the exclusion of the other, that does not wish that the other *touches* it, that demands its border to be *immune* from the other inevitably turns itself into a *prison* for the one who resides in it.

We would achieve an analogous result were we to "extol" the "transgressivity" implied in the notion of border by simply denying it. Many exodal-nomadic rhetorical discourses, many secondhand cosmopolitanisms constitute precisely the other side of "localistic" claustrophobias. By annihilating the border we annihilate the idea of our *own body*, we preclude the comprehension of the place as the extreme limit of our living body—we *reify* the place and prevent all authentic ground for the possibility of relation.

Ontologically, this possibility can be rooted only in the being-border of the place, in its being the site "where" the *cum-fines* touch each other. There can be relation because there is border. Otherwise, there will be no relation but rather a confusion of indifferent bodies in a homogeneous space.

And yet this seems to be exactly the current situation: the creation of one indifferent space to which closed identities seem to be opposed. In reality, a place that defines itself by eliminating its *limen* is a place that denies itself, and thus becomes maker, agent of that very process it would claim to oppose. The *idiotes* [particular] place, which *encloses* within itself the beings that constitute it, whose beings cannot express themselves at their limit, is *one and the same* with the notion of an indifferent (not *communis*) a priori space. They both represent the erasure of the border. Localistic idolatries[3] are on the one hand product, and on the other natural accomplices of abstract "globalization."

Is conceiving of only one space "inhabited" by places that are nonplaces, by ghosts of place, where no border can subsist, and therefore no relation can be established really possible? Can the globe be understood *without polarity*? Can the globe assume the image of a great plane, freely viable in any direction—some sort of an equivalent to the *aerial space* (to which, according to some, *earthly* mortals are anyway destined)? For a long time we have indeed been aware that the epoch when states acted in well-circumscribed spaces, on apparently well-designed *Schauplätze* [stages, theaters], the epoch of territorially determined sovereignty has ended forever. Yet, can this mean the empire of a single Leviathan,[4] uprooted from any land foundation and capable of resolving all polarity within itself? Could not this very epoch, instead, witness the arising of a new notion of *place-and-border*?

Let us start by asking, Does the "spatial crisis" of the Leviathan contradict "catastrophically" the logic of the modern state, or does it constitute its fulfillment? The contemporary universal *Mobilmachung* [mobilization] is the end of the systematic elimination of time and place differences, which already represented the "transcendental condition" for the sovereignty of the Leviathan. "Globalization" presupposes the systematic reduction of place to indifferent particularism [*idiotismo*], and the absolute sovereignty of a priori space. Thus, "globalization" presupposes the entire history of the modern state and therein the "Westernization" of the whole planet. The crisis of the Leviathan coincides with its full "success."[5]

The destiny, the ultimate destination of the state was certainly not to defend its own borders, and even less was it to conceive the notion of border according to the line of thinking we have put forth. The modern state moves toward its own overcoming. Thus it produces "closed places"; it transforms the border into a boundary—boundaries that are not so much, or no longer physical-geographical, or political-state related, but rather cultural, economic, ecological. The immanent logic of "globalization" eliminates borders and multiplies barriers; if the border is missing, in fact, the relation, which can take place only among *individualities*, ceases to be; difference, then, can only assert itself as inequality. How could a planetary sovereignty, which today exhibits as its only reason the economic reason, maintain itself, if the unachievability of its promise of "universal participation" to economic well-being for the inhabitants of the global space were to become increasingly clear? If it were to become increasingly evident that the elimination of the border (understood as obstacle, as element of separation—that is, ignored in its own truth), rather than producing "equality," produces a global, perfectly uprooted proletariat? That the elimination of the border produces "separatenesses"?

Might the reaction to these aporias of "globalization" open onto a new perspective on *place-and-border*? Not a "reactionary" perspective, but rather the opposite: the border as static container, and the place as its "particular" [*idiotico*] contained are the negation of border and place; hence they are simultaneously the makers and the products of "globalization." On the one hand, the idea of place as the "where" that is capable of reaching beings, as full expression of their form takes "globalization" "tremendously" seriously: it wants it to be such to the end, to the extreme, because it does not tolerate any limit that is separate from the *eschaton* of the living body. On the other hand, this body always constitutes itself "at the limit"; it can never transgress itself—and it is "here," outside of itself, that it enters a relation with the other, that it overcomes any separateness. This idea "concurs" with the form of "globalization," and it corrodes its domain/domination[6] from the inside. *Who* can *act* such a perspective? Certainly not the powers that are founded on a religion or gnosis of the One, of equality as elimination of the nonequal. Could Europe rethink and redesign itself in line with this sense of border? It is around the issue of its border that today Europe, as a matter of fact, discusses its own destiny. And what emerges ever more from this debate is that it is Europe itself that is border—that is, the place whose name is, exactly, "border." Europe will have to decide in which sense, in which direction to pursue its own *eschaton*. It will no longer be able to "remain within itself." This was possible for it after World War II, when it was forced between the two *non-European* winning titans. But even that period is over. Europe will define its space, and in so doing will define itself to the extent to which it will decide its border. If it erects a *boundary* to the east and the south, and it moves westward, then it will be an element, and nothing else, in that globalization-Westernization of which we have spoken. If it moves eastward and, simultaneously, toward the Mediterranean regions, if it assumes within itself east and south, then it will be able to be *place-and-border*, to be *confinis* and to recognize the *confines* as essential to its self-conception. Its sunset into the vast Western ocean would be its disappearance and nothing else. Its sunset into the east and into the Mediterranean could instead represent the "invention" of its own place.[7]

Notes

1. The un-limited, *apeiron*, is the originary condition for the appearance of places. Its notion is like that of *chora*, the "site" of all things that have birth (*Timaeus* 52b). In some ways Heidegger's *Raum*, space as *Freigabe von Orten*, as free donation of places, space as *making-space* for places recalls such a notion. Within the limits of this chapter, however, addressing either the relation *topos-chora* or the problems raised by Heidegger's rethinking of it will not be possible.

2. On the carpet as dwelling in relation to the overall phenomenological theme of *Lebensraum* see the essay by S. Bettini, "Poetica del tappeto orientale," in *Tempo e forma. Scritti 1935–1977* (Macerata: Quodlibet, 1996).

3. Or better, the ritual emptinesses through which one feigns "local autonomies" that are struggling for nothing else than to be "salient spaces" of "globalization" itself (because in the end globalization itself still needs to "land" somewhere).

4. What political form will "globalization" assume? That of the *Weltstaat*, which Jünger prophesized? But is the very term "state" not old when confronted with the total immanence of the domination by technics? And yet will this absolutely new form of sovereignty be able to avoid political *self-representation*? Will it be able to rule im-mediately, without a *representation* of itself?

5. This is true in general in all respects. The very domination by technics is the fulfillment of the "*dues artificialis*." The connection between the construction of the modern state and technical rationality is constitutive. Thus precisely the political is the ground for the unfolding of technics in its global sense. The "sunset" of the political is inscribed in the modern form of the political par excellence: the state. The epoch of de-politicization and neutralization (Schmitt) is the destiny of the political.

6. Trans. note: The Italian term "*dominio*" means both.

7. This would entail that "globalization" (if the globe will not accept liquidation of polarities . . .) may be defined on the basis of "great spaces" full of "meaning" (Schmitt). Or is the notion of "great spaces" inexorably tied to the age of imperialisms, that is, still to the past of the states and their wars?

Selected Bibliography

Ed. note: Only works in English are listed. For general information on the contributors' works in Italian, see the notes on the contributors.

Contributors' Works by Author in Order of Publication

Bodei, Remo. "Remota Justitia: Preliminary Considerations for a Resumption of the Debate on Ethics and Politics." *Praxis-International* 6 (1986): 124–47.

———."Farewell to the Past: Historical Memory, Oblivion and Collective Identity." *Philosophy and Social Criticism* 18 (1992): 251–65.

Cacciari, Massimo. *Architecture and Nihilism: On the Philosophy of Modern Architecture.* Translated by Stephen Sartarelli. New Haven, CT: Yale University Press, 1993.

———. *The Necessary Angel.* Albany, NY: SUNY Press, 1994.

———. *Posthumous People: Vienna at the Turning Point.* Stanford, CA: Stanford University Press, 1996.

Marramao, Giacomo. "Theory of the Crisis and the Problem of Constitution." *Telos* 26 (1975–76): 143–64.

———. "Councils and State in Weimar Germany." *Telos* 28 (1976): 3–35.

———. "Political Economy and Critical Theory." *Telos* 24 (1975): 56–80.

———. "Arché." *Planet: Technology and Culture* 1 (1999): 2–5.

———. "The Exile of the *Nomos:* For a Critical Profile of Carl Schmitt." *Cardozo Law Review* 5–6 (2000): 1567–87.

———. "Globalization, Conflict of Values, and Contingent Identity." In *Normativity and Legitimacy. Proceedings of the II Meeting of Italian-American Philosophy.* Münster: LIT Verlag, 2001.

———. "Self-Representation." In *Guggenheim Public,* ed. A. Sieff, 169–71. Turin: Hopefulmonster, 2002.

———. *Kairós: Apology of Due Time.* Aurora, CO: Davies Group, forthcoming.

———. *West Passage.* London: Verso, forthcoming.

Muraro, Luisa. "On Conflicts and Differences among Women." *Hypatia* 2 (1987): 139–41.

Olivetti, Marco Maria. "Comment on J. Hintikka, 'Contemporary Philosophy and the Problem of Truth.' " *Acta-Philosophica Fennica* 61 (1996): 41–47.

———. "Responsibility for Responsibility." *Perspektiven der Philosophie* 24 (1998): 345–55.

———. "The Third Party." *Philosophy Today* 49 (2005): 355–61.

Pagano, Maurizio. "The Universal and the Hermeneutical Experience." *Philosophy Today* 49 (2005): 362–73.

Rovatti, Pier Aldo. "A Phenomenological Analysis of Marxism." *Telos* Spring (1970): 160–73.

———. "Fetishism and Economic Categories." *Telos* Winter (1972): 87–105.

———. "The Critique of Fetishism in Marx's Grundrisse." *Telos* Fall (1973): 56–69.

———. "Maintaining the Distance." In *Recoding Metaphysics*, ed. Giovanna Borradori, 117–22. Evanston, IL: Northwestern University Press, 1988.

———. "The Black Light." In *Recoding Metaphysics*, ed. Giovanna Borradori, 123–36. Evanston, IL: Northwestern University Press, 1988.

Severino, Emanuele. "Aristotle and Classical Metaphysics." *Philosophy Today* 2 (1958): 71–81.

———. "Time and Alienation." In *Recoding Metaphysics*, ed. Giovanna Borradori, 167–76. Evanston, IL: Northwestern University Press, 1988

———. "The Earth and the Essence of Man." In *Recoding Metaphysics*, ed. Giovanna Borradori, 177–98. Evanston, IL: Northwestern University Press, 1988.

Sini, Carlo. *Images of Truth: From Sign to Symbol.* Translated by Massimo Verdicchio. Atlantic Highlands, NJ: Humanities Press, 1993.

———. "The Philosophical Grounds of Tolerance." *Philosophica* (Belgium) 2 (2000): 99–105.

———. "Gesture and Word: The Practice of Philosophy and the Practice of Poetry." In *Between Philosophy and Poetry: Writing, Rhythm, History*, ed. Massimo Verdicchio. New York: Continuum, 2002.

Vattimo, Gianni. "The Crisis of the Notion of Value." In *The Search for Absolute Values*, ed. I C F Press, 115–30. New York: I C F Press, 1976.

———. "Dialectics, Difference, and Weak Thought." *Graduate Faculty Philosophy Journal* 10 (1984): 151–64.

———. "Aesthetics and the End of Epistemology." In *The Reason of Art*, ed. Peter McCormick, 287–94. Ottawa: University of Ottawa Press, 1985.

———. "Nietzsche and Contemporary Hermeneutics." In *Nietzsche As Affirmative Thinker*, ed. Y. Yovel, 58–68. Dordrecht: Nijhoff, 1986.

———. "The Secularization of Philosophy." In *Writing the Politics of Difference*. Albany, NY: SUNY Press, 1991.

———. *The End of Modernity: Nihilism and Hermeneutics in Postmodern Culture.* Translated by Jon R. Snyder. Baltimore, MD: Johns Hopkins University Press, 1991.

———. *The Transparent Society.* Translated by David Webb. Oxford: Polity Press, 1992.

———. "The Truth of Hermeneutics." In *Questioning Foundations*, ed. Hugh Silverman. New York: Routledge, 1993.

———. *The Adventure of Difference: Philosophy after Nietzsche and Heidegger.* Translated by Cyprian Blamires and Thomas Harrison. Baltimore, MD: Johns Hopkins University Press, 1993.

———. *Beyond Interpretation: The Meaning of Hermeneutics for Philosophy.* Translated by David Webb. Stanford, CA: Stanford University Press: 1997.

———. "Hermeneutics and Democracy." *Philosophy and Social Criticism* 23 (1997): 1–7.

———. "The Trace of the Trace." In *Religion*, ed. Jacques Derrida and Gianni Vattimo. Stanford, CA: Stanford University Press: 1998.

————, and Jacques Derrida, ed. *Religion*. Stanford, CA: Stanford University Press: 1998.

————. *Belief*. Translated by Luca D'Isanto and David Webb. Stanford, CA: Stanford University Press: 1999.

————. *Nietzsche: An Introduction*. Translated by Nicholas Martin. Stanford, CA: Stanford University Press, 2001.

————. *After Christianity*. Translated by Luca D'Isanto. New York: Columbia University Press, 2002.

————. "Gadamer and the Problem of Ontology." In *Gadamer's Century: Essays in Honor of Hans-Georg Gadamer*, ed. Jeff Malpas, 299–306. Cambridge, MA: MIT Press, 2002.

————. "Knowledge Society or Leisure Society?" *Diogenes* 1 (2003): 9–14.

————. "After Onto-Theology: Philosophy between Science and Religion." In *Religion after Metaphysics*, ed. Mark Wrathall, 29–36. Cambridge, MA: Cambridge University Press, 2003

————. *Nihilism and Emancipation: Ethics, Politics, and Law*. Translated by William McCuaig. New York: Columbia University Press, 2004.

Veca, Salvatore. "Value, Labor, and the Critique of Political Economy." *Telos* 6 (1971): 48–64.

Vitiello, Vincenzo. "Desert, Ethos, Abandonment: Towards a Topology of the Religious." In *Religion*, ed. Jacques Derrida and Gianni Vattimo, 136–69. Stanford, CA: Stanford University Press, 1998.

————. "Hermeneutical Topology." *Philosophy Today* 49 (2005): 384–89.

Works on Contemporary Italian Philosophy in Order of Publication

Caponigri, Robert. "Italian Philosophy, 1943–1950." *Philosophy and Phenomenological Research* 11 (1951): 489–509.

Sciacca, Michele Federico. "Chronicle I: Present-Day Italian Philosophy." *New Scholasticim* 39 (1965): 69–83.

Nowicki, Andrzej. "Marxism and Phenomenology in Contemporary Italian Philosophy." *Dialectics and Humanism* 2 (1975): 157–75.

Borradori, Giovanna, ed. *Recoding Metaphysics: The New Italian Philosophy*. Evanston, IL: Northwestern University Press, 1988.

Silverman, Hugh. "Postmodernism and Contemporary Italian Philosophy." *Man and World* 27, 4 (1994): 343–48.

Barrotta, Luigi. "Contemporary Philosophy of Science in Italy: An Overview." *Journal for General Philosophy of Science* 29 (1998): 327–45.

Nuzzo, Angelica. "An Outline of Italian Hegelianism (1832–1998)." *Owl of Minerva* 29, 2 (1998): 165–205.

Parrini, Paolo. "Neo-Positivism and Italian Philosophy." *Vienna Circle Institute Yearbook* 6 (1998): 275–94.

Pellauer, David, ed. *Philosophy Today* 49 (2005).

Contributors

Editors

SILVIA BENSO is Professor of Philosophy at Siena College. She is the author of *Pensare dopo Auschwitz: Etica filosofica e teodicea ebraica* and *The Face of Things: A Different Side of Ethics*, published with SUNY Press. With Brian Schroeder she has coauthored *Pensare ambientalista. Tra filosofia e ecologia* and coedited *Levinas and the Ancients*.

BRIAN SCHROEDER is Professor of Philosophy and Coordinator of Religious Studies at the Rochester Institute of Technology. He is the author of *Altared Ground: Levinas, History and Violence* and coauthor with Silvia Benso of *Pensare ambientalista. Tra filosofia e ecologia*. He is also coeditor with Silvia Benso of *Levinas and the Ancients* and coeditor of *Thinking Through the Death of God: A Critical Companion to Thomas J. J. Altizer*, published with SUNY Press.

Contributors

REMO BODEI—Born in Cagliari in 1938, Bodei studied at the Università di Pisa. He was then awarded various fellowships at the Universität Tübingen and Universität Freiburg, where he attended lectures by Ernst Bloch and Eugen Fink, and at the Universität Heidelberg, where he attended lectures by Karl Löwith and Dieter Henrich. After being granted a Humboldt fellowship at the Ruhr—Universität Bochum (1977–1979), he became Visiting Professor at King's College in Cambridge, U.K. (1980), and later at Ottawa University (1983). He has taught on several occasions at New York University, and more recently at the University of California in Los Angeles. He taught for many years (1969–1993) at the Scuola Normale Superiore in Pisa, and since 1971 he has been Professor of History of Philosophy at the Università di Pisa. He is currently Visiting Professor at the University of California in Los Angeles. His books have been translated into many languages. Among his publications are *Sistema ed epoca in Hegel* (1975); *Hegel e Weber: Egemonia e legittimazione*, with F. Cassano (1977); *Multiversum: Tempo e storia in Ernst*

Bloch (1979); *Scomposizioni: Forme dell'individuo moderno* (1987); *Hölderlin: la filosofia y lo tragico* (1990); *Ordo amoris: Conflitti terreni e felicità celeste* (1991); *Geometria delle passioni: Paura, speranza e felicità: filosofia e uso politico* (1991); *Le forme del bello* (1995); *Le prix de la liberté* (1995); *Se la storia ha un senso* (1997); *La filosofia nel Novecento* (1997); *Il noi diviso: Ethos e idee dell'Italia repubblicana* (1998); *Le logiche del delirio: Ragione, affetti, follia* (2000); *Destini personali: L'età della colonizzazione delle coscienze* (2002); and *Una scintilla di fuoco: Invito alla filosofia* (2005).

MASSIMO CACCIARI—Born in Venice in 1944, Cacciari studied philosophy at the Università di Padova (Padua) with a dissertation on Kant's *Critique of Judgment* and later became Professor of Aesthetics at the Università di Venezia (Venice). He has been among the founders of some of the most important philosophical and cultural journals in Italy: *Angelus Novus* (1964–1974), *Contropiano* (1968–1971), *Laboratorio Politico* (1980–1985), *Il Centauro* (1980–1985), and *Paradosso*, started in 1992 and codirected with Sergio Givone, Carlo Sini, and Vincenzo Vitiello. He is a member of numerous European philosophical institutions, including the Collège de Philosophie in Paris. A former member of the Italian Parliament, a current mayor of Venice, and a former member of the European Parliament, Cacciari is now Professor of Philosophy at the Università San Raffaele in Milan. His publications include *Ristrutturazione e analisi di classe* (1973); *Piano e composizione di classe*, with P. Perulli (1975); *Metropolis* (1973); *Oikos: Da Loos a Wittgenstein*, with F. Amendolagine (1975); *Krisis: Saggio sulla crisi del pensiero negativo da Nietzsche a Wittgenstein* (1976); *Pensiero negativo e razionalizzazione* (1977); *Dallo Steinhof* (1980); *Icone della legge* (1985); *L'Angelo necessario* (1986); *Dell'inizio* (1990); *Geo-filosofia dell'Europa* (1994); *L'arcipelago* (1997); *La politica come servizio alla speranza* (2002); *Sulla responsabilità individuale* (2002); *Adolf Loos e il suo Angelo: "Das andere" e altri scritti* (2002); *Della cosa ultima* (2004); *Magis amicus Leopardi* (2005); and *L'incredulità del credente* (2006).

GIOVANNI FERRETTI—Born in Brusasco in 1933, Ferretti graduated in philosophy from the Università Cattolica del Sacro Cuore in Milan in 1962. In the same year, he also obtained a degree in Sacred Theology from the Pontificia Facoltà Teologica in Milan. He has taught philosophy of religion at the Facoltà Teologica dell'Italia Settentrionale in Milan and philosophy at the satellite campus in Turin. He has performed several administrative roles (Chair of the Department of Philosophy, Dean of Faculty, President) within the Università di Macerata, where he is currently Professor of Theoretical Philosophy. He is a cofounder and member of the board of directors of the journal *Filosofia e teologia*, and a cofounder and member of the board of trustees of the Centro di studi filosofico-religiosi Luigi Pareyson, of which he has also been the director. His publications include *Max Scheler: Fenomenologia e antropologia personalistica* (1972); *Max Scheler: Filosofia della religione* (1972);

La filosofia di Levinas: Alterità e trascendenza (1996), *Introduzione alla teologia contemporanea*, with F. Ardusso, A. Pastore Perone, U. Perone (1972); *Storia del pensiero filosofico*, with U. Perone, A. Pastore Perone, U. Perone, C. Ciancio (1975); *Filosofia e pedagogia*, with B. Bellerate, C. Ciancio, A. Perone, U. Perone (1978); *In lotta con l'angelo: La filosofia negli ultimi due secoli di fronte al Cristianesimo*, with U. Perone, A. Perone, C. Ciancio, M. Pagano (1989); *Ontologia e teologia in Kant* (1997); *Soggettività e intersoggettività: Le Meditazioni cartesiane di Husserl* (1997); *Identità cristiana e filosofia* (2002); *Filosofia e teologia cristiana: Saggi di epistemologia ermeneutica* (2002); and *Il bene al di là dell'essere: Temi e problemi levinassiani* (2003).

SERGIO GIVONE—Born in Buronzo (Vercelli) in 1944, Givone studied philosophy at the Università di Torino (Turin), where he graduated under the guidance of Luigi Pareyson. He has taught at the universities in Perugia, Turin, and Florence, where he is currently Professor of Aesthetics. Together with Carlo Sini, Massimo Cacciari, and Vincenzo Vitiello, he has codirected the journal *Paradosso*. Among his publications are *La storia della filosofia secondo Kant* (1972); *Hybris e melancholia: Studi sulle poetiche del Novecento* (1974); *William Blake: Arte e religione* (1978); *Ermeneutica e romanticismo* (1983); *Dostoevskij e la filosofia* (1984); *Storia dell'estetica* (1988); *Disincanto del mondo e pensiero tragico* (1988); *La questione romantica* (1992); *Storia del nulla* (1996); *Favola delle cose ultime* (1998); *Eros/ethos* (2000); *Nel nome di un dio barbaro* (2002); *Prima lezione di estetica* (2003); and *Il bibliotecario di Leibniz: Filosofia e romanzo* (2005).

GIACOMO MARRAMAO—Born in Catanzaro in 1946, Marramao studied at the Università di Firenze (Florence) under the guidance of Eugenio Garin, and later at Universität Frankfurt. After having taught philosophy of politics and history of political theories at the Istituto Universitario Orientale in Naples, currently he is Professor of Political Philosophy at the Università di Roma Tre (Rome III). He is also director of the Basso-Issoco Foundation and a member of the Collège International de Philosophie in Paris. As visiting professor, he has often lectured at various European and American universities: in Paris (Sorbonne and Nanterre), Berlin (Freie Universität), Vienna, Barcelona, Santander, Oviedo, Murcia, Granada, Majorca, New York (Columbia), Mexico City, Buenos Aires, Rosario, Cordoba, Rio de Janeiro, and Sao Paolo. He is the cofounder of important philosophical journals such as *Laboratorio politico* and *Il Centauro*. Among his publications are *Marxismo e revisionismo* (1971); *Austro-marxismo* (1977); *Il politico e le trasformazioni* (1979); *Potere e secolarizzazione: Le categorie del tempo* (1983); *L'ordine disincantato* (1985); *Minima temporalia. Tempo, spazio, esperienza* (1990); *Kairòs: Apologia del tempo debito* (1992); *Cielo e terra: Genealogia della secolarizzazione* (1994); *Die Säkularisierung der westlichen Welt* (1996); *Dopo il Leviatano: Individuo e comunità nella filosofia politica* (2000); *Passaggio a Occidente: Filosofia e globalizzazione* (2003); *Globalizzazione e politica* (2005); and *L'Europa alla prova del consenso* (2006).

VIRGILIO MELCHIORRE—Born in Chieti in 1931, Melchiorre taught moral philosophy at the Università di Venezia (Venice). Later, he became Professor of Moral Philosophy at the Università Cattolica del Sacro Cuore in Milan, where he had previously taught the philosophy of history since 1961. In 2000 he became Professor of Theoretical Philosophy at the same university, where he also directed the School of Specialization in Social Communications. He is the director of the series on Metaphysics and History of Metaphysics for Vita e Pensiero publishers. He retired in November 2003. His publications include *Arte ed esistenza* (1956); *Il metodo di Mounier* (1960); *Il sapere storico* (1963); *La coscienza utopica* (1970); *L'immaginazione simbolica* (1972); *Metacritica dell'eros* (1977); *Ideologia, utopia, religionede* (1980); *Essere e parola: Idee per una antropologia metafisica* (1982); *Corpo e persona* (1987); *Saggi su Kierkegaard* (1987); *Analogia e analisi trascendentale: Linee per una nuova lettura di Kant* (1991); *Figure del sapere* (1994); *La via analogica* (1996); *Creazione creatività ermeneutica* (1997); *I segni della storia: Studio su Kant* (1998); *Al di là dell'ultimo: Filosofie della morte e filosofie della vita* (1998); *Sulla speranza* (2000); *Ethica* (2000); *Dialettica del senso: Percorsi di fenomenologia ontologica* (2002); *L'ontolgia e la questione del fondamento* (2003); and *L'immaginario simbolico* (2005).

LUISA MURARO—Born in 1940 at Montecchio Maggiore (Vicenza), Muraro graduated with a degree in philosophy from the Università Cattolica del Sacro Cuore in Milan. She currently teaches philosophy at the Università di Verona. With other women, she started the *Libreria delle donne* in Milan in 1975 and in 1984 the philosophical community "Diotima." She is the principal Italian translator of Luce Irigaray's works. Her current area of study is women's mystical writings. Among her publications are *La Signora del gioco: Episodi della caccia alle streghe* (1976); *Maglia o uncinetto: Racconto linguistico-politico sulla inimicizia tra metafora e metonimia* (1981); *Guglielma e Maifreda: Storia di un'eresia femminista* (1985); *L'ordine simbolico della madre* (1991); *Lingua materna scienza divina: Scritti sulla filosofia mistica di Margherita Porete* (1995); *Le amiche di Dio, Scritti di mistica femminile* (2001); and *Il Dio delle donne* (2003).

SALVATORE NATOLI—Born in Patti (Messina) in 1942, Natoli's work engages the history of philosophy; more recently, he has devoted himself to the study of the relation between language and ethics. He is currently Professor of Philosophy at the Università di Milano-Bicocca (Milan-Bicocca). His publications include *Ermeneutica e genealogia: Filosofia e metodo in Nietzsche, Heidegger, Foucault* (1988); *Giovanni Gentile filosofo europeo* (1989); *Vita buona, vita felice: Scritti di etica e di politica* (1990); *Teatro filosofico: Gli scenari del sapere tra linguaggio e storia* (1991); *L'incessante meraviglia: Filosofia, verità* (1993); *La felicità: Saggio di teoria degli affetti* (1994); *L'esperienza del dolore: Le forme del patire nella cultura occidentale* (1995); *Soggetto e fondamento: Il sapere dell'origine e la scientificità della filosofia* (1996); *Dizionario dei vizi e delle virtù* (1997); *I nuovi pagani* (2000); *La felicità di questa vita: Esperienza del mondo e stagioni dell'esistenza* (2001); *Stare al mondo: Escursioni nel tempo presente* (2002); *Libertà e destino nella tragedia greca* (2002); *Il Cristianesimo di un non credente* (2002); *Parole della filosofia o dell'arte di meditare* (2004); and *La verità in gioco: Scritti su Foucault* (2005).

MARCO MARIA OLIVETTI—Born in Rome in 1943, Olivetti studied at the Università di Roma—La Sapienza, where he was a student of Enrico Castelli. He is currently Professor of Philosophy of Religion at the Università di Roma—La Sapienza, where he is also President of the Philosophy Faculty. He has been visiting professor at the Universität Freiburg, and has lectured throughout the world, including Berlin, Tübingen, Helsinki, Chicago, Atlanta, Tokyo, Osaka, and Buenos Aires. He is a member of the Accademia dei Lincei (Italian National Academy) and of the International Institute of Philosophy. He is the director of the philosophy journal *Archivio di filosofia*, and he is on the scientific board of several Italian and international book series and journals. For more than twenty years he has been the director and organizer of the international conferences "Enrico Castelli" on the philosophy of religion and has edited twenty volumes of proceedings of these conferences. Among his publications are *Il tempio simbolo cosmico* (1967); *L'esito teologico della filosofia del linguaggio di Jacobi* (1970); *Filosofia della religione come problema storico* (1972); *Analogia del soggetto* (1992); and *Intersubjectivité et théologie philosophique*, editor (2001).

MAURIZIO PAGANO—Born in Turin in 1948, Pagano studied at the Università di Torino (Turin), where he was a student of Luigi Pareyson, with whom he worked on editing Schelling's lectures on the philosophy of mythology. He is currently Professor of Theoretical Philosophy at the Università di Trieste. Among his main interests are German idealism, especially Hegel, and contemporary thought, with special reference to religious themes, intersubjectivity, intercultural relations and universality, spirit, and philosophy and globalization. His publications include *Storia ed escatologia nel pensiero di W. Pannenberg* (1973); *Hegel: La religione e l'ermeneutica del concetto* (1992); and *G. W. F. Hegel, Fenomenologia dello spirito: Prefazione, Introduzione, Il sapere assoluto*, translated with an introduction and a commentary (1996).

PIER ALDO ROVATTI—Born in Modena in 1942, Rovatti completed his studies in theoretical philosophy with a dissertation on Alfred North Whitehead at the Università Statale di Milano (Milan) under the guidance of Enzo Paci and Ludovico Geymonat. After working as a theater critic for the daily newspaper *L'Avanti*, he taught at the Università di Milano and later at the Università di Trieste, where he is currently Professor of Theoretical Philosophy. In 1979 he became the chief editor of the philosophy journal *aut aut*, which Paci founded in 1951. He regularly writes for the daily newspaper *La Repubblica*. Since 1983 he has elaborated the philosophical hypothesis of a "weak thought." In recent years, he was working closely with Jacques Derrida. He has often lectured at various European universities, including those in Paris, Barcelona, and Santiago de Compostela. Among his publications are *Bisogni e teoria marxista* (1965); *La dialettica del processo, Saggio su Whitehead* (1969); *Che cosa ha detto veramente Sartre* (1969); *Critica e scientificità in Marx* (1973); *Il pensiero debole*, with Gianni Vattimo (1983); *La posta in gioco* (1987); *Il declino della luce* (1988); *L'elogio del pudore: Per un pensiero debole*, with Alessandro Dal Lago (1989); *L'esercizio del silenzio* (1992); *Le trasformazioni del soggetto: Un itinerario filosofico* (1992); *Per gioco: Piccolo manuale dell'esperienza ludica*, with Alessandro Dal Lago (1993); *Abitare la distanza: Per un'etica del linguaggio* (1994); *Introduzione alla filosofia contemporanea* (1996); *Il paiolo bucato: La nostra condizione paradossale* (1998); *La follia in poche parole* (2000); *L'università senza condizione*, with Jacques Derrida (2002); *Guardare ascoltando* (2003); and *La scuola dei giochi*, with Davide Zoletto (2005).

MARIO RUGGENINI—Born in Mantua in 1940, Ruggenini is currently Professor of Theoretical Philosophy at the Università di Venezia (Venice). He is a member of the editorial board of the journal *Filosofia e Teologia*, and of the Comité d'honneur of the French journal of phenomenology *Alter*. He has spent periods of study and research in Cambridge and Oxford, and has lectured on questions of phenomenology and hermeneutics in Paris, Cerisy-La Salle, Freiburg in Brisgau, Halle, Heidelberg, Wüppertal, Bochum, Berlin, Lausanne, and Nice. He has been Visiting Professor of Philosophical Hermeneutics at the Theologische Hochschule in Bethel-Bielefeld, and has often lectured at the Istituto Italiano di Studi Filosofici in Naples. In Germany, he is a member of the Martin Heidegger-Gesellschaft, a guest at the Eugen Fink-Tagungen, and has collaborated with the Technische Universität in Berlin. Among his publications are *Verità e soggettività: L'idealismo fenomenologico di Edmund Husserl* (1972); *Il soggetto e la tecnica: Heidegger interprete "inattuale" dell'epoca presente* (1978); *Marx e la tecnica* (1979); *Volontà e interpretazione: Le forme della fine della filosofia* (1984); *I fenomeni e le parole: La verità finita dell'ermeneutica* (1991); *Il discorso dell'altro: Ermeneutica della differenza* (1996); and *Il Dio assente: La filosofia e l'esperienza del divino* (1997).

EMANUELE SEVERINO—Born in Brescia in 1929, Severino graduated at the Università di Pavia in 1950 under the guidance of Gustavo Bontadini with a dissertation on Heidegger and metaphysics. After teaching at the Università Cattolica del Sacro Cuore in Milan, he became Professor of Theoretical

Philosophy at the Università di Venezia (Venice). He is a member of the Accademia Nazionale dei Lincei (Italian National Academy), and writes regularly for the Italian daily newspaper *Corriere della Sera*. His publications include *Note sul problematicismo italiano: Heidegger e la metafisica* (1950); *Studi di filosofia della prassi* (1962); *Essenza del nichilismo* (1972); *Gli abitatori del tempo: Cristianesimo, marxismo, tecnica* (1978); *Legge e caso* (1979); *Techne: Le radici della violenza* (1979); *Destino della necessità* (1980); *La struttura originaria* (1981); *A Cesare e a Dio* (1983); *La strada* (1983); *La filosofia antica* (1985); *La filosofia moderna* (1985); *Il parricidio mancato* (1985); *La filosofia contemporanea* (1988); *Il giogo* (1989); *La filosofia futura* (1989); *Alle origini della ragione: Eschilo* (1989); *Antologia filosofica* (1989); *Il nulla e la poesia: Alla fine dell'età della tecnica: Leopardi* (1990); *La guerra* (1992); *La bilancia: Pensieri del nostro tempo* (1992); *Oltre il linguaggio* (1992); *Heidegger e la metafisica* (1994); *Tautotes* (1995); *Pensieri sul Cristianesimo* (1995); *Il destino della tecnica* (1998); *L'anello del ritorno* (1999); *La buona fide* (1999); *Crisi della tradizione occidentale* (1999); *La legna e la cenere: Discussioni sul significato dell'esistenza* (2000); *La gloria: Risoluzione di "Destino della necessità"* (2001); *Oltre l'uomo e oltre Dio* (2002); *Tecnica e architettura* (2003); *Dall'Islam a Prometeo* (2003); *Nascere—e altri problemi della coscienza religiosa* (2005); *Fondamento della contraddizione* (2005); and *La natura dell'embrione* (2005).

CARLO SINI—Born in Bologna in 1933, Sini graduated under the guidance of Enzo Paci at the Università Statale di Milano (Milan). In 1994 he was appointed member of the Accademia Nazionale dei Lincei (Italian National Academy). He is currently Professor of Theoretical Philosophy at the Università Statale di Milano. His publications include *Il pragmatismo americano* (1972); *Semiotica e filosofia* (1978); *Passare il segno* (1981); *Kinesis: Saggio di interpretazione* (1982); *Immagini di verità* (1985); *I segni dell'anima: Saggio sull'immagine* (1989); *Il silenzio e la parola: Luoghi e confine del sapere per un uomo planetario* (1989); *Il simbolo e l'uomo* (1991); *Etica della scrittura* (1992); *Il profondo e l'espressione* (1992); *La filosofia teoretica* (1992); *Pensare il progetto* (1993); *L'incanto del ritmo* (1993); *Filosofia e scrittura* (1994); *Scrivere il silenzio: Wittgenstein e il problema del linguaggio* (1994); *Gli abiti, le pratiche, i saperi* (1996); *Teoria e pratica del foglio-mondo: La scrittura filosofica* (1997); *Idoli della conoscenza* (2000); *La scrittura e il debito: Conflitto tra culture e antropologia* (2002); *La libertà, la finanza, la comunicazione* (2002); *Il comico e la vita* (2003); *Transito e verità: Figure dell'enciclopedia filosofica* (2004); *Archivio Spinoza: La verità e la vita* (2005); and *Il gioco del silenzio* (2006).

GIANNI VATTIMO—Born in Turin in 1936, Vattimo was a student of Luigi Pareyson, under whose guidance he graduated in 1959 in Turin with a dissertation on Aristotle. He studied in Heidelberg with Karl Löwith and Hans-Georg Gadamer, whose thought he introduced in Italy. After teaching aesthetics at the Università di Torino (Turin), he later became Professor of

Theoretical Philosophy there. He has been a visiting professor at various universities in the United States. Recently he was an elected member of the European Parliament in Brussels. Among his publications are *Il concetto di fare in Aristotele* (1961); *Essere, storia e linguaggio in Heidegger* (1963); *Ipotesi su Nietzsche* (1967); *Poesia e ontologia* (1968); *Schleiermacher, filosofo dell'interpretazione* (1968); *Introduzione ad Heidegger* (1971); *Il soggetto e la maschera* (1974); *Le avventure della differenza* (1980); *Al di là del soggetto* (1981); *Il pensiero debole*, with Aldo Rovatti (1983); *La fine della modernità* (1985); *Introduzione a Nietzsche* (1985); *La società trasparente* (1989); *Etica dell'interpretazione* (1989); *Filosofia al presente* (1990); *Oltre l'interpretazione: Il significato dell'ermeneutica per la filosofia* (1994); *Credere di credere* (1996); *Tecnica ed esistenza: Una mappa filosofica del Novecento* (1997); *Vocazione e responsabilità del filosofo* (2000); *Dopo la cristianità: Per un cristianesimo non religioso* (2002); *Nichilismo ed emancipazione: Etica, politica, diritto* (2003); *Il socialismo ossia l'Europa* (2004); *Nichilismo e religione*, with Santiago Zabala (2005); and *Il futuro della religione*, with Richard Rorty (2005).

SALVATORE VECA—Born in Milan in 1937, Veca graduated in philosophy at the Università Statale di Milano (Milan) under the guidance of Enzo Paci and Ludovico Geymonat, with whom he completed a dissertation on Kant's epistemology. After working as an Assistant Professor in Theoretical Philosophy at the Università di Milano, he taught at the universities of Bologna, Milan, and Florence. Currently he is Professor of Philosophy of Politics at the Università di Pavia. From 1974 to 1984 he directed the scientific activities of the Feltrinelli Foundation in Milan, of which he is now President. His publications include *Fondazione e modalità in Kant* (1969); *Marx e la critica dell'economia politica* (1973); *Saggio sul programma scientifico di Marx* (1977); *Le mosse della ragione* (1980); *La società giusta* (1982); *Una filosofia pubblica* (1986); *L'altruismo e la morale*, with F. Alberoni (1988); *Progetto Ottantanove*, with A. Martinelli and M. Salvati (1989); *Etica e politica* (1989); *Cittadinanza: Riflessioni filosofiche sull'idea di emancipazione* (1990); *Questioni di giustizia* (1991); *Questioni di vita e conversazioni filosofiche* (1992); *Dell'incertezza: Tre meditazioni filosofiche* (1997); *Della lealtà civile: Saggi e messaggi nella bottiglia* (1998); *La filosofia politica* (1998); *La penultima parola e altri enigmi* (2001); *La bellezza e gli oppressi: Dieci lezioni sull'idea di giustizia* (2002); *La filosofia politica* (2003); *Il giardino delle idee* (2004); *La priorità del male e l'offerta filosofica* (2005); and *Un dialogo civile* (2005).

VINCENZO VITIELLO—Born in Naples in 1935, Vitiello studied at the Università Federico II di Napoli (Naples) where he wrote, "Freedom and Justice in the Thought of Benedetto Croce." He has taught aesthetics at the Università dell'Aquila, and the history of modern and contemporary philosophy at the Università di Salerno. Currently he is Professor of Theoretical Philosophy at the Università di Salerno. He has also taught in several German (Berlin, Oldenburg, Osnabrück, Erlangen) and Spanish (Madrid, Valencia, Sevilla, San Sebastian, Murcia, Granada) universities, and at the University of Chapingo in Mexico. Among his publications are *Storiografia e storia nel pensiero di Benedetto Croce* (1968); *Heidegger: Il nulla e la fondazione della storicità* (1976); *Dialettica ed Ermeneutica: Hegel e Heidegger* (1983); *Utopia del nichilismo* (1983); *Ethos ed Eros tra Hegel e Kant* (1984); *Bertrando Spaventa ed il problema del cominciamento* (1990); *Topologia del moderno* (1992); *La voce riflessa: Logica ed etica della contraddizione* (1994); *Elogio dello spazio: Ermeneutica e topologia* (1994); *Cristianesimo senza redenzione* (1995); *Non dividere il sì dal no: Tra filosofia e letteratura* (1996); *Filosofia teoretica: Le domande fondamentali: Percorsi e interpretazioni* (1997); *La favola di Cadmo: La storia tra scienza e mito da Blumenberg a Vico* (1998); *Vico e la topologia* (2000); *Il Dio possibile: Esperienze di cristianesimo* (2002); *Hegel in Italia: Dalla storia alla logica* (2003); *Dire Dio in segreto* (2005); and *Cristianesimo e nichilismo: Dostoevskij-Heidegger* (2005).

Index